Blood Royale

(First Book of the Kahana Chronicles)

A Historical Novel by
Allen E. Goldenthal

Copyright ©1999 by Allen Goldenthal
First Published in New Zealand in 1999
by Charon Publishing Ltd.,
ISBN 0-9582098-0-4

2nd Edition released 2015
by Val d'Or Publishing
ISBN 978-0-9942559-2-1

To all my relatives and distant family members who were able to provide a few of the details and anecdotes over the past thirty years of my research. To their careful attention to keeping these tales alive within the family and which now will be carried on for all our future generations through the series of books known as the Kahana Chronicles. And especially to all my children Joshua, Evan, James and Charlotte, whose endless patience with me, as I dedicated my time and efforts to tell our story would have even tried the legendary patience of Job.

But this is not a tale of one family's fight for survival through the ages. Instead this is a tale of a people; a tale that grew out of the mud pits in Goshen, hardened in the desert winds of Sinai until such time that it could carve out a small territory to call its own on the eastern banks of the Mediterranean. A tale consisting of constant exaltation, reaching the pinnacles of civilization, followed by the inevitable fall into the chasms of desperation and desolation. A cycle engraved into the annals of history for perpetuity, evidenced by the events within a single family that was once promised on a windswept cliff of Mount Hor, that it would never fade from existence, continuous generations guaranteed for an eternity. This is the Kahana and this is their legacy.

Author's Note

The story you are about to read is based entirely on historical facts and details that are currently documented. The places, people and events all transpired in the most part in the manner by which they have been portrayed in this novel. The only mystery with this tremendous wealth of knowledge that can be accessed through numerous means is why there has been such difficulty for prior historians to tie down the details into a coherent chronology in order to clarify the confusion that abounds concerning the events of Southern France. This only fuels the conspiracy theorists with their outcry of "cover-up" or worse, which as the history as revealed in this book will demonstrate may be contentious and revisionist but certainly never eradicated.

Books such as the ***Holy Blood, Holy Grail,*** or the ***Da Vinci Code*** although very entertaining, have only exacerbated the myth making machinery that was already put into place centuries ago to conceal the actual history. Once the seeds of confusion were planted, whether it was by intent or merely the fertile imaginations of succeeding generations, it ensured that the initial kernel of knowledge became deeply enshrouded within the mystical and paranormal, permitting these aforementioned multiple conspiracy theories to become an industry all of their own.

The only mysteries that need to be explored are whether or not the knowledge of the events would have actually altered our present, changed people's perspectives, or even had any major detrimental impact on those organizations that were involved or was it simply their own fears that made them believe it so? It is the intent of this book to make the reader answer these questions and see if by chance it alters their own opinions and views of events they thought they were already familiar with and knew so well.

—A. E. Goldenthal

4

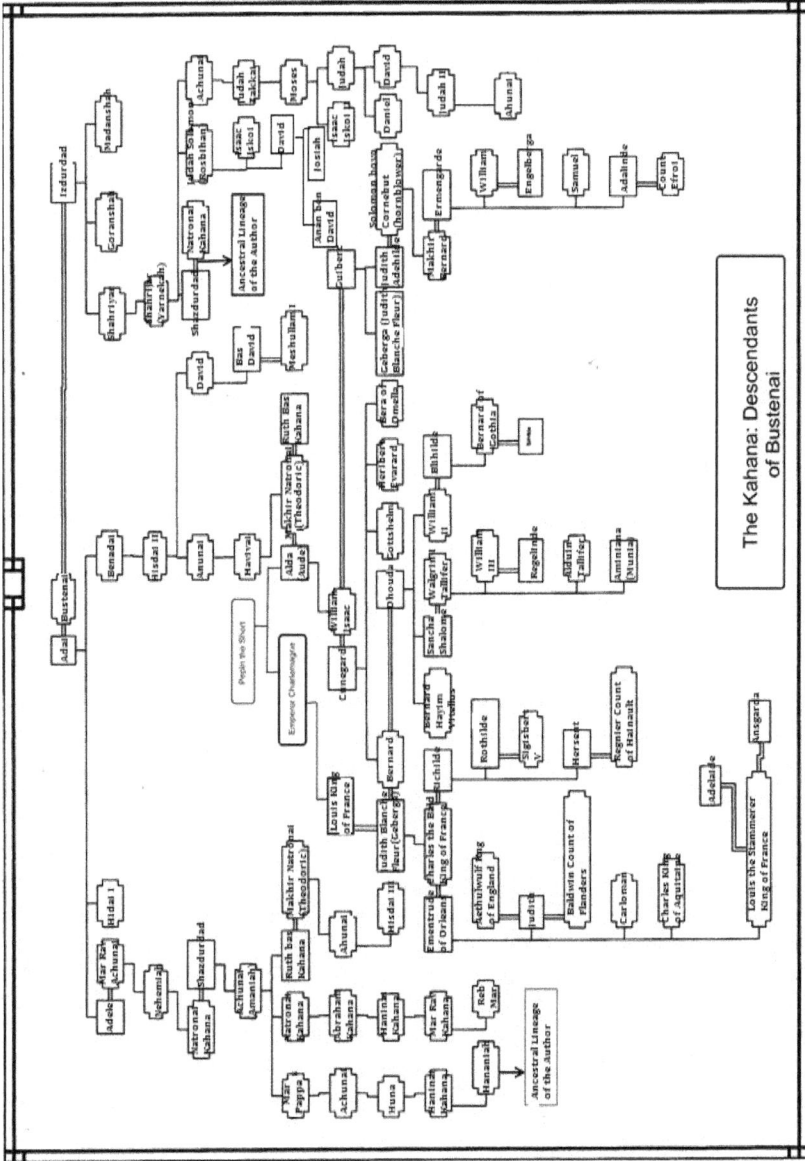

The Kahana: Descendants of Bustenai

PROLOGUE

Gottshelm lay sprawled along the ground, groping in the moist, clinging soil with toes and fingers, until every limb felt numbed by the effort. He prayed that he could magically cease his breathing; the tell-tale breaths resonating in his ears like the beating of a thousand drums. So loud, he cursed, assuming that they would be able to hear it too. In the distance, he could just discern the entrance to the cave, cleverly masked through the hand of nature by an overgrown juniper. Calculating and gauging the distance, he estimated the time it would take him to reach it. As a young boy, he had played in these same rock formations, hiding from his brothers in a mock game of hunter and prey. The difference now was that the game was for real and he was the prey.

Somewhere, in the darkness of the conifer forest behind him were his pursuers; before him, the beckoning mouth of the cave, appearing so close. He could practically feel the stale air from its depths blowing into his face. Raising himself into a sprinter's position, arms stretched forward, digging deeper into the red earth with his toes, knees tucked into his chest, he summoned his remaining strength to make that final burst for freedom. It was now or never, he told himself. The soil churned and sprayed with every driving step forward. Only a couple of more yards to safety and he through his body in a headlong dive through the narrow maw, scraping the flesh from his stomach and thigh as he flew past the razor sharp outcrop of granite. The pain was excruciating but he didn't care. He had to ignore it. Nothing could stop him now; not when he was this close to salvation.

Grasping his thigh, he pressed the torn flesh back into place; the gash foaming into an ugly pucker of blood and mud. It would heal. All things heal, he reassured himself as the time came to move deeper into the chasm. Gottshelm propped himself against the cave wall, forced to hobble now as he moved deeper into the cave, where he knew he would find the underground stream from his childhood. The watercourse utilized the cavern as a natural conduit to the nearby lake. He was convinced that he'd be safe as soon as he reached that stream. Thirty seconds of holding his breath under water and this nightmare would be all but over.

Immediately above his head a panic ensued; their rookery disturbed, the bats flew in blind terror, without any purposeful direction. Their attempt to flee the cave was unexpected by Gottshelm. He had passed by the cave's denizens numerous times in his youth when he played in the cave and they barely ever took any notice of human intruders. Something was obviously different this time; something else must have disturbed them. Just above the flapping of their leathery wings he made out the faintest of sounds; barely audible but definitely foreign to the natural sounds of the cave. At first he tried to dismiss it as nothing more than a constant gurgle produced by the stream but it wasn't long afterwards that the snarls and growls became clearly perceptible. 'Dogs!' Gottshelm silently screamed the word within his head in abject terror. He had completely overlooked the fact they would be using scent-dogs to follow his trail from the moment he made good on his escape.

"Mon Dieu! Mon Dieu!" he sputtered as he forced his battered body to move faster down through the tunnel. It was pointless, as Gottshelm knew that the cave was blind ended; nothing ahead of him except a solid rock face of impenetrable stone until he reached the point where the stream dove below a granite shelf. Reaching that orifice concealed below the cave floor would take time, precious seconds that he did not have. He was trapped!

The chorus of snarls now surfaced distinctly from behind. He could feel the hot blasts from their nostrils on the back of his legs. One of the pack moved instinctively, locking on to Gottshelm's ankle, taking him down like a wild boar. Before the searing pain of the teeth buried to the bone could even register, he found himself on his back, kicking wildly with his free leg at the attacking hounds. Catching the lead hound with the point of his heel across its throat, the dog shrieked in pain. Gottshelm could feel the cartilage and bone disintegrate with the force of his blow. Certainly it would be a death blow but that was of little relief considering there were others in the pack. Having released its anchoring hold on his ankle, Gottshelm seized the opportunity to shimmy along his back in a desperate attempt to elude his attackers. Automatically raising his arms to protect his face, kicking and screaming furiously against the remaining beasts he knew all too well his efforts would be in vain. If a wild board could not withstand the fury of these creatures, what chance did he actually have?

Suddenly two shrill whistles pierced the tumult and the remaining four dogs immediately sat, as motionless as onyx statues. Their eyes luminescent and piercing the darkness of the cave in a cold and heartless stare. The flickering of a brand slowly danced across the stone walls until it hovered eerily above Gottshelm like a grasping hand. His ankle swollen to twice its normal size, he knew that he could no longer bear any weight, even if he made an attempt to escape. His heart beat frantically against the wall of his chest as he tried to peer past the blinding flame to see his adversary but was unable to do so. 'So this', he thought to himself, 'must be the final sight seen by a hunted and wounded animal.' How many countless times had he felled one of those poor woodland creatures without ever giving a thought of how terrified it must have been? He never could have imagined it would be like this!

There was a sudden resurgence of pain as his attacker forced the point of his heavy boot into Gottshelm's swollen ankle. The intensity of Gottshelm's agonized shriek was so loud that even the dogs whimpered, taking a cautious step back from their prey.

The hound's master burst into the light, his face pulled into an anguished grimace upon seeing his dying pet. He threw himself to the ground, cradling the animal in his arms, as he began to weep openly. The other dogs gathered around his kneeling body, mimicking their master who was now engaged in a final ritual of mourning. Each in turn nuzzled him in an effort to console his grief.

"Oh, come now," Bishop Agobard mocked, his voice now identifiable as he spoke from behind the curtain of flames issuing from the brand he was holding. "It's a bloody dog! I'll get you another one if it means that much to you!"

Gottshelm grimaced at the sound of that voice, only to release another cry of absolute agony as Agobard dug the point of his toes deeper into the mangled ankle.

"Oh, shut up!" the Bishop commanded. "If anyone should have a complaint, it should be me. Do you know how long I have been chasing you across this bloody countryside? I'm not a well man, to be tramping in this manner," the Bishop snarled with disgust. "I have a frail constitution after all."

"Go to hell!" Gottshelm spat, but the spittle fell well short of the bishop, instead hitting one of the dogs along its muzzle.

"Do you not know dear boy, this is hell and I am its messenger? Hasn't anyone in your family realized that yet? I must admit, you are all very dull witted; not very smart at all contrary to everyone's opinion of your family. How long will it take any of you to finally understand that you are being eliminated to the point of extinction?"

"I'll be avenged." Gottshelm could only manage short bursts of words in between the searing spikes of pain that shot the entire length of his body with every downward press by the Bishop. "God will avenge me!"

Agobard laughed uproariously. "In case you haven't noticed, God has done this to you Almyeri. I am the scourge of God and your heresy is coming to an end!"

Tired of hearing the wails of grief from the hounds keeper, Agobard ordered the man to leash his animals and remove himself from the cave. "Annoying creatures! Even when they're just sitting there, they pant so heavily that I can't hear myself think. But useful, I'm certain you will agree. I thought we had lost you back at the river. A clever ruse. Fortunately, as I mentioned before, your family just isn't smart enough. Had you traversed further downstream, even by another hundred feet, the dogs never would have picked up your scent again."

Gottshelm could only respond with another terribly agonized groan.

"My sentiments exactly," Agobard scoffed. "But don't worry; it's all going to be over very soon. When I leave with my men, I'll have the entrance of this cave sealed permanently. No one will ever know what happened to you. And in a generation or so, no one will know that any of you even existed. The Almyeri will be a name forgotten forever. That is the power of my God! I guess he used to be your God but that is not the case any longer." Breaking into a hymnal refrain, the Bishop waved for his party to leave, glancing back on occasion to wave in a final act of humiliation towards his fallen quarry.

The Kahana Chronicles

Chapter One

Toronto: 1999

The rapid and incessant knocking at the front door managed to disturb what was now a rare and precious moment of tranquility in my life. All the excitement during the previous week provided only brief and very transitory interludes during which I could reflect upon what I had done wrong to cause this seemingly very public and embarrassing exposure. It was my own fault entirely. There was no doubt at all. It really was! I knew it but still that does not make it easy to accept.

I had not anticipated nor appreciated fully that this little game of cat and mouse I had been playing could and would be eventually deciphered. Perhaps it was arrogance but I never considered my protagonists in possession of enough grey matter to unscramble the carefully concealed clues. Oh, I was well aware that I had encoded them repeatedly into my scribblings but that was my little jest. A game I played for myself, really. A clue here, a clue there; I never foresaw there would actually be someone who would read them so thoroughly, as to have an inkling as to my intimations. In fact, why would they even bother?

Now I'm a victim of my own inclusion of these nefarious, teasing riddles. Subconsciously I must have known that I was tempting fate. So why does the unavoidable distress me so? After all, anonymity served no real purpose other than allowing others to bask in my glory; claiming my own hard work as their own success. I had grown weary of watching that happen repeatedly.

So why am I filled with this sudden dread and apprehension? Perhaps it's that I can perceive the world just isn't ready to accept the concept of my duality. My so-called skeletons in the closet will border on the sacrilegious to some. Some, who am I kidding? The entire construct of organized religion more like it as they prepare to burn me at the stake.

Then again, I might be overreacting. It may only be stage-fright. Then again, everyone knows that the limelight only serves to make oneself an easy target. I really should have taken more time and thought this out a lot more carefully. And I really have to stop talking to myself this way. Stupid! Stupid! Stupid!

Each annoying knock upon the door from my visitor reinforced my fear that it was all too late. I knew that once I open that threshold, there can be no secrets any longer. Was there another way? Definitely but too late now to think about that now! I am merely stating the obvious with the benefit of twenty-twenty hindsight. Sliding the deadbolt it has now become just a matter of fact. I pull the door ajar just the merest crack, permitting a blinding light to ricochet through the cloisters of my house. Not a light in the literal sense but still very intense and real; the metaphysical light of revelation.

Opening the door has bared my soul, stripped me of my protective cloak and exposed all that I am to this total stranger. I am suddenly feeling naked. He now stands just mere inches from me, looking sheepishly into my eyes. I am without words, a prospect that has rarely or more exactly never befallen me. I find I have nothing to say, no clever quip or snappy repartee to parry the foil of my real or imagined enemies. How totally unlike me this moment of silence truly is. I have become mute at the moment of my reckoning.

I wait for my unwanted guest to play his mischievous hand. After all, he requested this meeting but left me very little choice to decline. The gentleman cleared his throat and held out his right hand rather nervously. "I am John Pearce," he stammered. "I believe you were expecting me?"

"Yes...yes," I nod in affirmation trying to conceal any evidence of surprise upon seeing his diminutive, dowdy figure. "Forgive me, please come in." Definitely not what or whom I had been expecting. Oh, the ignominy of it all. That this...this obvious peasant will prove to be my undoing. I swing the door fully open and shake the hand that has been loosely hanging in midair for what could have been the better part of a minute now. I am now thoroughly convinced that time can at moments of its own discretion becomes suspended in purgatory indefinitely. I can no longer restrain myself. If my career is to be doomed then at least I should have the benefit of knowing how that had been accomplished. I am now suddenly as curious as to the background of my antagonist as he must have been in mine.

I managed to make what has been a near fatal shock to my system appear to be no more than a passing interest. "I really must confess that your call today took me by surprise."

"How so?" he inquired as I hung his water-stained beige trench coat on the hall stand. I point him towards the door immediately off to the right of the hallway, motioning for him to proceed ahead of me. I fail to respond immediately to his question. This bothers him but he says nothing. The arrival of John Pearce has made me think heavily for the first time on whether I am perceived as a lunatic or scholar for my theories. I wonder in which of the two views he has already cast me? Having taken a good look at Pearce's outward appearance, I can certainly state without hesitation that I doubt the two of us travel in the same social circles. Therefore I must assume that he must consider me the former and not the latter.

I find it far easier to switch my attention towards my library. The hand stamped leather with its gold embossed platings reflects the incandescent lights within the room. I lean against the oil polished wood, inhaling its rich lemon scented aroma, half sitting, half standing against the endless tiers of shelving. Books I can trust, this man is an entirely different story!

"Well, referring to your earlier question, I just didn't think anyone would be able to piece the riddle about my identity together. Or should I say, at least not this quickly."

Pearce laughed, "And that's the surprise Doc? Well, to be honest with you, I sort of backed into my little discovery. I got to admit, you had me really going there for a while. I had to follow a hunch. I know you're thinking that's probably the dumbest thing I could do considering I have this penchant for writing factual articles for the newspaper."

Dumbest thing? Hardly! I can certainly think of a lot dumber. How I got myself into this situation in the first place for example.

Pearce continued to ramble on, "But it just seemed to scream at me all of a sudden. Couldn't even tell you what it was that caught my attention at first, but it just all fit together; like a jigsaw. One minute it's nothing but a bunch of scrambled pictures and the next thing you know it's all there in black and white. Darnndest thing!"

"Oh, God!" I think to myself. I'm being dealt a fatal blow by an imbecile. This is not how I anticipated my exposure to the world would come about. I think I've always imagined some great theologian or antiquarian, working late into the morning hours. Their eyes damaged by years of squinting over mildewed fragments of decaying parchment barely illuminated by dripping candles. Only to come across a word, perhaps a phrase that made reference to my ancestry.

An esoteric clue leading them to my door to seek the missing words to their ancient tome and branding me the Antichrist or Satan himself; but not this. Not some bargain basement reporter who most likely works for the 'around town' section of a newspaper. That's if I'm lucky. This man could be one of those writers for the gossip rags. You know the type; those cretinous characters that spew out stories like 'Three hundred year old woman gives birth to orangutan.' God, I hope I'm not going to be the newest target for the Inquirer!

I decide that it's in my best interest to play along with him. "So what was this amazing and blinding enlightenment that bedazzled you in the first instance?" I try not to overdue my sarcastic tone, but that proves difficult. Those that know me say that it's a flaw of my character. But this Detective Colombo reject is after all altering my life forever. He deserves whatever I throw at him!

"Actually Doc, it was my wife. She loves your books! She has every one of them. She asked me to get your autograph for her before I leave today. I hope you don't mind." I nod courteously. "So, it's like this. I'm reading this article on the Dead Sea Scrolls. You know, how they're all fighting over who's going to release them and when. Nobody could care less for forty years, and suddenly, 'POW', they're all fighting, suing, cursing each other and it all becomes front-page sensationalism. It's as if suddenly everyone's looking for answers and they've all decided that the scrolls must contain them. I don't pretend to know a lot about this religious mumbo-jumbo but I do know when there's obviously something important being concealed.

Fortunately, my wife is there to help me with things like that. So, I'm reading this one part about how this biblical review magazine got hold of the entire set of prints and decided to release them to the public without Israeli government approval and with their own interpretation alongside the plates. Pretty nasty stuff from a bunch of guys wearing frocks if you ask me."

I didn't ask but that's a moot point.

"As I said, my wife's interested in this sort of stuff. I guess that's why she reads your books," he winks at me. "So I tell her to listen to this one part about the messianic order of events. Like there's this game plan to follow in order to become a messiah, a century before even Jesus was born!

We're talking major honcho stuff here. These aren't those guys on TV late at night, telling you to send money and they guarantee to improve your life. This is the real thing; a blue print from God. It then goes on to say that scholars think that this may be one of the reasons that the majority of the scrolls have been suppressed for almost forty-five years.

Suddenly Christianity isn't so unique any more. Buy a program and anyone can follow the script. Some guy named the Righteous Teacher tries exactly that and his followers were waiting for him to be resurrected too. I figure my wife's going to be absolutely astounded.

Instead she turns to me and says "I know." Then she goes on to tell me that this newly revealed game plan is going to talk about two messiahs; a priest messiah and a royal messiah. And the priest messiah is by far the greater.

So I say, "What do you mean you know? They just found this stuff out now!" Sure enough, I start to read more of the article and there it is in black and white; a priest messiah who will supersede the royal one. I'm sitting there, staring at her as if she's some kind of psychic or something. My wife loves it when she knows she's gotten me bamboozled. You know what I mean?"

Again he's winking at me. Oh lord, I can't stand it! The man's a moron! I should be talking to his wife. At least she has some understanding of the material we're dealing with.

"So Doc, I say to her, "What's the scoop? How do you know these things?" She then tells me she read it in one of your books, a while ago. Well, this reporter's no dummy! I can smell a story. There's only one way you could have known about this stuff. Since I could rule out you having any connections to the original group working on these scrolls, it was safe to assume you had access to the information in some other way.

But then came the hard part, tracking you down. You write under that pen name of yours, so obviously I just couldn't look you up in the phone book. So instead, I do the next best thing. I call your publisher. No luck! Confidential information they say, so I go to the library. You see Doc, I figured that name of yours must mean something to you. Why else would you use it? It's not as if you go make something like that up off the top of your head. I look through one encyclopedia set after another and then, finally, I hit the jackpot.

Eureka! There's some joker with the same name as your pen-name. Problem is, the guy's been a stiff for over two centuries and it was very unlikely that anyone would remember him, let alone use his name even if he was famous in the past."

"Very interesting Mr. Pearce but I still fail to see how you were able to make the connection. It's not unusual for an author to use the name of a person with some notoriety that is no longer alive, even if that person is no longer a household item, so to speak. It prevents us from getting sued as long as he or she's dead. It's actually done all the time."

"That may be true Doc but not too many people grab hold of a moniker like yours. ABROM ARYEH-ZUK KAHANA is not exactly John Doe. I figure there's got to be a connection somewhere. So, I'm thinking that maybe it's a family thing. What if this new Kahana guy really is a descendant of the old one? I start doing a search on the old man's offspring. Easier than I thought! But then I think, the guy's important enough to make it into an encyclopedia, so it should be easy. Christ, a God damn encyclopedia! Can you believe it?

This guy was a somebody back then even if nobody today would know him from Adam. The more I dig into his background, the stranger the facts become. He's got ancestors stretching back for miles. You think of a big event and sure enough there's some guy named Kahana involved. But I guess you know all this!

And then it hits me. I was looking at this all wrong. I'm finding Kahanas swinging from every limb in your family tree, each one more important than the last, but I'm not getting any closer to finding you. Obviously, there had to be a name change. Somewhere in this tree of yours, somebody grabs a new moniker.

I just had to look deeper. And there it was; Austria, 1846. Jacob Kahana is now known as Jacob Goldenthal. Never would have come across it if it hadn't been for the fact good ol' Jacob gets written up in the Austrian Royal Archives. Quite an interesting story there Doc about your ancestor and the Empress," he says slyly and winks at me.

"I'm glad you liked it. Remind me to tell you about it sometime." Although I can certainly detect the tone of annoyance in my voice, it doesn't even register with Mr. Pearce. "So, as to make an extremely long story short, Mr. Pearce..."

"Oh, yeah. So like I was saying, I now have a new name to work with and I have this talent of getting to the bottom of a good story. I phone your publisher again and I tell the receptionist that this is Mr. Goldenthal calling, playing the hunch that she'll patch me through to whomever you would normally talk to.

She doesn't fail me and the next thing I know your editor's whispering the most beautiful sentence in the world, "Yes Allen, what I can do for you?" Now I have a first name to go along with your last. At that point it was game, set and match. I look you up in the listing and there you are; Dr. Allen Goldenthal. There's only one of you in the phone book."

"Yes, I see. Well, so much for my anonymity. And I'll definitely have to talk to my publisher regarding the staff he's hired! I can't say that I'm exactly pleased with my exposure. It's an intrusion on my life after all. And then there's my family that I have to be concerned about as well. How do you think the notoriety you'll be causing will affect them, Mr. Pearce?"

I stare at him intensely, hoping to make him squirm with my obvious discomfort but I am quickly convinced that the man doesn't have a sensitive bone in his body. He doesn't even flinch as my eyes attempt to pierce his thick skin.

"Oh, Doc! Don't you think you're over reacting a bit? It's not like I've uncovered a mass murderer. All we have is a situation where you're obviously in possession of materials filtered down through time which no one else has a copy of. I just want to write about how you got it. Sure, it stirs the pot but my publisher will definitely pay for the rights to it."

I shake my head in mild amusement and what must be a huge smirk on my face catches his attention.

"What's so funny," he asks.

I throw my arms up and then clap them loudly. "Obviously, Mr. Pearce, you're clueless as to what you've stumbled upon."

He pulls a worn pencil from behind his ear. Reaching inside his plaid sports coat he pulls out an equally well abused notepad. "So, enlighten me Doc."

"What you think you can fathom about me, Mr. Pearce, and what is the truth about me are universes apart. I know that this is all a game to you, a challenge to your so-called investigative skills. The fact that you have come this far attests to the fact that these abilities may be considerable, but you have become involved in matters that are beyond your comprehension.

I know that I said on the phone that you could come over and we'd talk but I was somewhat in a state of shock when I made that comment and I now realize it was a big mistake. I think that it's best for all involved that we drop the interview and go our separate ways." I rock myself forward so that I'm no longer leaning in repose against the bookcase and begin to proceed towards the doorway, when Pearce suddenly grabs my attention.

"Doc, it's not that easy!" His tone was vehement. "I write this story with or without you." He began to wave and points the pencil like a loaded gun in my direction. "Either way, I get a story. You can help me and I'll guarantee that it will be your story that the public gets to read. Otherwise, they get a version that's just as entertaining. Your choice Doc!"

"You start printing lies and I'll have my lawyers crawling all over you and your publication."

"That's fine Doc. Then you'll have to tell your story in front of a courtroom. So what do you gain? The story still gets out, but it's the result of a messy legal dispute and instead of one, I get two stories."

I think I hate this man! It only takes a moment to consider all the possibilities. "So, what you're saying is that I have no choice; something in the vein of blackmail but without the extortion. Well, okay Mr. Pearce. It's your call here. Sit back, this will take a while."

"Ah, Doc. It's nothing like that. Just call it freedom of the press. And by the way, call me John."

"Well, Mr. Pearce, if you're a poker player, I'd say you won this hand. But the game is just beginning. So, I'll tell you something about myself and you can tell me when I'm shoveling it by the bushel and when I'm telling you the truth."

"Fair enough, Doc. You can play it anyway you want to. Just let me get my tape recorder started here and I'll grab my pencil and paper and we're all set."

I let myself fall backwards, deep into the cushions of my wing-back chair, prepared to give Mr. Pearce the story of his lifetime. I'll leave him with two choices. Either he'll consider me certifiably insane or merely an individual with an imagination far more vivid than anyone he has ever known.

There was a third option that he considers what I tell him the truth but I don't think he can handle that one. His choice to make but it's my game. But right now I'm thinking it might actually feel good to tell my story. I've kept it bottled up within me for so long, using my books as a release valve and now I'll have an opportunity to tell it all; to confess to another human being my sins of eternal suffering. "I guess you are fully aware of what I do for a living, Mr. Pearce?"

"John, please, and yes I do."

"Quiet please." I wave him silent with a flick of my wrist. "It was a rhetorical question. I'm going to tell you anyway what I do because it might help you understand a little more of what I'm going to attempt to explain to you." He merely nods his head in agreement. It's nice to see him silent.

"As you know, I work in the biologics industry, which has remained scientifically, fairly static until recently. Only now is it making considerable advancements based on entirely new concepts. Gene therapy for example. This includes a variety of specializations; knockouts, gene splicing, inversions, mutations and one that I happen to be particularly fond of, transgenics. This involves the transfer of genes from one species into a completely unrelated species. These are fully activated genes by the way.

In essence, Mr. Pearce, for the purpose of disease etiologies, I can make a mouse behave exactly like a human by transferring the human receptor sites. That small segment of the chromosome may be no larger than a couple of hundred kilobases and it can be incorporated into a fertilized mouse ovum. As the egg divides and develops, the end result is offspring carrying human genes. Are you following me?"

He nodded his head. I looked at his face to see how far his jaw had dropped. His eyes barely blinked. I knew he was out of his league. "Oh, don't be so shocked Mr. Pearce. It's done all the time and there's nothing immoral about it. All that is really being transferred is knowledge; knowledge that developed fifty, a hundred, even five hundred thousand years ago. That knowledge simply told us what it was that made us human. I and others have merely passed segments of that knowledge on to other animal species.

This is hardly new news. Rebecca Conn at Berkeley demonstrated in 1987 that all the mitochondrial DNA variants in the human population probably derived from an ancestral template about two hundred thousand years ago.

You probably don't understand any of this but what it translates as, is that the power sources for your cells, for the sake of simplicity let's call them the batteries, were all derived from a single manufacturer at around that time. What is significant is that our DNA has retained the original fingerprint, so to speak of, from that individual throughout all this time. Still following me?"

"I can grasp the gist of it, Doc. You haven't lost me yet."

Yeah, right, I think to myself. "Good, because here's where things start getting more complex. A fair time ago scientists demonstrated that memory could be stored at protein synthesis centers in the brain. What we remember is coded into our memory as amino acid chains which in turn are stored in gene alleles or segments and eventually incorporated into DNA so that brain cells produce protein when you try to recall past events.

15

The best analogy I can think of is your computer. You can load information into a database to perform a task, but unless you save that information, you won't be able to reuse it at a later date. Think of your hard-drive as being the same as the cellular DNA you're storing as memory and information. I know that this is a pretty simplistic comparison. Carrying the comparison even further, if you can download information from your computer then why not from the brain?"

Pearce was still nodding his head as if he understood so I continued with my dissertation.

"Let's look at an example. Investigators trained mice from a young age to run a maze repeatedly so that it became a learned response. They then removed cellular material from the brains of the trained mice and incorporated it into the cerebrums of naïve mice that had not seen the maze before. And guess what?"

Pearce was about to respond but I cut him off immediately. "The naïve mice were able to run the maze the first time they were exposed to it. Surprisingly, most people looked at the results of the test and adopted a 'so what' attitude. So memory is stored in a chemical form. Big deal. What else is new? That attitude has prevailed in science for centuries. Usually a scientist is dead and buried before anyone pays their research any attention."

"So you're suggesting that this was a major discovery," is all that Pearce could snap back in his limited response.

"If I'm moving too fast for you, Mr. Pearce, just let me know. Of course I'm suggesting that this was a major discovery. Why else would I even be telling you about it? It may have been relegated to the back page of some tabloid but that story had monumental significance."

I shook my head and regretted my outburst. As I said, sarcasm has always been a problem of mine. "I'm sorry. I didn't mean to sound off at you like that. I'm not used to talking about these matters. I guess it's made me somewhat impatient."

"Don't worry about it Doc. I'm a reporter. Trust me, I've had far worse blown my way. Keep talking. I'm getting it all down and it is your dime."

"Its significance is not readily recognized. Wasn't then and really isn't now. You see, neuroscience concerns itself with the function of the brain, rarely the potential. Neuroscientists sit within their own walls and don't extrapolate beyond their own interests. Chemical pathways are merely a functional reality to them; nothing more and nothing less.

On the other hand, I'm more interested in the encoding aspect; the ability to incorporate memories into our cells. And in so doing, the potential to pass these memories on down through time by imprinting them on genes, which are nothing more than blank slates waiting to have their base units assembled into an order that produces a memory."

"Whoa, Doc.", Pearce holds up his hands signaling a pause. "Let me get this right. You're suggesting that somehow, all the memories of my ancestors are swirling around in my brain and I don't know it. I mean, I gotta tell you right now, that's just not happening in me." He shakes his head in disbelief.

"Lots of examples," I counter immediately. "But in order to see them, I have to ask you to be open minded and throw away some of your preconceived notions."

Pearce displays a whimsical smile. "Doc, I'd have to be open minded to be here in the first place."

I rise from my chair and walk over to the bookshelf once more. "You know much about psychoanalysis, Mr. Pearce?" He shoots back a blank look which is pretty much what I expected. "Multiple personalities have been recorded since biblical times. First it was thought that the victims were possessed by demons. Many centuries later, they were thought to have experienced visitation by the Holy Spirit.

Several centuries after that, it was said that spirits of the dead were utilizing their bodies as vessels to communicate with the living.   Then came the dawn of modern medicine and these special people are all considered ill.   Freudian analysis would suggest that they were merely manifesting innermost desires in an effort to escape or supersede reality.

I'm not foolish enough to stand here and tell you that there's no such thing as mental illness.   Schizophrenics are prime examples of deviant behavior.   But in their case, behavior is the key word.   One person with two distinct sets of behavior patterns.   We have all experienced it at some point in our lives.   You know, that shy, reserved teenager who puts on the 'Joe Cool' act in order to attract the attention of the pretty girl.   Or what about all those people who after a few drinks undergo a complete Jekyll and Hyde personality transplant.

I'm not talking about the usual drunken behavior but the absolute extreme where an entirely new persona that no one had ever seen before manifests itself.   Are they crazy?"   Pearce raises his hand in order to respond.   "A rhetorical question once again, Mr. Pearce."   His hand goes back into his lap.   "Of course not!   They're merely drunk, right?   We all have at least two personality sets; that which we are and that which we wish we could be.

A schizophrenic can't distinguish between the two.   Reality is dream and dream is reality.   The dividing line is absent.   So they utilize each other equally but never overlap.

But what about the multiple personality, you ask?   Do not be mistaken, these are something completely different.   All of their personalities are distinct and separate.   They can overlap in attitudes, wants, actions, but each has nothing to do with its counterpart in the other persona.   Each façade has its own history and own set of memories.   And unlike the schizophrenic, they realize that they are sharing time and space with the other individuals trapped within their mind.

It's no surprise that most of these individuals go right over the edge.   Why would anyone want to deal with the fact that other lives have become incorporated into their own?   This would be truly insane but through it all, these individuals insist that they are as sane as you or I.   Rather than accept that there are other memories and intuitions existing as manifestations of past existences, the host individual tries to suppress them until they are finally overwhelmed, become despondent and often suicidal."

"Whoa, Doc.   Are you saying that these fruit cakes that all claim that they were Napoleon are legit?   I can't buy that one."

"Don't push it Mr. Pearce.   We're talking about entirely different situations here. I'm referring to those text book cases of multiple personalities which usually comprise personas of regular everyday people;   the scullery maid, student, girl-guide.   Nothing but regular mundane lives sharing a common host."

"Okay, Doc.   If you're saying that these memories are alive within all of us, then why don't more of us have these manifestations you're referring to?   I can barely remember last week, let alone events of lives that I lived before."

"You're still not understanding!   It's not your lives as in reincarnation!   It's the lives of your ancestors.   Genetic encoded memories that they passed down to you.   And you have already forgotten what I've explained to you, that the genetic coding is merely data storage.   You still have to have a decoder.   An activator; some form of antecedent which causes enzyme release that in turn tells the locus of these memories to start producing the manufacture of the proteins that are the memories.   In some cases it could be an emotional trauma or perhaps even a physical stimulus, like a concussion.   I like to refer to it as genetically linked, enzyme enhanced memories or GLEEM for short.

And let's not overlook the favorite past time of the upwardly mobile generation.   Life regression readings are all the rage. Hypnosis seems to be one way to activate this enzyme release but I can't tell you exactly why."

"But this hypnosis stuff they claim is evidence of reincarnation." Pearce interjects with the eagerness of a schoolboy attempting to correct his teacher in mid-sentence.

"An easy to make misinterpretation, Mr. Pearce," I counter, and I walk back to my chair, crossing my legs as I sit down. "The obvious is always the most difficult to accept. We know that if you hang a cord within reach of a newborn's crib, he or she will try to grasp the rope with their fingers and toes. Where did the baby learn this behavior? The answer is it didn't. Since we know that newborn chimpanzees exhibit this same behavior as they clutch to the underside of their mother's belly, does this mean that the baby is recalling a past reincarnation as an ape?

Of course not! And what about when we place a newborn in water, or even better, is birthed in water, and it instinctively knows how to swim. Does this mean the baby recalls a past reincarnation as a fish? Once again, it's a ludicrous assumption. The fact is we refer to them as instincts; patterns of behavior that have been passed down from ancestral forefathers by way of encoded genes.

So, when you refer to reincarnation, you have to carefully examine the readings of these people and see how detailed and specific they are. You may get a hundred people all claiming to have been Jesus or Napoleon, or even Cleopatra but you soon realize that the hypnotherapy has merely tapped into their hidden fantasies. Press the individual for details and you'll get a wonderful story with very little substance or fact. They're easy to identify and you can dismiss them right away.

But when you have an individual start telling you about how they were a mine worker, or house keeper, barely eking out a day's sustenance and then they provide you with minute details of where they drank their ale and with whom they drank it, you suddenly realize that this is no fantasy that you're dealing with. Press them further and they'll even tell you the address of the tavern and how to get there from their home, which is in a country and town they've never been to. You quickly realize that these individuals are legitimate as they reveal the utter insignificance of an ancestor's life.

And we can't forget that in some instances, the hypnotized person speaks in a foreign tongue, sometimes even in a language that no longer exists and you're amazed because they could barely master English, let alone another language. All you've done is tap into this store house of genetic information.

Sometimes the time frames that they provide create the suspicion that there is no possible way that the hypnotized person could be a direct descendant of the life they recall. So immediately we try to claim reincarnation. I would rather make the assumption that the time frame is inaccurate. A collection of memories may not use time in the same manner that we do. Time is actually a very ethereal concept. It is as long or as short as we tend to make it and, therefore, time may not have any specific reference within our memories."

"Okay, Doc. Let's say that I buy this argument of yours and I must say that you're doing a pretty damn good job of trying to prove your point, just where do you fit in to all of this. I can't figure that one out." Pearce scratched his head in a bemused fashion then stares at the carafe of coffee I have brewing on the side table beside my chair which I think is his way of signaling to me that he would like a coffee.

"Allow me to pour you some and then I'll explain everything you want to know, Mr. Pearce."

"John, please."

"Whatever." I reach over and fill a cup to the brim before offering it to him. "Where was I, oh yes? How do I fit in to all this? I thought it would have been ridiculously obvious to you. I am one of those unfortunates with all those memories just waiting to surface. You want to know about history, Mr. Pearce. I can tell you about history. You've already done some checking into the Kahana, so you know my family goes back a long, long way and has been involved in numerous history making events. But I don't think you realize just how ancient the family of Kahana really is."

Pearce shakes his head in confirmation.

"How does thirty-four hundred years sound to you? Over thirty centuries of memories, Mr. Pearce. All of them just floating around inside my DNA, just itching to be released."

"I don't mean to insult you, Doc, but isn't thirty-four hundred years stretching it a little bit?"

"Don't worry, Mr. Pearce. Your ignorance doesn't offend me at all. Why should I expect you to know what so few of my own relatives even know? As you discovered, my family comes from a relatively unknown Jewish heritage centered around the Black Sea. They were known as Karaites. Those that 'read' but there is another interpretation that is those that were 'called' and that would be the word's more appropriate translation.

Take my family back even farther and you find that they were from one of the twenty-four families of priests who served in the temple of Jerusalem. It was only after the destruction of the temple and self-imposed exile in Babylon that the name Kahana was applied to my family in order to denote a specific class.

I hope you're putting the pieces together and realizing that tracing one's ancestors back so far can be easier than you think. One of the customs peculiar to my family was that a male clan member could only choose a bride from one of two families initially. You either married the daughter of a priest, or the daughter of the king. As you can surmise, this limits the genetic pool; all those couplings, marrying within the same background, the same ancestry, over and over again. The same genetically coded memories combining hundreds of times over across the centuries. Can you even comprehend what kind of effect that would have through the hereditary chain, Mr. Pearce. I'll tell you. Your life becomes a textbook of facts and incidents that can be summoned on a moment's notice. You close your eyes and you see visions of battles, persecutions and celebrations, peopled by faces that have long since faded into the darkness of oblivion. What would you do with the ability to see through time?"

Pearce remained quiet, failing to respond to the question.

"This time it was not a rhetorical question, Mr. Pearce," I alerted him.

"I think that I'd be the luckiest person alive, Doc."

I look into Pearce's eyes and realize he is completely serious, which only infuriates me. No, I am beyond furious, I'm enraged. "Luck! You think this existence is something to be envious of? Do you believe that wading through a living nightmare is desirable? You have no idea what it's like to question every decision you make!

Not knowing whether you're arriving at it from your own judgment or because it's a course of action that's been programmed into your subconscious by some long-forgotten ancestor. Not knowing whether you still have freedom of choice, or is it merely a delusion since all your decisions in life have been laid out by your predecessors.

No, this is not a lucky or for that fact even envious life to live. To have dreams like normal men, now that is what I'm envious of. When I go to bed at night, I do so reluctantly because the dreams that I'm about to have are most often, not my own. People, faces, places, and I know none of them, yet there they are in glorious Technicolor panorama; life and death struggles playing out before my closed eyes from the mundane to the epical. I even have dreams in languages I don't even understand. People jabbering through the night without a clue as to what was being said.

There exists a volume of names and events that have no bearing upon my life except that they steal away the peace and oblivion that all of us are entitled to whenever you lay down and rest. Don't envy me! Pity me! That which you think is me is nothing more than a composite, a mosaic of all those that have donated their genes to my being and whom in some way have found their own resurrection through me.

It has become almost absurd. I no longer even have the satisfaction of my own signature. Several years ago I came across some papers written by my third great grandfather. Forgive my sarcasm, but it's becoming an ever present part of my nature or is it someone else's. I don't know any more. Lo and behold there's the very same signature. The very same squiggles and loops, the elongated double-crossing of the letter 't'. That which I had taken so much pride in developing as a youth was not even mine.

So who guides my hand when I write? A ghost of the past, come to be, by the sake of transferred chromatin? You tell me because I want to know! I want to know where I begin and all of the others stop! Because right now, I don't know where the defining lines are! So tell me once again how you would be so lucky to possess this gift."

"Okay, Doc, you've convinced me. No doubt about it. Honestly." Pearce flashes a smile to placate me but his eyes I can tell are saying, "What a nutcase!"

"Oh, shut up, Pearce! Don't try to patronize me. I'm not crazy and you know it. Otherwise you wouldn't be here. You wanted to know how I knew and now you have your story. So why not run along and see what your readership thinks about it."

"You know Doc, I was thinking", he pauses in mid-sentence, watching my reaction.

"I'll tell you what you were thinking, Mr. Pearce. It's pretty evident. You were thinking about getting the whole story; the thirty-five hundred year story. Am I right?"

"Not a bad idea. What about it. We could run it in installments. We'd have the readership begging for more."

"I know you don't totally believe me on this but why would you think that I'd give your paper my stories? I already have a career in publishing my stories in case you've forgotten."

"I'll tell you why, Doc. It doesn't really matter whether I believe you or not. What matters, if I'm guessing right is that you're tired of seeing your books shelved in the historical fiction section. You'd probably even like to strangle the next housewife who tells you how much she loved reading your book while she sat on the couch watching soaps and eating chips and wondering how you came up with such wonderful storylines. You want to make a statement and I can provide the forum for you to reach those people who would never dream of reading your books; historians, theologians, and even your fellow university professors that have scoffed at every one of your publications. Am I right?

Now you can use the media to challenge the establishment and their dogmas. And who knows, you may even come out on top. Yeah, they'll curse you, harangue you and crucify you. So what? What's most important is that they'll read you.

And if you're good Doc, if you can really give them something that proves indisputable; something that no one else could know but it checks out, then you've got them all. They'll hang on to your every word. And that's why you want my paper to publish your story. What do you say now, Doc?"

"Has possibilities."

"Sounds good to me! I'll take that as a yes. So where do you want to start telling your story? The beginning has always worked for me."

"I don't think you have that much time left in your life, Pearce. I think we're better off selecting a more recent historical period and concentrating on that for now."

"So, what period would you suggest?" Pearce pulls out another microcassette and replaces the one in the recorder which clicks to the finish.

I put my thumb and forefinger to my brow and close my eyes to think for the moment. "How about I select a time period that should prove easy for you to verify; one that everyone is talking about already. In that way, you can corroborate the details. If you're satisfied as to their authenticity, then we'll continue our task of rewriting history."

"It's your game, Doc. I'll play it anyway you want it."

"You may not like what I'm about to say. I may actually corrupt your perspective about matters you once took succor in. Your heroes will become false icons and those you perceived in the past as villains may turn out in a different light to be your saviors. Are you prepared to face that possibility?"

"Just give me a moment here, Doc." Pearce adjusts his seat on the sofa, making himself comfortable for what he knows will be a long haul. Loosening his coffee stained tie, he undoes the top two buttons of his shirt. "Okay Doc, I'm ready!"

"Be prepared for a long night, Pearce. I'm going to tell you a story about knights in shining armor and fair young princesses held prisoners by the evil dragons. The truth is that the dragons I'll speak of wore red or black robes and tri-cornered hats. But they most certainly breathed fire when they spoke and they made the people tremble with fear as they walked by.
A time of innocence and a time of deceit; when kings literally held the power of life and death in their hands. Let me welcome you to the Dark Ages. I'm going to shed some light on this darkness, but be aware, this is going to take quite a long time."

Pearce held out his cup looking for a refill. "Ready?" Pearce responded, nodding in anticipation.

"Sit back and I'll tell you the story of the Almyeri; a family of Kahana that journeys to the distant land of the Franks in search of a kingdom. Prepare yourself, Mr. Pearce. You're about to hear a story like you've never heard before . Are you ready?"

"Ready Doc, fire away!"

Chapter Two

Toronto: 1999

Closing my eyes, I lean back into the chair, the cushions firmly cradling my head. I need just the briefest of moments to collect my thoughts.

"Okay, Pearce, let's begin. I'll start with the ending."

"The ending?", Pearce parrots my words. "Why the ending?"

"Because it's my story."

Pearce sighs, resigning to the fact that he has to abide my whims if he wants his story.

"I'm glad you agree with me. As you'll come to realize, the ending is the only common ground for the entire book. All paths will lead to the conclusion. Then we'll go back two hundred years before that and you'll see how a bunch of isolated events taking place around the world actually led up to the finale. What I'm about to reveal to you is a determined effort to achieve a final solution to what the powers of that epoch deemed to be a serious problem."

"Doc, I'm looking to serialize this story in my paper. So providing the ending isn't exactly the way we sell papers. People like to start at the beginning."

"Don't worry about it, Mr. Pearce. I assure you, you're readership will continue buying. Sit back and I'll tell you about certain events of the mid ninth century; events that you and most everyone else don't even have a clue about. Trust me when I say, they didn't teach this stuff in your history class!"

Paris: 850 A.D.

"This is unpardonable! They cannot do this to you, My Liege!" the sharp, baritone voice, echoed between the cold, unyielding stone walls. "You are a prince of the blood. They have no right to disgrace you in this manner."

"Look about you, Charles. Where is my army to right this terrible wrong? Where are my brave knights to defend my honor? I cannot see them. Can you? Alas, you are all that has stood by me; my faithful companion; my one true friend. I shall never forget your fidelity. Your constant loyalty shall ease the heavy burden of death that hangs woefully around my neck."

"Your death? They would not dare to harm you, sire!"

The prince calmed the anxious look upon Charles St. Jean's face. "Who is going to stop them, dear friend? You? It is too late! It always has been a case of being too late. There is no escape for me. I cannot stay the executioner's axe any longer. It has been a good chase, Charles, but it is finally over."

Once more, Charles St. Jean grew alarmed. "The king will not let this evil thing happen!"

The prince responded with an amused laugh. "Not let it happen? Good King Charles is probably the very reason it will happen. And if not him, then it is Hincmar, and if not he, then the Pope. Perhaps even all three have mutually consented to my fate. Don't you see, my death is their release from their ancestor's bonds? I am the last of my line. Do you have any idea Charles what it feels like to be the last of anything? It is a feeling that defies description. They have most assuredly seen to it that none of my family resides anywhere within the borders of Septimania. I am a marked man. Accept my fate, good friend. I most certainly have. It will do you no good to become distraught over me. Now is the time for you to deny me, so that you do not have to share my fate."

"Deny you! Never!" St. Jean stamped his foot defiantly upon the rock floor of their cell. "The St. Jeans and the Almyeri have never been anything but steadfast friends. I shall not betray that friendship now. How can I deny you, William? Do you not see? I love you. From cradle to grave, I shall share the path you tread. Do not ask this evil thing of me. My neck shall be bared so that it too may feel the cold steel of treachery. I shall not forsake you!"

William reached out and embraced his friend within his all-encompassing arms. "And I love you, Charles! More than I even loved my own brother. And no two brothers shared a bond like we. But your death shall be my curse. Do not make me responsible for the deaths of all those that have dared to call me friend. Too much blood has already been shed on my behalf. Let me die with an eased conscience. If you truly love me, then live for my sake!"

"Do not ask me to forsake my vows, William. My allegiance is to none but you. I can serve no other man! What purposes have I in life if it be not to serve my prince?"

With the weight of his heavy hand, William slowly forced his aide to kneel upon the ground, then sat beside him. The cold dampness of the stone, forced the prince to coil his mantle about his body, preserving what little warmth remained within its folds. In the darkness that filled their cell, the scurry of rat's feet broke their moment of silence.

"Purpose? I will give you purpose. If we both are to die on the morrow, then who will sing the songs and praises of the Almyeri? Though my flesh die at the break of morn, will you be so cruel as to let my spirit die as well? You must live so that I might live through you. When children ask about the Almyeri of Septimania, it will be your knowledge that must tell the stories of our adventures together. And we have shared some of the greatest adventures of our times, have we not?" William elbowed his friend proddingly in his side. "You are the custodian of my being. Where you go, so shall be my presence. William of Septimania shall never die because he will live in the lore of Charles St. Jean. As loyal servants to my house, I entrust you and all your generations to bear the legend of the Almyeri for an eternity."

"Stories! What good are stories?" Charles began to weep openly for his master. "Let me die in battle, let me avenge your blood, let me share your fate, but do not ask me to become a weaver of tales. Who would listen to a man that sold out his prince for less than thirty silver pieces?"

"Those who witness the tears of your affection, they will know the truth. If you truly love me, good friend, then do as I request. No greater gift can I ask from you, than to give me immortality. What good is flesh if all I've been, all that I've accomplished is forgotten?"

William reached forward and placed his friend's head upon his heaving chest. "Listen well, sweet Charles, for soon my heart shall beat no more. No greater love for life has any man than I, but I do not fear my impending doom. I shall find sleep in a world that refused to give me rest. I have been hunted and dishonored, but I will not let those that availed themselves against me rest easy upon my death. Without you, my name shall disappear forever from the annals of time. That cannot be!

When my enemies go to war, I want them to hear the name of William of Septimania shouted among the ranks. When they go to bed, I want their dreams to be filled with images of my being. And when they make love to their women, I want their mistresses to call out my name in their moment of pleasure! I give you no easy task. No, indeed! I have set before you the most difficult of all. Will you not accept my demands of you?"

Tears streaming across his palled cheeks Charles St. Jean barely nodded his head in acceptance of his task. "I shall not fail you, my Lord. No matter how great the tide be that wishes to wash away the hallowed name of your family, I shall stand adamant in its path and give it no passage. Upon my life I swear this!"

William embraced his companion affectionately, kissing him tenderly upon the cheek. "I know you will not fail me, Charles. No man has ever had a truer friend and ally. In every campaign, you have stood faithfully at my side, unfaltering in your loyalty. You are the reason why I have made it thus far in my life. You have deflected every dagger that awaited me in the dark. I have not been an easy burden to you. So many times I have asked you to risk your life for causes only of a concern to me."

Charles broke free from his lord's embrace, straightened his soiled red tunic, and then rose as the proud, defiant soldier he had always been. "And I would risk my life a thousand more times if you requested me to do so, my prince. Just say the word! The St. Jeans have no masters save the Almyeri!"

"Say that it is not so. That all I have been through the years to you, Charles, is your master? A sacred duty? A regal responsibility?", the prince inquired, a wounded grimace upon his sorrowful lips.

"You know me better, my liege," Charles responded firmly, his jaw squared with resolve, "it has always been more than that! I have known no finer friend. No one is closer to my heart than you."

"I am glad. If ever I have treated you as a nothing more than a servant then please accept my apology, even if only it comes from the one they refer to denigrate as the Jew Prince.", William sighed then searched the expression on his friend's face.

"You wound me severely, my Lord. Have I ever given cause to show any attitude but love to you, whether you were Jew or not? Have I ever expected you to love me less because I am Christian? You have stung my heart." No sooner had Charles said his statement, William's mouth broke into a broad, comforting grin.

Rising majestically from the cell's floor he walked to the small window that hung just above head height, so that all he could see was the clear blue sky and a flock of swallows fleeing the autumn chill. "Yes, the Jew and the Christian who set out to conquer the world. My, we had our times! Such things have never mattered between you and I have they?" William smiled as he recollected the fondness of their shared memories but slowly the corners of his lips curled into a bitter snarl. "And yet, that very fact that we chose to overlook has been the cause of our ruination. No one but you, dear friend, has ever been willing to overlook that simple fact. Not even my wife! Come see the double cursed and blessed Jew; the freak of Narbonne!

That is why I have loved you so much, Charles. You defied them all and continued to stand by me. We were like those birds up there." William pointed outside the window. "Free to go as we pleased. Why has God allowed this to happen to me? Happen to us? I sometimes fail to understand the reasoning behind this world; a world that was clearly never mine." William's chin sunk to his chest, his eyes moistened with tears. "Is there any reasoning to this world, Charles, or is it simply madness?"

Charles placed his left arm around William's shoulders, one of the few times he had ever permitted himself to show such familiarity with his king; a reckless gesture that would have been frowned upon in the courts as indecent and a total lack of proper decorum. But he knew William had always been a man of flesh and bone and never one of the pompous, overstuffed aristocrats that ported themselves around as gods at the palace; too dignified to touch one of their subordinates, except for their servant's wives that is. That was one area of familiarity which was always condoned.

"We live in a world without God, my Lord. Certainly, we say all the prayers expected of us and the bishops bring to us the words of the Lord as they interpret them but the words are hollow and, our actions sinful. Was that not the reason your family was brought to us in the first place? Was it not because we were a land without God?

Therefore they sent messengers to lands unknown in order to find a living connection with God! In order to bring some of that God-like purity of your ancestors into permanence with our own souls, the blood of your line to be mixed with that of the Carolingians. Was not that the plotted deed of madmen? Rather than turn to God, they would try to inherit Him?'

"Are you also implying that they were mad or that my family was mad to have come here in the first place?"

"Not mad, your grace, but if you forgive my brashness, in the very least, foolish. This was not a world of your kind. The Almyeri failed to see the difference until it was too late. In this land there are no such things as eternal pledges. Bonds are made to be broken. Truths are made to be altered. Your family came from a land where an oath was kept in fear that God would make judgment. We had no God here in the west to ensure that our word was kept. There could never be any doubt that you would eventually fall victim to this deception.

Do you think that Pepin Herstel would have ever invited your family to our land if he did not know deep in his heart that eventually the Almyeri would be eliminated? You cannot have a country with two kings, especially when your family, being outsiders, were more royal than the reigning monarch of France. How could your ancestors have ever thought otherwise?"

"Well put, Charles!" the prince nodded in agreement. "My family has lived in a dream world, afraid to open its eyes to the reality that was always there. And you need not fear your brashness. I am hardly in a position where I could take any action even if I was offended," he laughed half-heartedly.

"Still, you try to make light of your predicament, sire. How can you laugh, knowing that tomorrow you will laugh no more? We must try to escape! It would be possible to overpower the guards." St. Jean mimed the method he would use to strangle the turnkey. "And if we should fail, at least you would die like a true king. They are not fit to stretch your neck before them."

"What then?" William held out his hands to the sky supplicatingly. "Where would we find refuge? Do you think that they would ever stop searching for me? No, my days are numbered. There is no escape. But it is also up to you Charles, to ensure the people that all that we shared together was not in vain. There must be those that will listen and wherever you can find such good people, you will find the God of the Jews and Christians. You must not hold it against them that those controlling their country and their minds are a godless race. There will come a time when the people will see for themselves that they were misled and they will turn away from their ministers and seek their own paths. You must work towards that day. That will be a fitting revenge."

"With God's help I will be the reaper of your vengeance, a curse upon your enemies, and a bane to their very existence. They shall have more to contend with the Almyeri after death than they ever feared while you were alive. I swear it upon my life and the lives of my ancestors." The normally sedate soldier made the sign of the cross across his chest, keeping his head bowed so that

25

his prince would not see the river of tears streaming across his face.

"Rise, Charles St. Jean, son of Remi!" William reached behind his own neck and beneath his mantle in order to untie the leather thong that he wore since the death of his own father. "I now proclaim you, Deus imperator servitudis. You are the servant of the Almighty God. You have no other master." Like a father giving his eldest son his most treasured possession, William knotted the thin thong that held a worn piece of stone around his companion's neck.

Charles choked back on his tears. He knew that this would be the last gift he would ever receive from his beloved friend. A gift so sacred that he had never questioned its purpose before, in spite of all the years he had served alongside his prince. "Excellency..." he gagged as he tried to swallow. "Though I know not the nature of this gift, I know that I am not deserving of it. I will see to it that your son receives it."

"No!" the prince screamed and hammered his fist against the yielding air. "No one is to have it but you! Especially not some bastard child who calls himself my son!"

"But sire, he is your flesh and blood?"

"Is he? That has never been proven by my wife of so little affection. I shall go to my death and never know the truth. I fear there will be no tears shed by wife and child over my grave. They are not of my kind. They are both of that world that you so angrily condemn." The taut expression on William's face suddenly relaxed and he smiled once again at Charles as he gazed upon the stone hanging around his courtesan's neck.

"Take care of that stone, good friend. It has been in my family for over two thousand years. You speak of a connection with God. That stone is the only connection that has ever existed. Even by marrying into the family of my ancestors, they have never been able to lay hold to that sacred relic. And now, it is up to you to keep it from falling into their hands."

"You know that I will, my Liege. But I still do not understand. It is merely a worn piece of stone. Does it have magical powers? Perhaps we can use it to escape from here. Or if it's precious then we may persuade our jailers to release us."

William shook his head in denial. "I am afraid that it is not like anything of that nature. Accept my word, that by wearing it, you have already escaped from this world of hate and deceit. You now wear proof of the legend of the twelve stones!"

A blank look spread across Charles St. Jean's face. "The twelve stones? I have not heard of such a legend."

Gazing deeply into the eyes of his companion, William began to unfold the legend that he had grown up with. A legend older than anyone could remember. "It is not a legend of your world, Charles. It is as ancient as the dawn of my people. I bring the story to you from the sages of the East. When you hear of it, you will know that it is no mere stone that you wear about your neck. Do you know of the covenant at Sinai?"

"I am not a pagan, my Lord", Charles quipped sarcastically. "We Christians too know of the covenant of the Lord with the children of Israel that took place upon the mountain of Sinai."

"Then the telling of the legend will be easier for you, as you will know of what I speak. When Moses first descended the mountain with the tablets written by the finger of God in his arms, he became disgusted upon seeing the people worshipping the golden calf, a practice they had brought with them out of the land of Egypt. In a state of fury, he hurled the twin tablets down to the ground still far below and they shattered upon the impact..."

"You don't mean that this stone...?"

William nodded his head in affirmation. "The very same. When it hit the ground it fractured into twelve pieces. Haven't you ever wondered what happened to the original tablets? It is common knowledge that Moses returned up the side of the mountain and the Lord gave him another set of tablets, but why no mention of the original. They still bore the imprint of God and for that very reason they are holier than any artifact the Church holds in its possession. The old sages knew that they could not be discarded having been touched by God, so they created the story that Moses put the broken tablets into the ark, along with manna and Aaron's staff. But the ark was made to hold the unbroken tablets, not the shattered pieces."

Charles began to fondle the stone that lay beneath his tunic, in awe of its enormous spiritual significance. Suddenly he began to fear its imagined power.

"Do not be afraid," William calmed his friend. "It will cause you no harm. That is not the nature of the stone. It was broken apart by an evil world and only when all twelve segments are brought together once more, will evil be purged forever."

Charles's eyes grew wide with excitement. "Where am I to find the other eleven pieces, sire?"

"The legend says that each prince of the tribes of Israel took a segment to themselves. The prince of Judah claimed that very piece you wear and it has passed down from father to son ever since. As for the other pieces, they have been scattered to the four corners of the world."

"Where am I to look?" St. Jean inquired of his seemingly hopeless task.

"It may not even be your task to search for the stones. All who have tried in the past have failed. Only one of pure heart and exalted faith will ever succeed. King David thought that he was the one to unite the stones and instead shattered his nation. Simon, the brother to Judah Maccabee thought the mission had befallen him and the jealousies of his court ended his life. Anyone who has ever tried has been made to suffer for their failure. So, keep the stone hidden, my friend and take care of those duties which I have entrusted you with after my death. Somewhere, sometime in the future will come a man befitting the task."

"But how will I know to whom I shall give the stone?" St. Jean's mind was filled with endless confusion. Question upon question racked his brain.

Very calmly, William answered his companion's concerns. "You will not know. It is not your part to know who, or where, or why. If the time should come, you will just know. Your primary concern is to see that the stone does not fall into the hands of those who represent the evil of this world. They would not hesitate to kill you if they knew the legend, in order to keep the pieces from ever becoming united again. The bishops must never hear of this sacred stone. Kings must never know of its existence. That is the only way that you can keep it safe. As custodian of God's presence on earth, you are greater than them all. Kneel to no man, for none is worthier than you. Upon that stone you shall build God's church!"

William withdrew his mantle, unclasping it from about his neck. Folding it neatly in a square he placed it upon the ground to cushion his head. Lying back he prepared to take his final sleep.

"My Lord!", Charles exclaimed. "Surely you do not intend to sleep these final few hours. There is so little time and so many things to say!"

"Not only do I intend to sleep but I intend to dream, dreams of youth and of better times, dreams of friends and family that live no more. I go to join my ancestors. Sweet Charles let me have my dreams of peace to soothe my troubled brow."

"Shall I wake you before the dawn?"

"See to it that I sleep, Charles. Promise me that you will not let me wake upon the morrow. I have taught you the manner of the Judaeorum Colaphus after the ways of my ancestors."

St. Jean looked upon his friend with horror on hearing the suggestion of the age's old art. "I cannot do it, my liege! This time you ask too much of me."

27

William gazed pleadingly into his companion's eyes. "Its manner is quick and painless. You have seen me use it and I know that you have studied it well and used it in your own fashion. A slight cupping of the hand and a swift blow to the back of the neck, which is all I ask of you Charles. I will be asleep and therefore my neck will be the most vulnerable. I will offer you no resistance. You, yourself stated that none of my executors was worthy of stretching my neck. But I deem you to be worthy, Charles. Only you shall have the honor to see me die like a man instead of a wounded animal. Do not look so aghast! Know it well that I join my illustrious ancestors. Now, I intend to sleep and dream of a noble past, relieved to know that I shall not have to wake and see this wretched world again!"

"But..." there were no words that Charles St. Jean could think of at that moment to fill his open mouth.

"Farewell sweet Charles. Know this with all your heart, that I loved you well."

William lay his head upon his furled cloak and shut his eyes to dream of his life and of better times; to dream where it all began. Of fair Narbonne, precious jewel of Septimania and the once famed capital of a kingdom soon to exist no more.

Chapter Three

Toronto: 1999

I could tell that Pearce was dying to ask a litany of questions but wasn't about to dare utter a sound until he was convinced that I had finished. He had been scribbling furiously with pencil and pad throughout my dissertation, all the while, his tape recorder whirring annoyingly in the background.

"So that's how it ends, Mr. Pearce. As they say, not with a bang, but a whimper. The end of a dynasty! A monarchy doomed to extinction!"

"But, Doc! How can you explain that there's no record of any such monarchy? They can't just disappear!"

"Can't they, Mr. Pearce? How many Egyptian dynasties simply vanished into thin air when the next ruling family chiseled their names over the older ones? History has always been subjected to obliteration in order to protect the future. That is the true history of mankind! The victors have always erased the vanquished."

"So, this Prince William of yours, if I should accept that he even existed, had to be a prince of somewhere?"

"Most definitely! The legends of the Almyeri are no different from the legends of Camelot. The names still exist into our time, but the facts are covered by layers of fiction. Even the somewhere, still exists. Grab your pencil and I'll take you back another couple of centuries to the 'somewhere and how it all began."

Pyrenees: 673 A.D.

Paul, Duke of Visigothic Spain, sat straddled across the inlaid woven and leather saddle that girthed his majestic dappled mount, as he surveyed the stretch of land that spread before him, reminiscent of the first maiden he had ever laid conquest to. Virgin lands with lush, green grass rolling forward to meet the foothills of the mountains that he had just traversed at the helm of his mighty army. It was the first time these soldiers had seen the lands on the other side of the Pyrenees; an unknown world enshrouded in myth and mystery. Paul had never had any desire or purpose to leave the rich pasture lands of his estate in Spain until now. Viewing this untouched paradise, he regretted all those years he spurned the urges to venture into these uncharted lands. These were lands well worth adding to his vast estates. Lands that would make him richer than even the king he served.

The southern extremity of the Spanish March in the spring was a landscape ablaze with color as flowers appeared in full blossom exuding euphoric fragrances, the seeds of which were incapable of blowing westward across the great mountains. Meandering streams coursed the life-nourishing soil. Eden had been rediscovered and Paul of Burgos truly regretted that it was now his sworn duty and mission to lay this beauteous land to waste.

The world was changing drastically but somehow this small isolated expanse of heaven on earth managed to avoid the transition. Wishing to maintain its status as an independent and self-governing entity, the cities of Septimania were adamant in providing nothing more than a nominal tribute to King Wamba of Spain. Every year they would send their contributions to his coffers with the expectation that it would buy them another year without his intrusion into their lands. In reality it was extortion but they gladly paid it to preserve their isolation.

But Wamba had grown greedy and in his desire to be recognized as the next Holy Roman Emperor he promised the Church in Rome he would Christianize these heathen lands to the east of his kingdom. To those inhabitants across the Pyrenees, Spain had been nothing more than a landlord they tolerated but now it was ruled by a monarch who knew little of his family's perpetual agreements and concessions with the lands bordering the south of Aquitaine. If he had been cognizant of any of these, he would have thought better of trying to divest these lands from the populace and placing them under the ownership of the Church in Rome. They were tolerant of many of the abuses by the Spanish monarchy but that was one condition they would never tolerate and they swore to make him regret his foolish decision.

For unlike anywhere else in the Spanish domain, Christians were only a minority in these eastern lands. Those few that did live in Septimania were strict adherents to Arian Christianity, having neither allegiance nor love for Rome and its power mongering bishop whom now called himself the Pope. To them, Wamba was a traitor to the religion of his own Visigothic heritage, bending knee to a faith determined to control all the kings and wealth of Europe.

These Arians stemmed from a proud race, a free people who had opposed every would-be conqueror since the Romans first invaded their lands over nine hundred years prior. Independence and freedom were the milk upon which they were suckled and concepts held sacred as they swore they would die before permitting Wamba to sell their birthright to the Catholic Church. Their faith was non-negotiable.

Hideric, the mayor of Nimes was the first to raise his voice and call for rebellion. Soon afterwards, Narbonne, Rousillon and Aniane heeded the summons to fight for the preservation of their freedoms and liberties. Before long dozens of cities had sent cohorts of men to join the coalition forces.

Wamba responded by hastily gathering his army to meet what he anticipated could only amount to a feeble and meager resistance. Placing the Spanish troops under Duke Paul, his most senior and capable general, the king's orders were simple; the entire district of Septimania was to be decimated. Not a single leader of the revolt was to be left alive. Fields and towns were to be ravaged and razed to the ground. Males were to be slaughtered without mercy and females enslaved as long as they were young and beautiful. The rest were to be left homeless or dead, the choice was left to Paul of Burgos to decide. There no longer would be a Septimania. It would cease to exist as if it had never been. Such was to be the price for resisting the kind offer from Rome to join their Church and it would be a lesson to all other heathens that refused Catholicism.

Duke Paul of Burgos rode swiftly across the plains surrounding Carcassonne, halting his troops barely a mile from the outskirts of the city. The lack of resistance encountered along the way made him uneasy. Although he knew the presence of his army would inspire fear in the Septimanians, he still had not anticipated a total unwillingness on their part to engage his forces.

Even the most ignoble of cowards finds the courage to resist when there is no other choice but death. The sheer silence emanating from the city was the most disturbing facet of all. Something was definitely wrong. He could feel it; he could smell it. Like all great military men, he had an inner voice that had guided him infallibly in the past and he knew it would be folly to ignore it. Everything he was feeling, shouted 'trap' inside his head.

Reports provided by Wamba's strategists concerning Septimania's defensive strength were sketchy at best and fairly antiquated, yet still, they had suggested the area was fully capable of mounting a sizable resistance. Where had they all gone? Retreated? Possibly, but Duke Paul could not accept that answer considering they had not even engaged in battle a single time. Where could they even possibly retreat to? No matter where they ran they would be eventually caught and cut down. The ominous silence began to weigh nervously on Paul's senses. Distancing him from the city until he scouted it thoroughly was best at this time. He was about to trumpet a return to base, which would be set several miles from the city, when one of his officers pointed excitedly towards the horizon. The enemy had been sighted!

They were like the waves of the ocean, approaching in the tens of thousands. The land they tread was blotted out by their presence; a human tidal wave of insurmountable strength and power. Soon every hectare was dotted in brightly shining armor that stung the eyes of Paul's soldiers with reflected sunlight. The Septimanian's had attained the first upper hand by approaching from the west. Not only had they placed the Visigoths with their backs to the wall of the city, but they were using the morning sun's rays to blind his men. By afternoon the same rays would be shining directly into the eyes of Wamba's army. For an entire day the Visigoths would find themselves not only fighting a superior force in numbers but against nature as well. Paul's inner voice now warned him about what every general fears most in battle; total annihilation of his own troops. As he scanned the battlefield, he saw that every route had been carefully sealed as if they knew his first reaction would be to try and circle around his enemy. Sounding their own trumpets, the Septimanians bore down quickly upon his forces, preparing to drown the Visigoths by sheer numbers which were incalculable.

Paul had never witnessed an army of its like before; units of Goths and Franks, Saracens and even other Visigoths, men of his own blood, interspersed throughout the main body of the enemy. Tribes and nations that he knew were sworn enemies of one another and now standing shoulder to shoulder in defense of Septimania. In his capacity to appreciate all things military, in spite of the dread of facing a superior enemy, Paul remained enthralled by the array of the various ethnic regalia of the opposing force. The hopelessness of his plight for the moment became secondary to his curiosity and interest in determining the nature of the enemy. What confused him most sorely was the identity of the enemy's main contingent, the likes of which he had never seen before. Their arms and regalia were totally unfamiliar. In appearance they resembled the Saracens of the North African coast, but their skin was fairer like that of the Goths. And their armor was most definitely Byzantine in manufacture. Of that he was certain. In his paranoia he began searching for the unseen hand behind the rebellion. Was the Eastern Empire somehow responsible for this uprising? How was it even possible for Constantinople to establish a Byzantine colony on the southern coast of Aquitaine without anyone's knowledge in Spain? Who were these strange people and why were they here? The endless stream of questions raced through Paul's mind as he grasped for an explanation of their origins. But the time for questions had passed as the front lines of each of the opposing forces engaged in battle.

Now positioned to the rear of his own forces, since initially he had been at the head of his army when approaching the town, Duke Paul had no other choice but to watch the enemy mow down his supply train and reservists that trailed behind his seasoned troops, like a scythe hacking through tall grass. It would only be minutes until his losses would number a couple of thousand but then the pitched battles would begin as the enemy reached the body of his main force. But by then the tide would have already turned as the enemy would have gained the advantage of pressing forward while the Visigoths would take a more defensive stance.

Looking beyond the encircling army no more than a tenth of a league from where he stood, Duke Paul saw in the distance exactly what his adversary's reserve forces consisted of; farmers hoisting scythes, peasants swinging axes, even young children ready to defend this land of theirs. They had all come to fight against the intruder. Soldier, farmer, civilian, all prepared to die for what they believed in. In his past experiences of conquest, this could only mean one thing; they possessed a prize so valuable that the value of their own lives was insignificant in comparison. It had to be a treasure beyond measure; a prize definitely worth fighting for if only his forces could survive the day. That probability was diminishing with each passing second. The front line of the enemy's charge moved steadily forward, forcing the Visigoths to be impaled upon the swords and lances of their own comrades that stood behind. There were so many fallen men that Paul could not even calculate where his losses now stood. Five thousand, perhaps ten, he had plenty of more men that could be sacrificed but to what end? A general knows when the battle is lost, and Paul of Burgos recognized all the evidence of a rout as he could see numerous cohorts from amongst his troops breaking rank to turn and run. It would be perhaps only an hour before he was counting his losses at twenty or thirty thousand. His army was being decimated before him and as the insurgent masses closed on Paul's forces, he abandoned any further thoughts of battle.

The enemy numbers were like grains of sand on the beach. No matter how seasoned his men were and bloodied in battle, there was not even the slightest chance of salvaging a victory today. There were only two options available to him. The first was to sound the retreat and flee for their lives. Paul of Burgos had never turned tail in battle before and the thought of doing it now left a bitter taste in his mouth. And even if they did attempt to retreat, the question that would immediately follow is to where? The stone walls of the city lay directly behind, the gates closed to them, to the right and left were walls built by the masses of enemy soldiers. They could possibly break through if they formed a wedge, but in doing so they would be decimated. He was neither so heroic nor foolish to see that he had no other choice but to select the second option. Ordering his men to throw down their weapons, a good commander knows when the odds are insurmountable. Surrender meant that he would live to fight another day. Kings always ransomed their nobles when taken hostage and today would be no different. There would be another time to return and fight for this unknown prize that these people of Septimania were willing to die for.

Duke Paul dismounted, handing his horse's reigns to the first officer of the Spanish force, then walked at a steady pace towards Hideric, the only familiar face amongst the sea of faces that he recognized in the crushing wave that swamped his own forces. Meanwhile the Visigoth trumpeters sound the surrender, responded to immediately by the clang of swords as they hit the ground as fast as the Visgothic soldiers could release them. An eerie silence draped the battlefield as the Duke approached the Septimanian leader. Men from both armies parted simultaneously to let him pass, not a single word being exchanged. Standing before Hideric's white stallion, Paul of Burgos knelt on one knee, humbled and respectful performing his act of surrender according to all the rules of war by holding up his sword in both hands and offering it to the victorious commander..

Hideric grasped Paul's sword and waved the captured weapon in a circular motion above his head, signaling an end to the battle. A rousing, thunderous cheer of jubilation and exaltation reverberated from the throats of the Septimanians. The Visigoths just bowed their heads in shame. Hideric dismounted, then reached down to pull the Duke to his feet, and embraced him openly. The sword was returned, symbolic of their mutual respect according to the laws of chivalry and the two armies then marched side by side towards the coastal plain where the city lay. As bloody as short battle had been, in this enlightened era, men lived or died by the rules of chivalry and that meant there would be no harsh words or exchanges between victor and vanquished. From this moment forward, Paul and his army would not be harmed unless the rules of chivalry were violated. Escorted by the town mayors, as demeaning and unpalatable as the surrender had been, Paul felt more like an honored ambassador than a conquered enemy as he relinquished the field of battle.

As they marched towards the city's gates, Paul's line of vision was drawn constantly towards one of the mayors that had been introduced by Hideric as being one Jacob ben Todros, the Berger of Narbonne. At first sight, he was a peculiar man, dressed in Byzantine garb. It was his contingent of soldiers that had comprised the greatest part of the rebel army. Based on first impressions, Paul's immediate thoughts were that this stranger and his unfamiliar people had leaped from a different world, a different time, into the lands of the Spanish March. He had not seen the likes of them before, not even in Wamba's kingdom which was for the most part a multicultural society.

Unable to restrain his curiosity any longer, Paul of Burgos broke his self-imposed silence. "Good sir, Hideric of Nimes, what manner of people does this Jacob of Narbonne command? In all my days I have not seen their likes. They are a peculiarity that I cannot easily dismiss. From whence are their origins for I can see clearly that they are not of our stock?"

Hideric laughed. "They are Narbonnaise, of course! They have always been Narbonnaise."

Paul winced under Hideric's mocking tone feeling that he was being ridiculed. "But they are not Goths! Look at their features. Anyone could easily tell that."

"Perhaps Goths are not Goths," the mayor continued the game of riddles in spite of Paul's annoyance.

"Sir, you have bested me in battle, but do not mock me in defeat, nor play me for the fool."

The game was allowed to go no further, being interrupted by Jacob ben Todros whom had overheard their conversation and felt it best intervene before Paul could press Hideric any further, which might lead to a breach of the code of honor that was now in place between enemy soldiers .

"Do not trouble thyself, Paul of Burgos. Even if the good Hideric could explain, it would not be easy to do so. Suffice it to say that my people have lived in this land for over ten centuries, long before there were Goths or Visigoths to spread their rule over Septimania. We came as seafarers, merchants and traders. Some even came later as refugees escaping persecution in our own homeland in the early days of Rome."

"If such was true, then why had I not heard of you and your people? What homeland could you have possibly come from?"

"Such impatience is not good for a man's internal peace nor for the preservation of this uneasy external peace between us," Jacob tutted. "Be patient good Sir and in time all will be explained." The mayor of Narbonne turned in his saddle and pulled away from the Spanish duke, replying as he did so, "Remember what I have told you, in time you will learn the truth."

For almost a month Paul of Burgos found himself moved from town to town until his transfers ceased and he was now confined to a small but pleasant enough room in the Palace of Narbonne. There had been very little communication with his jailers. Not a word had been mentioned about the remnant of his army or their whereabouts. Whether his officers remained alive or not he also could not ascertain. Certainly, he had been made comfortable, but despite all their careful attention to his needs, he knew that he was no more than a prisoner of high rank to be ransomed. And then he grew distraught wondering why it was taking so long for the king to make the ransom. Surely the price could not have been exceedingly high that Wamba could not raise the sum. The lack of progress and communication was most disconcerting, but he refused to let his captors see his mounting distress. He would remain stalwart in his resolve to be seen as nothing less than Duke Paul, their superior in every manner.

To idle away the time, Paul attempted to recall every detail of his initial shock at seeing Narbonne when he was led through its massive stone gates, just three days earlier. The architecture was clearly Eastern, far more intricate and lavish than the primitive structures of his own land. If there was a treasure, then this would be the city where they kept it hidden. This is where he would have to launch an attack if afforded another opportunity to lead the Visgothic armies. Then his mind jumped to other matters. When he looked up at the windows and the ramparts, it was the vision of the people that struck him most; they were from all races, all creeds, all apparently living harmoniously. They had not separated themselves into ethnic boroughs as was the residential manner in Spain. This was a mosaic of humanity unlike any that he had ever witnessed before. As they led him through the streets he heard tumultuous jubilation, voices raised in such joy that one would believe that they had just conquered an empire. 'Naive', he commented to himself, thinking how gullible they must be to believe this was truly an end to their problems. Wamba would make them pay. 'Let us see how much they sing then," he concealed his smile. Here, he was nothing more than a stranger in an even stranger world, but every detail was recorded to his memory; every weakness in the battlements and spots where the garrisons had their views obstructed of the field below. In time he would return with an army that would lay siege to its walls. 'Yes, let them sing and laugh now. Their time will come!"

On the eve of his fourth day in Narbonne, Paul was summoned from his room to attend a Diet comprised of the mayors of Septimania. His heart was uplifted by the news, fully expecting to be released, thinking that the King's representative had finally arrived and concluded the financial transaction of his ransom. He questioned the guard as to which of his peers had come but the guard simply replied that he knew of no such arrival. That was not too unusual. After all, why would someone of such low rank have knowledge of ambassadorial vistors?

Then as Paul thought about the situation, his mood grew black. Protocol was obviously not being adhered to. Any ambassador should have been brought to where he was being kept captive in order to properly seal the agreement by witnessing that he had not been harmed in any way. It was foolish to pay a ransom before seeing the prisoner, in case the prisoner was infirmed or perhaps in the worst case scenario, already dead. The circumstances of this Diet were not making any logical sense. He calmed himself by the thought that perhaps his belief that he would be released was premature. It was possible that this Diet was merely to confirm that a message had been delivered and that a ransom was to be paid soon. The wheels of affairs of state simply often turned slowly, thereby causing a delay. That was the only logical solution he could arrive at. Paul laughed silently at himself at his foolishness to have been so concerned thinking that his confinement was turning him into an old woman.

Before the assembled mayors of Septimania, Paul of Burgos stood silently, head cowed in shame as he awaited their decision to be delivered. The initial shock when the Diet had informed him that Wamba had refused to pay any ransom still sent shivers up his spine. How could he not even be considered of value to the King to merit a ransom? Apparently Wamba would not acknowledge that in the defeat of his army he had lost all claims to the lands of the Spanish March, holding the Duke personally responsible. Sentenced in absentia for dereliction of duty and cowardice, Wamba had annexed all properties belonging to Paul of Burgos, thus leaving the Duke as a man penniless, his name expunged from the aristocracy of his homeland. It was the final wording of the King's letter that cut him to the bone. It asserted that these penalties were inflicted for the crime of treason. Duke Paul was speechless upon the pronouncement of those words. Treason? How could the survival of his forces by surrender be considered treason? Was he supposed to let them all die on the battlefield? But now he had been condemned to a living death and the thought of letting himself die during the battle was not as bad as it had initially seemed.

The mayors shuffled the papers containing their final judgment between each other, without saying a word. Finally, Jacob ben Todros rose from his seat to break their silence. Paul swallowed with difficulty, preparing for the worst. He was now branded a traitor, unredeemable by his own king, a pariah amongst nations. Nothing had gone as anticipated. He had been betrayed by his own king whom he had served loyally all these years. He was now destitute and homeless. Harboring such a man was not even a consideration for other nations, else they earn the angst and animosity of Wamba. 'A death sentence would be most welcome at this time,' he thought to himself.

"Then it is agreed!" Jacob ben Todros nodded to the other mayors. "Paul, Duke of Spain, are you prepared to accept the verdict of this Diet?" Paul kept his head lowered in acquiescence. "It has been found that upon leading an army with no other purpose than to utterly destroy our lands that you are our sworn enemy. But it was our armies that first attacked and subsequently you surrendered your army to avoid further bloodshed. Therefore, according to all codes of honor and chivalry, you are guilty of no crimes under present laws. You have acted honorably and with wisdom, values which can be cherished. You are but a soldier of your nation, a reality which is not a crime unto itself. You follow orders but do not initiate such orders of yourself. It is clear from your King's reaction that the entire confrontation was a result of his greed and tyranny. If every general was to be held accountable for the transgressions of their kings, we would have none left in the world at all. You are highborn, and as such deserving of respect yet your king has dishonored you and seized all that you once possessed. This tells us much about your relationship with King Wamba. That you were as much adversary as you may have been confidant. As such, you could be of great benefit to us, or you can remain a threat. Ultimately the choice of former or latter is a matter of your own choosing. Therefore, it has been decided that your penalty, shall also be a matter of your own choosing. Should you see yourself as loyal to your King and a sworn enemy to our lands, then you will spend the rest of your days confined to the cell in which you have now resided, but if you see yourself as adversary, then there is much that we can learn from you and would welcome you amongst our ranks."

Lifting his head, the offer from Jacob ben Todros had most certainly caught the duke's attention. "What is it that you wish from me?"

"We are well aware that Wamba has not abandoned his desire to take our lands and that can only mean he will return with an even larger army in the future. You no longer have any allegiance to your former king but you are in possession of valuable knowledge concerning the strategy and manner in which Wamba's other generals wage war. We need you to use that knowledge in our defense if you are so willing. We want you as our protector."

"You are asking me to be a traitor as the price for my freedom."

"You are already branded as a traitor," Jacob ben Todros reminded him. "You have already lost everything. Your titles, your inheritance, even your country, now at least you will have an opportunity to perchance gain some of that back."

Throwing back his shoulders, Paul resumed the stature of the proud noble that he once was. "Lords, to be called a traitor is a shameful punishment to bear, but to be an actual traitor, that is an irreprehensible crime that will torment me for the rest of my life. To turn one's back on their homeland and take arms against their own people is neither a decision lightly made nor one that I can tell you at this instant. I am a man of honor, but to what end will honor prevail if I do such a thing? Such a decision can only be made when there is justification to clearly demonstrate that which is right from that which is wrong. Show me that justification and perhaps the fog will clear from my head. Prove to me that by aiding you and I am correcting some great injustice of this world and then perhaps I can override this feeling of self-loathing. You ask me to side with your cause and yet I do not even know who you are. Nothing of what you have showed me makes sense to me. The existence of this city, your world, does not make sense to me. So how am I to give allegiance to an enigma that I cannot even resolve? You beseech me to be your protector, then prove to me that you are worthy of that protection!"

"You want answers, Paul of Burgos, then you shall have those answers," Jacob ben Todros repudiated him. "You may not like what you are about to hear but it is the truth. It is the only truth of this land and it will expose you as having lived nothing but a lie for all the years of your life. Are you prepared to hear the truth! Are you willing to concede that perhaps you are a sinner, have always been a sinner and only now you have a chance for redemption?"

"I am", Paul stoically replied.

"If you and your King and all your men of wisdom had spent less time thinking of themselves as the center of the universe, then they would have realized just how trifling and small your kingdom is in respect to the world itself. You knew nothing of us because we wished to have nothing to do with you. Your pettiness and war mongering are an anathema to mankind. Your Church of Rome is nothing more than a corpse of rotting soles, worms eating their way from its core and spreading their pestilence across the Earth. If we had been more like you, then it is your eradication that we would have undertaken, smiting your kingdom in its infancy before it had an opportunity to leach its poison bile into our world. Only because of our benevolence, our mercy, and our beliefs in the greater good of mankind that we did not make it so!"

Paul questioned this perspective of the world according to Narbonne. "Where do you think you had the power to remove the stain of Visgothic Spain that you can brag about its eradication? By living in isolation, you have no strength to carry out your threat."

"Do not underestimate us," Jacob waggled a sharp finer before Paul. "Just because I said we had no dealings with your kingdom doesn't mean we are isolated. Again I state to you that there is a far greater world outside your Spain than you could ever imagine. We have set ourselves apart from your lands, relying heavily upon trade solely with Byzantium and the Caliph's markets in Damascus; two empires that render your little kingdom inconsequential. By maintaining these prerequisites for minimum exposure we have been endowed with the good fortune of being overlooked by your kingdom and its emissaries except for the payment of annual tribute. If some of your people ever grew suspicious by chance encounter with us, then they were told we were Goths. Who else would you expect to find in Gothia? A few well-placed bribes, to certain officials of your government, and we are even erased from all of your maps. It is that simple and therein lies the true traitors to Wamba. His government is riddled by traitors that serve our needs. Were you not surprised to see how prepared we were in advance of your arriving army? We knew of every movement you made before you even undertook it. You served a corrupt administration bankrupt of morals and you still believe they deserve your allegiance?"

Clearing his throat, Hideric rose to add a comment of his own. "If you don't mind Jacob, may I add a point or two?"

The mayor of Narbonne gave the floor to his companion.

"It was quite a simple matter to conceal our dual existence," Hideric explained. "We have everything we could want in this land. As an Arian, my people have prospered with the trade routes opened to the East by Jacob's people. To the Byzantines we pay a meager tribute as well, but never have they asked for a single dinar in taxes. Each man is free to pursue his own livelihood and to provide as he deems fit. Our people work their own land. There is no serfdom here! This is a land of freedmen. What could Wamba ever offer us. Except pain and hardship."

"Freeholders?" Paul shook his head. "It's not possible. Freeholders cannot farm their own land. They need to be told what to plant and when to plant it. Let them decide for themselves and they will fail to make the quotas. Without quotas, there'd be starvation. Nothing to trade or barter. This system cannot work! Absolutely, does not work. Slaves and serfs are needed to perform the tasks? That's what makes such endeavors profitable."

"So speaks a landholder that has profited of the backs of slaves! But it does work, my Lord,"Hideric argued with the resistant Spaniard. "And if it is any reassurance to you there are still slaves," Hideric confided to him, "but our rules of slavery are different from what you are accustomed to. No one is permitted to keep a slave after his sixth year of servitude."

"That is preposterous," Paul gestured with upturned hands. "A slave is always a slave. How could they know any different? Give them freedom and they know not what to do with it. Provide for them and they are happy, let them fend for themselves and they are miserable. That is the way of human nature."

"Ludicrous? Preposterous!" Hideric mimicked. "Do you not even know the commandments of God? Has the Church in Rome made you so ignorant that you cannot read the Bible for yourself? Six years is the limitation of one's servitude. Not a day more, lest you defy God and that would surely label you as an enemy of mankind. You say it cannot work, then show me another land where the people live in such bliss and contentment; where Arians live alongside Jews, who in turn live alongside Mohammedans. Every man is content with his lot in life. Neighbor loves neighbor. We have all done nothing but prosper and benefit by our alliance with Narbonne. If we had to die to preserve the secrets of Narbonne then I am prepared to gladly do so! So was everyone that you had encountered on the battlefield. You could have never won that battle because we were fighting for something far greater than your lust for power and profit!"

"Here, here," exclaimed the other mayors in agreement.

"The people of Narbonne are the life blood of Septimania," Hideric continued. "If we were to betray them, we would only be destroying ourselves. Our world would become no different from the one you live in. That is what your king wants of us. To give away our lands to him and to a church that tries only to divide us as it spreads its message of conquest. Your bishops claim only to be concerned with souls, but what about lives? Isn't the living worth more than the souls of the damned? Are we to let them tax us relentlessly? To let them take away our commerce because we trade with empires that your world considers enemies. Nay, we shall not give up all that we cherish. God has returned us to the Garden of Eden and not even Wamba can make us sacrifice the Lord's blessing and have us exiled from paradise again!"

Paul shifted restlessly as he stood before the mayors of Septimania. "I presume that you are not providing me with any other options. I either join your cause, become your protector, or else you're not going to allow me to leave here alive. I will be your prisoner, confined for the balance of my life." Gazing upon their expressionless faces, Paul could see that there would be no compromise. "I admit that I came here to destroy all of Septimania and lay it to waste, but I had no way of knowing what manner of society existed here. As you said, those that are traitors in my government have concealed your existence well. But I can assure you that I will not betray you if I was to leave. I swear to let your secret die with me. I will not beg for mercy from you because by taking arms against you I have forfeited any right to clemency but as a man of honor, let me return to my people and I forswear I will not reveal your secret."

"You have no land to return to. Your king is not about to return your property to you. He will hang you for treason. Do you not understand, Paul of Burgos, you are a man without a country. We are offering you one. Just remain with us and enjoy a new life of freedom, just as your men are doing now."

"My men?" It suddenly dawned on Paul of Burgos that no one had informed him regarding the fate of his surviving soldiers since the battle. "What about my men?"

Hideric answered calmly, "None of them were allowed to return to Spain but they do not seem bothered by that prospect. They have found life in Septimania to be better than what they left behind."

"You are suggesting my officers simply gave up their homes, their families, to take up new lives in a land totally unfamiliar to them," Paul refused to believe such a thing happened.

"Of course not," Hideric responded. "There are sacrifices that have to be made in order to maintain peace and anonymity. "It was not as if we wanted to take such action but we could not permit even a hint of insurgency to remain amongst your troops. Officers are a casualty of war. Without them the common soldier becomes compliant and willing to listen to reason."

Paul's expression grew grim. So you killed them. I had over forty officers under my command. Their only crime was that they followed my orders."

"Fifty-two to be exact," Jacob ben Todros interjected. "All good men but all a risk that we couldn't afford to entertain. You know the rules of war. Pardon the men, ransom the general, but execute the officers. Those in the middle always bear the burden. They could not be allowed to remain with their men because they would influence them and urge them to try and return to their homeland. They could not be sent back to Spain because as officers they had seen too much and would be able to relay that information to your king. You would have done the same if the tables were turned."

"You could have offered them the same opportunity you are offering me," Paul challenged.

"And why would they accept?" Jacob scoffed. "You have lost everything. There is nothing awaiting you upon your return except death as a traitor. They may have received the same punishment but as you said, they still had homes, wives and families waiting for them. The lure to return home was too great. As for the other option, keeping them prisoner, that would have never worked. Fifty-two men inside a prison is nothing more than a threat waiting to burst at the seams. We knew it. You know it. There is no denying it."

Why can't you learn from them?"

"And how do you know I would not consider doing the same," the Duke intimated at possible treachery on his part. "I could tell you that I agree to be your protector but instead I undermine your strength and resistance."

Jacob merely smiled before replying. "All things are possible but we are aware of this. We shall not let you betray us and therefore if you try to leave you or undermine our cause, then you will surely die. You will give us your word and as a man of honor we expect you to keep it. If you go back on your word, then you are a man without honor and the penalty of death is well deserved. That is your choice. Die for a crime of treason even if you escaped us and made it back to your forfeited estates, or live amongst us as a free man. A man respected for his integrity, his ability and his qualities. A man of whom we ask nothing more than to keep us safe from the savage that calls himself the king in the West. I will be honest with you. We have need of a man of your military knowledge and experience and you have need of us if you are to be protected from your king. He will hunt you down like a wounded animal no matter where you try to flee. Here at least we can keep you safe."

"I must have time to consider your offer." Paul refused to commit to the bargain.

"Time is a commodity of which neither of us has a surplus. The sands have begun to run out. We need you! And you most certainly need us!"

Riding at the forefront of his army, King Wamba made an impressive sight, bedecked in his polished gold and silver mailed armor. To his rear marched the entire amassed strength of Spain. Thirty thousand regulars and five thousand cavalry; battle hardened soldiers, each and every one of them. It was all that remained of the army he once boasted of being one hundred thousand.

It had been almost two years since Duke Paul's Spanish force had passed through the Pyrenees on its route of conquest, never to return. Only a few straggly survivors ever made it back to Castile; reporting the great battle from which they fled. They were all executed as deserters as soon as they had given their reports. As for the remainder of the tens of thousands that had accompanied Paul of Burgos, it was as if the gates of hell had opened up and swallowed them whole. Wamba never sent an offer to Septimania for release of his general or army. Part of the reason was that he never received a ransom request from the mayors of Septimania to respond to. He was left with no other choice but to assume that his general and the entire army had deserted to the enemy. There could be no doubt in Wamba's mind that Paul in some way had betrayed him. Why else would the duke not have made an attempt to have himself ransomed. The continued payment of tribute into the royal treasury from the province suggested that not even the Septimanians were uncomfortable with the defection and were still attempting to appease their king in spite of harboring the fugitive and all his men. It was a sorry state of affairs and Wamba was left with no other choice but to salvage his kingdom and reputation.

As word of the invaders crossing over the mountains circulated amongst the towns, the mayors of Septimania prepared to resist this new threat to their sovereignty. They immediately elevated Paul of Burgos to the newly established position of military governor. As such he was placed in command of all their combined armies. Swearing fealty to their newly appointed defender, they invested Paul with a confidence that only by uniting under a single banner could they successfully defend their domains against this new threat from the Visigoths.

Paul rallied new allies from the Gaulish tribes whose ancestors stemmed from the Roman divisions that were once stationed in the northlands, long ago. They didn't know Paul, but they were loyal to Narbonne, and more than any other people, they hated the Visigoths. From the forest lands came the Duke of Tarragon with a thousand men to strike a blow against tyranny. From the northern hill country, hordes of Frankish barbarians rained down, bent on battle with the detested Wamba, who even now was encroaching on their homeland. The war cry between once bitter rivals was now a united trumpeting under Paul of Burgos. No compromise! Victory or death! There would be no alternatives and certainly no retreats. This was intended to be the war to end any future wars. The plans drawn by Paul and his officers were perfect. They would engage in a frontal assault with about half of their resources, weaken the king's forces drastically and then retreat from the field as if they were fleeing, drawing the Visigoths deeper and deeper into their territory until they reached the first fortified city where they would teak refuge. Wamba would be forced to set up camp outside the city, weakening his forces even further by spreading them out until they completely encompassed the walls, not permitting anyone to enter or leave. That suited Paul's forces fine as they would simply wait until reinforcements from further east would arrive to attack the Visigoths from behind. Simultaneously Paul's forces would surge from the city, launching a frontal assault. It would be a massacre and the end of Wamba's threat once and for all.

Beneath the scorching heat of the late summer sun the two mighty armies clashed, the battle swaying back and forth at least a dozen times. Their polished blades drank their bottomless fill until every remaining soldier standing was drenched in the blood of his fallen adversaries. By day's end, the plains of Gascony were saturated with the thick red essence of fleeting lives. Mutilated corpses lay strewn across the wispy heather, buried beneath the thistle and hemlock never to be retrieved. The masses of corpses were so intertwined that one could not tell the Visigoths from the Septimanians. Wamba's forces dwindled rapidly, but their experience and training gave them a unique ability to persevere and keep taking the fight to Paul's men.

By sunset Paul's army of the united towns sounded the retreat fleeing towards the coastal plain just as they had planned. Without hesitation, the Wamba ordered the pursuit, never considering that the flight may have been a ruse. Relying on a superior strategy and knowledge of the geography the Septimanian army was able to out distance his pursuers easily as they fled towards the town of Nimes.

Hideric was instructed to place his city under a defensive mobilization as soon as the enemy arrived. This would not only force Wamba to lay siege to a highly fortified city for which he wasn't prepared but would quickly drain the king's might more by stretching it over several fronts to surround the city. Everything was going to plan. The Narbonnaise were under instruction to arrive from the east as soon as the siege was underway and slaughter the exhausted Spaniards. Their plan was perfect in every detail save one aspect. Only the armies of the combined cities of Septimania were aware of the details of their strategy. At no time had they informed the people of the cities for fear that somehow word would be conveyed to Wamba and the trap would fail.

Moving quickly at the head of his army, Paul arrived at the town of Nimes a half day ahead of Wamba's forces. Anticipating that he would just ride into the heart of the city, he was surprised to find that the gates remained sealed to his forces. Not all the pleading in the world by their mayor, Hideric, could persuade the townspeople to open the gates. When the people of Nimes saw the greatly reduced numbers in Paul's army and pondered the speed at which he and his men had covered the distance between Gascony and Nimes, they incorrectly assumed that Wamba had routed all the legion of Septimania and this was all that remained of their mighty army. Hideric pleaded and cajoled, threatened and scolded, but nothing that he could say, nor the beatings inflicted upon the people by the mayor's personal guard that still policed the city could persuade them to relent and open the gates. After all, Nimes was a town of business men and merchants; every last one of them a pragmatist. What would be gained now by continuing to side with the rebellion if it was failing. Now was the time to throw themselves at the feet of the Spanish king and beg for his forgiveness and mercy if such qualities even existed. They had no desire to die for a lost cause and if necessary they could plead to the king that they had refused entry to his enemies thereby proving their loyalty.

Closing their ears to Paul's exhortations, the citizens of Nimes sealed the fate of their own legions. Both Paul and Hideric had no other choice but to turn and face the approaching enemy in the plains outside the city, resigned to their impending defeat. There would be no opportunity to alert the Narbonnaise to the present circumstances and the change of plan. No chance to avail themselves on Jacob ben Todros and his men to come earlier than planned in order to affect a rescue. Paul offered his Frankish and Gallic allies the opportunity to leave the battle and return to their homelands before the Visigoths arrived, but both allies were stemmed from heroic races, knowing no other way to return from a battle other than in victory or carried back on the broad face of their shields. Here they would make their stand as brothers united in freedom; to die as they had lived, free men of Septimania. Steeling his spirit against the inevitable about to be unleashed, Paul was grateful for what little time he had lived in paradise. It truly was the Garden of Eden; a utopian society built upon ideals that could be found nowhere else in the world. From the moment he decided to accept Jacob ben Todros's offer to be their protector had had no doubts about his choice. For the first time he understood the true purpose of mankind. Not to wage war upon one another but to the contrary, how to wage peace, a much harder fought battle.

Even now as he looked up at the ramparts of the city, seeing the people huddled in fear while others jeered at the their own soldiers about to die, he bore no animosity against the people of Nimes. He understood all too well what unnatural fear could do to the heart of even the bravest of men. The people would be safe. The initial battle on the plains of Gascony and this battle about to take place would ensure that. There would be little left of the invincible Spanish army once they were victorious. It would be a victory in name only. Hollow and without any reward to carry back home. Wamba would most likely return immediately to Castile in order to prevent any insurgence within his own royal court as news of his own devastation would reach his castle before he ever returned with his men. The Visigoth army would be weakened to the point of falling prey to any other would-be conqueror that they met along the journey home. Wamba would just have enough strength to defeat Paul's abandoned army on the plain outside Nimes; barely enough to even consider it a victory. Afterwards, the king would not be able to sustain himself in Septimania any longer than it would take to end the ensuing battle. Without food and reinforcements, the Visigoths would be forced into an embarrassing retreat of their own. The war would be over. Wamba if lucky would still be able to retain his throne but Septimania will see the last of this would-be conqueror.

The iron pokers glowed red hot as they were pushed further into the blazing coals. The smith shifted the stones in order to spread them more evenly. Smug and sated in his hour of victory, Wamba taunted the only prisoner he considered worth taking alive and who now laid spread eagled upon the ground, his wrists and ankles tethered to immovable stakes hammered into the earth.

"Do you have anything to say now?" the king scorned. "Is there any last words you wish to say to me before my man takes the pleasure in removing your eyes? Perhaps a little pleading will do you some good? Let this be a lesson to all the plot treason against their king! I gave you everything and this is what I receive in return. Treachery, treason, rebellion!"

Paul refused to grant the king his request. There would be no begging to spare his life. Instead he waxed poetically in his final moments. "What need have I of eyes? I who have seen Paradise. The images of a better world are mine to treasure in both life and death. You, who dwell in sin and iniquity, shall never find the peace and contentment in which I have partaken. And what are you now? A bested monarch, barely able to protect your crown from hence forth. Beaten and cowering like a dog, waiting for the next upstart with a few men at his side to wrestle the throne from beneath you. This I have done to you. I have humbled you before man and God and your days are numbered. A curse upon your blackened soul."

41

"Enough of this prattle", the king shouted, motioning for the smith to do his handiwork. "I know not of what foolish blathering you spout. Your tongue shall be next." Whatever pleasure Wamba thought he would derive from this grizzly display had effectively been soured.

The glowing iron rod pierced the right eye socket with an audible hissing sound followed immediately by the scarcely human wail that echoed through the valleys of Septimania. The sight and sound caused the remnants of Wamba's own officer corps to turn away so that they didn't have to watch any longer. The seed had been planted. Who amongst them was fit to be king? The real insurrection was yet to come and open to all. Paul of Burgos had seen to it that the cities of Septimania would remain safe and secure for generations to come. Weakened from battle, injured severely from the many lacerations that laced his body, there was little left to torture after the first piercing of his eye. Paul of Burgos found eternal peace quickly but his spirit forever walks the winding roads that traverse the plains of Septimania.

Chapter Four

Toronto: 1999

"Well, that was most pleasant," Pearce comments.

"What do you expect? Happily ever after?" I berate him. "Do you think that history is all about the good reports and none of the horror?"

"So, let me see if I've got this straight. There's this city, hidden away behind the mountains of Spain and France, with a large population of people of unknown origin, most likely Jews but nobody knows about it." Pearce pokes his temple with the eraser end of the pencil.

"Exactly!"

"Exactly? Exactly what? What kind of word is exactly? I still don't get it, Doc. How can this place exist in secret? And not only that, I know your story is about them getting their own royal family because you decided to tell me the end of the story first! So, how does a hidden city end up with its own aristocracy? Why would the powers of the existing countries permit it to happen? This isn't making any sense to me! What's this got to do with anything? What's this even have to do with your family which brought me here in the first place?"

"Oh, I don't know, Mr. Pearce. I don't see it as that much of a conundrum. After all, the French permitted the Grimaldi's to set up their own little kingdom on the Riviera. No one seemed to get overly concerned about that. Don't you think that perhaps there was always a history of fiefdoms or kingdoms in southern France? Perhaps you should think of this as the precursor to those little kingdoms."

Pearce thumbs at his chin. "Even if it's possible, I still don't get it."

"No you don't," I reassure him. "I haven't made my point yet! You have to know the history of the Franks before you can see how this is about to unfold. There was far more going on at the time than merely a rebellious enclave that Wamba tried to put down. This is where the plot truly thickens. So many events were happening at relatively the same time, that uprisings in the Spanish March were merely a blip on the road at the end of some map. So much of the actual history has been papered over simply because far more crucial events were taking place elsewhere at the same time.

And that's exactly how all this could happen under the nose of those existing countries you speak of. What really served to ignite the subsequent chain of history was a carefully crafted subterfuge to exterminate the Merovingians. The true Kings of the Franks. This is the hub that the seventh century revolved around and most people don't even know it. All that I am about to tell you, precipitated from a Papal decision to eliminate an ancient clan of Frank chieftains. And once set in motion, there was no turning back."

"So why bother telling me about Spain then?"

"Because it was important!"

"But now it's not."

"It is but the Merovingians are more important," I answer.

"Merovingians?"

"Yes, the long hairs. Give me a chance to explain."

Gaul: 656 A.D.

"Find that little brat and bring him to me!" Grimwald shouted to his underlings, who stood gawking at the blood dripping from his unsheathed dagger. King Sigisbert lay motionless on the slate tiled floor, a gaping grin stretching across his throat from one ear to the other. "I am the king now!" Grimwald screamed. "Do as I say, now!" He motioned with his knife towards the reluctant guards.

The two men scurried down the castle halls, responding to Grimwald's barely veiled threat. The former Mayor of the Palace who now proclaimed himself to be king, knelt beside his victim. Tearing a piece of cloth from Sigisbert's robe, Grimwald wiped the blood from his soiled blade. His eyes grew large as he restored the weapon to its original brilliance, spitting and polishing several times before he was completely satisfied. With his fingernail he removed the last crust of royal blood that clung tenaciously to the hilt.

The night was over and the coup had been successful. As Grimwald sat himself upon the steps of the throne dais, he noticed an awkward movement behind the drapes along the wall. A devilish smirk settled upon his lips. "Immachilde." He spoke softly so as not to frighten his quarry. "Come here my little kitten. Don't worry. I wouldn't hurt you." The movement behind the drapes ceased immediately.

Grimwald rose to his feet and playfully crept closer towards the curtains. "Come to your loving uncle, my dear." He tried to toyingly coax the reluctant Immachilde from her hiding place but she refused to come out. Growing impatient, he reached behind the drape, but as soon as he touched her, a wildly swung blade nicked the back of his hand. He recoiled, more from surprise, than pain. Placing the back of his hand to his mouth, he licked the trickle of blood that oozed from the wound.

"Now it is my turn to taste the sweetness of your blood," he cooed. Drawing his sword he slashed at the heavy curtain, shredding it as he did so, but careful, oh so careful not to injure his fragile prey. He laughed heartily as each cut of the velvet drape was met with a small squeal of terror. With one final swipe at the rings, the curtains dropped, revealing the frightened creature that desperately tried to remain concealed behind them.

She was still a mere girl, her nineteenth birthday just passed and yet she was Queen of all the Franks. Sigisbert had claimed her for his wife at the tender age of thirteen and she had grown from a beautiful young child into a ravishing woman; not only in the king's eyes but in Grimwald's as well. Her long, flame hued hair enhanced a seductive beauty that entranced all who beheld her. Her round aquamarine eyes shone with a child-like simplicity. Grimwald had lusted for her from the day Sigisbert brought her back to the palace.

There were those that said he committed regicide in order to claim a throne but those that knew better understood that all he ever wanted was Immachilde. He wrestled the dagger from her petite hand, throwing it behind him, so that it clanged heavily against the quarried floor. The horrified queen shrunk back in terror as Grimwald unsheathed his own blade again. With an almost tender fondness, Grimwald caressed the skin of Immachilde's shoulder with the knife's finely honed edge. Slowly he slid the metal over the curve of the joint so that a fine rivulet of blood appeared across the flesh. The queen winced momentarily, pressing herself tightly against the stonewall, as if she could etherealize and pass through the bricks to safety.

Smiling through cruel lips, Grimwald forced his body over hers and lapped the droplets of blood that surfaced from her wound. "Nectar of the gods," he drooled, noisily smacking his lips. "You are as delicious as you are fragrant." His weight was too much for her to force from her fragile body. "You will learn to love me, Immachilde! Or else you will join your late husband and son in Hell! Is that understood?"

Her son! In the commotion she had lost track of the whereabouts of her only offspring! "Where is my son?"

"A good question but don't worry my dear. My men will find him and when they do it shall be the last you hear of your dear, sweet, innocent, Dagobert."

"No! Do not harm my son. I beg you."

"Beg, I like beg. Beg some more!" Grimwald was a man without compassion and Immachilde knew immediately that her pleading would be to no avail.

"He will find help. You will see. He will free me and avenge the death of his father."

Grimwald released a hearty laugh. "A five year old child? Be serious woman. He will not escape us."

"He will go to the Bishop and the Bishop will send troops. You will be made to pay for your treachery."

This time the former mayor of the Palace laughed until his sides hurt. "Oh, woman of such foolishness, can you not see? This has all been by order of the Bishop. Do you think that I would have perpetrated such a crime if I had not been promised total absolution by the Church? This coup has all been by the grace of your God!"

"That is not true! You lie! You lie!" She pounded her tiny fists hysterically against his chest.

"The best part is I don't even have to kill your little brat. His holiness, the Bishop has consented to fulfill that deed by order of his superiors. How ironic that your supposed rescuer will also be your son's executioner. But have no fear, little kitten. I shall protect you. You are mine! Now and forever." Enfolding his arms about the Queen, he pressed her to his chest. "Oh Immachilde. You will make me so happy. You will be my queen at last!"

———————————

Dagobert was brought to the residence of the Bishop of Poitiers soon after his capture. Having known the Bishop since the day he was born, the prince felt at ease with the brooding figure that sat across from him. Climbing down from his chair, the lad eased himself towards his old friend and clung to the loose sleeve of the Bishop's white cassock. "Why are you so sad Father?"

The Bishop looked into the big open eyes of the child and he could not find an easy answer. Aldred had no answers, just orders; orders that troubled him severely.

"Will you take me home now, Father? I would like to see my mother." Dagobert smiled with a child's innocence that only youth can display.

"Come here boy," the tired clergyman pulled him closer with a crooked and withered hand. Placing Dagobert on his lap, the Bishop rested his cheek alongside the boy's. "I have watched you grow over the years. It was I that baptized you in the name of Christ. I have loved you as if you were my very own son."

"And I love you too, Father."

"Hush child. You are not making this any easier." The Bishop began to lay his misery upon the prince, sharing his burden with someone too young to understand. "Sometimes the world can be a very confusing place, child. It makes no sense at times but it is not our duty to try to rationalize."

Dagobert could make no sense of the bishop's words.

The vicar immediately saw the child's confusion and he attempted to draw a correlation. "Do you remember the story of Abraham and his son Isaac?"

The prince nodded his head in eagerness of hearing another biblical tale. "Well, Abraham was told by the angel of God to take his son into the mountains where God demanded a sacrifice. Isaac did not realize until he was bound to the altar that his father intended to sacrifice him instead of a ram. When the reality became apparent, Isaac encouraged his father to obey the word of God. He knew that his father loved him more than anything else in the world but even so, it is not man's place to refuse to obey the command of God. Do you understand?"

"Yes, Father. Abraham loved his son too, but he also loved God. I have faith in God too, Father. Aren't you proud of me?"

"Yes. I am very proud of you, my son. You have learned your lessons well," the bishop responded, hugging the child.

Dagobert gazed into the fatigued eyes of the clergyman only to see a cascade of tears welling inside. "Why did you tell me that story, Father?"

"It is a very important lesson," the bishop sniffled, taking a breath before wiping away a few stray tears. "Like Abraham, I too have been commanded to sacrifice someone I love. It is a test of my faith and I fear that I do not love that faith enough, not to forsake it."

"But you must obey God," Dagobert interrupted. "God will be angry if you don't, Father!"

"Ah, yes, the command of God. I have tried to tell myself that. But which God?"

"Father! You know there is only one God. You are trying to trick me."

"One God, but many that claim to speak for him, child. How do I know which are the true voices? Lord, why hast thou forsaken me?" Aldred placed the boy back on the floor and shielded his face in the palms of his hands.

Dagobert stood by the priest and attempted to reach around his shoulders in order to comfort the old man.

"Father? Who must you sacrifice?"

The bishop looked up from moistened palms, staring haplessly at the boy. "It's you, my son. Heaven help me. It's you!"

The prince calmly patted the priest on the back. "I am not afraid, Father. I know that the angel will grab your hand before you bring down the knife. Just like in the story. God loves everyone. He will not let you harm me."

"Child, you have much to learn about this world. Those who speak for God do not always love everyone."

"Then they are not men of God." Dagobert squared his jaw in response. "But you are Father. I know you are!"

The Bishop wiped away another stray tear. "I do not know if I truly am. What they have asked I know is wrong and yet I have pledged fealty to their authority. If those in Rome are fallible, then what purpose do any of us serve? If I fail to obey them, then it would mean that I was living a lie!"

"I do not understand, Father?"

"Neither do I," the bishop smiled, the first time that he had displayed any crack in his grim veneer. The prince smiled in return. "Come back into my lap boy. I have much to shed from my heavy heart." Dagobert scampered into the clergyman's lap. "It is time you learn the realities of this world, child. You are young but there is no time to learn these things later. I am afraid that you must grow quickly into manhood."

"Will my father teach me?" Dagobert still knew nothing of the tragedy that had befallen the king.

"No, I am afraid that your father will not be able to instruct you. Sigisbert has gone away for a long time. He told me to tell you that he loves you very much."

"But where has he gone, Father?"

"On a very long journey; he has gone to see God. Only when you make the same journey will you be able to see your father again. Your mother did not go with him, but you must not try to see her. This is the time when all young boys must grow up! You can't do that hanging on to your mother's dress. Now, can you?"

Dagobert wanted to cry when he heard that he could no longer see his mother. He did not want to be a man yet. He thought back on all the nights he nestled into his mother's breast and fell peacefully to sleep. He was so secure when he was with her. The sweet melody of her voice would lull him and chase away the dark creatures of the night. He loved to play with her flaming tresses and especially enjoyed watching her comb her locks in the brass mirror. Why did growing up have to be so painful? Valiantly, he held back his own tears. "I understand, Father. Will I ever see my mother again?"

"In time, all things are possible. Now listen, child. I have much to tell you and very little time to do so. There are those in this world who wish to harm you." Dagobert was about to question why but the Bishop pressed a finger to his lips. "Men crave power and you and your family are in their way. I do not know if you father has ever explained to you that you are kings by way of your Merovingian blood and what that actually means. If he hasn't, it matters not for I will tell you a story which I doubt he even knew. Long ago, two kings of Israel were exiled to our land by the Romans."

"How long ago was that, Father?"

"Let me see...ah, yes. Just over six hundred years. The first one, Archelaus was removed from office by the Romans because he did not serve them as well as his father, Herod the Great, did."

"He was the king that killed the babies, wasn't he father?"

"Yes, yes. Now be quiet and listen. So Archelaus was exiled to Wien in Burgundy and there he lived the rest of his days as a king in all but name. Thirty-three years later, the Emperor Caligula chose to give his friend Agrippa, Israel over which to rule. To do so, Herod Antipas had to be removed from his throne in Galilee. He too was exiled and was transferred to Lyons. These Jewish kings took brides from among the princesses of the Franks and Teutons thereby mixing the royal blood of the east with those of the west. Merowig was such a progeny of mixed bloods and he was your grandfather of seven generations ago."

"Was my father a king of Israel too?" Dagobert was delighted to hear this unknown tale of his heritage.

"There are those that say he was and therein lies the problem."

"But why, Father? Was not Jesus a king of Israel too?"

"Exactly, dear boy! If Jesus be the son of God and therefore the last king of Israel, then how could there be kings to follow him? In the book of Genesis it says that the rod shall not pass from Judah, nor the scepter from between his feet until He has come to Shiloh. For Jesus to have been the son of God necessitates the breaking of the rod of Judah."

"Then I do not wish to be a king of Israel. I want Jesus to be king."

The old priest laughed heartily. "It is not as easy as that, child. It is not something you can give away. Those that wish to harm you, understand that. They see you as a threat to the Church. They know only one way to remove that threat."

"Am I a threat, Father." Dagobert shifted his frame in the bishop's lap as he grew restless.

"Not any longer, my son."

"Are you going to sacrifice me?"

"That will no longer be necessary. You have made me realize that my personal pledge to God is greater than my obedience to any church. I am a Vicar of Christ and I shall obey his laws before I try to preserve a lie. If it is His intention for the Church to fail, then so be it. I will take no part in murder of the innocent. Come. Let's hurry. There is much to do before Grimwald sends his men to see that the deed has been done."

"Where are we going, Father?"

"Me, nowhere. But you must be sent far away where the arm of Rome cannot reach you." Taking the young prince by the hand, Aldred rose from his seat and strode from the library.

Dagobert tried to match strides with the Bishop, skipping along as he did so. "Where will I go, Father?"

"I have friends that reside in Eire. They live in the monastery of Sloane. They will protect you."

"But where is Eire?"

"It is across the sea. You'll go there by boat. The Celtic church is not under the rule of the Pope. Rome has no authority there."

Dagobert grew all excited. "I have never been on a ship before. Will I be scared, Father?"

The vicar knelt and held the boy in his arms tenderly. "You are a man today, Dagobert. A man does not become afraid. He shields his fears and places his faith in God. I have put my faith in the Lord and I know that he shall light for us a path through the darkness that engulfs us. I will send father Aldo with you. He will report back to me as soon as you are safely at the monastery."

The little boy threw his arms around the bishop and hugged his neck. "I love you, Father. I will miss you. Tell my mother that I love her."

Aldred returned the embrace. "And I love you, my son. Neither Church nor Pope could ever make me desecrate that love. Quickly! You must be on your way!"

Down the torch lit hallway, the Vicar of Christ and the young prince disappeared into the flickering darkness.

"Is it done?", Grimwald growled at the Bishop of Portieres.

Revealing the boy's blood stained garments and a soiled dagger, the bishop hurled them at the feet of the newly proclaimed king. "This evil deed has been done. May God forgive us our sins."

"Where is the body, old man?"

"Am I to keep the body of an innocent victim within this house of God. Is it not bad enough that we have stooped to regicide, that we must also keep the remains of our foul deeds. If you want trophies, perform the deeds yourself. His body has been taken to the Loire and hopefully it shall be washed out to the sea. May the oceans conceal our crimes."

"Enough of your guilt, you old fool. Did you really think that you and your kind were above such things? You are no different from anyone else." Grimwald took pleasure in taunting the clergyman. "If anything, your kind are the worst offenders. I have no shame in what I have done. I do not try to hide behind a veil of lies. You and your ilk are all hypocrites. You preach one thing and do as you please. You are the lowest of the low. Do not look at me as if I am an evil wind that has blown your way. It was your kind that set the direction of this wind."

Aldred walked towards the study window that overlooked the river to the north. "I shall not try to wash my hands of my sins. It would be foolish to think that God would forgive me. But whereas I can feel shame in order to repent, you cannot. You have no soul. You bear no remorse. Your heart is cold and that shall be the curse borne by all your descendants."

"Remorse? Ha! What matters a cold heart as long as I have those that will keep me a warm bed?" Grimwald's laugh was cruel, his pointed beard and dark eyes casting a satanic reflection. "Remorse is the milk suckled by old fools. I am king. I am supreme. Immachilde shares my chambers from now on and none can dispute my power. My gratitude to you. You and your church have made it all possible."

"You have the power of king but you are not king," Bishop Aldred corrected the boasting mayor. "Childeric, Sigisbert's brother-in-law is to bear the title of king. That was part of the agreement."

"I know our agreement, old man! What care I of a puppet king that dances to my pulling his strings? I am the true power and that is all that matters. The Queen will be cleaved by my cock, making my sons heir to this land and that is the reality. What care I of Childeric? Your Pope made me supreme ruler and I fear no man."

Aldred returned his gaze towards the view outside the window, ignoring the ranting of his murderous ally. "Perhaps...." he muttered in a voice inaudible to Grimwald, "Perhaps not," as he watched the tiny boat float along the waters of the Loire towards the open sea.

Chapter Five

Toronto: 1999

I could veritably see the light-bulb going on in Pearce's head. The more I watched him, the easier it became to read his thoughts. And I knew that even though he thought he understood, he still didn't have a clue, as to what I was talking about.

"I've got it now! This Dagobert guy returns later and fathers this family you're telling me about. Your family, right Doc?"

"Wrong!" I shook my head in frustration, "Not even remotely related," I disappointed him.

"So the boy is the end of the line?"

"He does come back, but Dagobert belonged firmly to the Celtic Church, after his return from Ireland. He certainly wasn't destined to become the progenitor for Jewish royalty!"

Tossing his pad and pencil into the air, Pearce admitted defeat. "Then you've lost me! I can't understand how any of this is unfolding. Why talk about him if it has nothing to do with your family?"

"See, that's where you're wrong. It has everything to do with my family. Your problem is the same which most people have," I commented. "Everyone likes to think of history as a straight line progression. The reality is that it's not! Historical episodes are far from being sequential. Actually, a myriad of events, all taking place simultaneously, interweaving, influencing, and interconnecting with each other into an almost quilt-like existence.

For example, a relatively minor event may be taking place thousands of kilometers away, but it ultimately has a major impact when it encounters the event which you're studying on the other side of the world. It's completely overlooked because it's insignificant within the framework in which it occurs. Are you following me?"

Pearce shook his head. "Not one bit!"

"Now, I believe you're starting to get the picture."

"What's that supposed to mean?"

"Just what I said. It's confusing because history is not a straight line. It's a jumbling of events from which emerges a singular event of importance. Now do you understand?"

"I guess I'm just going to have to be more patient and wait for the who, what, where and how. Just there's part of my journalistic training that wants to know immediately."

"I understand. The who, Mr. Pearce, is key to the storyline. Everything which occurred was the result of 'the who' these people were. The where will tell you to what extent the plotters were willing to go, in order to succeed. The what is merely the curse of fate, as you will come to understand. But the how, that is very closely linked to the why. And to comprehend those two questions, it's necessary that I take you back to events transpiring in 7th century Iraq and the Arabian Peninsula. Then you will see how my family came into play."

Pearce was scrambling along the floor, looking for his pad and pencil.

"A new power had come to the forefront," I continued. "It was Islam, and it was sweeping through the Eastern Empires, replacing old dynasties with new ones. That's where we'll find my progenitor!"

Al-Kufah: 644 A.D.

The serpentine string of caravans descended upon the city of al-Kufah, originating from far off lands with names that few people would even dare to pronounce. Laden with gifts, borne by chieftains, princes, kings and ambassadors, they all flooded through the gates of the city precisely at this singular moment in time when the world changed.

A festival atmosphere greeted them upon their arrival; a gaiety and splendor without rival, in the civilized world. No expense had been spared. Dancing girls, jugglers, acrobats and magicians competed tirelessly for the crowd's attention and for the dinars they would throw. Children sat around grizzled old story tellers with high peaked turbans and gnarled canes. This was the land of the jinn and the hori, a land where all things were possible and a land wrapped in a mystical enchantment that excited both stranger and citizen alike.

From out of the desert sands appeared the King of Kings one day and all empires now knelt before this mighty emperor. Arabia was no longer a barren wasteland of windswept dunes and fierce Bedouin. Today it was a nation; reborn as a united people with a holy mission and a flaming sword. Allah was its war cry and death was its reward for all who refused to share in its glory. Those who came today from the far off places wished only to survive. They had witnessed the wrath of the King of Kings and they chose to bend their knees to the newly appointed monarch.

Within the ten year span since the death of the prophet Mohammed, Islam had risen to unprecedented heights, carving a swath of bloody victories across the eastern world. But with its rise also came the corruption and evil that exists in all fledgling upstart nations. Islam could not claim to be any different. Already the power struggle for establishing a line of succession had taken its toll. Omar, friend to Mohammed and successor to Abu Bakir had met an ignominious death at the hands of assassins. Who was responsible? It was well known to be the handiwork of Mohammed's son-in-law, Ali, who claimed the caliphate for himself.

But instead, Othmar became Caliph, and he moved his court to al-Kufah, far away from the dangers of Damascus. This was to be his coronation day. All who attended would be presented with the overwhelming impression that there was only one true Caliph, and his name was Othmar. Ali would be branded as a traitor to the Prophet and any that disagreed with the degree would meet the fate deserved by any branded as a traitor. But there was to be more! Not only would he be pronounced as King of Kings on this most joyous occasion, but he would also parade Yhosdergard, the captured King of Persia, in his triumphant march of honor.

God had once again smiled on Islam, and their most fearsome adversary was now delivered into their hands to do with as they pleased. The once proud and beauteous lands of Persia and Mesopotamia were now nothing more than smoldering ruins. The heir to Khusro now knelt, chained and bloodied before the mighty Caliph, his to do with as he pleased.

Othmar savored the pageantry and succored the success. Long lines of dignitaries eagerly awaited their chance to proclaim their loyalty to his newly established order. One by one they bowed before the master of the world and swore fealty to his reign. Gifts of jewels and silks bedecked the dais, as they were laid at the Caliph's feet. From India came rare spices and a baby elephant. Sian and Cathay offered jade, gold and the rarest of silks. From the Western lands, their ambassadors presented multi-colored gems of enormous proportions.

Othmar nodded gratuitously, as each entourage in turn bowed and retreated from his presence. By day's end, the pile of offerings began to obscure the platform. The Caliph ordered his servants from that point in time onward to scurry forward and receive the proffered presents and whisk them safely to his chambers where his accountants would qualify and quantitate each gift.

"The emissary from Bustenai Ibn Haninai, Scion of the House of David, and Exilarch to the Jews," the herald announced as the next guest to pay honor approached the dais.

Before the Caliph there stood a gnarled greybeard, bent and stooped with age. Yet his eyes still bore the traits of unbridled youth, sparkling while he spoke. "Excellency. On behalf of my Lord, I offer you this ancient Torah scroll in honor of your inauguration." The old man placed the silver bedecked scroll with its jewel encrusted ephod into the hands of the awaiting servants. The ambassador from Bustenai backed away graciously from Othmar's presence.

"Wait!" Othmar rose from his throne, traces of scorn tugging at the corners of his mouth. "Am I to understand that this is all you offer me? What use have I of a scroll I cannot read? Even if I was to melt the silver and pry the jewels from its breastplate it would hardly be a significant gift from so numerous a people under my care!" Othmar clapped his hands, signaling two of his soldiers to seize the old man and hurl him to the foot of the dais.

The old man struggled to prop himself upon his two spindly arms. "Excellency, it is our greatest possession. Even your Prophet has admitted that the book of the Jews is the word of Allah. And now your household will be blessed by having it lodge beneath your tent."

Othmar belched a hearty laugh. "What need do I have of your holy scriptures. I am already the master of this world by Allah's grace. I think that it is more likely that your people wish to cheat me of what is rightfully mine. Bring me your stateless king of the Jews so that I may make an example of him."

"No! Wait Excellency!" The guests gasped at the greybeard's audacity. No one ever dared to challenge a Caliph before; even raising one's voice towards a caliph in public merited no less a punishment than decapitation. The emissary continued to talk quickly as the royal guards unsheathed their long curved scimitars, awaiting Othmar's command. "There is far more than that scroll being offered, I assure you!

My lord, Bustenai, offers you the loyalty of over a million subjects. That is considerably more valuable than any of these other gifts offered to you by all these foreign dignitaries. Other princes have come but do they offer you taxes? Do they offer you men to fight within your army? Do they pay you yearly tribute? Theirs is but a solitary gift by which they hope to stave off your appetite to conquer their lands and take the tribute that would normally be yours."

Othmar held up a hand in order to halt the advance of his guardsmen. "Let him continue. There may be something worthwhile in what he says. I am not an unreasonable old man. In my seventy years, I have learned the value of loyalty. If not for my loyal Bedouin, I would not be where I am today. And I certainly know the value of taxes if I wish to build cities. Tell me more of this gift, your lord Bustenai offers me."

He pulled himself into a sitting position. "What my master offers you is the same unswerving loyalty that was enjoyed by the Persians. Where would the Sassanids have been if not for their Jewish subjects? We established and safeguarded the merchant routes. We developed and stabilized their economic growth. Our brethren in Europe, Africa and the Orient ensured that the Persians always had accessibility to foreign markets. What value can be placed on loyalty of that magnitude?"

"You have made your point well," Othmar lauded. "What is your name, old man?"

"Nathaniel, Excellency."

"Nathaniel, as your reward I give you your life. More importantly, I wish to meet this master of yours. Send word to Captain Ibrahim ibn Selah that he is to take his men to the city of Babylon and return with Bustenai ibn Haninai immediately." The King of Kings had spoken.

Babylon no longer resembled the ancient wonder of the world it was purported to be, its streets overcrowded and refuse laden. The fabled hanging gardens of Nebuchadnezzar were absent from the immense towers of the royal palace. In fact, the palace no longer stood defiantly at the city's center either. All that remained were the crumbling towers that clearly stated that once upon a time this had been a great city.

It had been a marvel to man's architectural skill, standing at the fork of the twin rivers, Tigris and Euphrates. Now the ravages of time and conquest had reduced it to nothing more than a suburb of the neighboring city known as Baghdad. But in spite of its downfall, Babylon harbored a large population and still served as a large merchant depot through which travelling caravans transferred their cargo to other trade routes destined for the silk roads leading east.

The chief magistrate of the city was Bustenai ibn Haninai, vizier to the now dethroned Khusro of Persia. He represented the last vestige of power from a failing dynasty, a man whose very word was law in what had once been the world's largest empire. But more than that, he was a king. A king without a kingdom but none the less, a king. His subjects inhabited many lands but no matter how distant, these people sought the wisdom and guidance of his divine rule. Even the Persians came to appreciate the extraordinary influence by which the family of Bustenai actuated over an entire race.

Scattered across the known world, Persia reaped the benefits from this close association. In fact, so great did their dependency on the family of the Exilarch become, that the Persians chose to overlook the matter of Bustenai's ancestor, Mar Zutra Kahana, who led a crippling rebellion against his Sassanid overlords a century and a half earlier. Instead, the Sassanids gave their Jewish community even greater autonomy, honoring the Exilarch as rightful king and worthy of sitting at the Emperor's right hand.

This arrangement was mutually reciprocated, creating an independent nation within a nation without the need to rebel as they had in Zutra's time. The Jews had their own courts, schools, even their own military units. Everything Mar Zutra tried to win through battle was granted after his death. Bustenai was heir to this unfathomable power. If his family legacy had taught him one thing, it was to never underestimate the value of his people and Bustenai was shrewd enough to realize that Othmar needed him far more than he needed the Caliph. Everything was going as planned. His spies had reached him long before Othmar's men and he knew that he was about to be summoned. Resplendent in an opulent purple robe, Bustenai strode patiently amongst the gardens of his estate waiting for his visitors to arrive. The gold and silver tumbrels that lined the borders of his garment chimed with his every stride.

It had often been said that the Exilarch was more regal in attire and appearance than the Sassanids themselves. Around his jewel studded turban, Bustenai wore the spiked, golden diadem that legend claimed was fashioned by King Solomon's own hands. The sleeves of his robes were hemmed with silk brocade interwoven with gold threads. His beard had been carefully coiffed and curled in the manner of the Persians, a sharp contrast from those worn by the Arabs, but intentionally done in order to make a statement to this new Caliph; not all things Persian are to be swept away. Settling comfortably into his metal chaise that stood beneath the gnarled date tree, Bustenai stroked his beard, ensuring that each ringlet was exactly as intended. Though only in his forties, his beard was streaked the color of snow; distinguishing him as a man of great knowledge and insight.

He thought about his withered servant Nathaniel, pleading for an opportunity to speak before the Caliph. How predictable it all had been. How contrived and how easy to achieve his true and intended purpose. Now all he had to do was wait. He would meet strength with strength, the only language that a man like Othmar could possibly understand.

No sooner did the Caliph's envoys appear at the Exilarch's estate, delivering their summons before Bustenai flew into a rage, feigning insult and assailing the envoys failure to arrive without gifts from their master. "Was he not a king also?" he threatened ibn Selah. For reasons he could not fathom, Captain Ibrahim ibn Selah felt compelled to bow in the presence of Bustenai, reeling from under the chastisement. Bustenai cared nothing for gifts; this was all still very much of his calculated plan of strength against strength in order to achieve the impression of a total lack of fear of the consequences. Ibn Selah was dismissed and he took the Exilarch's reply back to the Caliph. The message from Bustenai was simple, "I will come to the King of Kings once I have made proper arrangements."

Over the preceding fortnight, processions had come and gone through the streets of al-Kufah but none compared to the current spectacle being witnessed by the citizens of this dune swept city. The Scion of David had arrived. Not as a lamb, but as a lion! He strode proudly upon his mount, attired in the viziers garb known to all as the 'mantle of stars'. Embroidered into the silk woven hems were ornate jewels representing all the nations that once belonged to the mighty Sassanid Empire. Legend had it that the robe was not a gift from the Persian kings at all, but a prized heirloom passed down through the generations from the time of Solomon. Whether ancient or modern, it mattered not, as the jewels shimmered and shone, scattering the light into a rainbow of color that bedazzled the eyes. Surrounding the Exilarch was his own personal guard, four hundred men in all, with a reputation that was legendary in battle. It was a clear indication to all in Othmar's court that Bustenai ibn Haninai would not let himself be considered anything less than Othmar's equal.

The Caliph never uttered a single syllable nor flinched even a single muscle as he carefully scrutinized the advancing procession. Accompanied by his advisors and guard, the Jewish prince approached the presence of the King of Kings. Once he had come within fifty yards, Othmar ordered his archers to thread their bows. Bustenai watched calmly from his saddle as the desert marksmen raised their pointed shafts in his direction. No one even flinched. Neither Bustenai nor his escort showed any signs of concern, remaining perfectly still as a calm resettled over the crowd and everyone awaited a further signal from Othmar.

What seemed like hours was in truth mere moments, as the two adversaries stood motionless measuring one other. The throng of court officials and curious onlookers were stunned into silence. Othmar suddenly gave a second signal to his men and they immediately lowered their weapons. There would be no slaughter in al-Kufah this day. Othmar had weighed the man that sat in the saddle before him and found him every inch his equal.

The King of Kings rose from his throne and walked to the edge of the dais. He looked coldly into the former Vizier's steel grey eyes, breaking the silence with a hearty laugh. "Well met, my son! You have proven yourself worthy enough for Othmar to call you a friend."

Bustenai dismounted and approached the Caliph. He seized Othmar's hand and bowed so that his forehead caressed the rings upon the old king's sturdy hand. "I am Bustenai, son of Haninai. How may I serve my king?"

"Wisely, I hope." The Caliph laughed at his own joke. His laugh was infectious amongst his advisors. "But let me ask you this Bustenai. You took it upon yourself to wear the Vizier's mantle without my permission. How could you be so certain that I would consider placing you amongst my court and not placing your head upon a spike?"

"How could you have even considered otherwise, oh Lord of the ancient realms?"

Othmar slapped the younger man across the back. "You are a crafty one, Bustenai ibn Haninai. Already my heart feels a kinship towards you. Such audacity, such nerve! Reminds me of myself when I was your age. I was confident but not overly confident. I was arrogant but never rash. Remember that Bustenai. It will serve you well and in turn serve me well. I have lived a long life because I have learned to measure my friends and respect my enemies. Do I make myself understood?" The Caliph turned and seated himself once again upon his scalloped throne.

"Yes, I am arrogant and certainly I am overly confident, but I like all of my ancestors have learned to be humble before our rightful master. We have served the Sassanids well over the centuries and I pledge that same allegiance towards the Caliph. All I ask is for the same rights and privileges granted to my people by the Persians. No more and no less."

"In exchange for what? Every deal must have equal shares to the parties involved."

"For no more and no less than the Persians were given."

"Let me warn you young Bustenai, my people are renowned to be the best when it comes to seeking a bargain. We always achieve our price when we barter in the market. At first the price will be high but in the end both buyer and seller will negotiate a price they are both satisfied with. You have asked a high price and I have asked in exchange for what? You still have not answered me."

"The world." Bustenai's answer sent a shock wave through the Caliph's court. There was no doubt from his tone of voice that he could offer just that.

Othmar clapped his hands together gleefully. "My young friend, I expect no less to be delivered by you; we have struck a bargain. Let it be known to all that I have chosen for my court's Vizier, none other than Bustenai ibn Haninai. He speaks for me in all matters. His word shall be law. Offend him and you offend me! So I have declared!"

Bustenai had instantly become the second most powerful man in the world of Islam. "And there is one other matter that must be settled between us. You made it clear to my Captain that I violated the code of honor between kings when I sent him empty handed to you. I cannot allow it to be said that Othmar is an uncouth desert nomad who knows not the formalities of the court. Name it and it shall be yours."

Bustenai gave a moment's deliberation to his request. He knew what he wanted long before Othmar had ever summoned him.

"I ask that my lord be gracious in the granting of my request. He has offered me anything that I choose and I choose a life. Perhaps it seems strange to make such a request but long ago a good friend requested that I take care of his son should anything happen to him. We who are brothers of the desert know what it is to make an oath and the consequences to fail in upholding it. I have made such an oath to Khusro and it is his son Yhosdergard who I have sworn to protect."

Othmar wrung his hands in displeasure. "Do you know what granting such a request would mean. Yhosdergard is a threat to my throne. For him to live would mean preserving a dagger to my throat. And yet, we brothers of the desert do know what it means to make an oath."

"That is why I seek your wisdom, my Lord," Bustenai had successfully placed the delicate matter back into Othmar's lap.

"If I fail to grant your request then I have broken my own word of promising you anything you asked for. And in breaking my word, you will in turn break your oath. In our world a man that does not keep his word has no honor. And a man without honor will not stay long as a ruler of a people. No matter which way I decide, I have still pointed the dagger at myself. This shall be my first true test as Caliph. Have my scribes brought before me. A case has been presented that calls for judgment. You sought my wisdom, Bustenai, now I'll show you why Othmar rules the greatest empire in the world."

Once the last of the scribes and sages had gathered around the dais, Othmar began his dissertation. "A situation exists in which a man has given his word but by so doing he endangers the life of the Caliph. The Caliph has given his word to the man but in so doing has endangered his own life. When men of such high regard make an oath then the oath must be honored. To do otherwise would require punishment by our laws. There can be no exceptions. But for every dilemma there must be a solution. Come forward Bustenai ibn Haninai and answer for me this question. Is a man's duty to his family greater than his duty to a friend?"

It was a simple question but one which Bustenai could not even fathom the Caliph's motive. This time the sly old fox seemingly had the better of him. "It is written by our sages that loyalty to one's family exceeds even that to a nation. Such was the case when David married Micah, the daughter of King Saul. Because Saul had become his father-in-law, David could not take arms against the king, even though Samuel had anointed him as the rightful ruler."

"Exactly," Othmar shouted. "His responsibilities to his nation, his people, and his friends became secondary to the marriage contract and to the family of his wife. Although he would not abandon those responsibilities, he could not let them take precedent over the life of Saul. In fact, he had to preserve Saul's life at all costs so that his anointing by the prophet Samuel would not have resulted in Saul's death. Whether directly, or indirectly he could not commit murder."

The scribes eagerly recorded every word of Othmar's discourse while Bustenai nervously awaited the point that the Caliph was about to make.

"The dead king, Khusro, has two daughters. Both as you know were unmarried and both are beauteous. I have taken the one known as Scheherazade into my harem to become one of my wives. I was intending to do likewise with her sister, Izdurdad, but instead I have decided in my wisdom to present her to Bustenai ibn Haninai, to be his wife. My house and his house shall be one. We will be one family.

Therefore, greater than his oath to Khusro will be his loyalty to me and responsibility to my wellbeing. All oaths have been preserved and no man may make disclaimer. I have spoken and so shall it be recorded."

Othmar's courtesans broke into wild applause.

His wisdom had been masterful and even Bustenai could not shake the feeling that the wiley fox had gotten the upper hand. He bowed courteously to his master and accepted his decision.

"My Lord, your wisdom has truly been worthy of praise but I seek just one more piece of advice. How am I to explain what has just happened to Adai, my wife."

The Caliph laughed as he watched his Vizier wince. "Dear brother, I have given you the responsibility of an empire to manage. Surely you can run your own household!" The scribes chuckled as they recorded the old Caliph's final words.

Chapter Six

Toronto: 1999

"I need a coffee," Pearce stated as he rubbed his eyes, then reached over to the pot to pour himself another cup.

"I hope you're not finding this boring."

"No, not at all," he quickly responded. "I think I'm finally beginning to get the gist of the events. I still don't know how this is all going to lead up to a Jewish kingdom in Southern France, but at least I now know where the family originated from."

"You will have your answers in due time, Mr. Pearce. All in due time. As I said, it's essential that you comprehend the fate of the Merovingians before you can appreciate everything else that follows."

"And what about this Bustenai?"

"Picture this, two families in existence and both with ties to the royalty of ancient Israel. One is being hunted, living a quarter ways around the world in the west while the other is being exalted in the east. If we see life as a continuous see-saw of events, then we can appreciate that at some point in time that which was on top will eventually be at the bottom. Keep this in mind as your key to understanding what will happen."

I could see that Pearce was grasping this concept and mulling it over in his mind.

"So this kid, Dagobert, who escaped to Ireland, what happened to him?"

"He came back," I replied. "I told you that already. And that was to prove to be the prime motivating factor to what came next."

"And that is...?" Pearce was growing anxious for me to continue the story. The caffeine must have entered into his blood stream already.

"Drink your coffee, Pearce. This is going to take a while."

Languedoc: 679 A.D.

Squealing inanely accompanied by an occasional snort and exhausted grunt, the wild boar fled into the shelter of the winding thicket. The two horses were reined to a brisk halt as their riders dismounted. Gazing into the underbrush, they could only now guess as to the whereabouts of their prey. They withdrew their longbows from underneath the cloth saddles and refastened the cincture straps. The one rider with long golden hair falling around his shoulders, turned suddenly as if he heard a noise.

"Quickly Gilbert, hand me my quiver before I lose the sounds of our quarry!"

The other rider passed the quiver full of arrows to his master while he looped the second quiver across his own shoulders.

"I will try to flush him from the bushes. Stand ready!"

Gilbert threaded an arrow to the bow string as he assumed a stance in eager anticipation of their prey. "Be careful your Majesty," Gilbert warned. "It has been a long time since you last trod these woods. Remember that the boar is in his own habitat and you are the intruder."

"Save your concern, Gilbert. I know how to take care of myself. I've been doing it since I've been five years old. You just make certain that your arrow is ready for the boar should it come your way." Dagobert nocked an arrow to his own bow and waded into the deep green apron of the forest.

Gilbert waited impatiently, a nervous twitch in his bow hand as he watched the king disappear into the covering of fronds and bushes. It seemed like an eternity before there were any further sounds emanating from deep within the stand of trees. Suddenly he could hear the sound of snapping twigs, followed by a high pitch squeal. The steamy breath of the boar rose above the tall grass and Gilbert raised his bow in preparation. He thumbed the bright green peacock feather that trimmed the dorsal surface of the long shaft. The bow slowly bent as he pulled back on the string until it pressed ever so slightly against his tightly drawn lips.

"Still too soon", he told himself as he bided his time.

At first he could only see the snout and curved tusks protruding from the ferns and then came the jet black eyes staring directly at him. The expressive sounds echoed the animal's terror as it charged towards the strung arrow more concerned in attempting to elude its pursuer.

Dagobert's voice bellowed above the tumultuous din. "Shoot! What are you waiting for? Shoot, you fool, before he gets away!"

Gilbert waited until the boar was almost on top of him before he let the arrow fly. A deadly, hissing sound erupted as the missile sailed towards its hapless target. Suddenly, an all too human scream shattered the chorus of woodland sounds. The boar disappeared into the briar and bramble just behind Gilbert.

Writhing upon the ground, the king vainly tried to withdraw the iron barb from his thigh. With every twist of the shaft, the pitch of his scream rose accordingly. "My God! What have you done to me? I will have you killed for this! You are a dead man, Gilbert. Do you hear me? When we get back to the palace, you're dead! Dead!"

Gilbert made no reply, simply turning his back towards the monarch and slowly walking towards his mount. From where the arrow protruded from the leg, a rivulet of blood surfaced upon Dagobert's leather grieves, each precious drop of fluid falling to the moistened earth. The king tried to raise himself to his feet but something was gravely wrong. There was no longer any sensation in his right leg from the hip down. No sooner had he achieved a crouch position did he collapse to the ground again. The same result happened repeatedly.

"Come back Gilbert." The king's tone was surprisingly mellow and forgiving. "I will not punish you. Forgive my outburst but you shot me. Help me and all is forgiven! Don't leave me here like this. I beg of you. I am your king. We are friends. Please!"

Turning a deaf ear to Dagobert's pleas, Gilbert looped the wooden stirrup over his boot and vaulted onto his horse's back. He never looked back even once as he lurched his coal black steed towards the hills. If he had turned he would have witnessed the young monarch clutching at the grassy outcroppings and dragging himself forward in terrible agony, moving mere inches with each effort.

"Come back! Come back, you bastard," Dagobert sobbed, the excruciating pain causing his mind to spin relentlessly. Dirt streaked across his face as his sweat mixed with the cool earth. Fingers dug into the ground in a futile attempt to pull himself forward a few more inches. Finally, in an utter state of exhaustion, Dagobert sprawled in defeat, resigning himself to death's cruel embrace.

"Don't tell me that you have given up so soon. I am deeply disappointed. I had expected you to provide a far more valiant effort. I was enjoying your performance."

"Who's there?" Barely able to open his eyelids, Dagobert could see no higher than the pair of deer hide boots worn by his tormentor. "Who are you?"

"Mind if I sit down, my friend?" Finding a large rock a mere yard from the king's prone body, the stranger sat.

"The voice. I know that voice. So hard to think. Why is it so hard to think?" Dagobert's words were growing slurred and garbled with each passing sentence. "Pepin? Is that you? Thank God! Pepin of Herstel, Lord Mayor of Austrasia, I beseech you. Look what my valet has done to me! Weak, so weak. And dizzy. My head is spinning. No strength to move my arms and legs. Can't talk right. Can't think! Why? Take me back to the palace."

Pepin folded his burly arms across his green vested chest. "My dear king, still you make demands. This will not do. No! It will not do at all." The Lord Mayor shook his head disapprovingly.

"It is unfortunate that Gilbert, the dear boy, is not here to see the effects of his handiwork. Poor boy was so afraid of striking down your majesty that his missile landed a yard away from your heart. Fortunately, I anticipated this. I had to devise an alternate means of ensuring your death.

Coniine! Just a little bit entering the blood stream and viola. You lose control of your own body. What an absolutely charming potion from such an innocent plant like the hemlock. Gilbert, I knew was capable of inflicting a far lesser wound upon you with a tainted arrow. He really didn't know what it would do but none the less, he will be well rewarded. Can't leave any loose ends now, can we?"

Dagobert tried speaking, but all his lips formed were gurgling sounds devoid of meaning. The potion's effect was rapid.

Pepin paid the king no attention as he adjusted his feathered cap and stretched out his long legs. "I guess the big question on your mind is why. Why, why, why?" Once again, Dagobert emitted a flurry of unintelligible sounds. "Ah yes, eager inquisitiveness as always. It's a long story but I don't believe that you are in any hurry. The drug interferes with the muscle control exerted by your mind but it is terribly slow in causing your death.

It's your own entire fault anyway. You should have stayed in Eire where you were safe. Grimwald was a fool in the first place to have allowed you to escape but then it is well known that my uncle stemmed from the less intelligent side of the family. His carelessness was your good fortune. He was too involved in raping your mother, to have worried about much else." Pepin looked as if he was in thought and then began to laugh. "Rather fitting that your mother went mad from it all and one night in a state of rapture she stabbed him to death. Thirty-nine times I hear tell. Ah, the things we do for love!"

Summoning upon hidden resources, Dagobert raised himself upon his elbows and clutched towards his vulgar assailant.

With the merest of efforts, Pepin put the heel of his foot upon the back of the king's neck and forced his face back into the mud. "You really shouldn't try to do anything foolish," the Lord Mayor chuckled. "It wouldn't be right if you missed any of this story. Now where was I...ah yes. There is this strange effect your Merovingian women seem to have on the members of my family. Some sort of sorcery I would suspect. Just look at what Brunhilde did to my grandfather. He had her confined to his chambers, actually tethered to his bed and what happens? He ends up becoming her prisoner! Instead of governing Austrasia by manipulating her son Clotaire, Pepin of Landien can't bring himself to leave his own chambers. What manner of witchcraft do your women possess? Beauty can only be responsible for so much.

The way we Carolingians make fools of ourselves for the women in your family, I would suspect that there is a far more vile nature afoot. And each time we fall under their spell the plans of the Church go awry. Here they had guaranteed complete autonomy to govern to my grandfather as long as he invested them with the authority to be the sole religion of Frankia and he's too busy with Brunhilde to even see what Clotaire is up to. Well, as you are aware, your Arian heresy was allowed to stay firmly established in this land until the bishops tried again with the assassination of your father.

But they are gutless wonders, these Catholics! Something about your Israelite blood that sends a chill down their spines. You walk around with your long hair as some sign of a Nazarite vow like Samson of old and they're afraid to touch you. Oh, it's all right to kill one of you, that they can justify, but God will not permit them to kill all of you. Nonsense! You're a man like any other man. I don't care whose blood courses through your veins. It's red just like mine. It took a lot of persuasion on my part to convince them of that."

Pepin had grown angrier with each recollection and could no longer restrain himself. Removing his foot from the back of Dagobert's neck, he rose and began to pace restlessly. "It's just not right. I mean, all of this could have been avoided. Why didn't you just stay in Ireland? You come back here with some bitch of a Celtic wife and expect us to be overjoyed? The name of this game is power and you upset the balance, my friend. I ruled this land! I was king!

After Grimwald's death, his son whom he had appointed was never permitted to be king. By daring to call himself such, he brought down the wrath of that spineless Catholic Church upon his head. They feared the fact that you were still alive. They orchestrated your father's death and as penance set you free. The fools thought that divine retribution would cast them all into purgatory, so they plotted my cousin's execution in order to win your favor."

Pepin hurled his right foot against a clump of earth and sent it flying through the air. "Now what were they going to do? Well, they came to me. To me! Offering me ultimate power as long as I played their game. Fair enough! I can be king as long as I don't call myself king. What did I care? All I had to do was to establish their enclave as the official religion of Frankia. So what? Let them steal the souls and copper sous of the miserable peasants. Who cares? In exchange they were not to interfere with my governing of this country. But no-o! They could not leave things well enough alone. They felt obligated to seek out your official sanction of what they were doing. After all, your ancestry made you a demi-god. Bah!

Explain to me how being a descendant of some bastard Jew makes you divine! It only makes a joke of everything that they profess." The Lord Mayor stomped his feet in rage like a spoiled child. He glared at the sprawled figure of the monarch and his eyes shone with a hatred that did not even convey a fraction of its intensity.

"Inviting you to return to this land was a grave error of judgment on their part and making me bow down before you and your entourage when you disembarked was even a graver error. You weren't satisfied in returning only with your bride, Mathilde. You brought a gaggle of Celtic priests and bishops with you, spouting their Arian philosophy. Then suddenly the Catholic hierarchy awakened and declared, "What have we done?" The fools had invited disaster; that's what they had done! In this game one cannot afford to make mistakes of that magnitude.

Their cabal finally starts thinking of having you assassinated but your luck holds out. Mathilde can't bear you anything but daughters. The Archbishop of Ariens sees it as a heavenly manifestation, that God, himself had ordained   an end to your line and orders   the assassination attempt to be halted.

The hypocrisy of it all! From the moment you returned, they prayed for your demise. Your failure to produce a male heir was taken as a blessing in answer to their tainted prayers. But what did you think I was going to do? Wait until you died from old age? I am older than you. I don't have the time to wait."

A leering smile fractured Pepin's hardened lips. He laughed smugly to himself as he grew amused with the thoughts of his last comment. "So what did I do?" he repeated. "I killed Mathilde, that's what I did. Do you remember how she died soon after delivering your third daughter? She was so thirsty, she was prepared to drink anything offered her. She took the poison readily. And you did exactly what I thought you would do. You showed your grief by finding yourself a second wife; Giselle de Raz`es, niece of the Visigothic chieftain.

It took a while but after five years the bitch finally bore you a son. Had your seed not been so anemic, I could have taken care of this years ago.

Now, the Archbishop of Ariens grew very concerned. Sigisbert represents a possible end to the Catholic Church in Frankia. You even proclaimed him as the savior of the Arian church and celebrated your son's birth with the pronouncement that a tax was to be levied against all Catholics. That was enough to convince them that they had to take action.

But sealed away in Giselle's palace in Languedoc they couldn't reach you. You thought yourself so very clever. But not clever enough! Did you really think that I would just let you take away my kingdom? It took another four years but finally it has come to this. You grew careless. You thought this palace to be impregnable. You were wrong!"

Pepin continued to laugh as he walked towards the king's horse and withdrew the ebony lance that protruded from the girth sheath. He hefted the sturdy shaft in his right palm, seemingly testing its aerodynamics several times by arcing it high over his head but finally bringing it to rest across his shoulder.

"It really wasn't too difficult to arrange this opportunity to complete your downfall. It was only human nature that dictated that at some time you would make an excursion far from the protection of the palace guards. You always prided yourself in being a great hunter. I merely had to await your desire to butcher harmless animals to overwhelm your own self-protectiveness.

You may wonder how I knew. Your palace staff is so infiltrated with spies that work for me that it was impossible for you to even take a walk in your gardens without me knowing about it. Did you really think that by beginning your hunting expedition on the day before Christmas that it would ensure your safety? You always underestimated the Catholic Church my friend!"

Pepin arced the lance over his head once more, admiring its perfect balance. "An excellently crafted javelin," he praised. "I hope you don't mind but I intend to keep this. Anyway, as I was saying; to assume that the festive holy days would be cause for the church to suspend its plot against you was foolhardy at best. Since when has religion had anything to do with the love they profess?

Do you really think that I am a Catholic because I believe in the teachings of Christ? I prefer my enemies dead, not striking my other cheek. Why would I ever kneel to a god of weakness? I am Catholic because at this time it is smart politics to be one. You should have allied yourself with strength. The Catholic Church is strength. It is led by an enclave that are not afraid to abandon morality and scruples in order to achieve gain."

Pepin turned and started to lead the king's horse back to his own which grazed at the fringe of the clearing. "It really is too bad, you know. I really did like you, Dagobert. But after all, I am merely human and therefore I succumb to all the earthly pleasures." Pulling himself into the saddle, he turned towards the stricken king. "And you know what, if it's any consolation to you, once you're dead, Giselle holds absolutely no interest for me. So I bid you farewell, my friend."

The Lord Mayor thoroughly enjoyed the sarcasm evident in his remarks. Not paying attention to the stricken monarch, he failed to notice Dagobert had managed to crawl to the rock that he had been sitting on and was ever so slowly pulling himself upright.

Through the pain of straining muscles that still refused to respond fully, Dagobert could sense the trickle of strength returning to his weakened limbs and his mind began to shake itself clear of the heavy fog that had imprisoned it.

Still smitten with laughter over the sheer absurdity of those that proclaimed themselves to be the vicars of Christ, Pepin was oblivious to the king's slow recovery.

"Well, I will keep my allies happy," the mayor explained. "Your son, Sigisbert will sit on your throne after your death but only as a puppet of my rule. Don't worry! As I said, your wife doesn't interest me in the least. In fact, none of your Merovingian cows sway me in any way. That is why I will be successful, as shall be my son Charles Martel, and his son after him. This time we shall establish the rules."

"I shall kill you, you filthy, murdering pig." The voice was an anguished stutter but clear enough to snap Pepin from his thoughtful meanderings.

Alarmed, the Lord Mayor swung around to face his adversary who had now propped himself awkwardly against the huge rock. "What manner of demon are you?" Pepin was shocked to see the king working himself into a kneeling position. "You should be dead by now. You Merovingians just can't follow the rules! Whatever sorcery this is, I shall not let it deter me!"

Pepin raced forward with the lance firmly held in both hands, knees securely braced against the withers, piercing the king's cranium through the orbit of his left eye. The shaft buried itself in the skull until it emerged at the base of the neck. It was quickly followed by a reflexive vomiting of bile and blood. Falling to the ground, Dagobert's body convulsed wildly, his arms and legs flailing uncontrollably. Then as quickly as it had begun, the seizure stopped.

Pepin watched at first in abject disgust, but then his emotions finally gave way to bemused satisfaction. He reared his horse heavenward and shouted triumphantly, "Your Bastard king is dead. Do you hear me? Long live the new king!"

Chapter Seven

Toronto: Present

Stretching his arms behind his head, Pearce lets out a loud groan. "Not exactly the nicest of people we're dealing with."

"Since when did history concern itself with nice people? You're barking up the wrong tree if you want stories about nice people. History was made by the scum and bastards of our world."

Pearce has to admit I was right. "Just remember, it's the bastards that also get to write the history. That's why they call it..."

"I know," I interrupt as fast as I can. "His story! Old joke and not that good of one either."

"Can't blame a guy for trying. So, what happens next? What I have so far is a line of Jewish Kings in Babylon, these dead Merovingians in France and absolutely nothing in between."

"You're beginning to sound a little pushy Mr. Pearce."

"Don't get offended, Doc, but I still don't have a common thread to write about. As I see it, this other family is taking over medieval France, and they don't seem the type to want to share power with anyone."

"You still can't see it yet?" I mocked him. "Even Shakespeare recognized it. Why can't you see it?"

Pearce was now completely confused. "Shakespeare, Doc? What are we talking about?"

"Ghosts!"

My guest goes completely silent.

"The greatest fear of that all usurpers of power share," I explain, "Ghosts that will haunt them for the rest of their miserable lives; specters of past kings that frighten them to the point of death. Call it superstition, call it nonsense, but in the end, it still brings the mighty to their knees. These Carolingian bastards are no different. The year was 759 and on one particular night, the ghosts of the dead and murdered kings were particularly active."

Narbonne: 759 A.D.

The world trembled on its foundations as the great firs bowed to the howling winds, raining their needles like poisoned darts upon the tents below. The king turned restlessly on his cot, hearing not only the wind but the wails of the dying as well. He had followed the silent voice of a nameless God; a god that had promised him glory and now it had come to this. Seemingly abandoned at the edge of a forgotten world, the stench of decaying flesh from the corpses of his own men flooded his senses. The earth was now creviced by rivulets of blood that never appeared to drink their full. God had betrayed him to these nefarious heathens. As he closed his eyes, he mourned over the loss of a kingdom that never truly was.

Shadows stole whatever free thought he still possessed, leaving only the horror of demonically tainted dreams. How could the noble and righteous have been brought so low? It was his God that deemed him worthy to enlighten the heretics. He had beheld the future and it certainly was not supposed to end like this. Why had he been deserted now? The walls of Narbonne had not been broken and her people did not perish by his sword. He had carried that portent within his heart for almost seven years and now it was his people that lay wasted by the swords of foreigners.

Had he become a king only to die like a wounded dog, lying in some dark forsaken valley so far from home? He, who had made his path with emperors and had raised himself so high amongst the mighty, was he not Pepin, the son of Charles Martel?

Only five years had passed since Pope Stephen II had anointed him as the Patriciatus Romanorum, protector of the Church; the avenging angel of God. The Pope had knelt before him and honored him as no other man had been honored. He laughed as he thought about that day. He could feel the barb working its way towards his back and though he felt more like crying out in pain, he could only find another reason to laugh.

Conqueror of Nimes, Maquelonne, Agade and Beziers! Pepin the Great! Pepin the Magnificent! Who was he fooling? Pepin the Short! That's all he was. Pepin the Vanquished at Narbonne! And once more he laughed at his own arrogance, wincing as the slightest movement of his abdomen pushed the arrow even deeper from its point of entry. His bravery had been compared to that of the lion, his cunning to the fox and he was loved; loved by his family, loved by women, but most of all loved by his men. They fought not for his God but for him and now they were dying for him.

Each breath carried him farther from the reality of the world of the living. He closed his eyes to welcome the specter of approaching death. Where had they all gone? His doctor, generals and sons? Were they all not there by his side a second ago? Now he felt naught but the stunning silence and the warmth of the enveloping darkness. Had it been so long ago? Seven years ago in truth? Living outside these massive walls for seven full years, waiting for the stone blocks to come tumbling down as God had done for his anointed so long ago at Jericho. But they did not crumble and the days only grew into longer nights and all that he had inherited from his father had slipped through his fingers only to be lost in the mud and stench that grew outside this accursed city.

Scenes flashed before his failing eyes but they were not scenes from his own life. In some mystical manner, beyond his comprehension, he was witnessing a play from a distant past. Ancestors that had long since died paraded before him. Perhaps he was dead too? He could not say. All he could do was lie there helplessly as the series of dramas unfolded. A spectator to a past he barely knew.

Stepping forward from the gray fringed shadows strode a warrior bedecked in heavy armor and sealed visor. As he removed the helmet, Pepin released a silent gasp. It was him! Or it could have been him. The features were strikingly similar except this man was much taller and his hair was brown and shortly cropped, unlike Pepin's long blonde tresses. There was a knock on the heavy wooden door that suddenly came into focus.

"Go away!", the warrior shouted angrily.

"Open the door Pepin. I need to speak to you."

"I do not wish to be bothered now. Go away Bishop!"

"You cannot dismiss me like this, Pepin of Landien. Without me you are nothing! I am the Bishop of Metz! You will listen to me. None of this could have taken place without me."

"You give yourself too much credit, Arnulf. Without me it is you who are nothing. We have no need of your church. I have what I always wanted. Now go see to it that the boy is dealt with and do whatever bishops do."

The voice from beyond the door grew angrier. "You are a fool! Where once you were only the mayor of Austrasia, the Church has made you virtually ruler of this land. Think about what you are doing. Is she really worth it?"

Pepin of Landien unbuckled the shoulder clasps that held his breastplate and peeled the armor from his torso. Then he unfastened the iron and leather jerkin that hung from his waist. The bishop continued to hammer his fists against the solid wooden door.

"Yes, Arnulf, she is worth it," the tired warrior screamed. Next he removed the arm grieves and chainmail gloves, tossing them into a corner of the room with a resounding peal.

"Do not do it Pepin! You will destroy all that we have conspired for. Send her to a nunnery but don't make her into a martyr. The people will rally behind her. For god sake, listen to me!"

"God has nothing to do with this, Arnulf! What would you know about being a man? Have you ever been a man, Arnulf? Or are little boys more your style? Let there be no doubt about it, Bishop, I am a man. I fight my battles for spoils and she is my spoil of war!" Pepin continued to undress, removing his leg grieves and three-hinged boots. Slipping completely out of his linen tunic, the mayor of Austrasia stood completely naked before the four poster bed that slowly materialized from out of the gray shadows.

"Then you are a fool, Pepin", the bishop shouted through the door. "We offered you a kingdom and you will throw it all away for the flesh. What happens when Brunhilde grows old? Will you still want her then? We will raise her son to do our bidding. Clotaire will learn to serve us and not you. His dynasty shall prevail, yours will crumble into nothingness."

"What do I care of dynasties? Who knows if I'll even be alive tomorrow? I choose to live for today. And if I am alive tomorrow, I shall deal with Clotaire then." Walking towards the bed, Pepin separated the curtains of the canopy, revealing the luscious body of Brunhilde, stripped bare and tethered to all four bedposts.

"There are no tomorrows, Pepin! You are not the one that is important. Clotaire is! The blood of the kings of ancient Israel flow through his veins, not yours. You are nothing more than a petty despot. There are plenty of other power mongers to take your place. We do not need you!"

Arnulf screamed his last comments, piercing the eeriness of the bedchamber behind the sealed door.

Pepin halted momentarily as if he was suddenly contemplating his present situation. He looked from Brunhilde's seductive body to the door and then back again. "I curse you Bishop! I curse you and all of those like you! May Satan have your misbegotten souls. I will not be a tool of your deceptions." Pepin rolled on top of Brunhilde and squeezed her flesh between his powerful legs. "Once I am finished with the queen, I shall deal with Clotaire personally. And when all is done, I shall deal with you, Bishop!"

Arnulf laughed in reply, his voice slowly fading as he walked down the corridor away from the heavy door. "You shall do nothing to the boy. Without his royal blood there is no France. There is no unity of the tribes. Remember that Pepin. Remember it long and remember it well...."

Voices and images swirled into the myriad of nothingness; of shaded grays and muted tones blended on a canvas of memories. As one scene faded, another began to overlay itself upon the first. Pepin the Short found his own consciousness teetering on the brink between life and death. No longer could he discern between what was real and what was not; what was present and what was past. He had become merely a spectator to events that seemingly had some great import that only he would be privy to.

Brunhilde's image would weave in and out of the tapestry of unending thoughts. The taste of her breasts was sweet, her body swaying beneath his, thrusting skywards as she climaxed. He laughed inwardly. Even the conquered could not resist the pleasures of sin. Such was the way of the world.

Pepin remembered the bonds that held him firmly to her bed, an unwillingness to ever leave the security that nurtured him between her thighs. But no! These were not his recollection of a blinding, torrid love. They were the first Pepin's...his ancestor's; memories for which he had no right to recall. But in the blink of an eye he could now see himself striding that great Merovingian queen, riding her into the bliss that awaited him in the shadows of death. Nothing had changed he reminded himself. So it would always be, he reaffirmed his unyielding fate.

This was heaven! This was hell! Whichever, he cared little. He had penetrated the beauty that had enslaved his great, great grandfather and now he too never sought to leave Nirvana. He wanted to thrust, and push, and squeeze, until the bed and its heavy wooden posts shattered into a black oblivion.

There came a knock at the heavy wooden door. "Go away!" Pepin the Short tried to shout. "Go away!" After one and a half centuries he could understand why Pepin of Landien did what he did. Now was not the time to be disturbed by another manifestation, another haunting of the dim past.

"Quickly! We must go master. He awaits us." The voice was that of his esquire, Pierre St. Jean. Pierre was dead! He had died two years ago outside the walls of Narbonne while trying to breech the gates. Is this what it was like to be dead? Dream after dream from which you could never wake up. Pepin suddenly found himself fully dressed in his usual green chemise and brown britches but as he turned, he discovered the bed was now empty. He could not explain the feeling that overcame him. It was as if he had finally found the greatest treasure this world had to offer and now it was torn from him. Even after death, he reasoned, the fates could be cruel.

"We must leave at once, Sire."

"Yes, yes, I know. I'm coming Pierre." Pepin the Short paused momentarily. This was an all too familiar scene. Had those not been his exact words that night almost eight years ago? He was compelled to carry on, knowing full well whom he was going to meet and why. He opened the oak door and took off after his esquire.

"We must be very quiet, Pepin." St. Jean put a finger to his lips. He was a tall, lean man with baby like skin that could barely grow a hint of facial hair.

Pepin stared at him longingly. It was good to see his old friend again. He had missed him sorely. There were so many things he wished to say but the dream was in control and it would not allow anything to be said that was not said that night.

"He has requested that you come without your guard. The fewer people knowing that he is here, the better. He stressed that it is most urgent that you come immediately." St. Jean had always been the perfect esquire. In every facet of his work he would strip away the fat, leaving only the lean to be digested.

"I'm coming as fast as I can," Pepin replied. "It is an unholy hour that he has timed his arrival and I am afraid that he will just have to wait a little longer." He followed his servant down the long corridors and winding turret stairs that led to the sheep gate outside the palace walls. Few people used that entrance, meaning even fewer would be guarding it. Without even stirring a single sentry, the mayor and his esquire were outside of the palace compound and darted in the direction of the forest.

"I don't understand why he had to be so secretive, Pierre?"

"Apparently, he thinks that there are those in your household who cannot be trusted. He is the most vulnerable at this period of time. Without an army or a refuge, his enemies could dispose of him at any point they choose. That is why he arranged to meet only with you and no one else. Even now he has planted stories that say he is journeying into the land of the Germans. No one knows that he is here in Frankia, save us. Only by maintaining this pretense can he foil his would be assassins."

Pepin nodded his head. He knew all along that this clandestine meeting could only take place in complete secrecy and that was one of the reasons he had requested it. The fewer knowing of his own political ambitions, the better.

"How much further, Pierre?"

"He awaits you in that clearing just ahead."

Both men were about to enter the encampment when suddenly they were accosted by two very imposing sentries. "Who goes?" The guard to their left blocked their path as he scrutinized their appearance and awaited the password.

"One who wishes to learn how to fish," St. Jean replied.

"And what kind of fish do you seek to catch?" the other guard asked in answer to the reply.

"I wish to fish for men."

The guards stood back and allowed the strangers to pass, while a third man appeared from nowhere and ushered them towards the canvas tent.

"All kneel in the presence of his Holiness," the custodian of the tent instructed them in a completely monotone, gravelly voice. Both Pepin and Pierre St. Jean bowed and lowered themselves to their knees.

"The one named Pepin may approach his Excellency, The Pope Zacharias," the custodian instructed them.

Pepin approached, never rising off his knees until his forehead rested upon the outstretched hand of the Pontiff. He kissed the ring of St. Peter and waited patiently for Zacharias to speak.

The voice was old and edged with a trace of illness. Zacharias did not wear his sixty odd years well. His reign had been plagued with unrest from its very inception and now the entire Papal diocese teetered on the brink of extinction. "Rise, my son. It is good of you to have come. The church has fallen upon bitter times. We need a champion to raise it up once again."

"I know of this, holy father. That is why I requested this audience of you. It is I who am grateful that you have come. Your humble servant has need of your divine wisdom."

"Speak and let it be known how I can help you." Zacharias started to cough, losing his breath for a second or two before recovering.

"Once, my father, Charles Martel, asked permission of the Papacy to remove Sigisbert from the throne of Frankia. That permission was denied because of the superstitions that surround the Merovingian family. For all intents my father governed this land but was refused the title of king. I have a similar request. Childeric is a useless monarch who will only surrender this land into vassalage to the Moors. He is too weak to govern and yet I am powerless to depose him. Would it truly be sinful if I was to strip him of the monarchy? As Mayor of the Palace, it is I who control the army and the treasury. I have the power to defend this land and save us from the Moslem invaders. All I need is your permission to make it official."

"I am aware of your needs," the pontiff sputtered and coughed violently enough to knock the monk's cowl from his head. "In fact, I took the liberty to have a document drawn up to that effect." He coughed again. "You are a king without a throne and I am a pope without a diocese. We are very similar, you and I." Zacharias waved for a servant to rush forward with a large spittoon into which he spat a wad of phlegm.

"In answer to your question. No, it is not sinful. But remember that there is a direct connection between the life blood of the Merovingians and the life essence of this land. One cannot survive without the other." The Pope buckled over in a spasm of coughing. An aide rushed forward to keep his frail form from falling over. Assisting Zacharias back into a chair, the Pope continued his discourse. "If Childeric was to die your reign would be fraught with disaster. Therefore it is imperative that he stays alive at all costs."

"It is merely a foolish superstition, your eminence."

Zacharias pounded his crook angrily against the ground. "It is not a superstition; know this well for it is the truth. His ancestors were anointed by Samuel's holy oil. That oil was blessed by God! Man has not the right to question the will of the Almighty." Raising a gnarled hand to his mouth, the pontiff was successful in stifling a fit of coughing.

"We have held the evidence of this very fact for seven centuries in our possession. Though we despise the fact that these heathen Merovingians can raise themselves above us, it is nonetheless the will of God. This land can only exist as long as there is still one of the anointed to walk upon it. These are matters of truth that cannot be questioned."

"And in this document of which you spoke of, Excellency...?"

"In return for the Catholic Church proclaiming you as the rightful ruler of Frankia, you will in turn use your army to reconquer the Papal States from the Lombards who have taken possession of them and forced me into exile. In essence, we each get what we most desire."

"But that would mean splitting my forces at a time when I can least afford to. By sending part of my army to Italy, I am inviting the Saracens to attack on my home front."

Zacharias stamped his staff against the ground again. "That is our deal, Pepin son of Charles Martel. The needs of the Church must never come secondary to your own personal wants. If you wish the Church to approve of Childeric's abdication at your hands, then you must first ensure that the Church survives!"

It took two aides to restrain the Pontiff as his body shook from another violent bout of coughing. This time there had not been any warning and a volley of mucous shot from Zacharias's mouth and landed on the tent floor.

Pepin could not help but stare at the excreted phlegm. Its greenish, yellow tinge told him all too well that this pope would not be around for too much longer. Zacharias had fallen victim to the black lung disease that had victimized Europe for centuries. This opportunity might never become available again. Who knows who Zacharias's successor might be and how he would deal with such matters?

"I accept his holiness's most gracious offer and agree to all the terms in the document."

"Most commendable," the Pope congratulated him. "As soon as you have found proper accommodations for King Childeric, I will expect you to send troops to aid my cause. They will gather together in Aquitaine where I hope certain allies of yours and mine will send men to augment your forces. From there you will launch your attack against the Lombards."

"Agreed, your Excellency."

"Then let's get on with it." Zacharias waved his staff in the air, chasing the visitors from his tent and sending them on their way.

Pepin saw himself leave the tent but as soon as he stepped from the flap he entered the great hall of his palace. Time and space apparently had no bounds in this dimension of the afterlife. In truth, he had forgotten exactly where he had gone after his audience. He shook his head and within a heartbeat, he was nuzzled between Brunhilde's firm breasts, and that was all he cared to know. But the shadow of his forgetfulness now haunted and even the suck on the queen's turgid nipples was not enough to allay the uneasiness that plagued his subconscious.

Such a monumental event in his life and no matter how hard he tried to recollect where he had gone after leaving Zacharias's presence, he could not remember. Perhaps, he thought, this nether-world played havoc with his mind and only let him see what it chose for him. But why now show him the great hall? Surely, nothing of consequence ever happened there. Pepin was not one for magnificent banquets or lusty balls. In fact, he usually liked to eat in the great hall alone. He never enjoyed polite conversation while dining.

Perchance these were events that could have been. Now, he clearly saw himself gnawing at the breast of a roasted quail, sitting as usual by himself at the head of the table. He had just taken a swallow of mead when St. Jean came bursting into the hall. "My liege! A tragedy has befallen us!" Now it was all too clear. Pepin instinctively knew what was to come next. It had to be one of the most horrible days of his life. He wanted the visions to stop. He had seen enough. He shook his head violently but could no longer find his way back to Brunhilde's lithe body.

Why must he suffer through Childeric's death a second time? Why should he continue to bare the blame for a murder he did not commit? Using the power invested in him by the Pope, Pepin forced Childeric to abdicate and then confined him to a monastery. He made the monks shave the former king's head, thereby removing the sacred hair of the Merovingians. He only wished to taunt the king; embarrass him. Display him disgraced for the entire world to see. He had no way of knowing it would drive Childeric to suicide. It had never been his intention. Why must he bare this eternal blame?

"I know; Childeric is dead." That was not how it happened; he knew nothing until Pierre St. Jean had told him of the king's suicide a day after it happened. This dream was taking on a life of its own. A different reality from what Pepin had grown accustomed to. "We must restore the blood to this land, St. Jean." Pepin felt uncomfortable saying these words. He knew not why he was saying them now. "There is no Frankia without the anointed blood." How odd he thought that he would now be spewing the same superstitious nonsense that Pope Zacharias had uttered.

"Yes, we must restore the blood to the land," St. Jean replied.

"It is impossible!" Pepin shook his head regretfully. "Childeric was the last of his line. There are no other heirs to the Merovingian throne."

"There is blood even more sacred than that of the Merovingians, my liege. Why not bring the blood of the House of David to this land."

Was this specter speaking fact or fantasy? Pepin was at a loss to tell. This was not the Pierre St. Jean he knew. The real St. Jean had as little tolerance of the esoteric as he had. "How do you know of this sacred blood from King David?"

"In this realm there are no secrets, my liege. Look to the East for there dwells the Scion of David. His blood shall make this land bloom. Failure to lure him here shall surely mean the destruction of your household and the end of this nation. I must go now and you must return from whence you came."

"No! Wait! How will I know where to look for him?" Pepin tried to raise himself from his chair but no matter how hard he pushed against the armrests he could not move even an inch. The pain in his side surged and then subsided. He felt himself begin to black out.

"Farewell, Pepin. Until we meet again." Pierre St. Jean smiled benevolently and then closed the door behind as he left.

Pepin felt himself collapse deeper and deeper into the chair. Like a bottomless well, he continued to fall without end.

"I have it." The voice was triumphant. "As soon as I cut off the barb I want you to pull out the shaft." The physician grabbed a crude pair of pliers from the table beside him. "Now!" The aid pulled back on the broken shaft and it slid from Pepin's body effortlessly. "Well that's out. Hand me a tube filled with sulfur."

The aid passed the cylinder to the physician who then inserted it into the open wound. Filling the hole in Pepin's back with a pad of linen cloth, the physician then blew on the open end of the tube until it emptied the sulfur powder. "Now hand me the phosphorus." This was applied to the perimeter of both entry and exit wounds with extreme care. As soon as the physician completed the application he took a small blackened brand and touched it ever so carefully to both wounds.

A ball of fire erupted from the wound orifices, showering the cot in sparks. "There, that should do it. Bring me the light." Tilting the lit candle, the doctor allowed the wax to flow into the wound until it sufficiently sealed both portals. "He is one tough old bastard," the physician commented. "And all he could think of is riding some wench, named Brunhilde, under his saddle. I wonder whose daughter that one may have been. But certainly not a bad way to go for a man staring directly into the face of death."

"I heard that Peristes! Don't think that you have been with me so long that I will let you get away with saying anything you want about me."

The physician jumped back and almost kicked the small table with all his implements over. "My Lord, Pepin, I was not aware that you were conscious. You startled me."

"Of that I am certain. Just because you're the best goddamn physician around doesn't give you total liberty to say as you think. You better be more careful next time. I might catch you saying something really bad about me." Pepin winked at his old friend.

"Of you my Lord, never."

"Cut the bull-shit, Peristes. Give me something to drink. Whatever you did to me hurts more than the damn arrow."

The aide handed a jug to Pepin who eagerly grasped it and pressed it to his lips. After a quick swallow, he flung the pitcher across the tent and spewed the contents in his mouth over the aide. "Are you trying to poison me lad? This is water! When I ask for a drink, I mean a drink!"

"Here! Take this!" Peristes removed the gourd he carried on his belt. "You would think that someone who narrowly cheated death would be a little more courteous to those that saved him," the physician scolded. "This is something I carry around for my own medicinal purposes."

Pepin drank lustily, emptying the gourd in a single gulp before handing it back to the physician. "Peristes, if you had seen death as I have seen it I don't know if you would want to be brought back."

"Well for now be quiet and tell me later and hold still while I bandage your side. You'll talk too much and herniate your intestines through the wounds." The physician helped sit the King of the Franks upright as he meticulously began wrapping the dressing repeatedly around his mid-section. "There, that should do it." The physician tied a knot with the ends of the dressing. "No one else gives me problems the way you do. You must rest now. Your fever has not yet broken."

"Do not mother me, Peristes. I have rested long enough!"

Peristes ordered his aide to forcefully restrain Pepin from rising from the cot. "If you insist on behaving like a child then I will be forced to treat you like one," he warned. "The wound you suffered was far more serious than you give it credit. Be grateful that the barb must have only done minor damage to your vital organs. We are talking a matter of mere inches at best. If you insist on being noncompliant, I will have you bound to this cot." Peristes proceeded to place a cool compress upon the king's forehead.

Pepin swiped the doctor's arm away. "I will not be patronized. I did not return from a tour of the nether-world to have my mission delayed by your cajoling. We have known each other a long time, Peristes, and if you would like to go on knowing me then call my sons and advisors in here immediately!"

"But..."

"No buts! Summon them now!" The violent twisting of his body shot a spasm of pain through his abdomen. Pepin steeled himself against the sudden agony. As soon as the torment subsided he flashed a grin in Peristes direction. "Death has done its best and lost. Now go do as I say."

By nightfall they had all been gathered in the pale illumination of Pepin's tent. The Frankish King sat immobilized in his huge walnut chair. Though padded in every conceivable fashion, Pepin could not help but wish he had stayed in the cot as his physician had advised. Brandishing a clenched grimace, he nodded courteously to the assembled host. "As you can see, your king has survived another ordeal," he stated quite candidly. "But I grow tired of all these tribulations. That is why I have summoned you all here." He glanced from face to face only to see no one surprised or even interested.

They had heard this too many times before. "Bah! You have all grown weary of hearing of new tactics. Well, so have I! But this time we will do things differently." Now his comments had piqued their interest. "We have laid siege to Narbonne for close to seven years. Seven long years!" A low grumbling noise surfaced from the ranks. Pepin raised a hand to silence them. "We have lost many good men; many good friends. But most of all, most of the morale from our troops.

My dearest companion, Pierre St. Jean lies buried at the foot of that plain, my constant and faithful advisor." The generals nodded in agreement. "Well, he was a better advisor than I thought. While I was unconscious, or delirious, or dead, whichever you choose to pick, he came to me. He came across that great abyss and he instructed me on how to put an end to this siege once and for all."

Once again the murmuring began to stir but this time it was laced with sarcasm and mild amusement. Advice from the dead would be difficult at the best of times to accept. They loved Pepin but perhaps the experience of near-death had been too much for him. He would not have been the first warrior to suffer from battle madness.

Pepin caught their pitiful glances at him. "Oh yes! There are doubters amongst you. There have always been doubters. But there is no doubt that if we fail to take Narbonne then we have handed the Saracens the greatest victory of the war. They will rally their forces and utterly destroy all that we have succeeded in thus far. The Frankish kingdom will vanish and you will all learn to kneel and pray to a new god. Now, is there anyone still present who does not wish to hear what I have to say?"

No one dared to speak. Pepin was about to continue when his youngest son stepped from among the host and bowed perfunctorily. Slightly annoyed, Pepin still offered his son permission to speak.

"Father, we have tried every conceivable means to take this city. There is not a strategy we have not prevailed upon. Even if the ghost of your friend has offered advice to this effect, how can you be so certain that it would be successful?"

"He did not give me advice, Charlemagne; he gave me a lesson. A lesson in what kingship is all about. He reminded me that a king may wield the power of life and death but that still does not make him anything more than a man. Fighting against myths, or legends, and even curses, not even a king will fare too well. Therefore it is important for a king not only to know every aspect concerning his enemies but about his allies as well. Narbonne will not fall from any breech we establish from the outside. The key to Narbonne is striking from the inside."

"Granted, father but where do we find such allies."

"Half of the city is populated by Jews, is it not? They will be our allies."

Gasps of shock and revulsion spread across the lips of the generals. "Jews?" The mere suggestion made their stomachs turn. There had never been any love for the Jews in the Frankish kingdoms. They were an evil necessity; money lenders, traders, dye merchants and the lowest of the low. For centuries the Church had made their lives miserable; forced conversions, expulsions and even executions. It was all permissible for they had been declared a despised race that refused to accept redemption in Christ. How could Pepin even think of them in the same context as allies?

"Enough of your pettiness! Who here would not make a deal with the devil if it meant victory? When Childeric died, all chances of the survival of our kingdom went with him. There was a blessing bestowed on this land because of the Merovingian presence. Now we must seek the blood of Jewish kings to reestablish that blessing."

"But, father! There are no Jewish kings in Narbonne."

"Do you think that I am not aware of that! I'm wounded in my abdomen, not my brain!" Pepin's voice thundered in the direction of his youngest son. Charlemagne was taken aback by its tempestuous tone. "Tell our spies in the city to contact the leaders of the Jewish community. We shall strike a bargain with them. If they destroy the Saracen garrison for us and open the gates to my army then we shall let them live in peace under the rule of their own self-government. And in control of that government they shall have their own king; a king from the House of David. A descendant from that noble lineage of God appointed monarchs brought to them from the east. I shall make them masters in their own house and in turn they shall become valued and loyal allies of the Franks."

"Is there even such a king, father? After all, you were in a delirium!"

"Even if there is only rumored to be one, you are going to find him. As soon as the city is delivered to us I will be sending you on a mission of state to the Caliph of Baghdad. Take that pet Jew of yours , Isaac, with you as an interpreter. I want this king brought back to me. If he is a man, bring him here alive and if he is only a dead myth then bring him back in a coffin! Either way they will get their king!"

The generals broke into a series of salutes and hurrahs for their monarch as he concluded his commands. Narbonne's days as a Saracen base were numbered. Pepin had dreamed it so.

Chapter Eight

Toronto: 1999

Rising from the couch, where he had made himself extremely comfortable for a couple of hours, Pearce begins to perform some sort of ritual stretching exercises. His carefully choreographed movements suggest that this had been a precision development for some time. Like a crane, wading through a reeded pond, his swoops and exaggerated arm movements are quite amusing to watch. His ability to perform these theatrics without concern of what I might think, I actually find redeeming. For the first time, I find a quality in this strange man that I actually like.

"Am I to assume that you have reached your limit and would like to call it a night?" I suggest.

"Oh, you mean this...," he puffs trying to catch his breath. "I learned these tricks from a Tai Chi master. I'll be as good as new in a few minutes."

"Wonderful!"

"You should try it, Doc."

"Actually, I'm quite comfortable, right here, in my chair." I pad the thick cushioned arms, reassuringly. I thought there may have been a chance that Pearce would actually leave, but I realize that I am not going to have any such luck.

"So, Doc, I know this king who Charlemagne goes after is not going to be a myth. Otherwise, there'd be no basis for your story. But I find it strange that this guy is willing to uproot himself from being a king in his own country to come to a place that for all he knew might not even exist. Not too bright, if you ask me!"

"I think you'll agree with me that in his case, the circumstances and timing were right at that moment. As I tell you about him, keep this in mind, a year earlier, even six months earlier and he probably wouldn't have had the slightest interest. That is the remarkable thing about this episode in history. Everything had to be perfect for it to even have taken place. Coincidence? Providence? I'll tell you right now Pearce, I don't believe anything happens by coincidence. I believe it to have been much more!"

Baghdad: 768 A.D.

During his youth the maidens of this city dreamt that one day he would choose them to be his bride. Standing six feet and two inches tall, he towered over most men of his community, his powerful frame hidden beneath the loose fitting robes that were required to be worn by a man in his position. Many a young woman crooned over his auburn hair and ruddy good looks. Pale green eyes pierced deeply into all that they set upon and none could escape that penetrating, empathizing gaze. His beard was the short tapered cut, so fashionable amongst the Moorish nobility. Like all the members of his family, he chose its stylish sculpturing over the heavy bi-parted horns of facial growth worn by the orthodoxy. His father Havivai had worn his beard in exactly the same fashion but only recently had it become looked upon as a betrayal by the elders and they condemned him unjustly.

It was not so much the adopting of the mannerisms of his Muslim masters but more so his refusal to relinquish his hereditary authority to the new elite of the Babylonian Jews. He had willingly placed his divine prerogative in direct conflict with their heavenly inspiration and in the ensuing battle, he lost. The order had come from Caliph Al-Mansur the Abbasid that morning and now everyone knew that for Natronai ibn Havivai, the ordeal was finally over.

He nervously stroked his beard as he contemplated what his next move should be. So much had gone wrong in so little time. It was almost as if the entire world had risen up and turned against him. Alone, afraid, Natronai slowly shuffled to his olive wood desk and sat himself down. Lifting the ornate brass writing implement, he opened the small ceramic jar containing a mixture of ox blood and indigo and dipped in the pen's hollow point. At first he hesitated before the blank parchment on the desk as if his own mind was equally as blank. But then with a sudden flooding of emotion, he poured his very soul out upon the parchment.

> *"Blessed be the Lord God, the Merciful,*
>
> *In the year 4528 of the fourteenth day of Sivan, these are the words of Makhir Natronai ibn Havivai, the true and rightful exilarch of the Babylonian Jews. I am leaving this letter in the trusting care of my servant, Rafik, so that he may give it to you, Ahunai, my son, upon your entering of the covenant during your thirteenth birthday. It rends my very soul to know that I may never see you again, for I have perceived that my exile is permanent. I love you more than life itself. I shall miss you sorely but it is gladdening to know that this nightmare may finally be at an end. But fate has been cruel in forcing me to walk from one nightmare into what may possibly be another.*
>
> *Why has God done this to me? All is not as it was meant to be. If only my thrice great grandfather Bustenai had known what taking Izdurdad into his bed chamber would cause to occur in my lifetime, I think he would have rejected her comely advances. Now, the great rift has come about and the saintly rabbis have placed Izdurdad's whelping upon my throne. I do not contest Judah Zakkai's birthright, since the blood that courses through our veins is the same but he has become nothing more than a lackey for the rabbinical Gaonate. If the rabbis required him to lick their boots, I am certain that he would find pleasure in doing so.*
>
> *Oh, how the mighty have fallen! My God, why hast thou forsaken me? I could not bear to become like my cousin, Anan ben David. How many years has it been that he has sat in that prison cell? He openly defied the Gaon Yehudai and now he awaits execution like some common criminal. Is it a crime that he proclaimed the Talmud null and void because it was merely the work of men and not the word of God?*
>
> *By renouncing the Talmud he had portrayed the rabbis to be wicked men who sought power by distorting the truth. He told the people not to seek the wisdom of these patronized sages for God had given his word in the Torah for all men to know for themselves and not to rely on others to explain what does not need explanation. The rabbis say that theirs was the right to correlate and write down the oral law. But where did these oral laws stem from? Surely not from God for he told Moses to write down all that he had told him so that no man can brook difference.*
>
> *The Torah is the word of God and there is no other. Now I see, all too late that the*

path that Anan chose was the correct one. He resisted the Gaons of Suza and Pumbedita and by challenging them openly I am certain that God will show his mercy to him and Anan shall regain his freedom. Let all men open their eyes and see that there is treachery afoot. Should these esteemed rabbis gain complete authority they shall create a schism that shall utterly destroy our people.

The severity and harshness of their judgments shall make good men turn away from our laws and seek paths of lesser resistance. I am certain that at some point in the future these self-righteous men shall proclaim that only those who follow their decrees are true Jews. All the rest shall be chaff to be blown away by the wind. Woe to our people!

Though they preserve the guise that the Scion of David still rules in Babylon it is a falsehood that prepares our doom. Is it not written in prophecy that our nation shall stand amongst the mighty as long as the staff of Judah stays between his legs and the scepter does not fall from his hand. How long will Judah Zakkai remain as the staff and scepter? How long until the rabbis take upon themselves complete authority and eliminate our family completely.

Mark me well, my son. They are devious men and the generations of our family are at an end. Ever since the day the first Pharisee challenged a Sadducee they have prepared for our demise. Now that they possess this untold power, shall not the corruption in their souls rot the essence of our people. Jew shall be pitted against Jew. What true wisdom it was when Anan ben David proclaimed, "Whatever readest thou in the holy book, if it is perceived as good to you then it is correct." For this heresy of truth, the rabbis have placed him in jail.

And how terrible for me for that first I chose to believe their case against him for I feared that they would do likewise to all of Anan's kin. If only I had stood steadfast with my cousin; alas, all is but hindsight. The rabbis choose to place shackles upon our minds and like sheep we have allowed them to make our day to day decisions. They have raised themselves upon pillars of marble and bedecked themselves in dazzling lights which have blinded us.

When my ancestors established the Gaonate, it was for the sole purpose of providing judges and educators but these rabbis have chosen instead to reign as omnipotent kings. If theirs was truly the insight of the Almighty they would have learned that no man shall set himself before the people as king. He who the Lord anoints as king is merely subject to the people's will and that is why the history of our kings has always been different from the other nations. Where kings of other lands reign supreme, the King of the Jews has always been nothing more than a servant to his people.

Now, none may challenge the rabbis lest they be excommunicated or exiled. I have sat under house arrest for so long that I now welcome my exile. Woe to those that wish to think as free men! God condemns those that covet another man's property but did not these learned men covet my birthright. God shall condemn these sages for their perfidy.

I pray that Anan someday shall reset this wrong. His followers are many that come to the prison to hear him speak and day by day they grow weary and disillusioned with the rabbinate. All men shall come to know God without the need of these middlemen. Alas, I put my faith in Anan my cousin for I am too feeble of heart to face this challenge directly. I shall accept my exile without resistance, even though it means I relinquish my greatest treasure; you, my son. Such evil should not have befallen any man. I pray for God's mercy.

Who will stand with me to prevent my downfall? Not those that professed a love for me. Surely not them for they were the first to turn from me and cast me to the baying wolves. Those that should have been steadfast have been like the fleeting flakes of snow that fall once every seven years in our city; so beautiful to look at but such emptiness when you try to hold them in your hand. I bear no contempt for your mother but it was her that has seen to it that my exile is complete.

Please, my son, read the memoirs of your ancestor Bustenai before you wed. What wisdom he came to possess regarding the women of our race. His thoughts are like a beacon for all to find safe haven. If only I had understood his teachings in my youth, I would have saved myself from so much grief.

It is written that he came to love Izdurdad far more than Adai his first wife. One night when he came home from the council of the Sanhedrin, he found Izdurdad upon her knees, scrubbing the tiles by hand.

"Why do you do this my wife? Do not we have enough servants in this household to do all your chores?"

"The servants do not make the effort as if this was their own house. My husband is too important to have someone judge him by the cleanliness of his home. As woman of the house it is my duty to make certain that none of my husband's possessions cast an ill reflection upon him."

Bustenai was greatly pleased with Izdurdad's reply, especially the way in which she took such pride in doing things for him. But in order to be fair to both women that he had wed, he went to Adai's quarters so that she too could have an opportunity to display affection for her husband. When he arrived at her chambers he found her lounging upon her chaise.

"My wife, did you notice that the floors in this house do not shine with the same brilliance that they once did? What if someone should see them and make comment against us?

Adai turned to face him and smiled pleasantly. "If they make comment it will be against you only, my husband. They will say that Bustenai is slack in the disciplining of his servants. Or they might say that he is tight with his money and does not provide his wives with enough servants to manage all the chores that need doing. I would suggest that you remedy this situation quickly. Perhaps if you were to clean the tiles yourself, you would be able to show the servants exactly what you wanted."

"An excellent idea, Adai. I will tend to it at once."

Bustenai left her chambers but he was not upset by his first wife. Instead he was enamored by the thought of having a second wife that was so special. In another of Bustenai's memoirs he writes of a situation involving his two wives. One night, when he had not mentioned to either of his wives that he would be home late from his audience with the Caliph, he entered his house long past midnight only to find Izdurdad waiting for him in the kitchen. She was tending the low flame that she kept burning with constant blowing upon the embers, so that it would maintain a warm but steady heat.

"What are you doing up so late, wife of mine?"

"I was worried that you may not have eaten so I had the cook prepare this pot of stew that I have kept warm for your arrival."

"And how long have you been doing that."

"You made no comment that you would be late this evening, so I thought that you would be home for your meal at sunset, as usual."

"And you have tended the fire all that time. Your kindness is truly amazing."

Izdurdad blushed in his praise but sought to correct him. "It was not kindness my husband but my love for you that made me happy to do so."

Once more, Bustenai felt compelled to give his wife, Adai, the opportunity to demonstrate that she too would have done the same for her husband. When he confronted her in the morning he told her that once again he would be at the Caliph's palace until late in the evening. "I do not know exactly when I will be returning but it has been the habit of the Caliph to become so involved in matters of business that he forgets to have his servants prepare a meal for both of us. Could you be so kind to keep a bowl of food warm for when I return?"

"Ha!" Adai squealed a haughty laugh. "Will you have me chained to the bake oven too? Do not I do enough around here? We have a cook but even she cannot be expected to stand idly by the oven waiting for you to return. If you had any concerns for anyone but yourself you would make a point of being home when you are supposed to be. I will let the servants know that you will be late but if your meal is burnt then you can hold no one responsible except yourself. Is that understood?"

Bustenai shook his head in agreement. "It is understood far better than you think. I have my answer." The prince of the exile continued to shake his head as he walked from her presence.

In the last of his memoirs which I wish to comment to you about, our revered ancestor, Bustenai, is faced with a dilemma of grave import. A new Caliph had come to power upon the assassination of Othmar. Though everyone knew that Othmar had been killed by Ali, none would dare make that accusation. For twelve years, Othmar had been a kind and benevolent ruler but now all that was to change with the rise to power of Ali.

In order to curry favor with their new lord, all the nobles of Baghdad sought to ingratiate their way into the Caliph's favor. Fierce and irrational, even the slightest comment could offend Ali and cause one to forfeit their life. Not even Bustenai could deal with the unpredictability of this new overlord but as Vizier he had no alternative but to extend every courtesy and to continue to manage the reigns of the fledgling empire.

For his own protection, he arranged for Scheherazade's daughter, his niece, to marry Ali's son, Hussein. Since Othmar was no longer alive, Bustenai had become head of Izdurdad's family and therefore the marriage of his niece would be considered no different than marriage for his own daughter. Using Othmar's strategy that had been once utilized on him, he would bind Ali's life to his own, through the code of honor that pervaded the Eastern mentality. Bustenai would be forced to trust the Caliph and in turn Ali would be forbidden to take Bustenai's life. They would become family.

Now you may be thinking that Bustenai had just resolved his dilemma but this was not the problem at all. The true problem was which of Bustenai's wives would wear the spectacular gown of lights at the reception for Hussein's engagement. As adoptive father to the bride it was up to Bustenai to decide which of his wives would serve as adoptive mother. Now reason dictated that it should be Izdurdad since she was directly related to the niece but Adai was the senior wife and therefore by right, due the most honor. What was poor Bustenai to do? He hoped that each day some event of great insight would occur that would help him make his decision but neither vision nor revelation took place and the great day was growing nearer.

It was the morning of the affair and still Bustenai had not come to a decision. Already the guests had started to arrive at the city. Kings, princes, ambassadors and debutantes from all over the world had come upon the Vizier's bequest to attend the royal betrothal. Seeing to it that all was in order, Bustenai went from room to room in his palatial estate to check on the final arrangements. Wherever he went, there he would find Izdurdad, frantically racing about, ordering the servants in every direction to the point of exhaustion. "My wife, why do you take so much upon your shoulders? Surely, all will be in readiness by evening."

Izdurdad brushed her frazzled black tresses from her brilliant green eyes and wiped the sweat from her chin. "My husband, this is probably one of the most important events in our lives. Only if all goes as we hope can we rest easy and be assured that the reign of Ali shall be favorable to us. One mishap and we may not have an opportunity to make amends. You would not be the first Vizier to lose his head over some paltry issue. Until I am certain that all needs are catered to, I cannot rest easy. This is not just the betrothal of our niece but is in truth the marriage of our two families. My husband must be understanding of this one's concerns. Anything less than perfection is not worthy of Lord Bustenai. As wife, I must insure my husband's honor."

"But what of yourself? When shall you have your hair styled and your mascara applied? You must leave time for your own needs."

"When has this one's needs ever been more important than my husband's? There will be time for me but first I must tend to you. Now, get to our room and get attired properly. I shall be there as soon as possible. Go on!"

Like a child being scolded by his mother, Bustenai raced down the hallway to his bed chambers. He was bemused at the thought of Izdurdad treating him like a little boy that had to be checked on to see if he has washed behind his ears. He could not explain the sensation or why he liked it so much. Somehow, in a world where it mattered little whether a man cared for the woman chosen for him to marry, it made a world of difference knowing that Izdurdad cared for him. There was a magic: a kismet. The feelings he felt for her were so different from those he harbored for Adai. Adai! Yes, what about Adai? Where was she? Bustenai went in search of his missing first wife. She was nowhere in the house to be found. Only when he inquired of the gardeners who were busily sculpturing the hedges for the evening affair did he find out that his first wife was down by the brook with her attendants. Like an ill wind, Bustenai stormed across the grounds towards Adai. The servants scattered from his path, the scowl upon his brow warning them all to keep their distance. "Wife, there is need of you in our house." Bustenai's voice harbored a long standing resentment.

Adai did not even look up at him, preferring to concentrate on holding her hand perfectly still as her maidservant laminated her nails in gold leaf. Another carefully coiled her hair through the rings of the gold tiara that adorned her head. "Really, Bustenai. Can you not see that I am busy? Whatever it is can wait until I am finished."

"Adai! Are you not aware that there is still much to be arranged for tonight's betrothal? How can you lie here with your servants attending to your whims while my house is still not in order?"

"My husband," she sighed, immediately attaining control of the conversation. "Why do you worry so much? Everything will be taken care of but you must realize the importance of having your wife look absolutely ravishing. What would the new Caliph think if the Vizier's wife appeared no different from a street urchin?"

Bustenai tried to respond but Adai would not afford him the opportunity. "It would be an embarrassment," she continued," that could spell your dismissal. What kind of wife would I be if I failed to uphold my husband's honor by not maintaining a proper image? Now be a good husband and have your servants bring the gown of lights to my dressing salon." She dismissed him with a wave of her hand and then clapped a summons for the return of her maidservants.

Bustenai writes that he ran from her presence like a whipped puppy but he swore that this would be the last time would cower before Adai. He ordered his servants to take the gown of lights to his wife, but it was to Izdurdad that he had them bring it. And it was his Persian wife that he presented to the Caliph as his principle spouse, shocking the community which naturally sympathized with Adai.

To further promulgate the scandal that he had set in motion, Bustenai concluded the successful engagement with a toast to Hussein and his new bride. "It is with the wisdom of life's experiences that I can praise you on your fortunate choice of a bride, Hussein. I have two wives that share my bed chamber. One was born a princess but she has strived to be above all, a woman. She desires to be my wife and lover more than being a precious jewel of royalty. In my heart of hearts, I love her! The second was born no more than a woman but she has dreamt of being nothing else but a princess. Love and matrimony are low on her list of priorities. It is no wonder that in my heart I can say no more than I tolerate her.

You are a fortunate man to marry your princess. She too has come to know, like my Izdurdad, that a woman's greatest asset is being a woman. To a long and blissful life!"

With that toast the chapters of Bustenai's memoirs concerning his wives was concluded. They have tremendous value, Ahunai, as they will teach you much about the women of our society. I too have learned much but not until I succumbed to the same weaknesses that plagued Bustenai.

Since you will not receive this letter until you are much older, I feel that I can be honest with you. Your mother, my wife Rachael, was a woman much like Adai.

It grieves me to write these things about your mother, Ahunai, but it is best that someday you find out the truth about our marriage. I still remember the moment when I received the edict from the Caliph, ordering my exile. I turned to your mother and said, "It has finally come. Rachael, he has sent us into exile!" I was equally stunned by her reply.

"Why do you infer that he has sent us into exile, Natronai? Just because you are a failure and you have been banished, does that mean that I have to suffer along with you? I have my family here, my friends. I am not going with you. And I will not have our son living in the shadow of your shame as well."

She said it with such coldness in her heart, as if we were strangers or mere acquaintances. I knew that there would be no change of mind on her part. She had written me off as if I were dead. Now you know the truth of why you were left behind. My own wife had betrayed me! I should have known it would happen. My relationship with Rachael was no different than that of Bustenai's and Adai's. After all, is not your mother the daughter of the Gaon, the same man who stripped me of my throne and presented it to my cousin Judah Zakkai?

Even when our marriage was first proposed, it was her father who proclaimed that a star had finally come to shine in the house of David. Who was this man to even dare to think that the family of the Exilarch needed enlightenment? As long as I cooperated with your grandfather everything was fine but as soon as I tried to exert my own free will that was when he threatened to cause my downfall.

And throughout those terrible years of living under the Gaon's threat it was not I that Rachael supported but her father. She condemned me for raising my voice against her family. Who was I to defy the righteousness and virtue of her esteemed sire? She considered me an embarrassment and the more her father diminished my authority, the greater the distance became between me and your mother.

Sometimes I am astonished that you were ever conceived, Ahunai. In the last three years I have known your mother only scarcely and in fact I have not slept with her once in the preceding year. Like Adai, she has moved herself into separate quarters of our estate and we only see each other in passing. Truly, I exceeded even the humiliation that Bustenai endured from Adai.

Why did I permit it to happen? I cannot give you a reasonable answer, my son. Perhaps I feared the repercussions if I did not. The constant berating I would receive from Rachael or the further demise of my stature amongst the community at the hands of her father. A man can lower himself only so far until he begins to hate himself.

I'm not certain if you remember the time I had to stay several days in the care of the physician, Aisak of Constantinople. I remember it clearly as if it was only yesterday. My life had become an endless torment and the more I dwelt in the abyss, the further my body succumbed to my mind's ill humor. I returned from the Sabbath council with pains in my chest and my heart on fire. Upon entering our home, I called out for your mother but she did not heed my distress. Instead, she replied that if I was that concerned I should take myself over to the home of the physician, Aisak. Her mother and father had come to visit and it would have been rude of her to leave them, she explained.

Though I feared that I would not make it, I managed to reach the physician's home. Aisak grew gravely concerned and made me lie down in his abode for three days while he treated me with the essence of the poppy and foxglove plant. God was merciful and allowed me to recover not only in body but in mind as well. Your mother kept my whereabouts a secret so that none in the community would condemn her for her unsympathetic nature but it was not enough to stop me from condemning her. Surely, a woman does not love a man when she makes him face the specter of death all by himself.

I knew then that there was nothing that could be salvaged between us for we had grown too far apart. I needed only to await the final assault of her father, stripping me of the last remnant of my dignity to ensure that my wife would have no part of me. If I was to no longer be a prince of the people, then it was impossible for her to ever be a princess.

She was neither wife, nor woman, nor lover to me but at least I do not have to endure that torment any longer.

I do not know what the land of the Franks holds in store for me. I know little of its people or customs. I only know that it is far off, in a place beyond the Roman Empire and I pray that I stay alive long enough amongst the barbarians to find some enjoyment in this life of mine. Pray for me Ahunai, as I will pray for you. God permitting, we shall meet again.

> *I love you, my son. I always will.*
> *Please remember me.*
> *Your Abbah*

Chapter Nine

Toronto: Present

"And that's your introduction to Natronai. He is the integral cog to the entire story! The lynch pin which holds all of it together! Having made his monumental decision to sail to the West, he set the next two centuries in motion."

"Let's see. If I've got this right, he chose to abandon his own world and travel to a completely unknown destination because of his wife? Now, me and the missus, we have our arguments now and then, but this is a pretty extreme reaction."

"You will see, if you have the patience, that there was a lot more to it," I reassure him. "The biggest problem was that there were too many kings in the world; a plethora of kings, but only a handful of kingdoms. That's a pretty serious problem of the medieval times. It resulted in a tremendous number of squabbles, wars and assassinations. It wasn't too difficult to find a wanna-be king to rule over a newly made city-state, even if it was at the edge of the earth.

Natronai was no exception. Those who are meant to rule will sacrifice anything and everything in order to rule. I'll explain shortly, he didn't have much of a choice in the matter, either."

"It's hard to believe that this guy you're describing, writing this dear John letter to his son, would be capable of becoming a dominating figure of any time. Guy sounds like a wuss!"

"I'd like to believe that in the right environment, any one of us is capable of attaining greatness. and some of us, more so than others!"

"Doc, this Natronai is a long way from greatness!"

"Yes," I agree with him, which brings a smile to Pearce's face. "In his own environment, he was probably even worse than a wimp! He was doomed to failure. He knew it, his wife knew it, and the entire community knew it. Even his son knew it! That's pretty bad."

Pearce tries to rationalize the entire episode with twentieth century hindsight. "So, why does the son of the king of the Franks go all the way to Arabia, to bring back a loser?"

"For you to comprehend, it's necessary that I explain to you what the alternative was."

"Which was?" Pearce tries to prod me along.

"Nothing! It was either Natronai or a coffin holding the bones of some long dead Exilarch. All Pepin promised to bring the townspeople was a Jewish king. He didn't stipulate that he would be alive. They would have buried the coffin with a big fanfare and the people of Narbonne would have their symbolic leader. Dead, so much the better! He would have kept his promise."

"So why not just bring back a coffin?"

"He didn't have to! He was given a king to take back. Signed, sealed, and gift wrapped. Let me wind the clock back a couple of years, so you can witness a monumental meeting. East meets west! Watch how these events, occurring thousands of miles away, will eventually influence the Frankish kingdom."

Pearce flips to a new, clean page in his book and settles back into the sofa. "Okay, shoot!"

Baghdad: 766 A.D.

News of the five single-massed uniremes sailing up the Tigris River buzzed through the towns and villages along the shore. Two days prior they had been sighted, sailing out of a sunrise over the Persian Gulf. Their large rectangular white sails emblazoned with the rose croix bordered by three petalled lilies created a stir amongst a people who were witnessing the arrival of the western world for the very first time.

As the river narrowed, the order was given to furl the sails and take the crafts up river by means of long oars which churned the water furiously as they fought the current. Frankish ships sailing under a flag of truce in Arab waters. No one could have ever foreseen the day such an event would take place but these were strange days at best.

A new dynasty had seized the Caliphate of Baghdad, proclaiming an end to the Omayyads. All of Arabia was declared part of the Abbasid Empire which only served to anger those Omayyads that still held regional powers. Arab declared war on Arab and a never ending chain of events was established. In this time of turmoil, the Franks were seen as welcome allies by the Abbasids, even if they were infidels.

Coincidentally, on the day that Baghdad received Pepin's overtures, now some six months earlier, Damascus had just revolted and sent the governor's head in a basket back to the Caliph. Al Mansur considered the Frankish king's letter a divine inspiration from Allah. With the Moorish empire having grown so large, he required staunch allies in the west to safeguard his European holdings. What more could anyone ask for than to have barbarians actually serve this purpose?

Al Mansur quickly responded to Pepin's declaration of friendship and extended an invitation to the Franks to send a diplomatic mission to Baghdad to establish formal ties. For half a year the Abbasids had eagerly awaited this prearranged coming of the Europeans.

The Caliph's men carefully concealed themselves in the hills, spying on the Franks for days and reporting back to Al Mansur of their progress. The gossip circulating in Baghdad ridiculed the Franks for their stubbornness to not surrender to the impossible. When they had reached Al Kut, the point at which the river narrowed severely and began meandering haphazardly, the Franks would still not abandon their ships. Instead, the commander ordered his men to attach tow lines to the bows and masts and then having his men disembark on either riverbank, they literally pulled the ships up river. Scoffed at by the Abbasid admiralty, their Caliph did not share the same scorn and derision. Instead, Al Mansur was extremely impressed by the report of this commander's determination.

The Caliph sneered at his officers as they stood before him giggling like school girls. Grabbing the brass water pipe that stood beside his throne, he hurled it angrily in their direction. "You fools! What have you to laugh about? Are you all so blind that you cannot see what is plain before your face?"

The officers stood opened mouthed in abeyance. "Still, not even a single one of you can understand. How could I have been so blind. Nothing but incompetence! I am surrounded by idiots!"

One of the admirals cleared his throat sheepishly. "Oh, mighty one, sword of Allah, how is it that we have offended you? We are your willing servants. Let us understand our sins so that we may beg your forgiveness."

"Stop groveling. I hate it when you snivel like stricken dogs! Where is your foresight, ibn Shardiz? You all laugh at the writing upon the wall. How many of your men would tow a ship upon their backs at your command? These barbarians are putting on a display for your benefit and you don't even know when to applaud. Now they come in friendship but someday, who knows, they may come in war. And who will laugh then?

No army has ever made it to Baghdad by way of the river until now. How would we ever stop an attack by both land and sea? Such might of will and determination is sorely missed amongst our own men. This leader of theirs is truly an amazing man, able to summon such loyalty among his troops. When you can do likewise, then I will permit you to laugh. Until then, get out of my sight! I have had my fill of you today."

The officers quickly scrambled to the exits. Al Mansur was not a man to be argued with. His sullen moods were common and not even his best friends were safe to be near him during those times. The Caliph pulled upon his black braided beard in disgust as he watched them leave. When the last of them could no longer be heard clamoring down the marbled hallways, he lifted his eyes from the floor and turned to his vizier.

"You are not pleased, Rosbihan? You think I was too harsh with them?"

"I think you have been too hard on many, lately, Excellency."

"Why is it that you always find fault with what I do. I could have you scourged and still you do not fear me."

"I do what you expect me to do, Excellency. If your vizier will not be your conscience then who will be? Is that not so?"

Al Mansur looked squarely into the vizier's expressionless brown eyes. Rosbihan was a man approaching fifty years, of lean and slender build, who had served Caliph after Caliph loyally. But now, he appeared to be a man with little left to cherish; drained physically and mentally.

"Why is it that you Jews always make me feel guilty, even when I haven't done anything wrong? When I conquered this land I showed you mercy and granted you clemency. Being vizier to the last caliph would have been sufficient for me to demand your death. But instead I reinstated you to your old position and this is the gratitude I receive?"

"I serve all that have been my master to the utmost of my abilities. If you had found me wanting then you should have sought a vizier from elsewhere."

"You have become very trying, Rosbihan. I shall ignore your impertinence this time but do not persist in challenging me?

"If I do not tell you when you have wronged your advisors, then who will you rule if all flee from your presence. The mark of a good ruler is to appreciate those that serve him. Give them praise and in return they give you fidelity. Give them the back of your hand and they will plot against you!"

"Is this a warning of things to come or things as they are?" The Caliph squared his jaw in anticipation of the answer. His coal black eyes keenly scrutinized his vizier looking for any signs of trepidation, but Rosbihan refused to squirm. In fact he stood even more stolid before Al Mansur than he had been before.

"This is a warning of things that might be." Rosbihan flourished an angry finger in the caliph's direction. "Do with me as you see fit but heed my advice none the same. I serve you loyally and my words are for you alone. I have come to think of you as a friend, and as a friend your welfare is of concern to me."

"Friend? It is a strange word to me." Al Mansur's grim visage fractured into a warm smile. "I don't think I have ever had a friend. I have always ruled through fear and intimidation. That is how my father ruled and his father before him. He warned me that a caliph can have no friends. Perhaps he was wrong! You do not fear me and strangely enough I do not intimidate you. If this be friendship then it is good to have a friend. How is it that I have offended my friend?"

"You have not offended me but my people. In the same manner that you have not offended all your officers but enough of them to set them scheming. A wise old Greek philosopher once told me that for every action we take we can expect to receive a definite reaction. If we wish for these reactions to be pleasant then we must first weigh out the true value of our actions. Your actions to date have been impulsive and the reactions have not been very pleasant."

"You have humbled the ear of the Caliph. Tell me of my failings so that I may learn from them."

Rosbihan's grave expression lightened markedly. "You have already learned my liege. When one who claims to be omniscient can turn to a friend for advice then at last you have shown great wisdom. Humility is a virtue sorely lacking from most rulers."

"And who is it that you turn to for advice, my friend."

"To the one whom we must all turn to, Excellency; to Allah, to God."

"Allah is wise and Rosbihan has been enlightened by His wisdom. My eyes clearly see this. And though I know not what I have done to have offended thee, I wish that you will tell me so that I can make amends."

"You have done that which none but Allah should have done. You have anointed a king from among my people that may have not been worthy to bear the crown of David."

"But I did that which your learned Rabbis begged me to do. How could that be wrong which your own leaders have requested?"

"Perhaps like the rulers who know not humility, the Rabbis are not wise."

"I did not know this." The Caliph shook his head in apology.

"If you had consulted me first then you would have been made aware of this. The most I can do now is tell you as an afterthought what has come to pass." Rosbihan shook his splayed hands heavenward. "Oh, if only God would save us from those who claim to speak for him. This has ever been our doom. From time immemorial someone has always claimed to speak for God. Prophets, false prophets, seers, kings, queens, priests, sages, judges, messiahs, maniacs, fishwives, whores, devils, and now rabbis. When will we ever let God speak for himself?"

"And what would God have said, my friend, if we had listened?"

"He would say to leave things be as he had intended."

"Are you saying that I have interfered with Allah's ways?"

"You knew not what you had done. But the rabbis, they knew! In order to control our people they had to control the office of the exilarch. I fear to say it my lord, but they deceived you!"

"Then I shall surely make them pay!"

"No, that is the worst thing that you could do. You must turn their iniquity to your advantage. The situation can be extricated with but a little show of force. It will set the rabbi's back for a long time to come."

"What is it that I must do?"

"As the situation now stands, we Jews have three kings to contend with due to the rabbis trifling with the monarchy. Although Judah Zakkai is an intelligent man, and I say this without bias because he is my nephew, he is also a spineless jellyfish, incapable of making a single decision on his own.

Since the Caliph must appear infallible you cannot simply remove him from office after just recently appointing him. Makhir Natronai was by far the better candidate for the position but his strength of will could not be condoned by the rabbis. That is why they had you remove him. His own father-in-law was behind the cabal that opposed him. So as a result we must find a way of removing Makhir Natronai from your empire."

Al Mansur's eyebrows shot upwards in disbelief. "Surely you cannot be suggesting..."

"Of course not, Excellency! We need Makhir Natronai to be indebted to you. And we need him where he can do the most good for you. We need him in a place far, far away."

"You're not suggesting....ah, yes you are!" Al Mansur slapped his knees in amazement. "How utterly brilliant. You astonish me, Rosbihan. But wait. How do we keep Judah Zakkai under my control?"

"Very simple, we let the third king out of prison."

"Wouldn't that breed chaos?"

"Only if we were to have a situation where two kings were actually vying for the same throne. We won't have that because when you let Anan ibn David out of jail, he will be established as ruling monarch of his own following."

"What is to keep these two kings from fighting amongst themselves?"

"I ask your majesty's forgiveness but I have taken liberty to talk to Anan on several occasions. He is a rational person but who has a craving for power. After all, it was his refusal to accept his brother Hananiah as exilarch that landed him in chains originally. He assured me that he has had sufficient time to contemplate his iniquities. And true to form he had conceived a plan by which not only will you have to release him but by which he can establish himself as a king without necessitating the removal of Judah ben Zakkai."

"This is very intriguing, but why won't they fight?"

"Because Anan will be the leader of his own religion. Wait...don't say anything yet. Anan has confided it all to me and it is a good plan. We, in the Jewish community are well aware of the surge in the power of the rabbinate. This pleases some and angers even more. Anan will establish a parallel religion but without any so-called rabbis. Based entirely on the Torah there will be no Talmud by which the rabbis claim their authority. Religious duty and service would be placed back in the hands of the priests of the family of Aaron. In effect, he would re-establish the Judaism of the pre-exile age; a revival of the Sadducee teachings.

Such a sect may be condemned by the rabbis but they cannot abolish it simply because it is the root of the tree from which they evolved. If they cut the trunk, all the branches will come down too. All that is required is for you to give Anan and his followers your official recognition as a separate and distinct religious minority and the rabbinate cannot do a thing against it. Most certainly they will bicker and they will squabble but as a result of their distinct ideological recognition, they cannot lay a hand on each other without endangering their own standing as a state religion."

"And when do you envision my releasing of Anan from prison?"

"You can only do it once the third of the kings has been sent far away. He would be too much of a complication if he was still here at the time. He would side with one of the other two and that would shift the balance of power. We want neither side strong enough to subjugate the other."

"They will still try to subjugate the other," Al Mansur warned, "Even if there is only the two of them."

"Perhaps but the rabbis will never jeopardize their status. Instead they will all come to you when they have complaints about the other and as a result you become the power that pulls the strings. Not Anan and not the rabbis. By dividing you will have conquered. Three kings to kneel at your every whim."

"Won't it bother you Rosbihan that your own monarchs will be nothing but puppets dangling from the strings on my fingers?"

"I will tell you a little detail about my people, Excellency. What bothers me most of all. Whenever we get freedom we squander it. Whenever we get power we abuse it. The only time we have ever known peace is when some outsider has lorded over us. My world is a lot safer and a lot more secure when I know that there is a Jew behind the throne but not on the throne."

Al Mansur laughed heartily. "And that is exactly how I prefer it too! Let's go see this devil we are to strike a deal with!"

From their perch high in the hills, Al Mansur and his vizier watched attentively as the Franks strained their backs against the current that fought them for every inch that they advanced their ships. It was an event which had all of Baghdad agog. As entertainment, it was touted as the eighth wonder of the world. In the markets the wagering was fierce as to whether the foreigners would or could not defeat the river.

Some came to cheer, others to curse but whichever their leanings, the Franks under the stern command of their prince paid them no heed. The only statement they would make would be through their actions. Their straining muscles would speak of their indomitable strength, their precision and coordination would speak volumes about their discipline.

No one who came to the river banks could leave without sharing the overwhelming sensation of awe. These barbarians from a land that most could not even find on a map were putting on a display that would leave them with tales to tell to future generations. The Franks had come and they had made certain that everyone was aware of their arrival.

"Incredible! A truly amazing feat, is it not, Rosbihan? They have done the impossible. Only a few hundred feet more and they have crossed the narrows. From there on it is clear sailing to Ctesiphon and then on to Baghdad. Imagine, ships sailing right into the heart of our empire."

"Yes, your Excellency. They have provided a most entertaining feat. I think we should return now to the palace so that we can welcome your guests appropriately for the morrow. It would not be fitting if the Frankish prince should spy the emperor of this land concealed behind these hills like some common thief, stealing a glimpse."

"In due time, Rosbihan. I love watching that tall one as he takes command. That Charlemagne! If only all of us kings could look like him. He has an air about him that radiates royalty. His men would do anything for him. That is the true sign of kingship. He is the reason my people are so thunderstruck. He incites feelings of magnificence in all that behold him."

"That is also the true sign of an enemy to be weary of. Never underestimate your allies, my Lord. To snare a prince one must use special bait in order to entice him into the treaty." Rosbihan folded his arms across his chest in preparation for his preaching of another lesson. "So how does one ensure that his ally stays so?"

"You worry too much Vizier."

"And you worry not enough, my Liege. It was not a rhetorical question that I asked but a fact learned by my family several generations before."

"Your family has had so many lessons that I am surprised there are still things to be learned. So what is the answer?"

"He can be trusted only if he is family. Marry him to the most beautiful of your daughters and he will be your loyal servant forever."

"And what if he is already married and refuses to take another wife?"

"Oh, he most definitely is married, but it matters not. I have been informed that Charlemagne has been in conflict with his Church many times before but each time they have backed down against him. Even now they have condemned him, because of an incident of which I have recently been made aware of. He provides them with a country in which to preach their bible and in turn they leave his matrimonial bed in privacy. He already has a wife and three concubines. But I'm certain he cannot resist another wife especially since the marriage to your daughter is the condition of sealing the treaty."

"You are a devious man, Rosbihan," Al-Mansur commented.

"Why, thank you, your Majesty. It is always rewarding to know that you appreciate my talents. But it is imperative that we return to your palace immediately if we are to have sufficient time to undertake all the arrangements of both treaty and matrimony. And let us not forget the extra baggage that we wish the Franks to take back home with them.

I will require some time to carefully manipulate the rabbinate to agree to it. There will be those who will fear the thought of an unrestrained exilarch ruling somewhere in the Western world. Not to mention that Makhir Natronai may not be the most cooperative person when informed of his relocation. I do hope that our ally, Charlemagne will be pleased with our gifts."

They smiled conspiratorially. Climbing into the covered sedan chairs, twelve burly Africans hoisted the poles upon their shoulders and trotted towards the palace surrounded by the Caliph's armed escort.

Chapter Ten

Toronto: Present

Pearce wore a Cheshire smile spread broadly across his face, as I look up.

"So, what is so funny, Mr. Pearce?"

"Please Doc, John!   Don't you think by now you could call me John?"

"And as to what's so funny, John."   I draw out the pronunciation of his name to emphasize that I am finally willing to honor his request.

"Nothing.   Except for the fact that I now understand how this all came about.   I have to confess, I was worried there for a while."

"To tell you the truth, I was worried too.   I kept thinking, what if he doesn't click with how the puzzle pieces come together?   What was I to do then?"

"Fortunately for you, I'm a quick study," Pearce snaps back his response.   "And now I'll be able to explain to the readership how all the characters interplay."

I held up my hand to caution him. "Not exactly all!"

"How many more?"

"Just bringing one Jewish monarch to Frankia would hardly be enough to drive the Church into a frenzy.   You have to raise the stakes further to achieve that."

"I knew there had to be more of a threat than just one eastern king!"

"Sure, you did, John." Pearce laughs at my little jab.   "The threat was not the flower but the seeds."

"Ah...you've lost me again, Doc.   What seeds?   He was thousands of kilometers away and he was isolated from his family.   Wasn't he?"

"In order to achieve what they desired, the Carolingians required holy blood.   The flower was therefore required to cross-pollinate.   That's where the threat lay.   At first, it started simply with a symbolic marriage, but as you will see over the successive generations, it began to run far deeper.   So deep that no one could climb out from the pit that was dug!"

Aquitaine: 769 A.D.

"To think that I, Makhir Natronai, have come all this way only to find that you are repulsed by the sight of me.   Oh, cursed fates of my ancestors that leave me stranded on this foreign and backward coast.   If I had any tears left to weep surely I would flood a sea to wash me back to the shores of my homeland.   I who have given up the right to see my only son ever again for what?   For this!   God have mercy upon my wretched soul to think that I have come to such an ignoble end."

I snatched a quick glance in her direction to see if she was even paying any attention to what I was saying. In all my years I have never seen any creature in all of God's great creation that could stir my heart as she does. Her eyes are like two pale blue mirrors that capture my reflection and hold it captive. I think I must have spent half of each day as I sailed to this distant land worried that my bride to be would be a slightly feminine version of her hirsute brother.

"How was I to know that you wouldn't have a similar mustache to Charlemagne's or that you would stand well over six feet? It had been only the briefest of meetings when the Caliph's guards escorted the King of the Franks and his servant Isaac to my estate. Already I had been informed that the Caliph Al Mansur had intentions to send me into exile. There were just too many kings in Baghdad; especially when you consider that three of them were Jewish.

I can only think that Charlemagne wanted to see this King in exile, this Exilarch in order to test me for his own purpose. He did not find my abilities wanting in any manner. His proposal of my very own kingdom proved too enticing for me to refuse, especially when it appeared that my fate in Baghdad would be an adjacent cell to my cousin, Anan ben David.

The irony was that both mine and Anan's credentials to rule far surpassed my cousin Judah's but that mattered not for my very own father-in-law was later to brand me a threat to the community. Even my wife of twelve years petitioned me for a divorce on her father's advice for I had outlived my usefulness to him. If I would no longer allow him to speak for me then he had made sure that I would no longer speak at all in Baghdad. For over two years I endured this limbo until the arrangements were made for me to set sail.

Although Charlemagne was about to receive the most pure bloodlines available in response to his quest, he and his servant had no knowledge that my answer could have been anything but yes. He willingly made concession after concession in an effort to sway me but above all else it was his offer to give me his sister's hand in marriage that sealed the arrangement. Yes, you Alda. He offered me you! I would have come no matter what had been the bait but it was this arranged marriage that removed any fear and distrust that may have resided in my mind.

It was not unlike the stories of my ancestor, Bustenai, which I often told my son about as simple bedtime tales. I remember how the Caliph had told Bustenai that if you wish to remove the threat of a revolt against your rule then you simply marry your adversary into your family. Either Charlemagne feared me or perhaps your father, Pepin did, but nevertheless in order to ensure my fidelity to them they offered the flesh of their flesh and the blood of their blood as a seal to our pact. If they feared me that much then I knew that I had nothing to fear from them. It made my decision that much easier and now I am faced with my ultimate challenge. If only they had bothered to inform you of their arrangement instead of waiting until my boat had docked and then thrusting you towards me like a cattle beast being sold at the market. These Franks are truly barbarians in the manner that they treat their women. They place absolutely no value on the mother that bears them, considering them as nothing more than chattel upon which to beat their manhood.

How could they not see the beauty that shines from this goddess on earth. No sooner had my eyes settled upon your fair visage that I wanted to languish within your arms. To rest my head upon your ample bosom which clearly marked itself beneath your blue silk gown. Never have I ever seen hair like yours before; as soft as spun gold and the color of liquid sunshine. But alas, all is for naught for we have been in this manor for over an hour and you have not as yet even uttered a single syllable to acknowledge my presence.

There you sit, cowering with your maid-servant as if I am some wild predator on the loose waiting for the moment by which to feast my lusts upon your delicate flesh. Perhaps your servant expects the same treatment at my foreign hands. How little you know of me to think that I am some Vandal or Hun as you have come to know in this primitive land of theirs. How long will it be until you speak or even move? Or do anything to let me know that you will abide by your brother's bargain? Better yet, am I a man who will take advantage of a woman who has been sold to me as bitter goods? Would I be any better than the men of this outer world if I were to lose my sense of dignity?

I confess that I did not properly understand Charlemagne when he informed me that the women of his household could only marry on his say so. I thought only of the biblical context in which Jethro offered his daughters to wed Moses. That Charlemagne was only to give his blessing. But the reality was his ordering you, his sister to bed with me against your will. Perhaps I did not even take the time to realize that any relative of Charlemagne would have that same indomitable will that he constantly exhibits; that same aura of self-determination.

I will not try to tear that independence from you, Alda even if I could. In fact I must admit that I admire it. If you should ever come to me then I know that it will be by your own choosing and may perhaps even be for love. If Charlemagne thought that he could make his sister be a whore, even if it be a royal whore, then he is sadly mistaken. I commend you Alda. You have far more backbone than I ever exhibited back in Baghdad.

Oh, Alda, if only you knew of the pain I feel within. Is it not well known that both the emotions of pain and pleasure, and generally of all sensation, plainly start from the heart, and find in it their ultimate termination."

"You know of Aristotle?" Her expression was one of complete surprise as she stared at me unbelievingly. "Book two, chapter seven on the Parts of Animals."

"Actually it was Book three, chapter four," I corrected her.

"Are you certain?" For the briefest of moments a smile surfaced upon her moistened lips.

"Yes, quite certain. If you would like, I have a copy of Aristotle in my bags. I will get it for you." My heart is racing as I frantically search through my baggage for a book that I never dreamed I would ever be able to discuss with anyone ever again. "Here it is!" My hands are clammy as I hand the book over and for the first time notice how delicate her slender fingers are, their milk white flesh a sharp contrast to my own sun-baked skin.

"Thank you," she smiled. As she did so she looked into my eyes and I can feel a warming between us. "This book is so old!"

"Yes, it is. It is one of the original copies by Andromicus of Rhodes. Almost eight hundred years old to be exact."

"But how can that be? How could it be preserved for that length of time?"

"Actually, it is very easy to do in a desert-like climate. I have some books in my luggage which even predate that."

"More of the great philosophers?"

"Yes, Lucretius, Plutarch, and Marcus Aurelius. I have some of my own family documents which date from the time of the second temple in Jerusalem."

Her eyes suddenly lit like twin beacons. "I can't believe that there is someone else who likes to read the ancient philosophers. You do not know how long I prayed for the opportunity to discuss the Greek masters in their own tongue."

"But I have talked only in Greek from the time I disembarked and you did not say so much as a single word to me. In fact I have been standing here spilling my heart out to you and you never gave any indication that you understood what I was saying. I have embarrassed myself from the things I have said."

"How was I to know that it wasn't some performance you concocted with my brother in order to lure me into your chambers and then rape me?" She brushed her hair coyly to one side as she flashed me a subtle grin.

"How do you know that I will not rape you now?" I do not know why I said that. It was almost as if the words had a life of their own and just sprang from my mouth. I wish I could take them back.

"No one who can quote Aristotle would rape anyone. You are just too civilized to do that. That was the sign to me that you were speaking honestly; truthfully from your heart. And even if you did try to rape me, I would just lie in the bed and ask you a thousand questions about Aristotle's book on Metaphysics until you fell asleep from boredom."

I cannot help but laugh. She has me. It is true. Anyone who has studied Aristotle has in turn become too civilized to behave like a barbarian. Perhaps that is why the barbarians burn the libraries as soon as they ransack a city. If they were to read Aristotle, they could be barbarians no longer. I nod my head and concede her point. "You are right. But tell me. How is it that a woman, even more so a Frankish woman, is able to read Aristotle and not only that, read him in Greek."

"I can also read him in Latin or German but I have found no books to exist in those languages. So I have no choice but to read him in Greek." Again she flashes that teasing smile that entrances me. She has pushed her maidservant away, leaving a space between us that I believe she wants filled.

"You know that is not what I meant." Before I can even think about what I am doing, I find myself seated on the ground beside her chair and I am looking upwards at her bewitching beauty as both our hands meet around the book. "So how is it that you can read in all these tongues." I ask my question in Latin to see if I can catch her off guard.

She knows I was testing her and effortlessly, she too switches to the Latin tongue and replies.

"How wonderful!" She claps her hands in delight. "You speak Latin as well. We will have such wonderful fun together. Never in my deepest hopes would I think that my father and brother would find me a mate of culture and bearing. In case you haven't noticed, most men around this palace are a little uncouth."

"How could I not notice," I jest. "Some of them are still swinging from the trees in which they were whelped."

Her turn to laugh once again at my joke about her people. She winks at me suggestively while her left hand slowly coils the long tresses on the back of my head. My heart feels as if it is soaring through the clouds and all from the merest touch of her fingers.

"It was my father who insisted that I study both Greek and Roman history. Too many people were quick to accuse us Carolingians of being little more than savages or apes in trees as you have so correctly pointed out. Pepin felt that an education would still their tongues. Naturally the best way to learn these subjects was with tutors from those particular lands who were well versed in the classics.

It followed naturally that the ancient books and manuscripts be studied in their original dialect. The languages came so easily to me that it was not long before I was performing much of the translation of the Vatican letters and epistles for my father. I think that Pepin always knew that I was different in that way. My brothers were given the very same education but they did not take to it as well as I did. My father would use words cultured and refined but how could he be defined as an intellectual in a country populated by illiterates.

Any marriage to the local tribal chiefs would have been cruel torture for me as I would have died from within and without. Pepin knew this. He loved me too much to let it happen. Many an important alliance could have been closed with my hand in marriage but my father prized my happiness above all else. You can imagine how much of a shock it was when they revealed to me that they had arranged my marriage to a dethroned king from the East. I knew only of the Saracens from that part of the world and what I have learned of them is frighteningly harsh. In particular they are a slimy breed with coal black eyes and matted dirty hair.

Oh, it was true that Charlemagne upon his return made every effort to describe you to me but I would no longer listen. I had made up my mind. You would be one of these slimy loathsome creatures and it made my skin crawl to imagine you in bed with me, fondling my breasts as you drooled like a rabid dog. I felt betrayed by their underhanded manner in which they selected my future betrothed. Here I am twenty-three years old, literally an old maid by their choosing and condemned as such by the standards of my community with no prospects of marriage in sight.

Then it was also my fear that their selection would be limited to the kind of men that they themselves were and as much as I love the two of them, I could not bear to be wife to a man of their ilk. Have I spoken too openly?" She blushed as she put her hand to her mouth.

I want to reassure her that I am not such a man but I realize that she is not the type of woman that depends on a man's reassurances. She has already assessed me and though I think her opinion of me is favorable, I cannot be too certain by her comments. Do my dark skin and dark eyes make me one of these slimy loathsome creatures that she dreads?

"Am I to understand that you have consented to marry me? That in spite of all your hesitations you feel you must assent to your father' wishes."

"Nay, I have not. I have consented to let you court me and if you should prove to be the scholarly monarch that I have always dreamed of, then I shall consent to your proposal. This is the way that civilized men and women behave."

"Shall I presume that this would mean that there is a possible chance for me, though I may be one of those dark creatures for the East." I know that I am being pithy but I cannot recall the last time I have had a witty conversation with a woman. Especially one that would openly speak of a man fondling her breasts Back in my homeland, one grows accustomed to two types of women. There are those that are no better than maidservants and then on the other hand there are those that will abide with no less than complete domination. Alda presented a third option that I had not considered in the past. She was my equal in every way; intelligent, open, humorous and outspoken. It was absolutely refreshing and any relationship that might arise I would preserve and emphasize that equality.

"Silly boy. You are the only suitor that even stands a chance." Giggling, she lays my head in her lap and with a circular motion begins to stroke and caress my temples.

She is like a child in her responsiveness. So openly physical, unafraid to let our bodies touch. I feel like I am a doll in the hands of a young girl. Her outward display is genuine but childish. It is almost as if she has come alive for the very first time and is now exploring the wonderful world she suddenly finds herself in. But far more amazing is that her zealous inquisitiveness is contagious and I find myself caught up in the exuberance. I am both inspired and in awe of her rapturous beauty and capricious mind.

Now more than ever I am convinced God's hand has set me upon this path to this new land. There will always be those to claim it is nothing more than coincidence but I cannot believe that in even the slightest fashion. To find a woman that shares my most stolid interests, while still being a veritable fountain of beauty with a combination of an alert mind tinged with mischievousness would be virtually impossible if left to chance. This wonderful dream bears the hand of the Almighty firmly marked upon it.

Once more she is smiling at me and I know that from the twinkling light of her eyes that she is scheming; not in any malicious manner but in that playful way that young women are so oft to do.

"Will you make me try to guess what it is that you are thinking?"

Shaking her head, she lets me in on her secret. "It is with a great difficulty that I pronounce your name. It occurred to me that if we are to be wed, how terrible it would be if I could not whisper your name while we lay in our nuptial bed."

"How is it that a mistress of languages could have difficulty with a name like Makhir Natronai."

"See! Did you hear it when you said that Marir word? It is like a rumble in your throat. It is so guttural. It is impossible for me to produce such a sound."

"Well, don't. The word Makhir is a title only. It is not a true part of my name. It literally means Lord or Master. I would never expect for you to refer to me in either term. I have no desire for our relationship to be that formal. To be accurate, my entire title is El Makhir Natronai Kahana. But it is only Natronai which is my name."

"Almeryi Natrooney...almeryi nitronah...I will never get it right. What does the word for your name mean anyway."

I know she is playing with me. No one that is as talented a linguist as she obviously is would have any trouble pronouncing my name. "It is Aramaic and it means that God has given. A gift of God in other words. It is a name that has been long in use in my family."

"Then it is settled. I will call you Theodoric. Do you not find it to be an attractive name?"

"Ah, Theodoric; it is the direct Greek and Latin transliteration of my name. I am certain that you mean well but I have grown accustomed to my actual name."

"A wager then?"

"A wager on what?" I questioned.

The broad grin on her face tells me that I am probably going to lose. Her quick displays of wit and intelligence have drawn me to her like a lode stone to metal. Even to lose a wager serves only to bind us even closer.

"A test of logic. Pure Aristotelian logic which you are well aware is the nature of the universe and therefore should be adopted for it is the path to which life's journey is ultimately steered."

I nod my head. "Agreed and the prize to be lost or won?"

"Well, your name of course, silly. My question is in the form of a simple story that concerns our meeting."

"Go ahead. I am listening. But what if you lose? What do I claim as my prize?"

"If I should lose, of which I have my doubts then I will serve you in the manner of women of this land. I will not question, I will merely bend and obey."

She knows that this would not please me which only serves to guarantee her victory even more. If winning means that I break her spirit then I will ensure that I lose. My eyes blink in affirmation and I await her story.

"When my father first told me that a groom had been obtained for me I was livid with anger. Although I knew that the day was coming when a mate was to be chosen, as I explained earlier I did not consider any of the possible candidates from this part of the world to be of equal intellect to myself nor in possession of suitable social graces that I would wish to lie with them in love's embrace.

Pepin, being aware of my feelings, assured me immediately that the man chosen for me was not from this part of the world. That in fact he, being you, was from the Orient. Although this tidbit intrigued me it still did not convince me that this man would be any better than the rutting boars that populate Frankia.

He then went on further to explain that my brother, Charlemagne was purposely sent to the Caliph of Baghdad to arrange for the importation of one so-called, "King of the Jews." Now I am beset with not only some foreigner being selected for me but he also happens to be of a race that is thoroughly despised by both Church and state. How was I to reconcile my father's wishes with my own feelings?"

I want to say something but I think it best to wait until she is finished. Does she really see me as this loathsome foreigner? This despised Jew? I beseech her to go on.

"So all the time between my brother informing me and your arrival I am filled with painful and horrible nightmares which stare at me not only when I am asleep but awake as well. I beg Pepin to call off the betrothal but it is not possible. Our wedding has a far greater purpose than sealing a pact with the Caliph. Only recently have I come to learn of my family's obsession with obtaining an heir of David to rule in Narbonne. It would appear that the Jews of Narbonne would once again switch their allegiance if my brother failed to make good on his word. He was not willing to jeopardize the unification of Frankia over my protestations.

There is but one thing left for me to do. I make a deal with both Pepin and Charlemagne. I will go through with their betrothal on certain conditions. My husband-to-be would have to pass several tests in order for me to conjugate our wedding and to abide by the rules of marriage. First, was how you would look." She holds up her hand to stop me from saying anything.

"I know that this would appear a trifle vain but you must allow me certain quirks which flaw my character. I know it seems hard to believe that a woman who reads the great philosophers and speaks several languages would stoop to such a level as to base a decision on appearances but it is understandable. It was my own father's fault in a way. When he mentioned that you were a Jew I could only relate to those Jews who serve us, especially my brother's viceroy, Isaac. You have seen Isaac and you know I would not be exaggerating if I told you that visually he is a repulsive little man. After so many years I know him to have a heart of gold but he is so very unattractive. Therefore I concluded that all Jews must look like poor Isaac. The more and more Jews that came to the palace only served to confirm these beliefs. And then I saw you!

Your ship was just being oared into the slip and I could see you standing so nobly by the rail. My first thoughts were of how tall you were. My brother Charlemagne is huge among men and there you were but a couple inches shorter than he stands. Immediately, that dispelled any notion of your having a short bent stature as is common among the Jews that live here. And then I studied your features and found them to be pleasing like the statues of the gods of ancient Greece. Your face is so refined as if it were cut from the same marble as those ancient artifacts.

Although your skin is swarthy, neither your brow nor mane gave any hint of darkness and foreboding which again I must criticize of the Jews of this land. When asked by my father what I thought of my husband-to-be I quickly admitted that I found his appearance to be suitably pleasing."

"So it is safe to say that I passed the first test."

"Yes, but the second test was to be far more difficult. I told my brother that any mate that he selected must be intellectually stimulating. You can imagine Charlemagne's' and Pepin's reaction. If they could, they would have advised you to beat me at that moment in order to put me in my proper place but it was Charlemagne who calmed Pepin with but a simple comment. He advised him that I would not be disappointed. That upon his meeting with you in Baghdad two years ago he found you to be just as boring when you would elucidate upon all theoretical and historical matters as he finds me. He said we would be well suited in that regard.

We all laughed at the mere suggestion that you could be as stuffy as I can be. You see, I am considered quite an anomaly amongst the royal family. They never have been quite sure of what to make of me. Now that there might be two of us is a somewhat frightening thought, don't you think?"

"Terribly," I confirmed. "Then it is safe to assume that I passed your second test?"

"At first you had me worried. When we were initially brought into this room together you exhibited no signs of being anything but a sulking, morose debutante with but a single desire to return home. You said as much so in your open monologue, talking as if my maidservant and I weren't even in the room with you."

My initial reaction is to become defensive. After all, I was the one who travelled halfway across the world only to find that the princess to whom I was about to marry refused to say a single word to me for over two hours. She merely sat huddled in a corner of the room with her maidservant behaving as if I was some wild beast loosed in the room. If I talked out loud, it was more so for my benefit than hers, in order to calm my nerves. "Let us not forget that you were not entirely blameless for causing my behavior at the time. It was clearly evident that you had no desire to be alone with me and I think if it had not been for your brother posting a guard outside this door, you would have left long before we ever exchanged words. I do not feel I am wrong about this."

"No, you are probably not, but under the circumstances I would think that we both behaved reprehensibly. I was not willing to make the first move towards civility and you were far too busy feeling sorry for yourself."

I laughed as I conceded to her point. "Yes, you are right. Too often of late I have found myself wallowing in self-pity. I hope that you will continue to make me aware of when I do so."

"Rest assured that I will. You should know that as a fellow student of philosophy that I cannot tolerate one person maximizing himself to be the center of the universe which is exactly the nature of self-indulgent pity."

"I believe that was Epictetus commenting on Socrates' Man in the Universe?"

"No, that is Alda commenting on her future mate."

Her reply is so spontaneous, so incredibly wry and earnest that I burst into a fit of laughter. And then I hear the soft cackle of her laugh in return and we each feed upon the other's amusement until we are light headed and unable to stop the giddiness. "Stop it," I plead as I strain to catch my breath. It is a wasted effort. I laugh until I cannot laugh any more, the tears rolling from my eyes, my head resting upon her lap.

When all is done and we are both totally exhausted, while her maidservant stares at the both of us as if we are either raving lunatics or possessed by demons, Alda finally composes herself enough to continue with her tale.

So, it is evident that you successfully passed my second test for you and all that remained was the third and hardest challenge. I knew nothing of your customs and I think it is safe to say that you know very little of mine. I have my opinions as to the nature of men as I am certain that you have your own opinions regarding women. So my third test is one regarding customs. Some men like to treat their women roughly, as if they were beasts of burden suitable only for the bearing of children and providing satisfaction for their lusts.

I think that I have come to the conclusion over the years that most men are like this. Since it would be intolerable for me to surrender myself to such a life I would be faced with two alternatives. I made Pepin aware of both of these. If forced to accept such a man I would evoke the same choice made by Socrates when faced with the same decision of surrendering his individuality. I would commit suicide. Or, as I suggested to my brother, I would accept the marriage in name only, come to you on this one day when it happens that I am receptive in my cycle; have you impregnate both myself and my maidservant, Olivia, and be done with you. In that way, Frankia would obtain an heir to the blood of David and I will have fulfilled my brother's arrangement with you. My brother and father agreed that the decision would be left to me..."

"I do not understand what you wish me to answer. As to the manhandling of women, such behavior is offensive to me. It is not the custom from whence I came to commit such heinous crimes. I know it may seem difficult to believe since it is our custom to have up to four wives but I assure you that those who practice such customs hold all their wives in high reverence. In fact, the first wife is always considered to be in charge of the household and held in the highest esteem. Women in my land are granted the right to be heard in civilian court should they bear any grievances towards their husbands. Mistreatment of a wife is not considered lightly, I can assure you!"

"But therein lies the problem. My wants and needs are best suited to be a wife in your homeland but I cannot leave Frankia. You, on the other hand are not well adapted to survival in this land. It does not take me long to know that you are a man of kindness and generosity, capable of great tenderness and sensitivity. Easily hurt and often betrayed by those you felt closest to you. More than what you have spoken when you did not realize I understood every word, it was all evident in your eyes. But these are qualities I admire in a man; in fact, the man that I have prayed for all my life. But how are you to survive in this harsh cold land that will prey upon you from the moment others see what is considered a weakness within you? It would be wrong of me to force you to become someone you are not only to survive in this foreign land."

"I presume this is in some way the wager you spoke of? Something to do with doubts of how are two worlds can be bound over time. Is that not so? And if so, then I see it as not so much a problem of what to do about me but whether or not you fulfill your pledge to your father. You are wagering that our marriage will not survive!" She is right. There exists a great pain inside of me. A hurt caused by betrayal and once more I feel it swelling inside. The anger grows as I rise to my feet and begin pacing around the room, wanting to scream my fury to all about me. "So are you suggesting that we fulfill our conjugal rights and then part so that neither of us causes the other the pain of our mutual existence?"

"Are you still willing to wager?" she prods me.

I don't know if I'm hurt or angry or possibly even ashamed that she might be right. She has created a doubt in my mind that I did not foresee. How can I swear for an eternity what will be in the future when the future cannot swear to me that it will safeguard me within this foreign land? Then I remember, this is a test of logic, not one of emotion. She is challenging me on an entirely different level from the manner in which most would respond. How clever of her. She has preyed upon my own vanity, talking about my appearance and drawing me into her net. Then she hones her skills on my honor, seeking out how I would react to a woman that sometimes might even be my better. Now she tests my loyalty and devotion, the sly little minx. This is not a wager between us, this is a gamble on her part that I will fulfill her own desires admirably and my character is being tested. Well, I have an insight for her, I will not disappoint her. I feel the grin spreading across my lips as I begin my answer. "To do as you have suggested would cause me the greatest pain of all. I don't want you under those conditions. I know it is presumptuous of me but I have grown very fond of you, so very quickly. I am alone in a country that I do not have any knowledge about and I have only one friend who is now telling me that it is best that we have little to do with each other. In this, I do not agree.

I want you to be my wife. Not in name alone but as my companion, my consort and my friend. Do not take yourself from me for I will have no other recourse but to wallow in self-pity as you have so correctly pointed out to me. If you want me on my knees then I will eagerly do so but as husband and wife we should be walking side by side, neither of us ever to be on our knees to the other. I have no fear of living in this land because you will be my pillar of strength. There is no threat so great that we cannot face it together."

And now it is time to turn the tables. "But if you should ever find the my world, that which is an internal part of me, is so foreign that you cannot accept it any longer, then I will not chain you to live a life that is intolerable. To extinguish that free-spirit within you would be a crime that I would never forgive myself for. As much as your loss would be a crippling blow to me, your happiness will always be of greater priority. I can offer you love, and we can plant that seed together in our garden and watch it grow, but I cannot prune the tree unless we do it together, so that we both enjoy sitting within its shade and eat the sweet fruits of our labors. Where you are, will be my home and all I can ask is that you please stay with me!"

"Makhir Natronai, oh Natronai! Can you be so blind as not to see that I wish for no more than to be with you?" She has risen and with feet that almost float on air has glided towards me until I am now embraced tightly in her reassuring arms.

"You have said my name correctly!" I sound surprised but I am not really.

"I could always say your name. I was being cute. It was with your title that I had some difficulty but not enough from mastering the sounds. I am a linguist as you so shrewdly pointed out. What am I to do with you? Do you not see the problem that lies before us? You are from a different world than I and yet I fit more appropriately into your world which you have abandoned. To be with you I must give up my home, my religion and to a degree, the woman that I am. All these I will gladly sacrifice for your sake as long as you realize that which you were is now dead and your place will always be here at my side."

"So then, I have won our little wager." At least I think I have won but I'm not quite certain now.

She shakes her head, disagreeing with my assessment. "It was a wager that you were never permitted to win. Think upon it. You can no longer be Makhir Natronai! That person must die so Theodoric can live. That as you will come to see will be a necessity. There is no place for the one known as Natronai in Frankia. He would be scorned, ridiculed, and eventually driven from this land. I understand this land, these people far better than you ever will. Even if you accept my guidance, it is unlikely that they will ever forget who you really are. The only difference being that with my advice we should be able to preserve enough of a safe haven that they will not be able to touch us in our lifetimes."

I raise my hands placatingly. "I am not certain that I understand any of this." How is it that I can win and lose simultaneously.

"For our sake, you must! This is the real wager of which I spoke. You have been deceived. Can I make it any plainer than that? What you think is the reason for your being in Frankia is not truly the reason."

"And you are telling me this now because…" my voice trails off in anguish. She speaks of deception and immediately I think of betrayal.

"I tell you now because you have proven to me that you are the man I have sought all my life. You are the one I wish to share my hopes and my dreams with."

"So you tell me that I've won your heat but in so doing I am being deceived. This has no logical basis. I thought this was to be a philosophical discussion."

"Not all things in this world are based on logic. And that is why I must tell you this because it will defy any logical arguments you may attempt to defend yourself with. This is no longer about you but about us."

"How can it not be about me if I am the one being deceived? What is this great deception that I have fallen prey to? What can be so great that it defies logic and threatens the both of us?"

"Your soul is bound to an ancient Merovingian curse and not all the good intentions of my father, or Charlemagne will be able to preserve you. You have but one chance. I have shown you that opportunity. Just as I will sacrifice that which I am to meet you half way, so too must you make a similar sacrifice and try to meet me beyond the midpoint. Trust me on this! I know that we have only known each other for a few hours but you must heed my advice. I care about you, I care about us!"

I swallow hard. I don't know what has caused her this great consternation but I recognize whatever it might be will have serious consequences. I nod my head for her to continue.

"I have gauged the mood of the people, the stoking of the Church, and I can attest to you that there is no love for a man called Makhir Natronai amongst them. Heed me, listen to me, and even to a degree obey me and we will preserve our marriage and we will ride out the tempest together. But beware, as much as I may come to love and cherish you over the years, I will not bear the suffering of watching that which we build together go down in flames if you permit pride to cause us to stumble and fall."

"Surely you cannot be saying that I must fear the people I have come to serve. I have seen the agreement that Pope Stephen signed with your father. The church not only agreed to my coming but also sanctified it with their blessing. And what of the people of Narbonne? Is it not true that they overthrew their Moslem rulers only on the condition that I would be brought to reign over them? Are you suggesting that all this has been lies?"

"As a philosopher you should already know. The answer is both yes and no. The Pope Stephen III said yes but Pope Stephen IV, who now sits in the Vatican says no. If as Aristotle explains we exist in a dynamic, changing world then how is it that you expect it to remain static. This new Stephen is not as desperate to curry the favor of my father and brothers as had been his predecessor. Time changes all the pieces and this certainly is a game of chess.

This pope is so bold as even to condemn Charlemagne for his banishing of Desiderius, the Lombardian princess, and refuses to grant him his request for annulment. Already, the Pope's agent Aribert, archbishop to this diocese has begun to turn the people against you. You are not even aware of it. Here, look for yourself. I have kept one of the Pontiff's letters to my father for you to read upon your arrival."

She reaches under her leather skirt and removes a somewhat tattered parchment which she hands to me.

I carefully unfold it and scrutinize it's Latin script.

'To Pepin, King of Frankia and Ruler of the Western Hinterland.

I bring you God's blessing. I am deeply distressed by the information supplied by my Archbishop, Aribert, regarding the effect that certain laws of the Frankish Kings granted to the Jews allow allodial hereditary lands in the towns and suburbs to be held by them, though this be a Christian land.

Furthermore, Christians work the vineyards and fields of these Jews. Christian men and women even live in their houses, listening daily to the Jew's blasphemous talk day and night. We of the Papacy have been distressed to the point of death, especially since the promises made to the ancestors of the Hebrews by their legislator Moses and his successor, Joshua, were rightly abrogated as punishment for the Crucifixion of the Savior. What communion has light with darkness or Christ with Belial? What agreement has the Temple of God with idols?

Stephen, First Bishop of Rome

Upon finishing the letter I carefully re-roll it and hand it back to her. I sigh in a moment of disgust. This is all very new to me. "And how far has this madman gone with his campaign of hatred?"

"It is a pestilence that has reached as far as Narbonne. Do you understand my concerns now? If we are to survive as a couple, a unit, and eventually even a family, then I urge you to lose my wager and tread a new path along with me. We can do it. I know we can, Natronai."

I bowed my head in a brief moment of reflection and resignation. "I believe you should refer to me from now on as Theodoric." I have begun my life anew. A smile spread immediately across her face and she is satisfied the together we can make this work. She begins to laugh in amusement.

"What is so funny?"

"They say in the court that I am strange and boring. I can't wait to until they have to bear the two of us."

"Since when has the criticisms of others ever been a concern to people like us?"

"Never," she responded lovingly to her consort. "People like us only need each other."

Chapter Eleven

Toronto: 1999

Taking a deep breath, Pearce releases it slowly in a long, excruciating sigh. "Doesn't look like things have gotten much better for Natronai on the other side of the world either."

"Unfortunately, it was the blood which was important, not the container in which it was held."

"I guess he didn't expect that he would be expendable right from the onset."

"Only if he had a child," I interject. "As I indicated previously, the seeds were what the Church was interested in, not the flower."

"And the woman, Alda, did she really loved him?"

"Very much! And he, her. It was an all-encompassing love; the kind of love which we all dream about."

Pearce sighs at the thought. "So this Jewish kingdom was doomed from the very start," he deduces.

"Never had a chance," I confirm. "But strangely, it did serve another purpose. If there's one thing you learn about Jewish history, John, it's that we're persistent. Beat us down, and we'll rise again. Time after time after time! Likewise, if something works well once, we'll repeat it until it no longer works. We are very successful at duplication. So, if we can send one king off to the end of the world to establish a Jewish kingdom, then surely we could send another to the opposite end of the world and do the same. It's a survival technique that works very well."

"And did they?"

"Why, of course! It worked once, didn't it? So, why not try it again? Ironically, this second attempt is well known and is documented but the actual account of the event has been distorted significantly. Know anything about the Khazarim, John?"

"No."

"Then, I'll tell you. I'll take a little detour from our main story. It's all related but has no direct bearing on what's going down in France. Now picture this. It's the eight century and there's an entire race of people known as the Khazars, living in the Caucasus regions which decide to convert to Judaism. Legend says that their king sought council from a priest, an imam, and a rabbi. He asked the priest if he had the choice between converting to either of the other two religions or death, which would he choose. The priest chose Judaism, stating that it was closest to Christianity as they believed in the same commandments. The same question was proposed to the imam and he responded that he too would select Judaism because like Islam, there was only a singular God. When the rabbi was presented with the same question, he chose death, saying that he could have no other faith. The king saw it as a unanimous decision and converted all of his people. Now let me tell you the real story!"

Crimea: 769 A.D.

From her perch between the two great rocks, Thaliah watched the procession of leather and steel plated riders proudly saddled upon their stocky steppes ponies celebrating their victory. Their ponies were short-maned and swift legged horses, considered legendary for their ability to cross vast expanses without ever tiring or thirsting. The riders too had become the subject of numerous legends as they carved out an empire from the inhospitable wastelands between the two great inland seas. Long curved swords swung effortlessly above their crested helms, slicing deadly swaths through imagined and now dead enemies that hovered somewhere between heaven and earth.

Around and around they circled their mighty king as he posed triumphantly at the center of their spiraling masses, standing firmly upon a mountain of corpses heaped one upon the other as a stele to their victorious army.

"Savages! Barbarians!" she cursed under her breath. The thought of turning and fleeing back to whence she came crossed her mind but still she remained affixed to the rocks where she had concealed herself. How could the redemption of her people lie in the hands of this uncivilized people? If not for her promise she would have given the order for her servants to mount immediately and turn south upon the road back to Sura.

The king, bejeweled and crowned with a gold coronet encircling the low, flat cap he wore over braided black locks, began a merry little dance, balancing precariously upon the back of his slain enemies, much to the acclaim and applause of his men. Then, without a moment's hesitation he somersaulted into a forward twist, landing safely in the outstretched arms of his followers.

An order was given, and several men rushed forward, splashing naphtha over the mound of human flesh, all the while dancing dervishly, and spinning wildly out of control as they did so. The king was presented with a flaming brand, and with a leisurely arc of his arm, the torch sailed through the air, turning end over end until it came to rest upon the crest of the pyre. At first, only the crackling and spitting of oil occurred, but then suddenly, the entire pile erupted into a hissing pillar of flame. With each sputter of searing flesh, the army roared and cheered. Their nostrils flared as the black smoke spiraled in its path heavenward and they inhaled the sickly-sweet aroma.

The horror of the sights and sounds were too overpowering for Thaliah. Every now and then a faint, yet clearly audible scream of sheer terror would surface from beneath the pyre, from the choking voices of the wounded and almost dead. The smoke churned faster and faster in the circling winds that raced about the foothills. The tears welled in her eyes and she was even more convinced now more than ever that her presence here had definitely been a serious error in judgment.

The reassuring arm of her servant Eli come to rest upon her shoulder. "Come away mistress. This is no place for you." Thaliah let her eyes drop and turn from the foul desecration of human life. She looked into the soft brown eyes of her guardian. Eli held twenty years more than her yet to his credit he appeared to those that saw them together to be barely a few years older. His hair had not grayed and his skin was still smooth to the touch. When she was a little girl, she had often fantasized that Eli would come in the dark of night, cast her over his broad shoulders and carry her off into the distant lands where they would live happily ever after. But all along she knew that could never be more than a childish dream. Their castes were worlds apart. Royalty and servitude could never mix, only co-exist. No, her destiny had already been predetermined and here she was, in some nameless land, fulfilling a dream fueled by royal decree.

"Oh Eli, what have I've gotten myself into?" Her chest heaved with a sigh of defeat.

"Come mistress. The king's messenger awaits us. It is best he receives you before he and his men begin to celebrate too heartily." He flashed a smile that put her troubled heart at ease for the moment. Eli and Thaliah walked towards her entourage and the envoy that waited patiently for her return.

As she approached, the messenger bowed courteously. "I hope that your highness found the view quite spectacular?"

Thaliah knew well enough not to answer truthfully. She glanced quickly at Eli, to reassure him that she would maintain proper protocol and decorum, and then trained her eyes upon the king's richly robed courtesan. "Your king was a most impressive figure and surely his victory shall be exalted and praised by the singers of far off lands. You may tell your king that this princess has truthfully never beheld such a spectacle as this in all her life."

"His majesty, Bosiah, thanks you warmly and requests the presence of your company at his tent, accompanied by your servants, of course."

"I am most grateful for your king's hospitality. Please inform him that I will attend his tent as soon as I am properly attired in clothes more deserving of this honor."

"A word of wisdom your highness," the messenger overstepped the bounds of his position. "When the king makes a request, it is considered to mean immediately." Another bow, followed by a graceful leap onto the back of his horse and the envoy was ready to proceed back to the camp.

"Then the king will have to receive me as I am," she shouted at the envoy's back. "How dare they treat me in this manner!" she muttered as she turned to face her servant.

Eli helped his mistress into the ornate silver and leather saddle that nestled between the humps on her camel's back. Her mount had been the gift of the Caliph of Baghdad. He probably would have reconsidered his generosity had he known that his prized animal would now be making its way towards the camp of a most hated enemy. Thaliah handed the reins over to the messenger who had turned and coached his horse alongside. Demonstrating his gifted horsemanship, he walked the beast slowly down the side of the hill towards the encampment. Camel and horse pacing side by side was no mean feat and he did it expertly.

Her caravan of camels and donkeys followed a respectful distance behind, framed by the glow of the setting sun as she glanced back towards them. A glance that in some way said, this would be the last time she would see any of her family again.

"He's fascinated with you."

The sound of the envoy's voice caught her by surprise as she turned her head forward in response. "Pardon me. What was that you said?"

"You fascinate him. The king does not quite know what to make of your visit."

Thaliah cocked her head slightly, a look of bemusement crossing the lines of her face. Such forwardness by a servant was quite unusual. "How so?"

"Well, your highness. Firstly you must understand, we don't receive many visitors, let alone royal caravans in these parts. The mountainous regions of the Caucasus are treacherous and are not part of any established trade route. Those that do make it this far from the normal trade routes, we usually attack, not welcome." The messenger flashed a warm, jocular grin. "Secondly, not many women lead a caravan into parts unknown. One might say that you are either very brave or very, how should I say this kindly, stupid. Please pardon my openness but it is what he himself had said. "

Squinting her pale hazel eyes, she looked him squarely in the face. "For a mere courtesan, you would appear to know a lot of what the king has to say! And which one do you think I am?"

The messenger cleared his throat, his face flushed by the question. After a slight pause he responded. "I think that you are very beautiful. Therefore the other question does not matter."

Now it was Thaliah's turn to blush. She laughed. Perhaps this land populated by savages was not as bad as she had originally thought. They did have a natural charm about them. "Do you often pay such compliments to visiting princesses who have come specifically to see your king? I would think you could be put to death for such brashness."

"I have a certain amount of latitude as you might have guessed with Bosiah," his perfect white teeth flashed a devilish grin. "As his brother, he has grown used to my lack of decorum. I should have introduced myself sooner. I am Yusef, the son of Marzuk and inheritor of the kingdom of the eastern steppes. But I prefer to stay in my brother's court. He has more interesting visitors." Yusef winked.

The caravan quickly drew into a line circling the outside perimeter of the camp. Gray billowing smoke had replaced much of the fierce flames that had been so apparent but mere minutes ago. The sickly sweet smell of charred flesh filled their nostrils. Thaliah fought desperately to force the bile from the back of her throat. This was not the way of her people or the Arabians. It was forbidden to burn a corpse except under dire conditions. But even in that case, no one living in Sura could remember the last time such a detestable act had to be performed. She prayed that the pyre would quickly extinguish itself, in fear that she would embarrass herself before the king. As if in response, the breeze shifted to the east, blowing the smoke away from the camels and their riders. Thaliah wiped the sweat from her brow, thankful for the instantaneous relief.

"This is no sight for a Babylonian," Yusef commented as he watched the princess's face change from the white contorted illness back to its healthy glow. "My brother should have known better. Our ways sometimes appear brutal, but the cleansing flames prevent the spread of disease. There is some foresight behind our actions. I hope you understand."

"Please...," Thaliah apologized. "There is no need to make excuses. This is your land, your customs. I am merely a visitor. Do not feel that I have the right to judge you and your people."

"I don't," he dismissed her concerns. "I'm just trying to explain our differences. We are primarily a nomadic people. We have our cities but they are few. Burying of the dead would serve no purpose if you never return to the grave site. Not to overlook that the winds and the rains on the steppes would uncover their bodies in very little time. Cremation is the only logical solution. But I understand that your beliefs do not permit you to cremate."

"The body is a gift of God." Looking away from the pyre in the distance, Thaliah waited for her lungs to clear once and for all. "That which God has given us we have no right to destroy. As we come into this world, so shall we leave it? And if you knew all this, then why did you ask me if I found the view spectacular?" She looked into his azure eyes, waiting, searching for a response. His chestnut hair fell in ringlets about his bronzed features.

"No," she repeated over and over in her mind as she studied his handsome features. "This cannot happen. I cannot let it happen." She felt a strange heaviness fall upon her chest, her nostrils sucking back deep breaths as she struggled to calm herself. She quickly averted her eyes from his, breaking the spell in which he had enthralled her.

Yusef saw that the situation called for an abrupt change. He had seen that look in a woman's eyes before. Most often it would have been a signal for him to press the advantage, but this woman was very different. Not just because she was a princess of a people whom he had only heard of through the vaguest rumors, but she had been betrothed to his brother. Silence would be their downfall; an open invitation to think the impossible.

"Ah, yes, your God, of which we have heard so much about." It was a little lie. Like her people, her God was but one more tale heard told over a roaring fire, with eyes half closed after a night of heavy drinking. His people knew all the tales of all the great religions but chose instead

103

to worship the almighty Skyfather. "Though we have a belief in a creator, there are those amongst us that claim there are many gods, and even those which say there are none at all. Living in the steppes, it makes very little difference whether we believe or not. Life here holds its own rewards. You live, you die, and it's as simple as that. As for the spectacle, the term is without reference to good or evil. In your case, you've seen us at our worst. Our relationship can only improve from here."

Thaliah waved a finger of disapproval. "Then you have nothing to look forward to. Life is nothing more than a string of momentary pleasures and pains, leading nowhere. Our beliefs are very different. I shall have to tell you of them at some time." Her lips remained thin and taut, turned down ever so slightly at the corners.

"Our beliefs perhaps differ but our faith that tomorrow the sun will rise again are the same. That alone sustains us." Yusef looked satisfied with his answer.

"In Babylon, so little to look forward to would be considered depressing." She lowered her eyes, her lips now formed into a beguiling pout.

"In Khazaria, we consider Babylon depressing," he huffed.

She narrowed her eyes. Perhaps he wasn't as enchanting as she first thought. "My, you do have a tongue on you. Do you despise all of civilization or just Babylon?" Her arms were now subconsciously drawn tight into her body somewhat defensively.

They had ridden wide around the smoldering pyre of fleshless bones. "Have you thought at all about how these bones came hence? That is what remains of civilization's threats." Yusef's response was very calm, his voice carefully modulated so as not to upset the princess. "The Magyars considered us no more than barbarians. Why? Because we would not accept their Christian faith and by so doing, they declared war upon us. A blight upon their plans to expand their empire. Our way of life was unimaginable to them. Where they build roads, we know no boundaries. Why should we feel forced to become as they are?

Once they were like us, but the lure of civilization turned them on a different path and now they despise us because we remind them of their origins. Civilization is nothing more than a chasm of hates and prejudices. What could it possibly hold for us to envy?"

"Forgive me," Thaliah bowed her head. "It is not my place to make comment on your ways. I overstepped myself. I am your guest and I have behaved improperly once again." Her eyes became downcast as the shadow fell upon her countenance.

"Take heart, fair lady, there is nothing to forgive. I am not here to judge you either. You may possess your beliefs without fear of retribution. But I would suggest that you don't discuss your concept of civilization with my brother. There is no love for Babylon in his heart either.

Know this, that you are welcome here not as a courtesan of the Caliph's court but as a princess of a dethroned people. A once ancient kingdom held captive by a brutal regime that spreads itself through terror. Bosiah empathizes with your plight, though you may not consider yourself to have one." Extending his arm in supplication, Yusef cautioned her, "May I suggest that you do."

"I am grateful for your suggestion, Yusef. Contrary to appearances, my family has certainly fallen into disfavor at the Caliph's court. I commend your king for being very astute to see the truth of our situation."

"We have had our own disagreements with the Caliphate," Yusef clarified his standpoint. His reduction of three major wars to nothing more than disagreements proved that he was a master of the understatement.

"And here I am now," She explained, "Because one cousin has been sent into the unknowns of the Western sea and another has spent five years in prison. We are at the twilight of our existence and my family truly does seek your brother's aid. I don't know how we are to survive without his protection."

The words had stolen some of the fire from her eyes. Suddenly, Yusef saw not the obstreperous, proud royal princess as he imagined nestled in the lap of luxury in Babylon, but instead a true damsel in distress. His heart went out to her and her obvious need.

"My lady, I am truly sorry. I have misjudged your circumstances. I did not intend to upset you."

Thaliah suddenly bolted upright on the camel's back, reassuming her proud and majestic airs that she had originally shrouded upon herself. "Well, was that humble and beseeching enough for you," she inquired. "Will that be convincing enough for the mighty Bosiah? Never underestimate us, Yusef. We are a captive people but we are also a proud one. I come not begging but offering!"

Yusef clapped his hands in obvious delight. "A wonderful performance," he lauded. "Truly an effort worthy of myself I admit. I am afraid your highness that I am falling rapturously in love with you." The words rolled effortlessly across his tongue. He waved his index finger naughtily at her, entertained by the deception she had played upon him.

If only he had looked deeper, further into the limpid pools of her silver hued eyes, he would have seen the effect those words had upon her. She whispered unspoken psalms of the enduring warmth which engulfed her whenever she looked now upon his handsome and rugged features. Love at first sight? A childish notion and yet she knew there was no other explanation for the feelings she was experiencing. There was an instantaneous bond that existed between them and she knew he felt it too. She knew they were both doing everything possible to resist the urge since the first time they exchanged greetings. As he led her towards the king's tent she had but one plaguing thought, "What was she going to do?"

The tent that served as both domicile and great hall for the king of the Khazars was enormous. It had been designed with all the best materials that the trade routes had to offer. Silks from the East, flowed from ceiling to floor, bestowing a rainbow of hues and colors that seemed to dance and change with the slightest breeze. It was a truly magnificent structure, rimmed in gold brocade and silver tassels. Huge brass candelabrums hung from the towering cedar poles, illuminating the interior with the brightness of an afternoon sun.

Thaliah let her mind wander back to the stories she had heard as a child about the Tabernacle that the prophet Moses had erected in the desert. Could it have been possibly as ornate or even as large as the house of Bosiah? She doubted it. A kingdom of tents, she mused, and this one truly befitting of an emperor. What would the wives' tent look like? Like so many other Eastern despots, Bosiah would have a separate tent to house his wives, concubines and children. Would she have her own or would she merely take but one more place in his harem?

Just as it was traditional in her homeland, every inch of the floor was concealed by the artistry of hand knotted carpets. Only in this case they hid the earthen floor beneath rather than the marbled halls of Babylon. There were only few pieces of furniture, and those that were present were dwarfed by the immensity of the tent's chambers.

A large, low table, made from a black wood that she could not identify, stood at the center, surrounded by an ocean of pillows, some tasseled, and others cross-stitched with beautifully designed animal motifs. But it was the table that held her interest. Its top was carefully carved and painted with scenes from the daily life of a people she had also never seen before. There was a noticeable resemblance to the Tartars but the features of that particular heathenish tribe seemed to lie somewhere between her own and those that were carved into the table. But most striking of all was the serenity that seemed to surround this people depicted. There existed a gracefulness and placidity etched into every knitted brow and almond eye. There was so much of the world she did not know and having been forbidden by religious law to have any images of people within her home meant that her knowledge of mankind was limited to only those she met at her family's estate. Though she hated to admit it, as much as she thought of her visit to the Khazarim as a journey to a lesser civilized corner of the world, she now realized that Bosiah and his people had a far broader perspective of the globe than she had ever experienced. They were a doorway to unknown worlds that lived in the lands far beyond. Yusef may have been right; civilization can build walls within the mind just as easily as it does from mortar and clay.

The princess stood in awe of the elaborate surroundings and had become so preoccupied that she was oblivious to the movement directly behind, as Bosiah and his advisors took their positions in the great hall. "I take it that the Princess Thaliah is comfortable with her arrangements," the king interrupted, causing her to jump to the impact of his unexpected voice.

"The Princess has not yet had the opportunity to visit her tent but knowing of the King's generosity I can assure you that she is most grateful and delighted with her accommodations," Eli replied, recovering quickly.

"Do you always answer the questions directed to the princess?" the King's voice crackled with a hint of disapproval.

"Forgive me your Majesty," Eli immediately apologized. "We are used to the Caliph's court where he does not expect women to speak at all."

"Hah!" the laugh burst from the King's lips. "The Caliph is more of a fool than I thought. How does he think you can silence the chirping of birds? Is not a woman's voice like the sounds of the birds in the treetops? You must let them sing because it is the natural way of the world. But only when you ask them to, otherwise they will sing constantly." Bosiah bid the princess and Eli to sit around the low table while dismissing the rest of the attendants with a wave of his hand to seat themselves elsewhere within the chamber. Demonstrating how to pile the pillows properly, Bosiah adopted a reclining position. "I must ask the princess to forgive my lack of consideration of not even allowing her an opportunity to settle her belongings before my summons." The guests all followed the king's example, reposing around the table of carved figures of a people from unknown lands.

Staring at the king, the princess noticed how much he resembled his younger brother Yusef, and yet how dissimilar they were as well. Bosiah was heavier set, built like a bull, much thicker browed and definitely hairier. Thick tufts of his mane flowed down the back of his neck and across his shoulders. The same sparkle that glinted in Yusef's eyes was definitely there, but where those of Yusef indicated a mischievous scholar, Bosiah's shone more darkly as a tactful and skillful warrior. And where Yusef's smile flashed warmth, Bosiah's smile could be cold; as frigid as ice.

"As King of Khazaria, I can tell you how pleased we are to have you as our honored guest. Your father's letter and offerings were most welcome. I send warmest regards to King Judah Zakkai, exilarch of the Jewish nation. May his days be long and honored."

"His majesty, King Judah, extends his warmest regards and appreciation to the great King Bosiah and entrusts the care of his most favored daughter to the great king's care and mercies.", Eli responded. All the guests sitting at the table nodded in affirmation.

"Tell your good King Judah Zakkai, that the king of the Khazars is most pleased with his offering and shall welcome his daughter into my household with open arms."

Eli bowed his head in gratitude. "Speaking for the King of the Jews, I can tell the great King Bosiah how grateful we are that he is pleased with our gifts. The princess's dowry shall be found on the back of seven golden camels, all which are given freely to the great king in appreciation of his acceptance and ratification of a treaty between us."

"Answer me this," Bosiah interrupted the introductions, "How is it that your King was able to seek this alliance while under the watchful eye of the Caliph?"

Wise with age, Eli knew immediately that the king of the Khazars was fishing for a hidden trap in the arrangement. There must have been those in his court that were suspicious that the alliance would be taken advantage of by the Caliph of Baghdad. He had already prepared his answer for such suspicions. "There are those that think of my king as a puppet of the Caliph and a servant to the rabbinate but all along he has been an independent ruler, merely abiding his time, waiting for this opportunity to give you his heart and hand in friendship."

"But to do so would make him an enemy of the Caliph and at odds with his own religious leaders," the King's curiosity was peaked.

"Truthfully?"

"I would have it no other way," Bosiah insisted.

"He lied," Eli confessed. "He assured the Caliph that any trade agreements would be made on his behalf. The Caliph knows that you will not deal with him directly so he desperately wanted to believe that you wished to deal with him through an intermediary in order to save face."

"Shrewd, but what of these rabbis that have gained control of your people?"

"My king is well aware that they have their own agenda which is to undermine the authority of the House of David and the House of Aaron. He secretly works with his cousin Anan ben David to see that this will never happen. Your acceptance of the Princess Thalia into your household will ensure that this will not occur."

"Then let us drink to our mutual good fortune and acceptance of the contract between us," Bosiah raised his cup to toast in final acceptance.

At that moment, Thaliah stood defiantly and raised her voice above the conversation between the king and her guardian. "And when do I get a say in all this?"

There was a mutual gasp of disbelief from Bosiah's cabinet. Never had a woman had the effrontery to interrupt the court in this manner without first be asked a question.

Eli tugged at her dress, urging her to sit down. "Please mistress," he pleaded, "For your own sake, sit down! Do not show disrespect to the Great King." The more he tried to get her to sit, the more adamant she became in saying her piece. "Thaliah, please, in the name of your father, restrain yourself."

"Let her speak!" a familiar voice beckoned from behind.

"This is most unusual," one of the king's advisors commented. "A woman may only address the king in the great hall when spoken to first! This is an insult to our king and not even you, Yusef, can dismiss this act of discourtesy."

"And how many of those women to which this rule applies, also have been of royal birth, Vasqni? I say, let her speak. If she truly pleases the king, then he will welcome her words." Yusef strode defiantly forward towards the table. "Is that not so, brother?"

"Yes, Vasqni, my brother is right," Bosiah commented, "let her speak. She is a warrior born. I wish to hear what she has to say." The king waved his advisor's concerns away.

"Most unusual," Eli tutted, just audible enough for his mistress to hear. As he relinquished his grip from her dress, she pushed his hand away.

Yusef stood beside the princess in silent support. "Your majesty," she responded. "I am most honored that you are pleased with my father's gifts and his deliverance of his daughter into your hands. I beg you though, please do not lock me away in your harem, never to be seen or heard from again. I could not bear to be shunned from the courts.

What my courtesan has failed to mention was that my father saw our survival not only through my marriage into your household but by a mutual acceptance of our customs so that essentially we become as one people. That is why of all his daughters he picked me as I am well versed in the languages and literature of my people. I can be of great service to you in areas of diplomacy. Though my skills in mathematics and astrology have not been tested in quite a long time, I am certain that they too will be of value if I am given the opportunity. In theology I can provide you with all that is written in the Books of Moses in both Greek and Hebrew. Let me be a teacher to your court and your people."

Bosiah laughed at the suggestions. "Please Princess; do I look like a scholar?"

All of the King's attendants joined in the mirthful laughter.

"Perhaps not, Great King, but you do look wise to me. And wisdom outshines knowledge in any event. There is no reason that your court could not rival any in the world."

Bosiah nodded with approval. "A good dream Princess and what price am I to pay for your tutelage in my court besides the adoption of your customs?"

"I ask only that I hold position as a court princess. If I am to aid my people then it is necessary that I have access to the courtesans that pass through this chamber. My father has explained to you how the Caliph has taken control of the Exilarchate, placing my uncle Anan in custody all those years and divesting our inherited power to the rabbinate. In order to preserve our rightful privilege to rule we have sought this alliance with you, great king. But if I have not your ear, then I have failed in my own duty to my family and my people."

"I do understand, but how am I to explain to my most favored wife, the princess of Cathay, that she is being replaced by another princess? She has sat by my right side for two years now. Her father, the Sian Emperor would find it a great and terrible insult. I do not wish to insult the Emperor. "

"Then don't brother. I have a solution that all might find satisfactory." Yusef leaned over his brother, placing his hand upon his shoulder. "Furthermore, I know full well that neither you or your court would be prepared to accept the customs and beliefs of the Princess as the sole practices amongst you. That is not your way."

Bosiah reached across his chest to clasp his brother's hand. "As usual, my younger brother will find a solution." The king's cabinet laughed along with their ruler. "So, Yusef, what would you suggest to save me from placing my court in such peril." They continued to laugh at the King's suggestion that consideration would even be given to Thalia's request.

"I would suggest that it is time I live up to our father's expectations and rule the land that he gave me. I have been negligent in my duties."

Bosiah's hand quickly dropped from his brother's. "What are you talking about? What nonsense is this? You belong here with me. Have I not been a good provider and protector to you? Marzuk only said that when it came time for you to establish a royal line was it necessary for you to leave the court. You are my only brother, my only sibling and you have no wife. So of what foolishness are you now speaking and furthermore, how would such an action even answer the request by the Princess?"

Yusef threw himself to the ground in front of the king and lowered his forehead to the carpeted ground. "Oh Great King Bosiah, I have a request. A request so great that never has a brother asked for such a thing before. Please show me favor in your heart. Though you may be offended by the effrontery of my request, please remember the love in your heart that you hold for me and which I hold for you."

Bosiah quickly looked around the room to catch the shocked looks of his council. "Get up brother. You embarrass me to humble yourself thusly. What do you think you are doing? Have I ever denied you in all the years you have lived beneath the roof of my tent? You are blood of

Marzuk. Blood of my blood, I can deny you nothing. Quickly rise before you lose face before our guests. So what is this solution you spoke of?"

"I ask that you present me with a royal wife."

"Brother, do not suggest this! I would gladly provide you with the freedom to select any girl from my harem, but to take from the royal wives, how could I explain such an affront to my allies. They have entrusted their daughters to my care and I would do irreparable harm to cast one out from my household. How could I retain my honor, having broken my sacred pledge to cleave them to me?"

Rising to his feet, Yusef grew in stature, his jaw squared as he stood firm and proud. "Not if it was one that you have not yet wed, dear brother and brought in to your household. I have but one wife in mind, and by doing so it would certainly solve your present issue as well as solve the dilemma you would encounter afterwards."

"Careful brother, this is dangerous ground upon which you tread," Bosiah warned.

"Brother, I ask for the princess Thaliah since she is not yet betrothed to you and therefore you break no sacred vows of marriage. But rather than have you give her to me, I would ask for her hand directly and she would choose whether she leaves your court of her own accord."

"And this solves my problem? How? Am I to explain to her father that the princess chose to leave the court of the King of the Khazars after he bound our agreement with his honor. Her father would be humiliated and be shamed the rest of his life."

"She asked for a court in which to reign as a queen but you cannot have the Princess of Sian forfeit her position lest you offend the Great Emperor. She's requested that you and your court adopt her customs and I know that to do so would also offend those rulers that have added their daughters to your harem and drive the people that possess other beliefs away from you. But I can give the Princess Thaliah a court to reign over and I have no courtesans at the moment to take issue if I was to impose my wife's customs and faith upon them. You wish not to break the promises made between yourself and the kings that have sent their daughters to cement their treaties with you and that is also resolved if the princess and yourself choose to extend the treaty to include a third kingdom within the alliance.

You have the right to use the princess as the bargaining price for that treaty. Her father has placed her fate in your care. Not only shall Khazaria be an ally to the Exilarchate, but so too shall be the Tartar Kingdom."

"Brother, you have been absent from the eastern steppes a very long time. Calling it a kingdom may be somewhat of an exaggeration. You would seriously want to be king of that unruly mob?"

"If the Princess Thaliah was to be by my side, I would even rule in Siberia."

"But the court is a shambles. The Kaghan barely keeps any control. As our governor, he hardly met the task. For you to establish yourself after so many years of absence would be a formidable task."

"But not impossible! Not if I was to become Kaghan and therefore all authority still stems from you, their Great King. They say that the blood of the Princess Thaliah's family has already been intermingled with the dynasties of the East centuries ago. She will be received as a returning monarch. From the ashes a kingdom can be rebuilt."

Bosiah thought long and hard about the request. "A task certainly suitable for a son of Marzuk, brother. It has its merits. Would the world expect any less of us? Perhaps we have grown too fat in the luxury of Khazaria. Maybe this is the time to re-establish our dominion east of the Caspian?"

"And how say you Princess Thalia? Would you follow my brother on this mad dream of his?"

Eli started to answer. "The princess does not know what to say. This is a very unusual situation. She must consult with her father. This is hardly what the Exilarch Judah expected when he signed the arrangement."

"Oh, hush Eli. I can make my own decisions." Thaliah brushed her advisor aside. "If I was to marry Yusef, would I be recognized as the majestrix of his kingdom? Would I have the right to speak in the court of Bosiah?"

Bosiah leaned over his brother and whispered in his ear. "I think you have met your match with this one brother. I think you have done me a favor taking her off my hands. The tongue on her is sharp along with her wit and wisdom. Beware of which one rules and which one is ruled. I do admit thought, I like her very much. I'll regret giving her up."

Patting his brother on the back, Bosiah waved the princess closer. "You would be queen of this Tartar kingdom my brother has chosen to take as his rightful possession. He is a king by birth but he refused to rule until he had a proper queen. He has chosen you. As favored wife, actually his only wife, you would bear all the rights and honors of that status, including being a most welcome guest in my court. Though he chooses to call himself Kaghan he is still no less than a king in my eyes."

Thaliah fell to her knees before Bosiah and stretched out her hands beseechingly, "Great King, you who have wisdom beyond the grasp of most men, I humble myself before you with but one question more to ask."

"See, it is like I have told you," the king proclaimed to all in attendance. "A woman is like the birds. If you let them, they will sing endlessly."

Everyone laughed at the King's joke.

"Sing away little bird," Bosiah grinned.

"If you were me, would you accept your brother's proposal?"

Yusef shot an alarmed glance at his brother, concerned as to how Bosiah might answer.

Bosiah smiled warmly at his brother and nodded. "Dear Princess Thaliah. It is not a question that I ever dreamed I would ever be asked. If you are looking for a life without hardship, the comforts of Babylon, the luxurious gardens of the Euphrates, then the eastern steppes are not going to offer you that life. But on the other hand, I can clearly see the future, and in it you and my brother will build a kingdom to rival any other. For my brother to undertake this course of action, for him to seek a wife after having had the opportunity to have had so many in the past, then I know that he has offered you more than a kingdom, he has offered you his heart. Can you give him your heart in return? If your answer is yes, then you do not need my wisdom."

Thaliah looked towards Yusef and she immediately knew the answer for herself. "I will gladly accept."

"My princess," Eli interjected, "I really do believe we should send word to your father."

Bosiah did not wait for the princess to respond. "Eli, let me extend some of this great wisdom I am rumored to possess. I do not believe that there is anything that you or King Judah Zakkai could say that would change the princess's decision. My advice to you is to help my staff prepare a wedding like none that has ever been seen before in Khazaria. My little brother is getting married to your charge! I was beginning to think I would never see the day that he would find a bride."

Eli fell silent. He knew not how he was going to explain any of this to Thaliah's father.

Thaliah wrapped her arms around her trusted advisor, speaking softly so that none but he could hear. "Do not fret so, dear guardian. My father will be very proud of me. It will be his seed that spawns a new Jewish kingdom in Khazaria."

Eli urged his princess to take care in what she said. "My child, you may be somewhat premature to speak of Jewish kingdoms. The Khazarim have no state religion. And they have shown no urgent desire in the past to have one. You will only have a small kingdom to the east to start with and no guarantee that Bosiah's kingdom will follow suit."

"Oh, but it will, dear friend. My king and I will see that it will." With a smile she released her advisor and ran into the waiting arms of her future husband.

Chapter Twelve

Toronto: 1999

Pouring himself another cup of coffee, Pearce takes a moment to digest the storyline. "Another happily-ever-after ending I presume?"

"Actually, yes. For the next three centuries, Khazaria did become a powerful Jewish Kingdom. In fact, so powerful, that it stopped the advance of Islam through the region. The Mohammedans were handed one of their greatest military defeats during that time."

"Documented?"

"Yes, fully documented. I told you, John, the information which I'm providing to you can all be verified. Islam still bears a strong hatred for the Khazars even though they no longer exist, except they currently try to infer that all the Ashkenazi Jews are nothing more than the Khazarim and therefore not truly Jews at all."

"And are they?" Pearce jumped on my statement.

"Are they what?

"Are they Khazarim and therefore not Jews?" he responded.

"In truth, through genetic testing it's estimated that perhaps thirty percent of the Ashkenazi are from Khazar stock. But even so, how would that make them any less Jewish? When is a Jew a Jew you should be asking?"

"And what is the answer to that?"

"You're a Jew when you live as a Jew, believe as a Jew and die as a Jew. So that makes the Khazarim as Jewish as anyone else that marched out of the Sinai desert. Just a little later in arriving at that destiny."

"And this Khazarian Empire, it's an accepted fact?"

"You will have to dig deep into the archives, but it's all there. Masked by centuries of alteration and distortion, but when you begin to strip away the varnish that's been applied, you will find the original text. A lot of this varnish is haphazardly applied anyway, barely concealing what they intended to hide forever."

"So why hasn't it been done before."

"Because no one has had me guiding them before. What's buried deep in my mind provides the map for you to search with. Remember, I have the memories, hence, you'll know where to look!"

"And what was all that about her ancestors being in the East a couple of centuries earlier? Why wouldn't she have known about that? Sounds a bit far-fetched to me!"

"She wouldn't have known because all communication with the descendants of that line had been cut off from the West. But she definitely knew about her ancestor in the sixth century having a Chinese wife. But the rabbis had forbidden anyone to talk about that particular ancestor. They went as far as cursing anyone that even spoke his name."

"So who was he?"

"He's another story. Leave it at that. Another place, another time, but definitely not today."

Pearce takes a sip of his coffee and is deep in thought. In his eyes, I can see that he is cogitating a question that would seal his belief in my stories. "So, if you described a battle, at a certain time and place, I would be able to verify it through historical records?"

"Of course! And you will even realize that unexplained recorded occurrences, become easily explained when they are put into their proper context."

"Can we do that now?"

"That's not a problem. Natronai, or Theodoric as he now called himself, proved to be a great military strategist."

The surprised look on Pearce's face is priceless.

"I bet you never believed that would be possible. Yes, the wuss as you called him, placed into a different environment, proved himself to be a most capable warrior and military leader."

"You're right; I didn't expect that."

"Neither did Charlemagne, but thirteen years after his arrival, Theodoric commanded his very own army, which proved to be just one more grave concern to a very nervous Catholic Church."

Saxony: 782 A.D.

Theodoric pulled the fox-fur collar of his mantle as high as it would go. He still shivered in spite of the thick woolen blanket wrapped snugly about his shoulders, long enough that it covered most of the leather box-saddle. Most men of these parts would not have been bothered by the negligible bite of the approaching autumn but even after all these years, Theodoric had not lost his desire for the dry desert heat of his homeland. The south of Frankia was hot but it certainly was not dry like Persia. Somehow the desert found a way to crawl under one's skin generating its own brand of warmth and comfort. It was times like these that he longed for it.

This province of Saxony could only be described in his own words as a land fit for thick skinned individuals, too stupid or too sluggardly consider moving south. He had often heard his brother-in-law, Charlemagne, describe the Viking pirates in that manner, but he always felt it more aptly applied to the people inhabiting this land.

It was no surprise that his own men did not suffer to any significant degree the same discomfort that plagued him. As descendants of Jews, the felt they should still have inherited some abhorrence to the cold but by now they had been living in this land for well over a thousand years and were as pale as their Gallic neighbors. With time, they had become more like the Franks than the Hebrews from which they sprang. Over the passing of a millennium much had changed and he considered himself bearing little resemblance to these rugged, stout men, with their hirsute bodies and narrow set eyes.

Always analyzing, a characteristic that his beloved Alda cherished in him most, he theorized that a lot of inbreeding must have occurred between these two races from opposite ends of the Mediterranean. Too many similarities currently existed with the populations of Tuscany and Iberia to be mere coincidence. Not to mention that the eyes now came in a wide assortment of colors. In a way it was refreshing. Shades of brown or black were all that primarily existed back home. It was why his own eye coloring was considered such a novelty. Dark eyes that merely saw and had very little to tell. Not like the myriad of stories that one could glean from the colorful eyes of this land.

And as he dwelt upon the shades that abound, one set of eyes came to mind, immediately erasing all others. As he thought about those ice blue eyes staring deeply into the depths of his being, he longed even more to be back in Narbonne. They were Alda's eyes, soft and gentle, beseeching him to return. It was not an exaggeration to suggest that he could spend hours just sitting, without saying a word, just staring calmly and serenely into those wonderful, beguiling eyes.

Nevertheless, words were never a problem for Alda and himself. Even in silence, they would say volumes to each other by the merest touch, or sideways glance. They had grown inseparable, totally dependent upon each other. The thought of life without the other would be a living death. They had become two people merged into one. Theirs was a love that blossomed from friendship and respect from the first day they had been thrust in that room together and it had grown with unprecedented vitality only to become the subject of much gossip within the courts and courtesans both far and wide.

One such tale told of a young princess who had fallen in love with a frog who one day came to swim in the ponds of her private gardens. Though no one else ever heard the frog speak, the young princess insisted that it was not a frog but a prince from a far off land who had been enchanted by a wicked sorceress. The love of the princess for this frog eventually broke the spell, and the prince was even more handsome than she could ever imagine. In some of the palaces, the tale was told with an additional line that said that even after the young princess married her enchanted prince, the people would still look upon him and could see nothing but a frog. But none would dare tell this version of the tale directly to Charlemagne, ever protective of his sister and as close as a brother to Theodoric.

On the other hand, the version that included the extra little derogatory line was actually a favorite of Alda's and Theodoric's. They laughed heartily whenever they heard it, for it was gratifying to know that they had something together that so few people could ever understand or appreciate. God had given them each the gift that they had desired most in the world and then blessed it further with the birth of their son, Isaac, who like his father bore a proper Frankish name to appease the people and was therefore officially called William in the court registers. He was born a year after they had consummated their marriage and he was a source of unlimited joy; a living testament to their boundless love. There had been other births since then but they had all died shortly afterwards; mysterious deaths that could never be fully explained. Some claimed it was the curse but his father had other suspicions. Ever since, Natronai surrounded his son with a constant guard of his most trusted men that never left young William's side. No royal court physician would be allowed near his son, only the Jewish physicians from Narbonne had that task.

Theodoric's thoughts now turned fully to his son. He remembered trying to explain to William why he had to go to the Northlands with Narbonne's standing army of four thousand men. It was not easy to explain to a twelve year old boy that if his father failed to return that he would then have to assume the role as the man of the house. In fact, it was an impossible thing to do! It was not that long ago that he said his farewells to his first son, Ahunai. Even now he agonized over that letter he had left behind. If he had been the man then that he was now he would have never resorted to such a cowardly way to present the reasons for his leaving.

He could taste the bitter gall at the back of his throat; his first wife and her father had definitely won that round. It was unlikely that Ahunai would ever get to read that letter, let alone know of it. His father would become a distant memory, like the fog that was quickly dissipating from the Saxon countryside; soon to become nonexistent under the rays of the pre-noon sun. It was his own fault; he had let it happen. So why was he now in the middle of nowhere, breaking the heart of a second son who was more dear to him than life itself?

If there was any truth at all in this madness, it was that he owed it to William to come back alive. No son should have to live with only fragile, tattered memories of their father. He could not allow this inhospitable wasteland of shallow marsh and seething bogs, east of Friesland, deny him the privilege of ever holding his son again.

Damn Charlemagne! Damn him and his never ending campaigns to bring enlightenment to the barbarians. Who cared what the poor peasants of this flood plain chose to believe? Life was hard enough, trying to scrounge a meager existence from the land between the rains, the snows, and the floods. This was a land totally at the mercy of the North Sea. Whether it was Jesus or Woton who granted this wretched people a moment of mercy and respite in their miserable lives, what did it matter?

Any forays the Saxons made into Burgundia were done so only to secure food for their own survival. Surely a means of curtailing these raids by providing an exchange of supplies in return could have been arranged. It did not make sense that Charlemagne could be both fanatical in his pursuit of spreading Catholicism to the uncivilized world and at the same time have openly welcomed the despised Satan, as some bishops now referred to him, into his family. It was totally illogical but then Natronai knew that logic rarely applied to religion.

The thought of his own presence, married to the King's sister, ruler of his own Jewish city-state, and at the same time assisting in the spread of Christianity to a people who bitterly refused it for over three centuries had to be the culmination of the most illogical life ever lived by one man. To further add insult, he considered himself to be a philosopher as well. What bitter irony he thought. Surely God was laughing at him now; a philosopher with a sword, writing about the humanities in blood. Absolutely scandalous!

The men of Narbonne marched rhythmically to the sound of the beating drums. Their leather armor was poor protection against the great iron war axes of the Saxons. With a single blow they could cleave the wooden shields carried by the Frankish armies and just as easily separate a man's head from his shoulders at the same time. The heavy two-handed long swords hung from their belts and in their free hands they carried the long spears that had been handed down since Roman times.

At least five hundred of his men were promoted to the elitist ranks. In their hands they carried not the awkward pikes like the others but instead the beautifully carved long bows of Moslem design. On their backs were slung the square, box-like quiver of arrows so often seen in the Empire of the East. To be an archer was a most sought after position in any army. Whether an archer or a foot soldier, they majority wore leather helmets that hung down below the nape of the neck, as few were able to afford a helmet made of metal. It had once been calculated that for a man to go to battle outfitted in the best there was, chain metal armor, bronze buckler, helmet and grieves, would cost nearly forty head of cattle. Narbonne had its wealthy citizens but most of those had bought their way out of serving in the army.

Theodoric was grateful for having a herd so large that he could easily afford that much. As he glanced at his men, most under-equipped and over-burdened, he wondered how many would not be making the long march home with him. If only he had a unit of cavalry, like the Muslim armies maintained. But the horses of Europe were poor examples of equine flesh, bred from a long line of draught horses that were nothing more than plodders, sure of foot but slow of pace.

The Mohammedans selfishly guarded their own horses, refusing to let but a token few fall into the hands of a very small group of select infidels. Good relations with Al-Mansur allowed him to obtain a half dozen of these Arabians that he spread amongst his officers. Give him a horse unit like they had in Baghdad and he would show these Franks what warfare was all about. War in this part of the world resembled nothing better than a brawl, where combatants lined up against each other and slugged it out until only one of them was left standing. Luck was the greater part of strategy and assurance of victory was usually obtained by having the larger number of infantry to sacrifice and absorb the losses.

In that respect, Charlemagne had the greatest reserves to call upon, summoning all the princes of the Frankish kingdoms to come with their armies and join him in his trail of conquest through the Northern provinces. Already they had lain to waste the land of the Bavarians but Theodoric was weary of this new challenge. The uncertainty of the land, sometimes solid, other times alluvial flood plain, added an element that had not been encountered previously. Too many times his men had wasted precious hours pulling the wagons out of the ruts their wheels had dug a foot deep into the loose soil. Every cautious step meant a further delay in a war which had already kept him away from his beloved Alda for far too long.

The advance scouts having returned now jogged in their heavy leather outfits to the rear of the army, where Theodoric had taken up position. They informed him that several armies under Frankish ensigns were camped about a mile ahead. Theodoric was relieved. It had been a constant worry that he and his men would be ambushed along the way, long before he joined with the other units, but now it appeared he would be able to relax soon under the shelter of his brothers at arms. Word quickly passed through the troops that they had arrived at their intended destination. Now all that remained was to engage the enemy, defeat them and then prepare for the return to Narbonne. Charlemagne's campaign of empire building would soon be at an end and as far as Theodoric's soldiers were concerned, it was not a moment too soon. What place would they ultimately have in the king's Christian Empire? They were well aware of their tenuous position. As long as Theodoric remained a favorite of Charlemagne's they were safe, but how long would that be? None could say if the sons would inherit the tolerance of their fathers.

Having his army prepare camp, Theodoric rode towards the main tent at the center of the Frankish encampment. He had been hoping to find Charlemagne, but upon entering the field headquarters he could only find three of Charlemagne's generals present. Nodding his head, Theodoric acknowledged Adelges, Gailo and Worad. "I have come looking for Charlemagne," he informed them.

Worad looked up and down at the recent arrival and then spat in the other direction. "What need you be seeing Charlemagne about."

"It is a matter of concern only to the two of us. Have you forgotten that I am not answerable to you Worad? Best you remember that next to our King, I am second in command." Theodoric knew that he was presenting a false bravado that would probably not fool Charlemagne's generals for very long. Unless he could force them to back down quickly they would be looking for an argument; anything to pour fuel onto a constantly burning fire. Though by marriage he was truly next in line after the king, such would only be the case until such time that Charlemagne's sons were old enough to be designated as heirs apparent. What little authority he did possess was whittled away constantly by his detractors. It was one of the reasons that Theodoric had his men set up their camp a quarter mile from the closest allied troops. The distance provided a buffer between two forces that cared very little for each other even though they fought under the same flags.

Most Franks had never been to Narbonne but such a minor detail was easily overlooked when it came to formulating an opinion regarding the Narbonnaise. The Archbishop Aribert had been very active in transplanting his vicious prejudices into the devout minds of the Frankish people. Perhaps it was the way it always was and always would be. Theodoric couldn't spend any more time contemplating the source of the antipathy between his forces and the others. It was his duty to report to the generals' encampment and await the arrival of Charlemagne. And duty always took precedent over personal dislikes.

"Did you hear that gentlemen?" Worad guffawed, "The frog prince wants us to recognize him as second in command. I say we teach him a thing or two about seniority in our ranks. "

"I would suggest that you think twice regarding any rescission of my orders. No matter how long you may have served your king, and no matter how loyal you are to him and his cause, you had better remember one thing, he and I are family through marriage. If you choose to forget that fact then I cannot be responsible for any of the consequences that might follow."

Again he was bluffing. Truth was that Charlemagne would never raise a finger against his generals. If any were worthy of being family it was those three men. Over the years they had fought in countless campaigns, suffering their share of wounds all in defense of Charlemagne's realm. No one could ever question their loyalty. The King was well aware of their devotion and had rewarded them handsomely. Why would Charlemagne ever even think about handing the reins of the combined forces over to him, an imported prince from an ancient prophecy? These generals could far outstrip him in command given the opportunity to prove themselves.

Certainly, Theodoric could pride himself in having been an apt pupil in the art of military warfare as fought in the Orient but the barbarians of Europe conducted themselves by a completely different set of rules of conflict. As well versed as he was in stratagem, it was of little use in a land without proper horses. Theodoric could only hope that they were not aware of how truly feeble his position was within the kingdom.

"So what do you want, Theodoric?" Adelges grew steadily impatient with the foreigner who pretended to be next to the throne. "We do not need your assistance against the Saxons. I have no idea why your brother-in-law bothered to send for you. Your kind should stay in Narbonne where we don't have to be bothered by the likes of you."

"Perhaps he requested me to come because he had so little faith in your ability to lead after the campaigns in the south that you three were responsible for conducting," retaliated Theodoric. He regretted making that comment as soon as it left his lips but it was too late to retract. It was a sore spot easily picked upon by the prince of Narbonne but one which only festered the relationship between him and the generals even further. It was now four years since that disastrous march into Spain. Al-Mansur had requested that his allies, the Franks, help put down an insurrection led by an Omayyad pretender to the throne, who had been an affliction to the major cities of the peninsula.

Toledo, Granada and Cordoba suddenly stopped sending tribute to Baghdad and instead anointed the rebel Emir as the Caliph of an independent Spain. The request from Al-Mansur arrived through the multitude of traders that navigated the sea between Narbonne and the Muslim world. Theodoric was compelled to deliver the message to Charlemagne but consistently counseled against attacking the rebel forces. He was even so bold as to suggest to Charlemagne that to do so would only serve to install himself as an official puppet to Al Mansur, but the Frankish King would have no part of Theodoric's implication. 'This was a matter of honor," the Frankish king insisted.

He had made the deal long ago, sealed it personally by marrying Al-Mansur's daughter and he would not dishonor himself or his family by turning his back upon his father-in-law. It was to be a fatal and foolish mistake in retrospect. Theodoric was well aware of the Saracen battle strengths and knew that even if by the rarest of chances the Franks happened to be evenly matched against the Muslims it would be of no consequence once Charlemagne's men had entered the

Spanish plain.

Crossing the Alps on foot, there was not enough strength to muster from the men to repulse an attack from the Emir, who had been waiting for them in the foothills of the mountains. The ensuing battle proved to be an ultimate disaster for the king of the Franks. Out-maneuvered and harassed by a disciplined cavalry, Charlemagne's men were quickly routed and sent fleeing. The combined efforts of a raging storm and the pursuing Muslims was enough to send a resounding message of defeat. It was almost too easy for the Spanish archers to pick off with ease those that trailed too far behind the main body of Franks.

Years later, Charlemagne would be overheard to comment that he obtained nothing of value from that mission into the Iberian heartland, except for the blessed event of his Arab wife bearing him twins while he had been away. As for his generals, they could find nothing but shame in recalling their flight before the Saracens.

"Are you suggesting that it was entirely our fault that we were routed in our attempt to free the peninsula?" Rising in pitch, Worad's voice betrayed a nagging guilt that had followed the general around all these years.

"I am suggesting nothing other than the fact that no one should ignore nor slap the hand of someone who offers to help."

"And how is it you can help us," Gailo inquired. "After all, it was you who undermined us when we initiated our war against the Saracens. Had you spent more time in aiding our cause than criticizing our efforts, perhaps we would have fared better than we did."

"The invasion had been ill conceived. By not considering the disadvantages of the terrain, it was virtually impossible to take the Spanish mainland. We didn't require an army. Instead we needed a navy. An attack by sea would have met with better success."

"So where was this great wisdom when we required it." Worad's hand crept slowly to the hilt of his sword, guided instinctively by his desire to force Theodoric into a challenge.

Theodoric pursed his lips into a faint smile. His eyes did not fail to see the eager fingers of the general caressing the carved handle by his waist. "Wisdom is like the wind. It blows about constantly but who is able to catch the wind?"

Adelges scratched his head. "And what is that supposed to mean?"

"It means whatever you wish it to mean. I did not come all this way from Narbonne to argue with you good gentlemen. My army is here to fight. Either we are comrades in arms or we are destined to return to our homes without bloodying our swords. I shall not force our acceptance upon you. That is for Charlemagne to undertake. Personally I agree, you are correct, I would rather be home with my wife than fighting battles which are of no benefit or concern to me!"

"Yes, that is right. Of what concern is God's work to you, Jew? Go back to your Jew-loving wife and let us not have to soil the banner of good Christians with the blood of unbelievers for allies."

Suddenly a voice thundered from behind where they were gathered. It's very sound forced them to attention. "Is it true that my ears have heard such tripe from you, Worad? Am I to be forever burdened by childish antics from my generals? What plague is this that has so cursed me from battle to battle? When shall I be rid of such abysmal behavior?" Striding towards his general, Charlemagne shook with unmitigated fury. His mailed hand shot out like a cobra, striking Worad squarely across the chin. The force of the blow toppled the smaller man like a tree falling in the forest. "That is for insulting my sister! If I should ever hear you talk of her in a derogatory manner again, I will have your tongue cut out. Friend or not, is that understood?"

Barely able to pull himself onto one knee, Worad grunted his assent as he rotated his neck in an effort to clear his head. "Forgive me my Lord. You of all people know that I meant the Lady Alda no ill will."

"Very well then," Charlemagne's responded in a most forgiving manner as he helped raise his general to his feet by placing a powerfully built hand underneath Worad's shoulder. "Do not let me hear of it again. And now I would think that an apology is in order to our good friend, Theodoric. Is that not so?"

The generals all uttered their apologies halfheartedly but they were enough to satisfy their king. Charlemagne learned long ago that pride was both a strength as well as a weakness. To achieve greatness a man had to discover the balance between the two.

"Now what is this all about?"

Adelges was first to respond. "My Lord, there exists a reluctance amongst the men to fight alongside the soldiers from Narbonne. They consider their presence here an ill omen. The Church has already advised us against letting them fight as our allies and although I do not accept all that the Archbishop had to say, I cannot entirely say that I disagree with him. An army of Jews fighting under the Christian banner is reprehensible. It is a mockery of all that we hold dear. How can our Savior be pleased with us if we let unbelievers spread his Good News. The inherent lie that is the Jews birth rite would only serve to confuse His message of peace.

And Theodoric represents an even greater threat to your own authority, my Liege. If he is as he claims to be, a direct descendant of good King David, then how can we spread the word of Christ who clearly stated that he was the last of that hereditary line? Does this not imply that our Savior was wrong? Does this not also make Theodoric of higher nobility than yourself?"

"You always were the shrewd one, Adelges," Charlemagne mused. "I think that you have tried to antagonize me with your little game of rhetorical questions. I have a better question for you. If Theodoric stems from a line of higher nobility than myself, then so what? I am king of the Franks, not he." A wide mocking grin spread across Charlemagne's handsome face. "It matters only if I felt insecure in my own being. I do not. Likewise, the presence of the Jews amongst us is only threatening if we feel threatened and insecure in our own beliefs. If this is found to be the case, then perhaps it would be better to re-examine why it is we believe what we believe. Would not the rest of you agree?"

"I for one, your Majesty do not feel threatened by the Jews but is it not more important what our men choose to believe and not ourselves?" Gailo stretched his open hands placatingly towards his king.

"Yes, I tend to agree," Adelges responded. "Above all else, we must consider the attitude of the men. Whatever should upset them would ultimately reduce their fighting effectiveness. We must not allow anything to confuse them before the battle. I for one feel that it is imperative not to include Theodoric's men within our ranks. It would prove too difficult for our own men to accept unbelievers fighting our cause. Call it superstition, or the foolish rantings of old women but I feel that such an inclusion would be ultimately detrimental!"

"Is that how you all feel?" Charlemagne looked from face to face of his generals. As they nodded in agreement he suddenly realized how little he believed in the holiness of his mission. In the rivalry between monarch and church, he had always considered himself to be supreme. For the first time he realized the degree to which Rome had made inroads into his once heathen nation. Glancing away from his generals, he looked dejectedly at Theodoric. "Come and take a walk with me brother. We must talk."

A bitter and biting wind scurried across the rugged coastline bearing with it the salty brine of the northern sea. His men shivered against the cold, huddled beneath tattered blankets, as they sat gathered around struggling fires. Pacing along the delta shoreline, Theodoric privately wrestled with his own inner feelings. Had he and his men covered hundreds of miles only to find themselves in a losing battle with the elements upon some distant shore by the mouth of a river that they did not even know the name of? The locals didn't even seem to know the name, referring to it as the Weser, meaning nothing more than water.

He would have sooner been on the march heading south towards warmer climes and eventually to his hometown of Narbonne, but to do so without explanation to his troops would only serve to invite mutiny. They had come to fight, to do themselves proud and win themselves honor but none of them could even remotely guess why they had been placed in reserve and their entire force sent on a forced march into the lowlands further north.

Theodoric thought it better to let them speculate as to the true purpose of their mission rather than try to convince them with any of the excuses that he had already provided for himself as alibis. These were proud men and proud men do not take lightly to being ostracized. On their own, they could draw conclusions of secret missions and believe that every minute they suffered under the cruel and harsh elements was for some crucial and essential purpose.

In truth, Charlemagne had convinced Natronai of the importance of avoiding internal divisions amongst the generals and the rank and file, during their little stroll away from the encampment. He knew that it was not Charlemagne's desire to send him away from the field of battle but that did not make it hurt any less. The king expressed his desire for the army from Narbonne to remain out of sight for the next few days, while he and his army engaged in their attack upon the Saxons.

Once victory was secured, he was confident that the Jewish forces could then reappear without any dire consequences. The generals would have been assured that their good fortune was ordained by an entirely Christian God and their men would be too busy celebrating their victory to pay any attention to the return of the Narbonnaise.

Such a plan may have been satisfactory for the Frankish King but it did little to placate Theodoric. As he forced his men on the march north his mind would wander endlessly in the other direction, taking him back on a route south to where his Alda eagerly awaited his return. It would have been so easy. Fate may have even ordained that Charlemagne would fall in battle and suddenly, he, Theodoric would be crowned as the new king of the Franks. It was entirely possible, even plausible. But he knew it could never be allowed to be anything more than a daydream because Theodoric knew that its eventuality would not be permitted to happen. Forces within Frankia and the Church would see to it that it never happened.

No, he would do as Charlemagne had suggested but with one difference. He would never let his men know that they had been ordered away from the battle. Better to make them believe that their true mission was to engage a reported Saxon troop movement coming from the north to reinforce their initial assault force. The report was fabricated, as was the size of this supposedly lethal auxiliary force, which they would never encounter. As concerned as Charlemagne might have been for his own men's opinions, so too was Theodoric concerned that the Narbonnaise force preserves its dignity as well. Honor must always come before death. He was their king, not Charlemagne and upon his shoulders rested that mantle of responsibility.

The time had come for Theodoric to begin moving his forces south to meet up with what had been calculated to be a victorious Frankish army by this time. It would take a further day and a half to return to the plains east of Aachen where Charlemagne would be waiting. What spoils would be left for his men after their week absence would be minimal but they would have to suffice. Whatever trinkets could be removed from the dead bodies of fallen Saxons would be better than returning home with nothing to show. Theodoric released a heavy sigh as his men assembled for the long march south. The campaign had unfolded miserably. To war for God and country; only in his particular case it was for neither.

The return march was shrouded in an air of anticipation. Envisioning the ensuing battles, his men broke repeatedly into a medley of war hymns, which raised their spirits. Still believing that they were still to encounter the Saxon reinforcements along the way, they prepared themselves emotionally for the anticipated encounter. Theodoric's mind stretched back to a time when he was Natronai, only to see a world as perceived by his ancestor Bustenai, only to hear the resounding notes as they fell upon the ears of Zerubbabel, an even earlier ancestor, leading the return march to Jerusalem from Babylon. And then finally he was David, marching his men against the sea-faring Philistines as soon as they had disposed of his arch-rival, Saul. So many centuries had separated them yet all these memories were still alive and embodied in his soul. When his men sang, they sang for him, they sang for their own ancestors, and they sang for a heritage that weaved through the millennia like the cord on a rug weaver's loom. He looked heavenward and prayed for a battle still left unfought, a unit of Saxons still unscathed by Charlemagne's massive might. Mists filled his eyes as the rhythm girded his loins, his horse prancing to the steady beat. "God, let there be a battle, let there be a song for Jews to sing in the present and not of the past! Let my men have their moment of glory."

Then, almost as if in answer to his prayers, horse and rider came darting from the thick cover of the forest ahead and drove in a maddening rush directly towards their king.

"My Lord, my Lord," the frenzied voice hailed, "They are down by the river!"

"Whom, Absolom? Whom are you talking about?"

Halting just several strides short of his prince, the rider dismounted and bolted the remaining distance to Theodoric's side. "Everyone! Charlemagne, the Franks, the Bavarians, the Saxons, absolutely everyone!"

"What is Charlemagne doing? He shouldn't be this far north! Especially by the river. This part of the Weser is nothing but bog."

"He is caught my Lord. His army lies between the arm of the river with the Saxons to the north and the Bavarians to the south. I can only think that he pursued the Saxons northward after engaging them. Those few cohorts of Bavarians that had not yet been vanquished were tracking him all this time."

"I cannot believe that Charlemagne had fallen for such a ruse. He was never one to be so easily ensnared. Assemble the troops. Gird them for battle! Today we fight for God and Narbonne!"

Positioning his forces behind the wall of trees that stood like a monumental blockade to the east of the Weser River, Theodoric and his officers watched the careening battle from the safety of a concealed knoll.

"Shall we engage the enemy yet sir," inquired young Solomon Cornebut, somewhat disgruntled.

"Not yet, horn blower," Theodoric replied. "When the time is ready I know that God shall give me a sign."

"But my Lord, the Franks are taking heavy losses. If we do not act soon there will be none left to save!"

"Not yet!"

"I do not wish to question you either," Absolom interrupted, "but do we have a plan, my Lord?"

Theodoric cast a penetrating stare at his officers. "All these years and still you do not know me. Have I not led you wisely that you heap doubts upon me? Am I the only one to trust in my own abilities and in the power of the Almighty?"

They shook their heads like scolded children until Absolom spoke up. "We do not doubt you, my Lord, but we must know your intentions if we are to enter this fray."

"We wait."

The shock waves reverberated from officer to officer. Why was he being so secretive? Had they not earned his trust repeatedly in the thirteen years they had served him. To sit idly while the Franks were suffering terribly in the combined pincer movements of two barbarian armies was more than they could tolerate. Was he afraid? Could this be what stilled his hand from combat?

"Enough of your pathetic stares! Must I be surrounded by doubters? Is there not one amongst you who can perceive my intentions?" He looked one by one into their blank faces. "Alas, I live in a land of unschooled heathens. Is there no one here that has even looked into the books of the great military masters?" Again, he saw nothing but blank stares of ignorance. "Oh, woe upon woe! If only Charlemagne had taken the time to study the past he would not be in his current predicament. Scipio...look to Scipio if you seek answers to your questions; Scipio, greatest of all Roman generals. He knew each situation before it even transpired. Once he was engaged in such a battle. The Carthaginians were arrayed before him and began to fall back as soon as the encounter began. He pursued them for miles until the enemy had crossed the Seine. At that moment the Carthaginians suddenly turned and made their stand. Fresh Carthaginian troops which had been concealed in the hills suddenly appeared and stood to the rear of the Romans. Scipio would appear to have fallen into the same trap that our good King now finds himself in, save that the Romans did not have to contend with standing knee deep in the swamp. But unlike this situation, Scipio was no fool. He knew his enemy better than they knew themselves! By carefully studying the history of Carthage's military conquests he knew that the Carthaginians frequently used the ploy of feigning a retreat at the start of battle. This apparent rout was always combined with the concealment of troops along the path of retreat.

Knowing this, Scipio had only attacked with one third of his army. Of the remaining two thirds, one half he sent out the previous day with orders to circle behind the enemy and to stay behind them until they stopped their staged fall back and the other half were given orders to follow him but to stay several hours behind the main attacking force. The rest, as you know was history. Scipio went on to burn Carthage and Rome dominated the world."

"So, we will split up and attack," Absolom assumed was the plan of the lesson. "Shall we do it immediately?"

"It is not yet time. I want Solomon to take the archers and occupy a line on the north bank of the river. As soon as the Saxons are within range he is to blow his horn which will signal the rest of us to charge northward from a position south of the Bavarians. I will lead all those on horseback, as few as we might be, in a mounted attack, to be followed by the infantry who will quickly dispatch the scattered enemy. We will then continue our cavalry charge and pass straight through the Franks in order to engage the now harassed Saxons. I know that most of the horses in our possession our not much for speed but I think what they lack in fleetness of foot we will easily make up for with the element of surprise. Are there any questions?"

"Yes," Solomon responded. "How am I to get the archers close enough without setting the Saxons upon us?"

"That is what we are waiting for," Theodoric waved his forefinger omnipotently. "In order to be successful we must wait for the last of the Saxons to cross the river onto the south bank, so that a fast moving body of water lies between our archers and them. They will not be able to turn and disarm us because the water acts as a natural barrier. If they should be foolhardy enough to reenter the water then the archers will make easy sport of their stupidity."

"How can we be certain that they will all cross over to the south bank?" The surrounding officers nodded in agreement with Solomon's question.

"Why shouldn't they when they see the Franks about to be crushed?"

"But that means that we have to allow the Franks to sustain injuries in the thousands while we sit hidden in this forest. It galls me to think of what kind of men we have become to allow such an occurrence. I say we enter the fray now and save our allies before it is too late."

Theodoric wrapped his arm around Solomon's shoulders and squeezed him tightly until Solomon squirmed from the pressure. "Solomon, oh Solomon, have I not loved you like a son? Have I ever counseled you wrongly? You are still a young lad, full of youthful enthusiasm and dreams of chivalry Trust me now, if you ever want to see your homeland again. You do not fully understand the futility of encountering the Saxons at this moment. The advantage of the terrain is theirs. Not only will they annihilate Charlemagne's forces but ours as well if we should do as you brazenly suggest. Hot heads do not win wars. We shall move to action when I say and not a moment before! Make sure that is understood by the rest of you."

"I cannot say that I agree with you, my Lord but I will follow your lead as always." Solomon bowed in apology then gave a sharp salute to his prince.

"I ask no more of you than that. Do us proud and I promise you we shall be returning home in triumph. I rely on you, Solomon Cornebut, to blow your horn precisely at the moment the last Saxon sets foot on the south bank. Your role is the most important than any others. Do that and God shall do the rest for us. I salute you all. Now let us muster the men and prepare to move into positions." Theodoric vaulted into his saddle and drew his sword so that it pointed skyward with the hilt but a few scant inches before his face. "To Victory!"

"To Victory," they shouted in return.

Like a demon possessed, Theodoric and his small cavalry unit charged into the rear of the Bavarians upon hearing the long blast trumpeted on Solomon's horn. They had waited for hours, patiently patting the broad necks of their mounts while but a few hundred feet behind them the body of their infantry stirred uncomfortably as they lay face down upon the cool, moist grass of the forest apron. Like the raging waters of a flood, the Narbonnaise were upon the enemy before the Bavarians were even aware they were being attacked. Meanwhile, a steady shower of arrows launched from the longbows under Solomon's command rained down heavily upon the equally surprised Saxons.

The battle weary Franks who thus far were being decimated by the barbarians, discovered a new well of vitality upon which to draw, and their swords began to sing as they were sunk into the bare chests of their adversaries. Where once Charlemagne's men were falling to the heavy war axes of the Saxons, it was now heathen blood which poured in rivulets to mix with the chilled marsh waters. The pendulum of battle had swung completely.

Arrow after arrow found its mark burrowing deeply into a Saxon warrior, causing their tribal chief, Aufred, to flee from the battlefield, as he attempted to escape under the cover of panic and confusion. A terror fell upon the leaderless barbarians and they threw down their weapons in great numbers as they vaulted from the flood plain in pursuit of their fleeing chieftain. Using both javelin and bow, the Saxons were easy targets for the Frank and Narbonnaise marksmen. Thousands fell before they could reach the beckoning arms of the forest cover. Others were hunted for miles until they collapsed from exhaustion only to be decapitated by their pursuers' thirsty blades.

Unlike the Saxons, the Bavarians had no direction in which to run. Theodoric's horsemen charged into the center of the enemy while simultaneously his foot soldiers completely surrounded them, cutting off any opportunity to escape. By the strict Bavarian code of warfare, there was no choice but to stand their ground and fight to the death. Using his steed as a living battering ram, Theodoric waded into their midst with war mace and broad sword flailing to and fro as he chopped the enemy down like so much tall grass. One after the other fell to either blade or spiked club, crushing their skulls and cleaving their collar bones until metal clashed against hard unyielding bone.

Theodoric submitted to the exhilarating surge of the bloodlust, overpowered by the pounding in his head and chest that refused to let him sense the weariness of his arms nor the bruising blows of enemy clubs that attempted to knock him from his mount. There comes a time in every battle when sword and man become as one; neither knowing where the other starts nor ends, until they are one and the same, an engine of pure destruction; a force that transcends both good and evil, dealing in nothing more than death.

Sensing an aura of invulnerability, Theodoric plunged further into the melee, watching in slow motion as combatant after combatant fell about him. A trick of the mind, a plateau beyond pain and suffering as the euphoria pushes the warrior beyond normal limits until he is able to perform superhuman feats of strength and endurance. It is a level from which heroes are created and legends are born. And precisely at that moment, all eyes are riveted to the mighty one who now has become the singular focus.

Just as spontaneously, the enemy becomes consumed with the stratagem of stopping but one man. As if the death of that one hero would result in the total deflation of their enemy's strength. It is a natural thought because one man had assumed a value and importance far in excess of normal rationalization. One such archer stood firm in his resolve, in spite of the inward crush of his beleaguered colleagues, sending a single shaft whining through the air towards the invincible Theodoric. That was the moment that time had stopped and all the combatants froze, focused only upon the iron tip of the missile hurtling towards Charlemagne's champion.

The arrowhead cleaved through the chainmail garment, slicing neatly into the leather jerkin. It was a death blow and the light of life quickly faded from Charlemagne's forces. The Bavarians cheered in anticipation of Theodoric's falling from his saddle. The arrow struck with a shattering force that bolted Theodoric upright in the saddle and if not for the stirrups he would have probably been toppled from his horse. The Franks, Bavarians and Saxons stood motionless, swords raised and eyes transfixed. Not even the Narbonnaise could react to the turn of events and rally to their stricken leader. Everyone on the battlefield had become rooted to the shifting soil, immovable, paralyzed with either dread or anticipation.

Inexplicably, the shaft of the arrow stopped in its forward progression, quivering uncontrollably and then simply dangling from where it had become imbedded in the leather jerkin. Theodoric looked down at the limp projectile and tore it from the leather, then raised it over his head while he released a blood-chilling scream of triumph. All that anyone could think of was that they had witnessed a miracle. Even the enemy was stunned into silence by the supernatural occurrence.

Sensing that it was God's will, the Franks turned and fell upon the disillusioned barbarians, whom were easily routed, offering little if no resistance after what had transpired. Jabbing, slicing, impaling, the Franks dispatched the Saxons and Bavarians to their vaunted Valhalla without compassion and certainly without mercy.

"El Makhiri, El Makhiri," the Narbonnaise shouted repeatedly as their victory cry. God had given them a sign in the presence of his servant, the Makhir Natronai. Even the Franks took up the war cry. "Almyeri, Almyeri." Over and over they screamed the name as they slaughtered their enemies. "Almyeri!" It was the best they could do in pronouncing that strange and foreign tongue, but nonetheless it warmed Theodoric's heart to hear the adulation in their shouts. For the first time the Franks had hailed him as more than the foreign devil that had impinged on their world. When he could no longer find an enemy to engage, Theodoric rode to the high point of the plain and waved his blood soaked sword over his head in a sign of victory. The cheer that went up was deafening as Frank and Jew broke into triumphant praise.

Charlemagne rode to Theodoric's side and in an act of extreme honor removed his gold buttoned cloak and placed it over Theodoric's shoulders. Leaning over the saddle, Theodoric embraced his brother-in-law. It was then he realized just how much his chest hurt beneath the stone medallion he wore about his neck.

Several days passed before all the spoils of their victory could be divided fairly amongst the men. Raiding the nearby towns, the soldiers obtained food, wine and women. For one of the few times in their lives, Frank and Jew shared a meal from the same pot and laughed to the same joke told around a common fire. The victory served to unite all of the Frankish allies beneath a single banner. For the time being they were willing to overlook their differences and enjoy their camaraderie in battle. As they drank, they sang, and they sang an ode to the might of the Almyeri.

"Do you hear that, brother? Already they have made you into a living legend. The song of the Almyeri has become part of Frankish heritage overnight." Charlemagne clasped his arm jubilantly around Theodoric. "But I am curious. Was it magic? I must know how it was that the arrow failed to penetrate your chest."

"I thought you believed in the hand of God, brother?"

"I do. But I also believe that sometimes we can help steer the hand." Charlemagne's eyes danced with insatiable curiosity.

"If you must know, it was by the merest of inches that the arrow struck precisely upon the stone about my neck. A fraction either way and victory could have just as easily been defeat." Theodoric waved the incident casually aside with a back stroke of his hand.

"If it was that simple, brother, then let me wear the stone. I will at least appreciate the luck it manifests if you cannot."

"You are right. The stone does brings more than luck. It has protected me numerous times in a multitude of ways. That it has certain powers cannot be denied."

Charlemagne looked keenly at the inscribed piece of stone that hung by a leather thong around Theodoric's neck. Holding it in the palm of his hand he sensed an unexplained pulsation and quickly released it. "I have seen this stone since the first day we met in Baghdad but in all that time I have never asked you about it. It looks as if there are runes engraved into it. Normally, something as unusual as this is would have prompted a question from me immediately."

"Believe it or not, this stone is the one true sign of heritage. Neither my uncle, Anan ben David nor my cousin Judah Zakkai has anything like it in their possession. But if this object confers the right to be king then how is it that I am here and those two are still engaged in a contest of wills to determine who rightfully leads the Jewish community of Persia?" Theodoric laughed but the bitter taste of his comments burned uneasily in the back of his mouth. "This stone is one of twelve remnants of the original Ten Commandments brought down from the mountain by Moses. Those aren't runes, they are letters inscribed by the finger of God!"

A gasp of astonishment escaped from Charlemagne's open mouth. The King reached out and held the stone more firmly this time, as he attempted vainly to decipher the inscription. "This has been touched by the finger of God?" His comment was both statement and question made in awe of the worn rectangular stone.

"Yes, by the finger of God and by every one of my ancestors from the time of Moses to my father who preceded me. There is far more than a mere chunk of lime-granite. That is why, when the council of Baghdad requested that I leave the stone behind for my successor, I did not comply and sailed away before they would become aware of my deception."

Charlemagne listened intently, then pursing his lips he nodded his head in agreement. "You did right, brother. The shard of rock can be no one's but yours. Too often we sacrifice our birth rite in order to appease the other powers that be. But there exists no higher authority than the Lord and on that battlefield he demonstrated to both ally and enemy alike that you were his chosen instrument. I am envious of your anointing, Theodoric."

"I am forever at your disposal, your majesty. Upon this earthly plain I am your servant." Theodoric desperately tried to appease the Frankish king lest he see him as a threat to his own throne. "The Lord has no other intentions for me to be other than what I already am."

Charlemagne laughed as he firmly clasped Theodoric's shoulder affectionately. "I think you have misunderstood me, brother. I have no doubt of your loyalty. It is all right to serve two masters, as long as God, Almighty, is one and I the other. What I think I was trying to tell you and obviously I was not too successful was that I am in your debt. I wish to reward you. I lost two generals and four counts on that battlefield. I know that you did not get on to well with Adelges and Gailo but they were good men; knew exactly what they were doing in the command of men. That's a rare talent that I admire in my commanders. You have that ability, Theodoric. Those men singing your praises in their odes have seen that special quality. I need you!"

"I am honored, my Lord but I fear that I cannot accept. I am prince of Narbonne and as such, my people need me. I cannot perform both duties equally well. In time of need I will always be at your side but I cannot be there permanently." The sad expression in Theodoric's eyes conveyed his regrets without further comment.

"Well, you would have surprised me if you had said anything different," Charlemagne struck his chest in feigned disappointment. "We are both kings, Theodoric. Our duty lies with our people above all else. You are a good prince. The people of Narbonne have a lot to be proud of. I will have to look carefully amongst my officers and see who is worthy of a promotion. But how then can I best reward you?"

Theodoric jumped at the opportunity to name his own reward. Having thought of absolutely nothing else for two days, he quickly responded to the king's appeal. "I ask nothing for myself, my Lord. All I seek is assurances for my people. That will be reward enough."

Cocking his head sideways, the puzzled look upon Charlemagne's face revealed that he did not quite understand the prince's request. "Assurances of what, brother?"

"For three days now I have heard nothing but the screams of the prisoners being executed down by the river..."

"So what of it, Theodoric? They were offered a choice. Be baptized or be beheaded. If they chose to refuse the enlightenment of Jesus, then their deaths are upon their hands, not ours."

Theodoric rested his forehead in the palm of his hand and momentarily closed his eyes.

"My Lord, over four thousand chose not to be baptized, clinging to their beliefs in Woton. Already the river is red with their blood as they willingly stretch their necks beneath the executioner's axe. How can we be right about this when both you and I believe in a merciful God?"

"It is not the Saxons you are concerned about, my friend." Charlemagne sensed the deep hurt swelling within his brother-in-law's soul.

"You are a wise king. My men choose not to be baptized either, Charlemagne. Is this to be our fate sometime in the future? Are we deluding ourselves in believing we are different from the Saxons?"

"Do not be absurd! These are barbarians, heathens, and pagans! They refuse to accept God. My God, your God, our God. As long as I live, no one shall ever lay a hand upon your people." Charlemagne's anger seethed with conviction.

"Then I hope that you have some arrangement with God to live forever," Theodoric replied sarcastically. "I am afraid that is the only way I would ever be fully assured of my people's wellbeing. You know yourself that you have repeatedly been an obstacle to your own church's intent to forbid slaves from adopting Judaism if that be their master's religion. Why would they cease their efforts after your death?"

Charlemagne had never thought too much about it before. He had always been there to protect the needs of the Narbonnaise against such men as Aribert. How was he to know and feel the fear of Theodoric's people when he had placed himself so far above the papal authority? "What is it you would have me do?"

"All I seek is some means by which the rights and privileges of my people can be legally entrenched within the laws of the land so that no future king can take away that which we have earned. Can this be done? Assurances of hereditary land rights, basic freedoms, even tax privileges. Whatever can be arranged? And these guarantees must be in force before you transfer the seat of the government to Aachen. Otherwise, the distance that will separate us will automatically present itself as an advantage to our enemies."

"You should know that I will do everything within my means. Aachen will present itself as a problem if we have need of immediate communication. But even what may be considered a monumental obstacle can be removed with careful consideration. It might be of the best interest to all if I had a man placed highly within your court who would report directly to me. Not only would he relay messages from my court to yours but he would also be empowered to speak on my behalf in my absence."

"Do you really think such a man can be found?"

"There is someone I already have in mind. With his prominence well known amongst the nobles, it is unlikely that those opposed to you would take the chance of incurring my wrath."

"Who would you be suggesting as you envoy?

"There are very few people that I have come to trust over the years and when I do find someone with whom I can share a confidence, I tend to surround myself with these people. In this particular case my selection would be Michel St. Jean, my squire and personal valet."

"St. Jean? I could not possibly conceive the thought of one so noble, agreeing to become little more than a decoration in my palace. He is too intelligent to accept what you have in mind."

"Brother, I am trying to help you with a problem and I do not appreciate your reluctance to accept a possible solution."

"Forgive me, your Majesty but although I see the worthiness of your intent, to insist that St. Jean stays with me may only weaken your own position. He is and always has been the best advisor you have had. His presence in my court would give it the sovereign authority it presently lacks if my enemies were to challenge the legality of my government but I fear the price you are willing to pay may be higher than you can afford."

"Then compensate me for my loss! If I send you an ambassador of my good will then do so likewise. Let me take your second in command, Isaac Iskoi, back to Aachen with me. I have all the confidence that he is just as able to handle my affairs as Michel St. Jean. After all, he used to have a similar position in my court before I sent him with you to Narbonne."

"Vizier for vizier, it has a ring of the East for me. I believe it will work. May not settle my fears for Narbonne in the far flung future but I am certain that it will benefit my children and my children's children. And I don't think Isaac would mind returning to your palace. He was, after all, spoiled by the lavishness of your court."

"You must believe that I would never let any harm befall you or your people. I will do everything in my power to see that that day never happens. You have my hand on it, brother." Charlemagne stretched out his huge mitt which easily engulfed the strong but more delicate, long fingered hand of Theodoric's. "It shall be done!"

Chapter Thirteen

Toronto: 1999

"Absolutely brilliant," Pearce yawns. "Excuse me, Doc," he quickly recovers. "I must be getting tired."

"Well, we have been at this for a long time."

"I don't want to stop now." Pearce reacts very strongly to my comment, feeling threatened that I am about to usher him out through the door that very moment. "I love these battle tales. Best part of a story."

I hear my wife calling from upstairs. "Excuse me a moment." Dragging myself from my chair, I lumbered over to the bottom of the staircase. "What did you say?" I shouted into the empty chasm of hallways that sprouted from the top landing.

"I said, are you coming to bed yet?" comes her gruff reply.

I take a backward glance at Pearce, only to see him shaking his head fervently with hands cusped in a pleading position. I figure that I could hold out a little longer. "No. Not yet," I respond. I am met with cold silence. Well, so much better than an argument. I return to my library and wedge myself back into my comfortable chair.

"Thank you," Pearce mouths as he restarts his recorder.

"Best we move along before you become a permanent house guest," I quip. "The wife will have both our heads then."

"So, this Natronai, or Theodoric as he now calls himself, lived a pretty charmed life." Pearce was baiting me to tell him another battle story.

"Pretty much so...as long as his wife was alive, that is."

"And after she died?"

"After she died..." I paused in reflection. "After she died, for all intent and purpose, he died too!"

Narbonne: 793 A.D.

Protected beneath a banner of truce, the lone rider strode towards the gates of the city, putting as much distance as he could between himself and the Saracen forces that had completely surrounded the walled city of Narbonne. This day had been Theodoric's nightmare for many years. His people's customs had become too well known and now they were being used to tighten the stranglehold around his city.

The holy days of the New Year for the Narbonnaise had always been a joyous time since his arrival in his new homeland. It was a time for families to re-unite and share the bountifulness of their lives. Now, his desire to have his son, William partake in the glory of their Lord, would be the downfall of them both. With both of their armies cloistered within the confining quarters of the city, they were trapped as the enemy's forces gathered outside. Unless he could find a way to maneuver the troops beyond these same walls that now afforded them protection, they would be starved into submission.

Their devotion to their God had been exactly what Emir Hisham had been depending upon. His only opportunity to breach the defenses of the southern Franks was to discover a means to negate the influence of the Narbonnaise. With both Theodoric's and William's armies constantly patrolling the Pyrenean boundaries, it had thus far proven near impossible. Only if both armies were out of commission simultaneously and unable to reposition themselves before an attack, could the impossible theoretically become possible. It had been a brilliant idea and the Emir thanked Allah for the illuminating insight.

Over several months, small units of men moved across the border from Muslim Spain into the south of the country. These men would bivouac in the forests that dotted the landscape, having taken enough rations to see them through the late summer and early fall. Having sufficient supplies they were able to conceal their presence until the appointed day. That day according to the plan was the tenth of Tishrei. To the Jews it was the holiest day of the year; The Day of Atonement. A day that the Emir knew would stretch the Narbonnaise forces to their thinnest as most of the men would fill their synagogues and prayer houses.

Through his network of spies, Emir Hisham, son of Rahman, had come into possession of knowledge that claimed that William was to join his father behind Narbonne's massive stone walls to celebrate the festivals. It was only a matter of waiting; waiting for the Day of Trumpets to pass and then count the ten days until the Yom Kippur, the Day of Atonement, began. He knew that on that particular day, the Jews of Narbonne would be oblivious to all else. Heads bowed in continuous prayer, the world on the outside would be completely shielded from their senses.

The other third of the city comprising Christians and Moslems would equally be lulled into a false sense of security. Having lived so long under the protection of the Almyeri, they had come to fear very little and would not be paying much attention to what occurred outside their city walls either.

The Emir knew that his plan would work perfectly. Allah had guaranteed that it would proceed flawlessly. He had not overlooked a single contingency as far as he was concerned. The conquest of the Franks was to begin that day in Narbonne and finish six months later on the cold, gray coast of Brittany's shores. All the dates of anticipated battles were recorded neatly in his diary. Everything was unfolding according to the vision he received.

Yet the rider, sent by Theodoric, under the banner of a truce had not been factored in to the unfolding of events. The diary had made no allowance for what transpired that morning beneath the Emir's colorfully striped tent. An oversight of little consequence he consoled himself. Surely Allah knew it would happen, otherwise why send the vision?

The note from Theodoric invoked the ancient right of battle by champions. Although none had called upon it in almost a thousand years, still it featured well amongst the tales and old traditions of the Eastern story tellers. As a matter of honor, it could not be refused; as a Semitic code, it could not be ignored. There were no available options but to accept the challenge, otherwise the Emir would lose face. To lose face amongst his men would be a greater tragedy than the loss of his life. Once word of the challenge had spread, there was no avoiding the code!

The loss of his life was not even being entertained by Emir Hisham. The champion of Narbonne was to be none other than Theodoric, an old man by this time. Hardly a threat was the Emir's passing comment as he retired to his tent. He had sent the messenger back with his agreement to the challenge. When the sun was hanging half way through the western sky they would meet on the plain outside the city in a battle to the death. To the victor would go the city of Narbonne but the people were to remain unharmed.

Within the palace, the war council paced restlessly while their commander demanded an explanation of his king. In total indifference to their concerns, Theodoric stared laconically beyond the open window.

"This is insane!" William screamed. "I cannot let you do this. I will not let you do this!" William defiantly stomped his capped boot against the stone slabs of the floor until he finally forced his father to respond.

Natronai seized both his son's wrists in his strong grip. Not an easy task considering that William's forearms were massive beams and Natronai's hands at this age were no more than long and slender tendrils. "Are you going to tell your father what he can and cannot do? Is that how things are to be from now on? The father subservient to his offspring? Know this well, William Isaac, you cannot stop me!" An angry furl crossed Theodoric's brow. With a minimum of effort, he threw his son's arms forcefully away from his talon-like grasp. "I will not allow you. I have given a response to the Emir and as men of honor, we shall abide by it. That is all I have to say."

"We owe no debt to the Saracens, Father! The Saracens are lying pigs."

"This is not an issue of debt. If I don't do this, he will destroy our city. Thousands will die. I have the power to stop that. Do any of us that have the right to rule also have the right to place our lives above that of the people we rule over?"

William pleaded with Theodoric. "He will kill you! You are no match for him, father. Perhaps you may not see it, but you have grown older with the passing of time. Single combat is not for a man of your age. Do you want to die? Is that what you wish? Anyway, he gave no guarantee to spare the city. He only accepted your offer of single combat."

Theodoric's eyes pierced deeply into his son's heart. "I do not fear the netherworld. In fact, I welcome death. I can only pray that it brings me once more into the warm embrace of your mother. Will you deny me that which I long for? I miss her so much, Isaac. Since the day she died, I feel as if I have been in a deep slumber from which I cannot awake. I only dream of her and when I awake, I weep. To die now would be a blessing. Why have I being so old lived on, while she so young died in the cradle of youth I cannot fathom. I do not want to be of this world any longer. Can you not understand that?"

"You are not the only one to miss mother. But do you truly believe that she would wish that you would die for her? Mother was always about life. She was the song of the morning sparrow. She radiated like the sun that rose each dawn. She would not encourage your death. Let me take you place. It will be our best chance to defeat the Saracens."

"And shall they say that Theodoric was not a man of his word. Shall they spit on our family name because we have no honor amongst men? Without honor we are as good as dead. No, Isaac! We shall win but not as you think because of a contest between champions. The Saracens are not bound by the rules of chivalry. That much we both agree is true. This ancient rite which I invoked binds only those words which were spoken at the time of challenge. That is why I never made a request that either force surrenders to the victorious combatant. Only that the s=city will belong to the victor. I am positive that my opponent has already made arrangements with his field commanders to burn the city should he fall by my hand. It has been a well-known trait of the son of Rahman throughout his entire campaign in North Africa to scorch the earth wherever he has been. As long as he has us surrounded, we are trapped within our own city. Your troops, my troops, all of us! Trapped within these same walls that were intended to protect us. Our deaths are imminent if we cannot go beyond our own walls. He, most certainly will not let us leave here alive. Our only chance at survival is to lull the Emir into a false sense of security."

"What am I to do, father? Tell me what you wish of me?" William Isaac fell to his knees, clutching at his father's tunic. "Tell me father."

"Listen carefully, Isaac. It has not been my intent to best the Emir in combat. I am not foolish enough to hold out that false hope for myself. I only wish that God grants me the strength to draw him into a long contest. I know the Muslims well. They are no different here than they were in Baghdad. They are a gambling lot. The longer the duration of our battle, the more engrossed they will become in their wagering. As they are drawn towards the scene of the conflict, they will leave gaps in their siege of our city.

You must have your men ready for battle. As soon as the tower guards identify a weakening in our enemy's deployment of men, they will signal your officers and you will exploit that weakness. Pour your men through the gates and do so without hesitation. You are to break through their lines and force the Saracens to take a position between your army and the wall. My men will rain down missiles upon them from above. We will catch them by surprise and set them to flight as soon as they see their siege has failed. But my men shall not leave the protection of our city in honor of my pledge to the Emir. Our destiny shall be in your hands alone. Do you understand what I am asking you?"

"I will lead my forces to your side, father." William looked up beseechingly into his father's eyes, hoping for approval, fully acknowledging the wisdom of the plan but seeking an alternative ending.

"No! Absolutely not! You will not come to my aid. Use your army to decimate his forces away from the main body of his men. It will provide you with the advantage of time. The main body of Saracens will not be able to distinguish the cries of the slaughter from the shouts of their gambling. Then, you will progress forward through his ranks, killing without mercy until they finally realize that they have been set upon. Spare no one. Tell your men to take no prisoners. They have two choices; fall to your swords or flee. Chase these devils from the borders of our land."

"I do not believe that I can abandon you as easily as you suggest," William Isaac warned Theodoric.

"There comes a time to let go of me, son. Release me to your mother's bosom. I am not afraid to die. I have been so close to death, so many times, that the dark angel seems to be my constant companion. Perhaps, it is best that I let him take me this one time. But I do not wish to die without compensation. I want my death to have a price. Our city must survive. Our armies must prevail. Do as I have instructed you. Honor your father."

With tears welling in his eyes, William stood and embraced his father, "I love you father. I do not wish to let you go. Without you I will perish in fear and despair. "

"You will live! Just as our family has always lived! Do as I say! Do not tie me to this earthly existence. I have had a full life. I had only one hope unfulfilled. It has always been my wish to have my two sons unite in my old age but now it has become only an old man's foolishness. But know this, William Isaac, you have always been the son of my one love.

No father could ever be prouder of a son. Never forget that love and secondly, never forget your birthright. You are an Almyeri. You are Kahana. You are God's anointed. For eighteen hundred years we have been so blessed. Now, help me on with my greaves. The hour quickly approaches and I do not wish to keep my opponent waiting."

"I shall bring you honor throughout my life, father. I shall not fail you!"

"No son could please a father more. Be ready and bring me honor this day. This is all I ask of you."

As the sun settled its position overhead, the gates of the city drew back and spat forward the armored champion of Narbonne. His polished helmet reflected the sunlight like a beacon in the night, blinding his opponents when they first gazed upon him. Theodoric suffered under the weight of his chainmail that covered his body from head to toe. Only his forearms and shins bore any plate, while his chest was encased in hammered metal. Seated firmly in his right mailed fist balanced the hilt of his iron broad sword, while his star emblazoned shield hung from his left arm.

The weight was exceedingly heavy, movement restrictive and the heat within the mail suit excruciating. In marked contrast, his opponent emerged from his tent and was proceeding to the valley, wearing the traditional battle dress of the Moors. Flowing robes crossed the leather jerkin at chest level, while a black and red coiled turban sat firmly across his brow, the metal peak of its crown extending skyward. The huge, curved scimitar remained slung over his left hip, its jewel encrusted hilt protruding well in front of the enormous silver buckler that covered most of his midriff.

The Emir smiled cruelly as he approached his adversary, stroking his pointed black beard as he did so. He knew that his opponent would be weighed down by the mass of the armor he bore, slowed by the ravages of age, and weary from carrying the burden of his city under siege. What more could he have possibly hoped for? The challenge was recognized as a last desperate act of a monarch witnessing the final days of his empire. He would quickly dispatch the Almyeri to his merciful God and put an end to this Jewish kingdom that defiantly resisted passing into extinction like all the Hebrew kingdoms that preceded it. This he had sworn by Allah. By the Prophet, this would be done!

The two combatants moved within ten feet of each other and then slowly began to pace the circumference of an imaginary circle as they probed each other for an opening in their defenses. They were quickly surrounded by the Saracen officers, eager to watch their leader slay their most bitter and scorned enemy. Both took a moment to size the other, weighing the obvious strengths and weaknesses prior to engaging.

"You know, that it did not have to end like this," the Emir called out in Arabic.

Responding in an even more perfect Arabic tongue, Natronai replied, "There was never another option. This can be the only conclusion. Neither of us has a choice in our fates. For that is the curse of kings."

"You are wrong. If you had surrendered your city to me, I would have let you leave with dignity. Your death was not necessary."

Natronai looked his opponent squarely into his eyes. "In surrender there is no dignity, merely dishonor. Would you have done any different from me if it had been your city?"

"I think we are men cut from the same cloth, Makhir Natronai. I will take no pleasure in this combat. To fight an old man, whom I think not of as an enemy but as a brother of the East leaves only the hollowness of victory. Whereas my men have only tasted the bitterness of defeat that has befallen them in the past at the hands of the Almyeri, I have harbored no other feeling but admiration."

Raising his sword mere inches in front of his face, Natronai saluted the Emir. "Then we are both men without choices. I would suggest we engage our swords. And let this old man prove to you that your victory is hardly assured."

"You know the advantage is mine," Emir Hisham cautioned.

"Then you should know that I will not make it easy for you. You need not grant me any leniency in your blows." Upon uttering the last word, Natronai rushed his opponent swinging his great broad sword in a descending arc aimed at the Emir's peaked cranium.

With but inches to spare, Emir Hisham wedged his curved blade between himself and the oncoming sword. The broadsword slid down the length of the Moorish blade and bounced harmlessly of the metal guard protecting the Emir's hand.

Back and forth they stepped, parrying thrusts and exchanging blows. Metal clashed and clanged against metal, while more and more of the Saracen army gathered to watch and wager upon the outcome of the spectacle. Every now and then the tips of the blades would breach the other's protection, leaving behind small rivulets of blood that flowed from superficial wounds cut below the fabric of their armor. Each blow began to quickly sap the strength of the wielder until after performing their bizarre entwining dance of death, both the Emir and the Prince could barely lift their blades in order to exercise a simple maneuver.

The throng that had gathered about them voiced its encouragement for their leader, hurling a cascade of insults at his Jewish adversary, yet still admiring the determination and fortitude of the elderly opponent. Using the advantage of youth, the Emir Hisham would unleash a barrage of blows, severe enough to force Natronai back but not enough to penetrate the superior defensive skills garnered over a lifetime. Now even more and more of the Saracen troops gathered about the battling warriors, deserting their posts so as not to miss the excitement of the encounter that had reached a feverish pitch.

Their shouts were deafening, drowning the sounds of the motivating voice within Natronai's head. If he could not hear himself think, then he knew it was time for his son to make his move. Already the sun had begun to arc behind the crest of the Pyrenees. How long had they been fighting? One hour, perhaps two? Long ago the arms had grown sore and weary. The ground they stood upon was now spattered with their blood. The cuts and bruises had gone beyond sensing any pain. Their legs were bandy, barely able to support their own weight but neither man was willing to let the bone aching weariness take hold and bring an end to the confrontation.

Concentrating beyond the cheers of adulation, the curses from his opponent and the metal reverberations of their weapons, Theodoric thought he could hear something else in the distance. It possibly was the sound of panic. He could barely recognize it, extremely faint and almost imperceptible but certainly different from the sounds of the past couple of hours. After straining his hearing as much as humanly possible he concluded that it could only mean one thing; William had penetrated the human siege wall that held his forces captive within Narbonne. But if he could hear it, then how many of the Saracens surrounding him would do so as well? It was a worry that they would return to their posts in time to repel William's breakout from the city.

Theodoric detected the slight hesitation in his opponent's onslaught. He knew immediately what that meant; obviously the shouts and screams from the Saracens on the far side of the city had also caught Emir Hisham's attention. This would be the turning point with only seconds before the Emir would register exactly what these new sounds were emanating in the distance. Another few seconds and Theodoric caught the penetrating gaze from the Emir; the Emir now knew that the motivation behind the entire challenge was nothing more than a colossal rouse.

"Now is the time, Hisham!" Natronai shouted loudly so as to catch the attention of all the onlookers as he charged directly towards the Emir's outstretched blade. The metal pierced the weld in his breast plate and sunk deep into his belly before it struck solidly against backbone. The Emir tried to dislodge his blade, to withdraw it, but Natronai seized its sharp edge in his gauntleted hands and refused to let it be withdrawn. Stunned into silence, the Emir stared at his wily adversary, knowing that the prince had successfully brought his plan to fruition. The surrounding Saracen soldiers, not realizing that Theodoric had intentionally brought about his own demise, broke into a riotous cheer, their voices singing praises to Allah in a deafening roar, tongues shrilling sounding the ululation and drowning out any other perceivable sounds.

Exactly as the Almyeri prince had intended, none would hear the advance of his son, before it was too late for them to stave off the attack. "Sing," he smiled and whispered to the Emir, "sing to your deaths, you foolish carrion. Sing you bastard hell-spawn. Allah curses you today!"

Still unable to retrieve his sword, Emir Hisham finally recovered his voice and screamed for his troops to return to their stations, but his words only fell upon their deaf ears, sounding to his men as being nothing more than his own victorious elation. They rushed towards him, chanting his name, singing his praises and all the while, William made steady advances through their ranks, slicing a huge swath of corpses as he steered towards the main gates of the city. Preoccupied and unprepared, the Saracens fell in massive numbers to the young prince's army until the valley outside the city became nothing more than a sea of slaughter.

It wasn't until William Isaac, charging at the forefront of his army was within a hundred yards of the Emir, did the extent of the ensuing massacre register with the Muslim leader. "A curse upon your head, Almyeri," the son of Abd ar' Rahman spat at his slain opponent, who now sat upon his knees, the sword projecting upwards from his torso as if frozen in time. Natronai's body remained motionless, a grotesque statue of life ebbing swiftly away.

"You are not a man of honor, Natronai Kahana. You have lied. May the curse of your lies extend down through your generations until the end of your line! You gave me your word! You said your men would not attack under the banner of our agreement. I will burn your precious city before we leave. I spit upon your accursed soul and its lying tongue."

Hands still resting upon the blade that he had driven into his own body, Natronai summoned his remaining strength to lift his head and smile mockingly. "I did not lie and I have not betrayed my honor," he gasped. "Not one of those men is mine. You face the army of William the Avenging Son and may he send your accursed soul to hell!"

Natronai closed his eyes as his body slumped backwards upon his heels until the sword transfixed him to the ground where he had fallen. "I am coming, Alda, my love," he whispered with his final breath.

Chapter Fourteen

Toronto: 1999

"Still consider him a wuss?" I challenged Pearce's earlier comment.

"Like you said, Doc, people can change. You must be pretty proud of your ancestor?"

"If he had been my ancestor, I certainly would have been."

"I thought this was all about your family," Pearce asked, somewhat befuddled.

"He was part of my family but I'm not part of his. My family intercrossed back and forth with Makhir Natronai's for several generations before he was born. But the last time we crossed was not with his family in Narbonne."

"So that would mean..."

"Yes, the wife who rejected him back in Baghdad, she was in my ancestral line as was the Persian line of Judah Zakkai. Actually, her brother Mar Pappa was my direct ancestor, so essentially she was my very distant aunt. That's why I'm here today and what was born in Narbonne was doomed to slaughter. The Catholic Church ensured that they became extinct."

"Everyone dies?"

"We all have to die, John. Unfortunately for the Almyeri, they had to die in ways that would be inconceivable for us to even fathom. The easiest victims to strike at were Natronai's grandchildren and that's exactly who the Church went after."

"Why not his own children," Pearce inquired.

"He only had the one son, and William was too powerful a match for the clergy to deal with. It was far easier to strike at William's children. No, they were the weak links in the chain that would break first. So let me tell you about them."

Aquitaine: 821 A.D.

The beautiful spring day unfolded its tendrils of Eden-like splendor across a vapor shrouded glen engulfed in crystalline hues while the air was fragrant with scent of ambrosia. A perfect day to dip beneath the turquoise waters of an artesian fed pond that sprouted to life each year precisely at this time; the ultimate blend of melting snows and little streams that danced with their first signs of life from the ancient underground riverbeds of Septimania.

For the young princess, this was far more than just another annual welcoming of spring's awakening. During the confines of an unusually harsh winter she had grown extremely restless; subtle changes to her demeanor began expressing themselves in response to her body's transformation into womanhood. Miraculous changes which paralleled the budding blossoms now seen upon the once barren trees. During winter's embrace, the little girl had faded away along with all the ice laden boughs and the new spring had brought a total emergence of newly discovered femininity.

Today was not destined to be just another dip into chilled waters but a baptism into adulthood; a celebration of the cravings she now possessed and associated with freshly kindled desires and passions. Today was destined to be far more than a simple reenactment of annual spring rites with maidens wearing opulent floral arrangements underneath rainbowed skies as they danced through the mystical forests. That was the tradition of little girls of which she considered herself outgrown. With each excited breath she scurried along the road, running far ahead of the carriage which transported her maidservants within the far too claustrophobic cabin. The nervous women brayed for their mistress to cease this nonsense immediately and climb back inside but their pleas went unheeded. Geberga drew too much pleasure from the sensations of the smooth pebbles and soft dewed grass caressing the soles of her feet with each footfall.

As she ascended the small knoll which surrounded the pond she could no longer withhold her unbridled enthusiasm this spring day had unleashed. Without a second thought or hesitation, her linen blouse was unstrung and pulled over her head, then flung wildly onto the brambles that dotted the hillside. Next shed was her corset, tossed even further than her blouse, her upper torso now fully exposed to the warming rays of the early morning sun.

It was at that precise moment that her maid servants ordered the carriage driver to stop; their mistress's behavior was now deemed by them as being totally unacceptable. Had they been empowered to do so, they would have taken a length of hickory to that white behind of hers to teach her the proper way for a lady of the court to behave. If anyone was to see her in this state they would think that their mistress was nothing more than a common strumpet, working the back alleys of Narbonne. Already the carriage driver had seen too much and would be talking as soon as they returned to the castle. Shaking their heads, they tutted and scuttled like a flock of distressed hens.

What were they to do with such an impetuous young woman? Had she no shame? What would her father say and do once he heard? Alas, it was hopeless. If only from the day of her birth they had been more strict, but they loved her dearly and she had been allowed her every whim. Geberga was the total focus of their lives and if it was any consolation, she had ensured their lives were anything but mundane.

Stepping down from the carriage, the maid servants pursued the princess across the hill, gathering up her lost clothing as they did so. Huffing and puffing, they eventually climbed to the summit and stood alongside Geberga. Their young princess stood immobilized, her arms angrily placed upon her hips, but it was not with them that she was displeased. Something else, someone else had warranted her displeasure.

Standing naked from head to toe, her skin beading with pearls of sweat that scintillated in the morning sun's rays, she scanned the periphery of the pond to assess the situation. Somewhere, concealed in the reeds was this violator of her personal paradise.

The pond had always been off limits to strangers. In fact the only way to access it was by knowingly trespassing upon her family's property. It was part of her Almyeri land holdings for over a century, passed down through her grandmother's lineage. Everyone knew that! How dare anyone have the gall to violate the sanctity of her estate? Such an effrontery could not be allowed to go unpunished. She would see to it immediately as soon as she could locate the concealed felon. Her skin crawled with the uneasy sensation that the trespasser's eyes were probably focused upon her that very instant. As she considered that thought, it made her both nervous and something more; a sensation that she couldn't immediately find the proper word for. Eroticized! That was it, she smiled internally. What was most alarming she thought was she enjoyed this new feeling more than the guilt she should have been experiencing simultaneously.

The scoundrel had neatly piled his clothes by the southern edge of the pool. She scrutinized their fabric and cut and concluded they were certainly those of a nobleman but that only made the act of trespassing far more insulting. Which possible peer would openly display their lack of respect for the family of the Almyeri? Her father would definitely hear about this effrontery. Geberga refused to allow even the slightest crease of fear or apprehension cross her brow. No intruder would ever be allowed to make her afraid upon her own lands. After all, she was a warrior born, just like her father William. She once again scanned the surface of the pond, searching for her elusive voyeur but without any luck until noticed a ring of expanding ripples emanating from behind the rushes. Now she had him.

Whoever it was, he managed to conceal himself successfully behind a stand of tall grass from where he had been watching her. Tracing back the source of the ripples, she thought she could possibly make out his shadowy figure amongst the reeds where he had camouflaged himself. Despite her own lack of concern, her maidservants had determined that the stranger surely was a threat to their mistress and were pleading hysterically for her to put on her clothes and race back to the waiting carriage. Geberga continued to ignore them, refusing to acknowledge any of their concerns. Pinpointing the likely location of her silent watcher, she defiantly challenged him, if not so much in words as in her gestures and posture. In a manner dictated more by anger and crude insult than by common sense, her body suddenly responded in a way that had little to do with aristocratic or proper behavior and certainly not in a manner that any of her tutors would have taught her.

Thrusting forward her pale upturned breasts, she cupped her newly endowed bosom within the palms of her hands, somewhat concealing but mostly accentuating the line of cleavage. A previously unheard voice resonated in the back of her mind and pushed its way through her lips, hurling a flurry of insults upon her cowardly voyeur. Upon the wind she could detect the spoor of his nervousness; his fears wrapped in tiny whiffs of pheromones that attached themselves to the wafting breeze. If he had not known it before, he knew now that this little prank challenge he had accepted at the goading of his friends was turning into something far more. Many had known of the young girl's tradition of spring baptism, some may have even watched in the past, but none had ever entered into the pond prior, leaving themselves to be discovered.

"Are you still not satisfied," she screamed. "Did you want to see more, you perverted bastard? You're a coward! Come on to my land to feed your perversions will you? Men like you must hide in the shadows because you have no manhood to brag about. Get off my land while you still have a chance. Wait till my father talks to the Emperor about you!"

Why she behaved in a manner so crudely, she couldn't really say. It didn't matter any longer that he had seen her naked, the damage was already done. Stories would circulate on the streets and they would try to ruin her reputation. There was nothing she could do now that would make it any better, but as far as she was concerned she couldn't make it any worse either. Might as well do and say whatever she pleased from this point, that being the case. But strangely, she actually wished to flaunt that which her voyeur had obviously desired so much to see in the first place; an overwhelming desire on her part to emphasize that which he will never have. Her hands moved rhythmically in small circles, squeezing her now turgid nipples enticingly, while her taught hips, rigidly carved and defined, swayed to an intoxicating melody that rustled amongst the reeds each time the breeze passed softly across the water's surface. The insults still poured from her mouth like a flowing fountain but were now interspersed with a wicked, almost naughty laugh. Harsh, indignant words, both threatening and challenging; words that she did not fully comprehend, herself but which she had heard time and time again in the hallways and passageways of the court. They now sprung forth from her mouth upon their own volition.

Still the stranger refused to show himself, frightened that once identified her father would certainly be able to exact punishment from the Emperor. "Is this what you wanted to see?" she taunted. "Do you not think I know that you have been staring at me all this time? I know exactly what it is you want! Things which you can never have", she spoke in thick, seductive tones, continually tightening and relaxing her sinewy thighs so that every muscle stood chiseled prominently, like the statues of the goddess Aphrodite from ancient Greece.

Frantic, her servants had become speechless, gasping in horror at their mistress's apparent loss of sanity. How horrible! It was not enough that she had been seen naked by a complete stranger, but now she was even displaying herself in this most vile and lewd fashion. Fearing for her wellbeing they finally bleated like lost lambs, urging her to step out of the water and wrap herself back into her clothes. Geberga refused to acknowledge their concerns, deaf to their wails of impending doom, choosing instead to strive relentlessly with her hidden assailant until she could force him to show himself.

Her obvious attempt to tantalize rather than flee was more than the trespasser had considered and it was beginning to have an effect. Slithering below the waterline, the intruder attempted to conceal himself behind the sparse outcropping of elephant grass and watercress that sprouted between the long reeds. He never quite succeeding in blending totally within the veil of green, now that Geberga could finally pinpoint his location and even more so, she was surprised to discover that he was succumbing to the ravages of her sexual onslaught. It was as if she had taken complete control of his body, forcing him to react involuntarily, and in a manner that would surely raise the ire of her father. How easy it was, she realized and she reveled in the thought of having such power over men.

What she had not anticipated was that she would become equally enthralled as she watched the stranger's upper body thrash wildly, churning a thick froth in the pool. Like a speckled trout struggling valiantly but vainly against the pull of a lure he bobbed up and down repeatedly upon the surface of the water all the while never failing to hold the turgid beast ensnared within his circling grasp. It was not her first time to see the manhood so often bragged about by the men in her father's court but this admittedly was the first time she had seen one that actually lived up to its reputation. As miraculous as it was to witness the extremes which that dangling piece of flesh could achieve, nothing compared to how quickly the beast deflated to the size of mouse after it had exhausted its seed. Catching his breath, the stranger rose to his feet, slow and unsteady, his chest heaving from the exertion, totally exhausted and body drained of its life-spawning energies.

Geberga eyed the situation greedily, rolling her tongue across her upper lip. Whatever embarrassment he may have originally thought he would cause her was now completely reversed. Whereas she bore no discomfort with her nakedness, her adversary was suddenly overcome by feelings of overwhelming shame and humiliation. Fear had been the only advantage he had assumed in his favor when he accepted the wager and that was no longer an option. The girl proved to be a rock of defiance and as long as she remained standing at the edge of the pool, he knew that he would not be able to maintain his anonymity for much longer. His was a face that most could recognize.

With the prancing grace of a dancer, the princess pirouetted jubilantly savoring her victory. Truthfully, she did not know at first how to react to what she had just witnessed. Yes, she knew the stories of how one made love, having heard the gossip regarding such things but never had she seen the likes of such a ridiculous spectacle before. Her eyes still focused upon his shrunken genitals, examining, evaluating, and ultimately realizing that this changeling appendage truly was not as miraculous as she first thought. How ridiculous she thought that it had excited her in the first place. Certainly it bore no resemblance in size or stature to the stallions in her father's stable. This after all was only a pathetic shadow of that belonging to those majestic animals. Not even a hand's breadth she calculated when she thought back to the moment prior to its release. Hardly as incredible as she first thought.

"Girls, girls! Come hither! Look!" Geberga shouted to her attendants, pointing in ridicule at her stalker. "The hunter has emptied his quiver without even a nick to his quarry." The servant girls tittered nervously as they tried to look away from the man and his exposed manhood but found their eyes drawn mystically back to the shriveled shaft which swayed limply between his well-muscled thighs. "Surely all men cannot be as poorly equipped," she jested. "Otherwise, why would any woman even bother with such a thing?"

He attempted to cross his thick arms in front of their line of vision but to no avail. Red-faced he slowly let himself slink below the crystal-clear waters up to his waist, head sheepishly turned away from his tauntor. Where he had always thought of himself as suave, beguiling and most assuredly desirable, to have his masculinity ridiculed in such a manner was an experience he never thought possible.

"It will take a firm straight blade to cleave my maidenhood, Milord, a thing which you are obviously sorely lacking! A eunuch displays more stamina than you have exhibited," Geberga laughed impishly. The phrases merely words she had heard used by others at the court. But her wicked smile taunted him more so than even her acrid comments. She knew instinctively that her barbs were cutting deeply. Male ego, she heard them call it. So easy to wound and so hard to repair! Even when she knew that what he did possess was impressive by any standard, yet she could wound him grievously with words sharper than any sword.

"Let us be away girls and tell the pathetic tale of this poor wretch that dared to spy on me. But what worry have we of a man that would wear an empty codpiece?" Geberga strode from the edge of the waters, her long legs prancing with exquisite precision, as she shook her mane of auburn hair enticingly. Upon reaching the bank's crest her servants quickly wrapped her within her linen robes and proceeded to whisk her towards her waiting carriage which stood at the foot of the forest atoll.

Before disappearing beyond the grassed knoll, Geberga turned to offer a parting repartee. "Should you ever learn to approach a woman properly, good sir, then come again and perhaps I will re-examine your qualifications. Otherwise I demand you never set foot upon my property again lest you be prepared to forfeit your life or perhaps even that pale ornament of your manhood."

"Milady!" shouted one of her servants in exasperation, "how can you say such a thing? Quickly, we must reach your carriage before he comes after you because of your naughtiness or your threats. Your behavior has been most unacceptable!"

"Marie, you are such an old maid. Honestly, was he not pleasant of face to look at? I think I fancied him. In fact, he was a better specimen than most that have displayed themselves at the court. And you must admit that you are well aware of what goes on at court. I have overheard you many a day talking about certain indiscretions between maidservants and masters. I've bet you've seen quite a few in your time."

The servants made the sign of the cross upon hearing their mistress's words. "It is the devil that makes you talk so. No good shall come of this thinking. It is evil and vile," Geberga's chief handmaiden scolded her.

"Nonsense!" Such discussions between the princess and her handmaid had been addressed many times before. After all, Geberga had been raised from infancy by Marie. It was Marie's breast she had suckled upon when Marie was no more than fifteen years of age. As a servant she was taken into the house of the Almyeri as a wet nurse when her own family had turned her out onto the streets when she delivered a dead child of unknown siring.

Some say that it had been Geberga's father who had actually fathered the child for it was well known that he often had his way with many of the village's womenfolk during the hunts each fall. Whether her child had been stillborn as she had been told or had been eliminated as a potential source of embarrassment as had many of the children born to such rumors, it would never be known. It was the young princess Geberga whom became her only child but Marie could never deal comfortably with the impetuousness of the girl placed in her care.

"Nonsense," Geberga continued. "It is womanhood that makes me say such things and the cravings I feel within my loins. Seventeen years and I have not even so much as touched a man. My best years are almost forfeit and I have not even seen a plough that I wished to furrow my field. Few have caught my fancy, and even fewer have made it obvious that they wished to violate me. My father has made me virtually untouchable. Is it so wrong to desire to grasp that writhing snake and let its venomous bite sear the path into my womb?" Geberga made a motion with her hand simulating her intended action, as she winked wryly. "What was it like, Marie?"

"Mon Dieu! Mon Dieu! Gardez nous!" Marie covered her ears, looking fearfully at the heavens above. "Such a terrible thing to say! And you, the daughter of a prince talking with the tongue of a tavern wench. A harlot's gossip! Votre mots est tres terrible!"

"Is it so wrong to desire what other women take as a matter of course? My loins ache like any other woman's. Is my groin tempered any differently than that of a barmaid? Where is the sin to have a man embraced between my thighs? To sense his warm bodily issue surging within me." Geberga glanced precociously at her frantic servants. "Tell me truthfully. Would you not prefer to have a man's engorged member within you rather than whatever else may be at hand?"

"Enough, Milady," Marie scolded her. "This is devil talk!"

"It is no more a sin to make love than it is to eat or breathe. God did not give us such an aura of pleasure so that we would hide ourselves away from such sheer ecstasy. I have heard your breathless wails in the night and know that you think no differently than me."

"Please, princess. I beg of you. Climb into the carriage and let us be off before the Count de Bourbon catches you. Such talk would surely grant him power over you. The demons would claim your virgin soul." Marie windmilled her arms towards the open sedan door, urging her mistress to climb the step quickly.

"What did you say?"

Geberga froze immediately mid stride upon hearing Marie's words, refusing to take another step. "You knew who that was? You knew it all along and you didn't tell me. How dare you! What gave you the right to hide his identity from me? Not to tell me of his birthright! Why have you concealed this from me?"

"Forgive me lady. I have said too much. Forget that I even said he was such a person." Marie covered her mouth with her hand as if to ensure nothing else escaped her lips. "He is evil! They say that he can cast the eye upon you. Please do not give him a second thought."

"That was Louis de Bourbon?" A smile of delicious surprise spread across Geberga's lips. "I have heard so much about him. He's far better looking than the rumors say!"

"A plague upon him and his wicked deeds!" Marie spat upon the ground with the very mention of his name. "Such shamelessness! Not a woman or girl-child of the courts is safe from his vile clutches. Wench, maid, mistress, not even a duchess is shielded from his unholy designs. And married as he is to the Baron of Avignon's daughter, a most beauteous and pious soul. He is a sorcerer, Milady. They all fall under his unearthly spell, bringing shame upon their Lords and households. I beg of thee. Do not fall prey to his evil handiwork."

141

"Louis de Bourbon," Geberga repeated. "Call me for the fool that I am, the stallion does come from good breeding after all." Geberga shook her head in disbelief as a mischievous smile crossed her ruby lips.

As soon as they climbed within the carriage, Marie propped her head out the window and shouted the order to return quickly to the castle. Whips snapped sending the team of six perfectly matched dapple grays hurtling down the path that led home. All the while, Geberga sat quietly with an impish grin of satisfaction spread across her lips. It had been a most beautiful spring day.

It was several days later when the first of the many surprises arrived at the front gates of Geberga's summer home. Before the young princess had even risen from her bed the shouting of her butler at the unexpected intrusion into their lives was echoing throughout the stone mansion. She overheard him saying such things as, "We don't want it! Take it back to your master...my mistress is unavailable..." Just enough to peak her interest and send her sailing down the winding staircase towards the foyer.

From behind the open door she peaked into her courtyard to see what the commotion was all about. Rearing its head magnificently, the coal black stallion pulled the young page clear off his feet before he could brace himself. Within the brass ring of the harness a small waxed sealed parchment was rolled, the name of Geberga clearly scrolled upon its outside.

Still dressed only in her nightgown, Geberga leaped from the doorway, ran past her butler and reached towards the halter. Immediately the horse settled quietly into a calm stance as if recognizing and acknowledging its new mistress. There was an unseen mystical bond that instantly connected between animal and young woman. On the other hand, the butler became frantic at his mistress's apparent disregard for both dress and safety. The disheveled page stood both wide eyed and open mouthed, overcome not only by the exhaustion of having to wrestle with the stallion the entire length of the journey but more so by the comeliness of the maiden that had now taken its possession. As he carefully regarded the fine curves of her body beneath the thin woolen garment, the pains of his travels became inconsequential and well worth the price. He was in the presence of a goddess.

Geberga threw her arms around the stallion's neck. It was a magnificent beast and as she unrolled the note it confirmed instantly what she had hoped; it was definitely hers. A present of apology from one count Louis de Bourbon. And written below his name was a simple wish that he could see her again under less embarrassing circumstances. He wrote that since that fateful day a spell had besotted him and he could not live without seeing her beautiful visage. Geberga ran her finger over the impression of his name, tracing the fine curves of his signature as if she was caressing the man himself. She sighed openly, then rerolled the note, tucking it safely between the cleavage of her breasts. Tittering with girlish fervor, she raced back to her room, scaling the stairs in leaps and bounds. Shouting from the window for the butler to fetch her groom and have him prepare her new mount for a quick morning ride she rummaged through her clothing to find some more suitable and appropriate attire. "And reward that page," she yelled from the half balcony. "Reward him handsomely, Philip. Do you hear me?"

From that day onwards the river of gifts flowed with precision timing. Each Friday a new surprise was delivered to Geberga by a succession of squires and pages and without exception an exchange of notes took place between Louis and Geberga. It was not long until they were discussing their secret desires for one another within those letters. An unbreakable bond had been established and not long afterwards a note arrived which announced that Louis could no longer live without seeing Geberga, he would be coming to her villa in a week or so to be with his little princess. It was an open invitation for a young girl to get involved in wickedness and Geberga could not resist the temptation.

The attendants to the princess were shocked when they heard Geberga's request that they prepare for a visit from Louis de Bourbon. Everyone knew of Louis's penchant for pretty young things. Their mistress was just one more amongst a collection of what the whispers described as hundreds. And then there was the matter of his wife. How could this liaison be taking place without her knowledge? No one knew the answer to that question. Poor Geberga! Poor Justide d'Avignon! Two women at the mercy of the Count's lewd and devilish behavior.

Her closest confidante, Marie, threatened to send a letter to Geberga's father, describing what was about to transpire. Certainly, William would put an end to her foolishness. The Prince of Narbonne was still a giant in the eyes of his daughter. Almost as powerful as the Emperor, if William forbade Louis De Bourbon to see his daughter then it would be made so. Not even the family of Bourbon could challenge an edict from the Almyeri. Though threatened, Geberga chose to ignore her threats. "What would be would be," she responded to each rant by Marie.

The solution became now one of timing. Marie knew that she could arrange for the letter to be sent out the next day but whether Prince William could respond in time would be the issue. Narbonne was several days by horse and there would be no guarantee that William would not be on another of his forays against the Spanish Moors, across the Pyrenees. "What to do...what to do?" she pondered, "Two letters." That was the solution she concluded. She would still write one to Geberga's father but at the same time she would also send one to the Bishop Abrogard. He would most certainly prevent this travesty from taking place before God's eyes. She would explain what had happened and how her mistress had fallen victim to Louis de Bourbon's mystical arts of persuasion. Surely he would understand how easy prey the young princess would be. Though Marie knew that the Bishop had no great love for William the Nasi, he was still the guardian of the church and as such, preserver of its righteousness. It was his holy charge to prevent de Bourbon from deflowering her little princess and bringing shame to all involved in the eyes of God.

The week flew by as Geberga stared anxiously from her bedroom window, each time a rider could be heard approaching; Marie guarded her nervously, expecting at any moment a delegation from the bishop to come over the horizon. When that knock at the gates finally came, Marie's hopes and prayers were dashed. Alas, the Church had failed her. William had obviously abandoned her too. Now, the devil stood menacingly in the archway, leering lasciviously at her mistress, who pranced naively before the wake of her ultimate desecration.

No sooner had he stretched his arms towards her, she was hanging about his neck, swooning to his every breath upon her cheek. The touch of her skin invigorated him after his journey. His arms clenched in the hollow of her shoulders, forcing her lithesome body to meld into the flesh of his chest. Brushing back the hair that fell across the crest of her ear, he nibbled ever so gently upon the lobe, whispering words of passionate intent that only she could hear.

Marie cringed at the very sight of her young mistress, now apparently hapless and at the mercy of her captivator. Everything about Louis suggested that he had done these same maneuvers countless times before. It was so easy for Marie to recognize the signs of a man more animal than human in his lust. Each movement rehearsed and reduced to an art that he could duplicate time and time again. A master of seduction, celebrating his proficiency in every hand movement, each word carried upon heavy sighs and the sway of his body as the simplest of steps became exaggerated into a pirouetting ballet. He was everything a woman would crave and everything that they would learn to despise given enough time to recover from a broken heart.

Geberga took Louis by the hand and raced down the road leading from the castle gates. "Oh, Louis, there is so much I want to share with you. I have a very special place that I go to. No one else except Marie knows about it. It is the most special place in the entire world. It is so beautiful and peaceful there. You must see it, you must!"

"I am coming, little one. You are pulling and I am coming."

"Faster Louis. Run faster."

"Mon Dieu. You are like an antelope. How is any man to keep up with you?"

Geberga turned from the path and raced through the waist high heather with Louis in tow. Her voice squealed with delight as the puffs of milkweed shattered in her wake, painting the sky with a sea of white fluff. Further and further she led her paramour into the deepest part of the fields. The trickle of water could be heard in the distance, becoming louder with each step between the timothy and clover. The little creatures of the forest scurried in every direction as the two lovers raced towards the mist that rose like a multicolored umbrella above the tops of the small shrubs and bushes.

Penetrating deeper beneath the oasis canopy, the sound of water now crescendoed as it fell twenty feet from the top of the rock face to the black lagoon below. All around the skirting of the lagoon was a clearing approximately ten feet wide. By all appearances it was a place where ancient gods would come to frolic amongst mere mortals. The fragrant flowers sprouted from the rock face behind the veil of water that showered from above.

"Is it not beautiful, Louis?"

"It is magnificent, Cherie! How did you come to find this place?"

"This was my mother's favorite place. Whenever the world would become too much for her she would bring me to this place. Here we would like down in the grass and watch the clouds fly above the rainbowed mist. I remember laying my head upon my mother's lap and just staring upwards from dawn to dusk. Birds would sing and then my mother would sing in response. It was as if the entire forest came to life when my mother sang. Her voice would harmonize with all the sounds of the lagoon, weaving in and out amongst the trees, while flowers danced with every note. Oh, Louis, they were the happiest days of my life. I miss her so much." Geberga released an anguished sigh.

Louis cradled her in his arms, resting her head upon his shoulder as he softly caressed the back of her neck with his fingertips. "Oh, little one shed no tears of pain or sorrow. Know it well that your mother shall always be with you, both today and for the 'morrow. We do not lose the ones we love, they merely burrow deeper within our hearts. And there they leave us their greatest gift, becoming one with us as they give a little sliver of their own souls to remind us of their love and caring. Their tenderness is such a rare gift that we must treasure it even when it is no longer with us. You honor your mother by remembering her so fondly."

Geberga stopped tearing and looked appreciatively into Louis' sea blue eyes. Louis curled his body around hers and kissed her passionately. Geberga did not resist, giving her own sliver of her soul freely.

"Are you afraid", he whispered with a shallow breath?

"Afraid," she mused at the thought. Again his lips fell upon hers and then quickly probed the rest of her face, delicately resting for a moment upon her closed eyelids. She brought her arms behind his neck and pulled herself more tightly against his heaving chest. The kisses came in waves of exaltation. His fingers were upon the laces of her bodice, managing to maneuver themselves through the intricate pattern of eyelets until finally her upturned breasts were exposed to the rays of the morning sun. Hungrily, his lips raced along her neck and found succor upon her coppery nipples, now turgid with excitement.

Geberga's hands searched desperately for the ties on his jerkins, clawing and tearing at them once they were found. Within a moment they were nuzzled in the soft heather, warmed by the clutches of each other's naked embrace. With every rise and fall of Louis' hips, Geberga released a faint chord of delight, raking his back responsively with her nails. Geberga kept her eyes shut, listening to the sweet song of her mother that was still carried upon the wind. She laughed with newly discovered pleasure, safe in the knowledge that her mother approved of her happiness; happiness so long sought and now found by her little girl.

Satisfaction brought contentment, followed by a peaceful slumber beneath the floral canopy, while the hum of the insects and the melodic songs of birds carried the two lovers to a place where time and sorrow did not exist.

As dusk was settling upon the meadow, Marie came looking for her mistress who had been absent all day from the castle. She knew instinctively where to look. There were many times that she had found her little princess huddled in a fetal position, having cried herself to sleep in her mother's favorite spot to picnic. "Geberga, ma petite fleur. Ou es tu? Where are you?" she shouted, her voice resonating between the water and rock formations.

Hurriedly, the two lovers raced to pull their clothing back on before Marie would clear the underbrush. Pulling a trouser leg here and tying a lace there, the two rushed to make themselves presentable but Marie had entered the clearing long before they had the chance to do so.

Upon seeing Geberga's youthful bosom protruding above her hastily tied bodice, Marie let out a horrific scream. "Diable, diable," she hurled her fury at Louis as she ran to her mistress and valiantly tried to conceal her nudity. "What has he done to you, princess? Please tell me that he has not done what I think? Lord protect you!" She made the sign of the cross over her chest as if to keep Louis at bay. "Oh, my silly girl, what have you done? I have failed to keep you from harm. It is all my fault!"

Marie's words were tainted with both tears and fear. All her adult life was dedicated to protecting the princess from the ills of the world and in one brief afternoon, she watched all those years come to naught. What would her father say? Worse than that, what would he do?

"Hush, now, Marie," Geberga commanded. "I am not a little girl any more. I know what it is to be lonely and I know what it is to want a man. I do not want to be treated like a little girl any longer."

"You think that you are so smart that you know everything now," Marie questioned. "Do you think that lying with a man means that he loves you? Oh, you foolish little girl, of all the men to have chosen, this one knows nothing of love. He is the devil. La Diable!"

"Silence woman," Louis ordered. "I have tolerated enough of your insolence. Do not tempt me to silence you wicked tongue forever. Who do you think you are speaking to? I am one of the most powerful men in all of Frankia. Be grateful that I care for your mistress so much that I would not harm her guardian. But you have wounded me gravely and I will not permit you to assassinate my character any further. I love your mistress and it is my intent to take her back to my castle with me. There, she will live with me. That is if she's willing to go with me." Louis looked deeply into Geberga's starry eyes, awaiting his answer.

"Do not do it, milady. You do not know this man. He is the devil. I swear it to you. This is but trickery. There is not a word of truth in any of his promises. Please do not go with him. I will die of shame when your father returns. Do not leave us princess!"

"Yes, silence Marie. I have listened to your prattle long enough. Have Philip prepare my carriage for travel. I will be accompanying the Count de Bourbon to his home in Avignon." Geberga clapped her hands together. "At once now, do you hear me?"

Marie wept and wailed even louder upon hearing her mistress's commands. But in the maidservant's mind, this was far from over. She would have to let justice take its course and deal with Louis de Bourbon. She would make certain of that.

———

"Come, we are at our destination," Louis spurred his horse into a gallop and set off in front of the inlaid rosewood carriage. There, set high upon the north bank of the Seine, rising hauntingly out of the evening mist stood the castle of Avignon. Its gray towers loomed over the small village nestled within the confines of its massive walls. Standing as a monument to early Iberian architecture, its bricks were so massive and precisely cut from the local quarries that they stood against the elements without any mortar between them.

Geberga leaned forward to stare out the curtained window and to admire the sights and sounds of the town but her enthusiasm waned quickly as the road fell beneath the cold shadows of the palace walls and she felt a chill run the length of her spine. She realized there could be no turning back now; she had entered the den of the lioness that Marie had carried on about endlessly. She had made her commitment, in spite of the pleas and threats from her handmaid. How much of her decision had been defiance of the rules she had to always abide by and how much was true love, she began to question as she contemplated what might happen next. She was about to face her greatest fear, a conflict entirely based on emotions over one man, still wrestling with the fact that Justide was Louis's wife by law. He had already explained to her that his was a marriage in name only, but still it was inscribed in the church and court registries as being official. It was a fact, it was documented, so how did she manage to let herself into this situation?

"Are you nervous?" Louis questioned as he turned to see Geberga's concealed anxiously behind the curtain. She nodded without comment, staring only at the stark roughhewn stones that confronted her with this new harsh reality. A crowd had gathered upon the parapets and shouted their salutations of joy to the returning Count. Geberga carefully scrutinized their faces, searching, evaluating, and digesting the situation in which she had placed herself. Then her eyes darted towards a single face that outshone all the others. One woman in particular stood out from the rest as if a beacon radiated from her eyes. Her coronet of golden braids fell across silver mantled shoulders.

"It's her", the phrase replayed itself over and over inside Geberga's consciousness. Transfixed by the face of her adversary, she watched as the woman waved enthusiastically, as soon as Louis laid his eyes upon her. Geberga sucked back a deep breath. Holding on to it as if struggling to prevent herself from the inevitable bursting inside. The taste of sour bile rose in the back of her throat.

"What have I done," she screamed within the confines of her mind. "The way she looks at him." It was obvious that Louis was still the center of his wife's affections. This was not a woman scorned or rejected. What she saw was a woman still deeply in love. This was not at all what she had been expecting. How could Louis have been so wrong about his wife? How could he not have seen... not have known? Are all men this blind and stupid?

She could not answer, only ask. Question after question; hurt after hurt; searing pain on a trajectory through her heart. The pain forced her to close her eyes, so that she wouldn't have to look any longer. Justide d'Avignon was not beauteous in the sense that one would think. Neither the perfect face nor the deepest blue eyes but what she did possess was a powerful and majestic aura. It illuminated in a corona surrounding her, inspiring poets to sing her praises and men to fight their battles in her name. Clad in silver and blue, her small features were the pinnacle of femininity; a classical beauty in the fashion of the ancients.

Forcing herself to open her eyes, Geberga could not remove them from the Countess afterwards. Even as her carriage made its way into the courtyard of the castle, along with the entourage which rode alongside their mistress, she found herself turning in her seat just so she could continue to observe Justide. Her mind began playing tricks as she thought she saw Justide smiling and waving at her but that could not possibly be.

As soon as the princess disembarked from her carriage, she was ushered into the great hall of the castle. A frenzied activity energized the room all around her, as servants prepared the seating for the castle's honored guest and entourage surrounding a huge oak table. Entertainers practiced their routines, awaiting their cue to perform; dancers, jugglers, and magicians, all waiting their turn, while a string quartet played softly in the background. It was a reception fit for a queen and all taking place directly under Justide's very nose. Geberga found herself surrounded by the household maids, fawning over her every gesture, when suddenly a hand reach out and grasped her forearm. "You must come and sit beside me, my dear. I insist!"

Geberga gazed upward into the crystal blue eyes of her hostess. Justide's thin lipped grin made the princess tremble. It was neither sinister nor malicious but still threatening in its own manner. What was not being said was far worse than any confrontation Geberga had imagined would take place. She searched frantically around the room for Louis, but he was nowhere to be found. She was left entirely to the tender mercies of her hostess.

Justide d'Avignon led her special guest to the head of the table where three large wooden chairs stood out prominently from the backdrop of benches that were set for the other diners. Seating herself in the middle chair, Justide patted the seat on her left, urging the young princess to sit.

"Louis has told me so much about you," Justide purred. "I have been looking forward to meeting you for so long."

"I really don't understand," Geberga responded, confused by her hostess's openness. "I thought you would be angry with me."

"Why would you think that, silly girl?"

"You said that Louis told you about me. Why aren't you angry?" The princess was startled by Justide's total lack of concern. She could only reason that Louis had not mentioned a word of their illicit relationship, describing it as nothing more than a normal social encounter on behalf of her father. But now her own admission that there was definitely something more had sprung the trap by which the truth must be revealed.

"Of course he told me about you. Louis tells me absolutely everything, my dear. He has not talked about anyone else but you for the longest time."

Shaking her head, Geberga still could not fully comprehend Justide's total lack of concern regarding the situation. "And still you're not mad at me?"

"Mad? Of course not! I encourage my husband to have his little friends. He is far more than I can handle. I'm actually grateful for the attention you have lavished upon him." Justide squeezed the princess's hand firmly between hers in appreciation.

"This is all too confusing?" Geberga confessed. Nothing like this had ever been overheard in the gossip in her father's court. Slanderous tales, inflamed jealousies, even murder were how such matters were dealt with by the nobility in her father's court, but never had anyone

147

considered such matters acceptable.

"It's very rare for Louis to bring his friends home," Justide continued. "For him to do so, means that you are very special. That's why I couldn't wait to meet you. And he's described you in detail, down to the very curl of your lower lip. I am so pleased that you are here. I want us to be such good friends." Justide rolled her tongue across her lips as she spoke, which made Geberga even more nervous as it brought to mind a wild animal about to devour its next meal.

"In detail?" Geberga questioned apprehensively, her voice quivering as she did so.

The steward approached from behind, proffering a pair of silver chalices on an ornate tray to the two women. Justide passed the one chalice to the princess, then took the other for herself. She clinked the two cups together in a silent toast. "In every detail," she now grinned devilishly.

Looking frantically for a sign of Louis, the princess scanned the entire room, peering over the rim of the chalice. He was nowhere to be found. Desperate to find even an ounce of strength and confidence, she downed the wine in a single gulp.

"I'm so glad that we'll get to know each other," Justide continued. "Louis's trips have left me so lonely at times. Sometimes, I think he forgets that I have certain needs and would like particular affections too."

"I don't understand," Geberga blurted once again, holding her stomach as a wave of nausea swept over her and her head began to swim.

"Oh, I do so approve of you my dear," Justide cooed. "I think we shall have such a good time together. Louis and I hope that you will be with us for a very long time. Wouldn't that be nice?"

The room began revolving uncontrollably, faces circling around and around, spinning ever faster, while Geberga's bowels felt as if they were being forced into the back of her throat. Her body had gone numb and all went black.

Geberga awoke to find herself laying naked upon a goose down comforter. Justide d'Avignon knelt beside her, rubbing scented oils over her smooth skin, spreading it evenly between her breasts, across her stomach, and along her thighs. The reflection of the chamber torches danced in the shimmering oils that delicately coated her body.

The countess smiled beguilingly, and as the princess raised her head from the pillow, she gazed upon Justide's firm body, bowed and taught with anticipation. Panic initially seized her, but Justide's gentle touch pinned her to the bed. Geberga found her body was frozen with confusion as the countess's mouth searched and explored, like a wolf savoring its prey. She felt the moistened lips on her breasts, her stomach, and slowly moving downward until she felt the soft caress of the tongue within her labial folds.

Opening her mouth in protest, she found her mouth immediately filled with the ample flesh of Justide's breast, as her hostess slid upward, along her immobilized body. The nipple grew turgid between her lips and subconsciously she gave suck, sending repeated pulses of gratification through Justide's tensed musculature. The countess forced Geberga's hand between her legs and the princess felt the warm and moistened lips swallow her fingers without resistance.

Soon afterwards, Justide wedged her own hand between Geberga's thighs, massaging the tender skin of her groin. Geberga moaned, as undesired waves of pleasant shivers shot the length of her out stretched body. Her back arched reflexively while her hips thrust repeatedly against the touch of Justide's inquisitive and exploring fingers. Deeper and deeper, the slender digits delved, writhing to and fro, as they tickled the fleshy internal ridges of her vulva.

The countess pressed her torso firmly against the princess's, palm against palm, and mound against mound. Justide forced her lips over Geberga's, showering her with kiss after kiss. Geberga felt the tongue weaving its way between her partially closed lips. Soon it was fully within her mouth, teasing and intertwining with her own tongue. She was helpless to stop it. She wanted it to stop. She did not want it to stop. She didn't know any longer what she wanted.

"Why are you doing this to me?" Geberga whispered between trembling pulsations.

"Because you belong to me," the countess replied. "All that Louis has also belongs to me!"

"I want to go home," the young girl cried in pleasured anguish, failing tears staining her cheeks.

"You will dear. Once I tire of you, you will go! Like all the rest."

A fortnight after her return, Geberga ended another restless night with an early morning walk with her maid servants to the bathing pool where all her nightmares had begun.

"Princess, it is not necessary for us to walk so far. You look tired and should rest."

Geberga brushed away Marie's concerns. "I am fine. This is something I must do. I cannot hide from what I have done. We must go to the pond."

The maids fell in behind their mistress as she led them along the path she had taken so many months ago with Louis. For about a half mile there was nothing but silence until the Princess spoke again.

"I have been so stupid, Marie. I listened not to your good counsel and now I am tainted with wickedness. Why did I choose not to listen?"

Marie rushed to the side of her mistress, caressing her gently and softly brushing her long hair with her fingers. "Hush now, my child. You are not tainted. You have come back. For that we rejoice. These are the cruel lessons we learn in life. God has set those in our path to lead us into temptation but he watches carefully to see those that stumble and fall, only to rise up again and choose the path back to his love and kindness. Those of us who do so He cherishes above all others."

"Do you really think so, Marie?"

"I know so, Princess. I was one of those that stumbled but God set me back firmly upon his path and gave me someone to love and care for, all the days of my life."

"You have no concept of what they did to me. The obscenities, the horrors, they terrify me! I can't close my eyes without reliving them!"

Marie wrapped her arms around her princess. "It matters not, little one. What others do in their sinful ways can be cleansed through time. Most importantly is that you have returned. Here you are safe. Here you will always be safe!"

There was a distinct rustling at the edge of the clearing and Geberga readied to release a scream of absolute fear, when suddenly a pair of pheasants emerged from the forest apron. "Look, mistress, aren't they the most beautiful birds in the world?"

But the young princess could not see the beauty, only the shadows of haunting specters hiding behind the rushes surrounding the pond. Meanwhile, her maidservants became so enthralled watching the majestic fowl spread their wings into flight that they failed to notice the hooded riders ascending the roadway to her ancestral home.

"Run, we must run!" the shout from her servant immediately disrupted Geberga's thoughts. Marie was pointing towards the approaching riders. Four guardsmen from the Holy See could now be clearly identified, mounted upon identical black horses; their long pikes firmly grasped within gloved right hands and nestled in their leather supports which hung from the saddles.

"Oh, Mon Dieu. Que, je faites? What have I done? What have I done?" Marie cried out over and over again.

Geberga stared at her maidservant, confused by her exclamation of guilt. What had she done? Without breaking stride, the guardsmen rode directly at Geberga. Her maids began to frantically scream, grasping their mistress and forcing her to run to stay in front of the charging horses. "Run, Milady, run!" Marie screamed again but this time in terror.

Within several heartbeats, two pikers were along either side of Geberga and the long net that they unfolded between themselves, scooped the young woman in a single motion. Geberga found herself tossed to the ground and dragged until the horses finally came to a halt. Though her body was now bruised and battered, she felt nothing, her mind convinced that this was somehow all in due course; part of the punishment for her wanton sins.. Marie and the younger servant Christa assailed the guardsmen with a fury of fists but in their heavy leather plates, it was perceived as no more than the stinging of fleas.

Finding a moment of lucidity, the princess wailed. "Why are you doing this? What have I done! There must be a mistake. I am the Princess Geberga. My father is William of Narbonne!"

The guards ignored her pleas, securing the ties on the netting, ensuring that no matter how hard she struggled and clawed, she could not set herself free from the snare.

"There's been a mistake! A terrible mistake," Geberga cried but the guardsmen paid her no heed. Marie was still pummeling the one picket until a mailed backhand to her face quickly sent her flying backwards into the long grass.

"Marie! Marie! ," The princess shouted upon witnessing her maid's assault. "Cretans! Monsters! Why are you doing this to us?" But as Geberga looked into the eyes of her assailants, she fell silent, a shiver of icy loathing scrawled across their faces. The eyes she saw were bottomless, without pity; eyes that were cold and murderous; the eyes of sadistic animals, not even remotely human.

"Be silent witch!", were the last words she would recall before the pole end of the pike swung towards her followed by a quick crack to the back of her skull.

Each movement, every thought caused severe pain as Geberga valiantly attempted to open her eyes and analyze the strange surroundings when she awakened. There was not a part of her body that did not ache. The place in which she found herself was foreign and the stench of urine unbearable. The eerie torchlight flickered from without, outlined a large oak door centered in the far wall. She was aware that her wrists were tied together in front of her body. There was no strength left in her legs to even make a feeble attempt to stand.

How long had she been unconscious? Time had no measure in a windowless room. Even more perplexing was how long would she have to remain here? With her brothers all gone on separate battles and their separate ways, and her father returned to Septimania after his long crusade against the Iberians and now tending to his own wounds, who would even know that she was missing from her private estate?

"Witch!" The word surfaced in her mind. It was the last word she recalled the before her arrival in this dank hole. What had they been referring to? What nonsense was this talk of sorcery? Surely there had been a mistake. She tried to raise her spirits by reassuring herself that it would be cleared up shortly. She was frightened and alone. Burying her face in the palms of her hands, she wept openly.

'Could her father's old enemies have come back to exact their revenge by striking through his defenseless daughter?' She knew over the years her father had garnered numerous enemies. It was not unexpected that one day one of them might try to topple her family. She wanted to cry but she found that now even an attempt to cry would hurt as her body craved water. The thirst was unbearable. Two days! Two days she recalled her father saying before the body craved liquid replenishment. Had she truly been here that long? She began to pray to God; to the God of her ancestors. Praying for a sign, any sign that would signify her redemption would be forthcoming.

An eternity of waiting ended when the heavy oak door with its iron braces rolled back upon its hinges. At first Geberga could not see anything but a glaring torch held aloft and moving swiftly in her direction. Once her eyes adjusted to the sudden infusion of light she could identify the scowling, scarred faces of two prison guards. One of them carried an offering that she could not immediately recognize until it was tossed to the ground, unfolding as it fell to reveal a sackcloth dress that would become her prison uniform from then on. The other guard cut the leather binding from her wrists and grunted for her to get dressed. They made no effort to turn away as she suffered the ultimate humiliation of removing her dress and replacing it with the hard hemp clothing in front of her jailers.

Once she had changed her vestments, her wrists were retied and a long leather leash was connected to her manacles in order to pull her from her cell and down the rough stone cut hallways. Geberga's only saving grace was that she could no longer sense her suffering; she had grown beyond pain, beyond fear, beyond concern any longer.

Entering the tribunal's chamber, Geberga gazed attentively at the macabre little shapes dancing upon the walls, shadows cast by the smoky, flickering candelabra. She caught glimpses of the withered half faces that waxed and waned with each furtive flame. She could see it in those corrupt faces that leered from beneath red caps. The outcome was stamped indelibly in her mind; she was going to die. All of the faces were bereft of any evidence of justice. The verdict had already been decided long before she had even been dragged from her cell. She was merely fodder for their legislative appetites, a footnote in some ledger to record their decision and account for their payment. The prison guards forced her to her knees upon the hard stone floor. The chief barrister then rose to his feet, the papers firmly clenched in his thick fingers. His hands were trembling with religious maniacal fervor. His opportunity to speak had arrived!

"It is the opinion of this esteemed tribunal that the accused, Geberga d'Almyeri, daughter of William Naso of the Almyeri is guilty of practicing sorcery, that most vile of black arts condemned by the Almighty." There was an immediate outburst of laughter from the assembled tribunal over the pronunciation of William's title.

Chief Magistrate, Cardinal Julian Giscard corrected the barrister. "I believe, Abrogard that you meant to say, William Nasi of the Almyeri."

"No he didn't", shouted another cleric. "Have you ever seen the nose on that man!" Once again the august assemblage burst into laughter and applause. The chief magistrate waved for silence and for the barrister to continue.

"And of this crime did use her Satanic influences to entrance Louis de Bourbon and cause him to commit the following crimes; adultery, for which he shall make offering to the Church and do penance; the bearing of false witness, for which he has been exonerated as we deemed this to be the result of the witch's influence; and the murder of one Marie D'Uberville, servant to said sorceress and therefore in most likelihood in league with her mistress. Therefore, for that act the Duke holds our esteemed appreciation having saved us the need for future trials that would result from bringing this maidservant to justice which would only have served to inflame the public furor even further."

The pronouncement penetrated her state of mortification like a cudgel slamming against her head as she realized that her beloved Marie had been killed while she lay unconscious within her cell. Poor, poor Marie! Always protecting her little princess and yet no one was there to protect her when she needed her mistress most. And then to accuse Louis of their heinous crime; what better way to guarantee his silence. Or perhaps he did commit the murder and that was his means of gaining clemency from the Church. Either way, he was responsible for Marie's death.

The archbishop issued a barely perceptible sigh upon reading the sentencing. "Geberga in her sorceries was witnessed to have summoned Satan, for the purpose of fornication in a cesspool one May morning upon her estate. Almost immediately his tone and appearance grew even more sinister as he twisted his face into a wretched sneer as he gazed upon Geberga, hapless before him. Barely able to lift herself from the floor, a mass of bloodied bruises and riveting pain, his words by this time had little influence on the princess.

"How responds the accused?" But no response was forth coming from the young woman.

"For all these accusations, your Holiness, we have testimonials, attesting that all we say is true and beyond dispute. The barrister approached the magistrates table and placed the testimonials before Cardinal Giscard.

"Oh, Marie," Geberga sighed. "In all your love for me, what has your protection done?" She now fully understood Marie's outburst prior to her capture. Marie had loved her beyond any earthly riches and now condemned her with that unselfish love. The princess made an attempt to speak but the words were choked behind parched and swollen lips; unable to even reach the tribunal's ears.

Learned and scholarly men all dressed in red or black, sat impatiently in the dock behind the tribunal's chief barrister. The archbishop ordered the bailiff to raise Geberga's head so that they could hear her inaudible confession. Grabbing a fistful of hair on the back of her scalp, the bailiff tugged her head into an upright position. "Repeat you response for the tribunal!" the archbishop shouted. "The crimes of which you have been found guilty are quite serious. You stand accused of blasphemy against the Father, Son and Holy Ghost in the most vile of acts. Is it true that you were seen summoning the Dark Angel with the intention of fornication?"

Though approaching total exhaustion and growing steadily more dehydrated and debilitated with each passing minute, Geberga's lips parted into a whimsical smile as she summoned her father's courage.

"Is this amusing to you girl?" The chief magistrate shouted at the defendant demanding obeisance. "Wipe that smile from her face!"

The fist of one of the jailers hammered against her cheek. Her jaw trembled as she tried to speak again. Perhaps it was the angle of her head, or else the massive welt that now covered her face and forced her eyelids shut, that she knew instinctively that her jaw was likely fractured but she was well beyond feeling any pain.

A new voice broke the increasing tension within the room. Louis de Bourbon rose from the witness's box, forcing the restraining hands upon his shoulders upward until he was standing, staring in utter horror at the girl he dared to love. "Dear God! Your Excellency! Why are you doing this to her?"

Geberga's head tilted in the direction of the familiar voice, seeking the comfort of its concern, the obvious intonation of perhaps an element of love. She had not noticed earlier that Louis had been sitting in the chamber. Though the room was chilled, she felt warmth for the first time since being led from her cell.

"Remove the Duke from this hearing." The archbishop dismissed the guards and Louis with a wave of his hand. "His presence here is no longer required. He has served us well and we do not require any further statements from him. Your Holiness, we must excuse his outburst which results from a most arduous experience." The Duke struggled to break free of the soldiers' grip but the effort was futile. With imperceptible ease they seized him again, lifted him off the floor and ushered him towards the door. "It is obvious that the witch is still able to exert an influence over the Duke. It is imperative that we separate him from her sphere of power."

"You are the evil ones," he shouted as he was escorted from the chamber. "Forgive me, Geberga, forgive me!" Louis screamed guiltily as the guards pulled him through the open doorway. "I love you, Geberga! I will always love you! I'm sorry. Please forgive me for what I have done!" The distance muffled his final words as his voice trailed off into nothingness until his presence was no longer felt within the courtroom.

"He loves me," she managed to whisper repeatedly, "he loves me." That much her frail heart had heard.

"What did she say? I want to know what she said. How says the accused?" the archbishop hammered his question once again. One of the guards bent forward placing his left ear to her parched lips.

"She says your honor that she is an Israelite. She doesn't believe in such nonsense as devils except for the human kind." Chattering like nervous squirrels, the assemblage reacted to her statement.

"Silence," Giscard commanded. "Continue Abrogard."

"No devil indeed," the magistrate huffed. "She wishes to confuse the issues by denying the existence of that which we all know and accept as true. Speaking with an air of heavenly authority, the chief magistrate began to read the sentence, "Geberga, daughter of William Almyeri, you have been found guilty of the crime of witchcraft and blasphemy against our Lord, most High. Furthermore, you have now denied the truth of our religion and attempted to use your sorcerous ways to confuse us and thereby escape your crimes. How plead you to the findings of your guilt?"

Geberga summoned what little strength remained, and replied in a faint whisper. "I am guilty of no witchcraft." The effort to speak caused her chest to spasm and a clot of blood shot from between her teeth and landed at the foot of the docket. "He loves me. Don't you see he loves me?"

"We will hear no more of that", the archbishop stamped his gnarled staff against the floor. "The sentence has been predetermined. The accused will not admit to her sins and therefore it is necessary that she be given a test by which to establish her innocence. Her legs are to be tied to a rock and she will be thrown into the courtyard well. If she floats then it is proof of her witchcraft. If she sinks, then God will have mercy upon her soul. It is the will of God. Let the law be done! Glory be to God and the Son and the Holy Spirit. Amen"

"Amen", the council stamped their approval.

Justice had been done.

Chapter Fifteen

Toronto: 1999

Pearce looks horrified. Pallor spreads across his face as he looks down upon the scratchings that covered his pad of paper. "I can't believe they could do that." He's muttering to himself. "I'm not a religious man, Doc, but to be told that the Holy See and the Bishops were this evil, it's awfully hard for me to accept."

"You're Catholic I'm guessing, John?"

"Regular choir boy," he chuckles.

"Probably goes against everything you choose to believe, doesn't it? But remember, this isn't about good and evil, this is purely about power. Men of power are a law unto themselves."

Standing, Pearce begins to pace restlessly, his demeanor somewhat perplexed. "If we go ahead with this story, I may have to make some changes."

"Getting too hot for you to handle? I'm surprised John."

"You can't tear down walls in a single day," Pearce cautioned me. "I have no doubt in what you're telling me, Doc, but this is going to make a lot of people nervous. *Caiaphas Letters* could be taken as fiction. It didn't offend anyone's beliefs. Now you're saying, 'look everyone, here's one of the world's great religions and it's committed every one of the seven deadly sins.' This is not going to make any of us too popular."

"The truth will never win you a popularity contest," I state stoically. "Religion is ruthless. Any religion! The situation they were facing would have been devastating to the future of the Catholic Church in France. If Geberga had become a consort of Louis de Bourbon, they were faced with the situation of both houses that were heirs to the throne being tainted. The probability of a Jewish king sitting in Aachen was already looking like a good bet."

Pearce walks over to the coffee pot, lifts it, and then shakes it to indicate that it is empty.

"Let's go to the kitchen. I'll fix up another pot and make some sandwiches. All this talking is making me hungry." I pat my stomach in sympathy.

"Sounds good to me." Pearce grabs his tape recorder and dogs my footsteps. "Honestly, Doc, was she really that much of a threat as they supposed?"

"What I haven't told you yet is that the poor girl was a Christian, raised as a Jew." I open the fridge door and buried my head in the shelves, looking for the sliced meats. "She wasn't William's real daughter!"

"I don't think I heard you correctly," Pearce comments as he leans over my shoulder and peruses the fridge contents. "Hey, can I have some of those." He pulls the jar of sour pickles off the shelf. "So, what's this about her not being the real daughter?"

I watch as he wrestles with the lid of the jar. "I haven't gotten to that point in the story yet. It has to do with a whole other plot conceived by the papacy. But before I go down that avenue, there's far more I have to tell you."

"Been holding back on me, eh?" With a major exertion, he finally pries the top of the pickle jar.

"Quite intentionally," I comment. "Other matters take precedence. You see, matters can and did get worse. The secret conclave could not have even anticipated this one!"

"What secret conclave are you talking about?" He looks at me with that confused look I often see on his face.

"If I tell you now, it wouldn't exactly be a secret, would it now?"

Narbonne: 822 A.D.

I cannot comprehend exactly what is drawing me along these hidden stairs. Perhaps it is her eyes. Yes, that must be it. When I look into those eyes I sense myself melting into oblivion, as if I do not exist nor ever have I existed. I am merely some molded clump of wax that bends to her whim and touch.

It is definitely her eyes! They were my mother's eyes. I do not comprehend how they can bear this uncanny resemblance, but they are most definitely the eyes of my departed mother, the fair Guiberc. I can feel my soul rise in those green-black orbs as if I was a little boy sitting in my mother's lap once again. How I have missed her reassuring smile, that faint laugh, as my mother's eyes sparkled and danced, as she spoke. In the showering warmth of those eyes I was safe and secure. Though I am now a well-seasoned man of seventeen years, I wish I could still be that little boy who gazed assuredly into those captivating eyes.

Oh Judith! Do you even know that I am ascending these stairs outside your room in order to commit the unpardonable? Do you have any place in your heart at all for me? Does one of your noble stature and alluring beauty even know that I exist? What a miserable wretch you have made me by your being here. Why did Louis have to send you here of all places? Could I have not been left alone in my period of mourning?

Shall I defile the black of my sackcloth with the white of a lusting effluence? Can my father ever forgive me for my failure to mourn his departing spirit properly? Forgive me dear pater. It is those eyes! My resolve has been sapped. I can no longer resist. The King's magnanimity has been my undoing. His fear for his young bride's safety, while he is campaigning, has delivered her to my castle. His love for me has given her as a companion to my orphaned loneliness. Shall I slap his hand so callously, as to take his queen into the embrace of my loins? Where is my guilt? Where is my shame?

Alas, I am already at the top of the staircase and behind this wall lies the beating breast of my desires. Be not so foolish Bernard! Turn back before you do this heinous crime! Shall the queen be made an adulterous harlot for your own pleasures? Damn the day I looked into those eyes! I know that I am a drowning man who holds out no hope of salvation. I must pursue this path for it is my destiny to do so. Oh what a pitiful creature I have become to actually contemplate stealing the wife of my godfather. I pray Lord that you will forgive me as I have succumbed to my temptation.

Judith Blanchfleur must belong to me! She is only my senior by but a few years, but Louis's younger by almost two decades. What can he offer her that the flame of my youth does not fulfill in greater measure? Can he hold her more tenderly or caress her more gently? Can he arouse the savage beast which rides the hell bent mount more assuredly than I?

My hands move as if they have a life of their very own. They reach into the cleft of the wall and pull the concealed lever causing the great stone slab to roll forward on silent hinges. Into the yawning stillness of the chamber, I swallow repeatedly to gain the courage which has begun to desert me. The faint glow of the draped torches dances all about me, as if taunting me to turn and run from their devilish flames.

My legs have turned to stone, impossible for me to lift my feet from the cold marble beneath them. Is this how it is all to end? To be slain by fears that I have manufactured within my own mind. I must not! I cannot! To turn now is never to know the promise of paradise. Let not my courage fail me. Move feet! Slide if you must but do not keep me from the bed of the fair Judith. I know not how but in some manner my limbs have been liberated and her bed is stretched out before me. The raising of my eyes takes an eternity, as the struggle continues within me. My neck twists, as if to separate my head from my shoulders, but I have come too far and fought too strenuously not to be rewarded for my perseverance.

She has curled herself tightly about the fox-fur cover that stretches between her breasts and tucks into the cleft of her long and slender legs. Her skin is so smooth that it shimmers and radiates a bronzed warmth from the flickering fires. How remarkable! For the first time I notice that the hue of her flesh is the same as my mother's had been; so many similarities. How could this daughter of Languedoc and Aquitaine bear characteristics that Guiberc had gained only by being birthed in the Far East? Surely this is a sign of heavenly approval. No man could desire more than a woman to offer the same love, which had once been his to suckle and nurture from childbirth. To thirst upon the breasts that had ushered us into a cold heartless world, until the end of our days would be a most blessed event.

This could be no mere coincidence that Judith's alluring body can usher forth such sacred memories from my past. Her pert nipples, surrounded by rings of deep magenta, are but sacred memories. How familiar they are to me, even after the passing of so many years, though never before have I set my eyes upon the queen's nakedness before.

Kneeling, I cannot restrain my hands from exploring the smooth lines of Judith's hips and wandering across fields of anticipated pleasure. My tactile senses are flooded with a surge of emotion, coursing through my every fiber. I am alive with energy of immense proportion. My mind is reeling in a multitude of images that urge me to press my advantage.

The softness of her chestnut hair is like the rarest silk upon one's skin. Coiled about my fingers, the subtle scent of powdered rose petals escapes from her captive tresses and fills my lungs. I find myself, hovering over her, and burying my face into her delicate locks.

Too late, I realize that I have applied the weight of my chest upon her shoulders and she begins to stir. My heart begins to race frantically. Fear has overcome me. A sudden need to hide, an uncontrollable panic seizes upon my heartstrings. What shall I do? Where shall I hide? No time to escape through the secret passage! Question after question; doubt after doubt. I try to collect my thoughts and find myself standing and ready to flee, but with nowhere to go! I have been undone!

"Bernard? What are you doing here?" She wipes the sleep from her eyes and stares questioningly in my direction. She shows neither shock nor disdain, which unnerves me even more. Too late! On her merest of wishes, my life is forfeit now. Her voice keeps ringing relentlessly in my mind. I want to speak but I cannot. My mouth is but an open orifice with not a sound to utter.

"Dear boy, do not be afraid." Her words seem reassuring, but how can I be certain of a woman's true intent.

"Forgive me my lady. Let me go! I have done wrong and I must flee!" My breathing is such a heavy pant that I doubt she can even understand a single word I say.

"Please Bernard, don't go."

I am half way to the concealed doorway when my heart registers her plea. Have I heard her correctly or did I merely hear what I had so fervently wished she would say?

"Don't go. Please!"

She said it again and this time I am certain. I wheel about on my heels and there awaits the breathtaking vision of Judith sitting upright, her torso fully exposed and her hands beckoning to me. Oh God, you have answered my prayers. No man could ever be further in your debt. The wave of her hands pulls me forward, like an object dangling from an unseen cord. I rush forward and bury my face in the full cleavage of her pear-shaped breasts.

"Forgive me," I sob for reasons I do not fully comprehend. "Forgive me."

"There is nothing to forgive." Her hands stroke and caress the back of my head, as she holds me tight against her throbbing chest. "Foolish boy, do you not see that I have waited anxiously for days for you to find your way? The seed was planted upon my arrival and now we can reap the harvest. I am here to ease your anguish."

"Then you knew?" How could I not have suspected? I am young and do not fully understand the games of love. This is all so new. I feel ashamed of my ignorance.

She kisses me softly and lets her tongue roll across my left ear lobe, sending a shooting sensation racing along every sinew of my body.

"It had not been Louis's intention to send me here. Since when has he held compassion for any of his friends or allies? The passing of William meant no more to him, than does a fly caught between hand and wall. But I made him realize that you will be the inheritor of much that William possessed and therefore you must be groomed properly if the king was to take advantage of your assets. It is too late to win over Bera, Heribert and Gottshelm. Who better than his sweet-tongued wife to ensnare you in his trap?

That is how Louis wishes things to be in his perfect world of marital bliss. Little can he imagine that I see him as a kindly old man who treats me well but wants me to be nothing more than chattel to be fawned over by dukes and courtesans sitting at our dinner table. I am reluctant when he takes me into his chambers but I am relieved to admit that such occasions are rare and extremely fleeting when they do occur. Since the birth of Giselle, two years ago, the King has not been amorous. Louis has come to an age where he can no longer rise to the occasion." She titters ever so softly at her final comment.

My mouth begins to move spontaneously across her flesh, searching, gnawing, and fighting for a hold. Her back quivers reflexively to my stimuli and I feel her pulling me on top as she lowers herself into her bed. My breaths became short and snorting and I find myself totally losing control. Instincts guide me completely as I wrestle to remove my leather jerkin, all the while, never removing my mouth from her suppleness.

She arches convulsively, thrusting her pelvis in harmony to my gyrations; pressing, releasing, pressing again until I find myself swimming within her; lost inside her flesh and wishing to sink more and more until my entire body is contained between her encircling legs. If only time would stand still and I could remain enfolded within her limbs for an eternity. Her every movement is designed to drain me of strength and will, until I lay like a hapless babe, barely able to lift my head from the searing heat of her seductive torso.

"I love you," I moan over and over again until the words are fluid and indistinct.

"Oh Bernard! Do not ruin this moment with talk of love. Who am I to love or to know love? What we have done is wrong but I would do it all over again if the opportunity should arise."

"Then do not leave! Stay with me! We can always be together."

She laughs annoyingly, like a teacher musing at a student's failings. "So much the man, yet still a boy. We have committed adultery. Not only that, you have committed it with the wife of the king. Our lives are forfeit at the slightest hint of our affections. Do not destroy what we share with talk of forever." She places her finger over my lips preventing me from speaking. "When I first saw you standing in the palace beside your father almost two years ago, I knew then that this day would happen. I am glad that it has come to pass. I shall cherish it beyond all else and if ever we should embrace again, then that time will be just as special. There is an indescribable bond between us. I know not what it is but you're lying in this bed had made me complete. If I did not know better I would swear that I have known you forever."

Though she speaks openly and frankly, I grow angry at the thought of our love being consummated but never fulfilled. Is this to be my reward, a sporadic love that would gnaw at my sanity? Why has this been done to me?

"Stay with me, I beg of you. I do not care if I have to die as long as I can be with you."

"Would you slay me as well, Bernard?"

She has made her point. I care for her far too much to wish to see her die for my lusting desires. I choke back the tears. "But will you not stay with me if even for a little time."

"Oh dear boy, I am with you now. And I am with you tonight. And I shall be with you for a fortnight to come, until Louis returns from his campaign. We have each other for that time. Love me to the fullest, until the day comes for me to depart and learn to be grateful for all that we share until then."

I lower my head upon her soft shoulder, burrowing my face into the nape of her neck. "I will try," I swallow. "I will try."

"Sleep, my love and dream of a life where no restraints bind us. A world in which kings do not make the laws and love is all that governs our lives. How sweet a life we would have!"

Time has passed far more quickly than I ever thought possible. What I would give in order to turn back the hands of time and relive these past two weeks during which I have grown from adolescence to manhood. I have been riding upon the crest only to find myself plummeting at this very moment into the depths of despair. Never had I thought that I could be any lonelier than when my father passed away, succumbing to the wounds he suffered in Iberia and leaving me a master of all he possessed; a master of nothing of consequence if I cannot fill this hollow castle with the laughter of love.

Now these last few hours pass haltingly at the sill of my window as I wait for her carriage to be brought forward. Judith Blanchfleur, fairest of the flowers that grow wild in the forest, you have given me so much and now the hour comes nigh when you shall take it all away. The carriage men have sounded the bell and reluctantly I must attend your departure. My god, why have you forsaken me?

With a wave of my hand, I dismiss my servants who have come to fuss over me and rearrange my disheveled appearance. Fools, can they not see that my dress merely mirrors my feelings on the outside. Let the world see and know that this is a most unhappy day for me. If my cloak is rumpled then so much more is my heart crushed like the velvet of my collar. Be gone and beware my wrath, you wretched curs who laugh at your master's sorrow!

"Count Bernard, I have been awaiting you." Judith curtsied and held out her hand for me to kiss softly. Her gown was stunningly beautiful, trimmed delicately with red and gold bows upon its white silk front piece. The laced skirt accented her slim waist and long legs. Dressed so becomingly for such a morose occasion, such is the nature of women and I doubt I will ever understand it. "My Lord, are you ill? You look so wane?"

"Yes, my Lady, I am ill. My heart is failing, the black gall coursing through my veins with the poison of loneliness."

"Do not say such a thing, Bernard. You must remain strong if not for yourself, then for me. Do not falter, my Lord or else we shall both be cast into that bottomless hell hole for sinners like us. Rejoice, rejoice in the memory of what has been and what will be some time again. Be strong for me! Then and only then will I be able to carry on. Now walk me to my carriage and wear no frown so that others might guess at our secret."

"I will make no promises. All I can do is try. But the burden I bear is heavy and I do not carry it well. Beyond these doors awaits the vehicle that will take you from my castle and may possibly be taking you from my life as well. How am I to make light of this?"

"You must believe! Believe in me, believe in love and most of all believe in us!"

It is with thoughts of anguish that I help her into her coach. She rolls away the shade to say her final goodbyes to me. "I believe that I am the epitome of sadness. At this moment I do not know if I can believe in anything else." I am trying so hard to restrain the tears that are bursting within. If I break down I know that she will be displeased but I sense only that I am losing to my feelings. What bravery is there in a man who refuses to yield to his emotions? Only an empty sac of flesh could stand so stolid as not to shed a single tear.

Her hand reaches down and caresses my cheek so very softly. I tremble at her merest touch. My soul screams in agony as the coachmen snaps the whip and the big iron rimmed wheels lurch forward. She tries to wave me away but my feet involuntarily begin to give chase.

Keeping pace with the still slow moving carriage, Judith strokes my fingers that clutch for the frame of the coach-window. "Oh Bernard, what am I going to do with you? You are making everything so difficult. Why can you not just believe in our love working a way out, on its own?"

"Because you are so far away and you are married to the King of France. And I am merely a boy who feigns being a man. What is there for me to believe in? What concrete evidence is there for me to believe other than this be our final parting?"

"I had not wished to tell you this, my prince but you leave me no other choice in the matter. If it is proof that you want then proof it shall be. I have missed my time!"

At first the words fall on uncomprehending ears. Time? Time for what? And then it dawns on me. Now I am at a loss for words. My legs begin to falter and I have lost my grip upon the window. Sensations of mixed and varying natures swarm across my body and I want to howl and cheer simultaneously. "Do you mean...?" I call out after the coach, which has left me standing in the mud of its tracks.

Judith propped her head out of the window and I can unmistakably discern the wide grin on her lips. "Yes," she nodded. "Yes!"

I leap into the air and swipe at an imaginary gadfly way above my head. My landing is hardly eloquent as I end up on the seat of my britches. But I don't care. I can hear her laughing at my current dilemma and I am laughing just as loudly. "I shall see you in Aachen. Can you hear me? I shall come to Aachen!"

Chapter Sixteen

Toronto: 1999

Stuffing an entire hero sandwich into his mouth is quite an amazing feat to witness. Pearce is obviously displaying some of his finer honed skills. We head back to my study with our food and our coffee in tow. Suddenly, the weight of exhaustion seems lifted and we both feel rejuvenated. Caffeine is an amazing drug. We're ready to talk into the wee hours of the morning if necessary.

"I can see your point," Pearce nods in concession to me. "The Queen getting pregnant by one of the Almyeri wasn't anything they could have foreseen; complicates matters considerably."

"More than you think."

"You mean it gets worse?"

"It already is worse! In order to appreciate to what degree holy men will go in their lust for power, you have to journey into hell!"

"We got an illegitimate heir to the throne about to be born. A well as a baby girl that wasn't born Jewish being raised as one. Just, how bad can it get?" Pearce questions not realizing what I am intimating.

"The victims are always the innocents. You don't find more innocent than babies. You're asking the wrong question. You should have been thinking to yourself, if Geberga wasn't their real daughter, then where was the real girl." I wink at Pearce as the plight of the whereabouts of the other child sprang to being.

"That's right!" he shot back. "There's got to be another child! Was she dead?"

He still hasn't caught on. "The real daughter was very much alive."

"So..."

"Remember, to keep a secret, you must live the lie. What did the Church want? Holy blood," I answer my own question before Pearce has a chance to. "If that blood could finally be contained in a Christian vessel, they would be ecstatic. Geberga was as much William's daughter as any one of his other children. She would be totally imprinted by her family's beliefs as if she was their naturally born child. Now picture the opposite! Let's go back in time; the year's 797 A.D. This is what they did..."

Bordeaux: 797 A.D.

It was possible to sail a small boat from Narbonne, which lay in the shadow of the Gulf of Lyons, to Bordeaux, located at the tip of a huge inlet that stretched for miles, from the great ocean to the east. The Garonne River had become the lifeline to thousands that lived, washed, and died by its banks. Stretching from sea to sea, it would constantly renew itself, cleansing itself of the waste and disease which mankind chose to carelessly create and abandon within its nourishing life-giving waters.

It had become common place for the trader ships to ply this route in the depths of the night, their small lanterns seen as floating ghosts, moving silently across the still waters. Few would have suspected or even hazard a guess at the cargo which one of these small sailboats carried this evening. Into the heart of southern Frankia sailed the Lion of Rome, unannounced and scantily attended, on a mission of the utmost secrecy.

The vessel showed extreme signs of its age, the splintered deck badly in need of repair. Anyone who would have seen this boat would mistake it for nothing more than the lifeline of a poor trader, trying to eke out a meager existence by transporting the cheapest of goods to be sold in the poorest of the local markets. Thus, under the cover of inconspicuousness, the crude ten-manner rowed quietly through the blackish waters towards its destination, the magnificent cathedral of Gironde-Bordeaux.

Careful plans had been executed so that only a select few would ever know that the Pope Leo III had come to Frankia. Those few consisted of the monks of St. Jerome, and the bishop and abbot, all whom nervously awaited his arrival. Disembarking at the small port of Langon, an insignificant speck along the river, arrangements had been made to travel the remaining forty miles by closed carriage. Neither the carriage driver nor the coachmen had been informed of the identity of their passengers. They were scurrilously transported by way of back-roads and little known paths that only the most skilled horseman would even dare to traverse.

Monsignor Morenci's greatest fear was not so much of being robbed by the bands of highway men that plagued these parts, but of being discovered as unwelcome guests in Charlemagne's domain. For if such an event was to occur, there was little doubt in his mind that none of the papal party would ever see Rome again. In Charlemagne's kingdom, Charlemagne ruled supreme and it would have been obvious to all that Leo had not come in the dead of the night to bring offerings to that great and mighty king.

It was a mission of vital importance to Vatican survival as far as the Pope was concerned. The Carolingians had drawn the line over which neither Pope nor King was to cross but agreeing to such callous dictates would ensure the eventual demise of the Catholic Church. Already, Leo found himself in the awkward position of requesting troops from the Franks to guarantee that his election as Pope two years prior would not now be revoked due to certain improprieties. The support came, but not before the Holy See had to agree to a list of demands by the Frankish king which only created further, more complicating problems for the papacy. Something had to be done quickly before the matter of state versus church assumed proportions totally out of control.

Fifteen years earlier, following the victory at Saxony, Charlemagne had granted for the minimal sum of seventy silver marks, a request by his boon companion and brother-in-law, Theodoric, the privilege of making his princedom of Narbonne a permanent hereditary kingdom; a kingdom where the Catholic Church had no authority and no sway over the day to day lives of his citizenry. In spite of the urging by the Pope, the King refused to even consider revoking the installation after the death of Theodoric but instead reaffirmed the hereditary right to rule upon his son, William Isaac. The Vatican became frightfully aware of the problem of a hereditary Jewish kingdom. Now it was threatening to grow into a monstrous uncontrollable nightmare that would ultimately engulf them.

The existence of a Jewish monarchy went against every fiber of their beliefs even if they had been responsible initially for its existence in France. If a Jewish kingdom continued to exist, then Leo had come to the fervent belief that such a state would negate the need for the coming kingdom of the Lord. That the presence of either kingdom excluded the possibility of the other and it was the Jewish Kingdom which had arisen first. As such, it was their Catholic kingdom that now appeared to be the interloper.

If the Church considered Theodoric to have been a thorn in their sides, then William had to be considered the entire briar patch. He had chosen, most definitely, not to assimilate into Frankish culture, but selected instead to establish his own retreat in Gellone where he actively sought followers to adopt his heretical way of life. There he spent his time proselytizing an existence that was the antithesis of everything Catholic. Not only did he choose not to go by his Christian name of William, nor even call himself Isaac as his father had lovingly called him, but instead he responded to the self-appointed nom du plum of Evarard and later simply Nasi.

Both were to be considered titles of royal significance, indicating the bearer to be either the potential heir to the throne of Narbonne or its reigning monarch respectively. As soon as his father Theodoric had died in single battle against the Emir on the plain of Panronia, William adopted the title of "Prince of Narbonne", leaving the title of "Evarard" to his eldest son Heribert.

The importance of the titles had not been lost upon the Pope and his bishops. There's was a society where titles and stature meant all the difference in a noble's personal empire and wealth. They were also well versed in Hebrew language and Jewish history. The first to adopt the title of prince or "Nasi", were the Hasmoneans who later decided to take upon themselves the responsibilities of being kings. It would be no surprise to them if some day William decided to expand his title to include King of Frankia. To one seeking power, it would be the next logical step; a step that they would make every effort to prevent from happening through every available means at their disposal.

If the translation of Evarard meant "knight of valor" as the Hebrew would indicate, then the leaders of the diocese concluded that Theodoric's clan was already in the process of developing its own system of feudal government. Drawing conclusions such as these led the Bishop of Bordeaux to write to the Pope of his concerns. Leo deemed the worries of his bishop serious enough to bring him into the shadow of the cathedral this very night. Once and for all the heresy would have to be stopped and God had delivered into their hands the means by which to accomplish this feat.

The carriage took its passengers as far as the monastery of the black hooded monks of St. Jerome. As soon as Pope Leo set foot upon the ground, the bishop threw himself to his knees and kissed the pontifical ring upon Leo's crooked finger. The Pope bid him to stand with a mere flick of his aged hand, reducing the Bishop Agobard to a level of either nuisance or insignificance. To Leo, there was very little difference. Agobard had been a disappointment ever since he acquired the office of Bishop from Aribert who had been ignobly forced from office by Charlemagne.

Whereas Aribert had been belligerent and condemning, Agobard was non-committal. Although Leo blamed most of what had occurred on his predecessor, Pope Adrian, he could not help but feel that if Agobard had been more vocal and alarmist, the situation would never have gotten this far out of hand. Where was his outcry when Charlemagne decided to send his son Louis at the age of three to live in Narbonne with Alda and Theodoric? That had been the first tell-tale sign of undermining the Church.

The King envied the education his sister and brother-in-law were providing for their own son, William. By the age of twelve, William could speak and write five languages fluently. Franco-German, Hebrew, Arabic, Greek and Armenian flowed off the tip of his tongue effortlessly. Louis, on the other hand, seemed to have difficulty in mastering his own mother tongue. If it had not been for the frequent visits to see his father in Aachen, the bishopric would never have been confronted by the disturbing changes in Charlemagne's son's beliefs.

By removing Louis from the influences of the Roman Catholic Church, the future emperor began to adopt many of the foreign customs of his uncle. Harmless as they may have been, their appearance were considered strange by all of the royal retinue in Aachen, thus seriously damaging Louis's right to rule upon his father's eventual death. Sadly, as he himself had been a lover of languages although he had never learned to write, Charlemagne sent for his son and had him return to Aachen permanently in order to protect his son's future inheritance.

It was Leo's opinion that none of this would have happened had Agobard been more vehement in his opposition to the King's plan to send his son away to be raised by heretics.

Walking through the corridors that led from the monastery to the cathedral, the monks scurried about the papal party, holding their candles high above their heads, begging for an opportunity to touch the flowing red robes of their Pope. Perhaps even to be so lucky as to lightly kiss the ermine lined cape that trailed majestically behind. Leo appeared oblivious to their antics, his mind clouded with other matters of grave importance, the least of which would be dealing with his errant bishop.

A torch suspended from the stone wall at the end of the tunnel illuminated the large antechamber that formed the outer wall of the cathedral's foundations. At its furthest point, a huge winding staircase led into a small reading room situated behind the altar of the assembly hall. Agobard politely offered Leo the throne chair which had been his to occupy and then sat himself down by one of the many reading tables that formed a semi-circle in front of Leo. The other members of the party as well as the Abbot and the monks filled the remaining chairs in anticipation of the Pope's first words.

Leo waited until there was complete silence before uttering a sound. "I cannot tell you how very disappointed I am with events as they now stand. I hold you entirely responsible. Would you not agree with me, Monsignor Morenci."

Morenci nodded, his silvered hair waving in response thereby signaling his agreement. "Most certainly, Excellency!"

Agobard appeared shocked by the accusation, while simultaneously a rumble arose from the quick chatter between the monks.

"Surely you are aware of the problems, Bishop Agobard, otherwise you would have had no reason to send me your letters of complaint and I would not have had a need to be here."

"Excellency," Agobard pleaded, the prayer beads squeezed tightly in his hands, "I have no idea of what you are referring to."

"Oh, come, come now, good bishop," the Pope tsk-tsked under his breath. "Do not take me for a fool, at least not for an old fool. I am well aware of events in this part of the world. We are one Church and I am its head. It would be unforgivable of me not to know what transpires in this barbaric country of yours. And what I have seen, I am not pleased with!"

Agobard dropped to his knees, dragging the black hooded abbot down with him. A look of total surprise swept over the abbot's face as he was pulled from his seat. "If we have offended you, Excellency, then we ask your forgiveness and appeal to your Grace." The bishop bowed his head as he spoke, avoiding Leo's penetrating stare.

"The abbot has done nothing to offend me, Agobard. After all, he is merely an abbot, a source from which we choose new bishops as you are aware. Perhaps he would not be as likely to commit as many mistakes in judgment as you have taken the liberty to commit?"

"If only your Excellency would take the time to enlighten me, perhaps then I would fully understand the error of my ways." Agobard was sincere; his tone of voice clearly indicating that he had no concept of how he was responsible for current events. "I will gladly do penance in reparation for my sins."

Leo shook his head and sighed. A look of disgust creased his ancient craggy features while his beady dark eyes stared harshly from beneath the papal miter.

"How is it that I could have surrounded myself with such incompetence? Not only do they commit error after error but they have no insight as to what they are even doing. What were you thinking when you agreed to let Charlemagne divorce Disiderata? Did you even take a second to consider the consequences? So what if he wanted to marry Liutgard? The king already has more than one wife and God knows how many concubines! What manner of idiot would insist that he has to obtain a divorce annulment before agreeing to let him marry again?"

"But, but, your..." Agobard tried to speak in his own defense but was quickly cut off in mid statement by the Pope."

"But nothing! It was inexcusable. I read your report. You thought you would teach the Carolingian the proper way of doing things. Well, in case you aren't aware of it, the proper way of dealing with Charlemagne is letting him do as he pleases and turning a blind eye to it. When Desiderata returned to her father, who do you think Disiderius blamed for the insult to himself and his daughter...not you, me!

The greatest threat to the Vatican are the half-savage Lombards who have us totally surrounded and you in one quick sweep of your feathered pen destroy everything that it took years for us to develop. The marriage of the Lombard princess to Charlemagne was our greatest coup. It almost ensured the Lombards would adopt the Catholic faith and accept me as their spiritual head and now we are practically at a state of war!

So, spare me your innocence bishop and instead tell me something that will appease my wrath. You have put me in a position where I must ask the Carolingian for assistance in repulsing our mutual enemy and knowing the King, he will use my request as a negotiating instrument by which to extract further concessions from me. Already he considers himself above the Church. What will he think now that we must ask his aid another time? We appear weak and foolish to him. You, most certainly must appear weak and foolish to him!"

Agobard found the courage to speak in his own defense. "Excellency, I think that we might be too premature in judging what the King's attitude is towards us. I personally feel that the relationship between Charlemagne and us is based upon a mutual and healthy respect for the other. The King has expanded the Catholic Empire into regions we never dreamed of accessing before. Saxony, Brittany, Burgundia, all are now areas of practicing Catholicism. This does not strike me to be the deeds of a man who lords himself above us."

"And do you not remember what concessions have already been granted to the King in exchange for his cooperation?," Leo spat in front of the prone bishop. "He gives with one hand and you have let him take back with both. He and his Jewish relatives are laughing at you this very moment, my dear bishop."

The bishop straightened and stiffened his resolve. "The situation with the Jews is no fault of mine. If you recall, it was the secret dealings of the papacy with the Carolingians that brought them here in the first place. That was long before you were pope and I was bishop. I will not accept the blame for matters which have gone beyond your control where the Jewish Nasis are concerned."

"Nasis, Nasis! We wouldn't have any of these Hebrew princes to deal with if you had been a little more alert and calculating. How many score of fair, young, Catholic ladies of the court are there in this country? Twenty? Fifty? One hundred? All are the daughters of dukes and counts and perhaps even a few of the Carolingian family itself. And what happens? When William goes looking for a bride, rather than arrange one for him, you sit idly by while he imports some Hebrew harlot from the east.

164

This Guiberc is apparently a Yemenite tribal princess and now we have more of these cancerous children being born constantly. Soon the situation will be totally out of control. There will be a Jewish prince child for every town in Frankia that has a congregation of Jews. This is utterly inexcusable!"

Agobard was staggered by the verbal onslaught. "There was nothing I could do. William is a very determined man. Theodoric was a convert in comparison to William's passion for his own religion. He has turned his citadel in Gellone into a virtual sanctuary for religious studies. He's brought sages from as far away as the Indus River to study and teach their Tanakh. They even refer to the community that continuously resides there as Beth El or as Casa Dei. When I begin to ask too many questions they turn a deaf ear to me. Now how was I to convince a man like William, who is so strong in his beliefs, that he should have married one of the court ladies of Frankia?"

"Hrrmph. Well you should have tried harder. Instead we get Guiberc and her brother Reneward. The man goes as far as claiming that he is blessed and he was never baptized. What kind of message do you think this relays to the people? And then there is the matter of Reneward's son, Guischart. How many times must I hear about the oath he swears every time before he enters a battle. How does it go? God deliver me from my enemies..."

"...and if I should die, keep me from the arms of Jesus so that I may die with honor in your eyes only," Agobard completed.

"I see that you have heard it," Leo replied sarcastically. "If you don't feel we have a problem then might I suggest that you, dear bishop, may be the problem."

The abbot pulled back the hood of his habit and boldly interrupted the conversation wishing to speak. He was young; younger than anyone the pope had ever seen as abbot of a monastery before. Perhaps it was his age that caught most off guard, or his extraordinary physical beauty, but odd as his request had been, Leo granted him permission to speak.

"This is probably very presumptuous of me, but I think I have a solution to our mutual dilemma."

His lyrical voice easily swayed the papal party to urge him to continue. "Finally we find a man with some intelligence amongst your followers, bishop. I was beginning to think that the conversion of the Franks was a colossal mistake."

Agobard opened his mouth and raised a finger to reply but then decided to wait. To be insulted by a man that was considered by most in the Church to be the epitome of everything non-Christian was the ultimate in humiliation but he knew any response would further aggravate his precarious position.

"Please continue," the Pope leaned towards the abbot. "Your name, good abbot, before you start, so that I may make note of it in case any opportunities arise that require a man of a more cerebral nature." Leo quickly flashed a poisoned stare towards the bishop.

"My name, Excellency, is Hincamar, abbot of this humble monastery dedicated to the good works of St. Jerome. I know that it is forward of me to even suggest that I have a solution to a problem which surely outweighs one of such lowly standing, but I can only fathom that being in the presence of one so saintly as yourself has inspired me to excel beyond my usual position."

Agobard watched as Leo's mouth cracked into a fractured smile. He quelled the surge of bile that began to rise in his throat. There was nothing to say now, but he would have to talk to Hincamar alone, once Leo and his party were far from Bordeaux. To think that after sharing so much of himself with Hincamar, that he would turn on him so casually. It was as he had always thought. A pretty face belies a rotten soul. Better he should have bedded one of the lowly monks than have his face slapped so sharply by this one.

Hincamar began to lay out his nefarious plan before the Pope. It was well thought out, thorough in every detail, and devious to the most righteous thinking mind. How long had Hincamar been conceiving his ideas, was all that Agobard could ponder at the time. Surely, he could not have been planning to betray him all the times they had been together. What had happened to friendship? To love?

The thought of betrayal by someone that had he had shared everything with haunted Agobard. Nausea flushed over the bishop as he reached out, grabbing one of the nearby monk's tasseled belts in order to steady himself. It was taking all his effort to stand but he was well aware that he could not let himself collapse while all eyes were upon him. He could not show any sign of weakness. His will steeled itself against the churning in his gut.

"Are you having some difficulty, Bishop Agobard, with the suggestions being presented?" Leo's tone was taunting. The words were easily brushed aside but the penetrating eyes beneath that beetled brow, searching for leverage, scrutinizing for a weakness were what bothered Agobard the most. How could one so evil be ruling all of Christianity?

"No, your Excellency," the Bishop replied. "I merely began to feel slightly dizzy. It is possible that the suggestions being made regarding what might be considered less than righteous actions by men of the clergy have upset me somewhat."

A hoarse, dry laugh ushered forth through Leo's thin lips. "As it should do, my dear Bishop. After all, we are all men of the cloth and what has been proposed would be considered unworthy of us under any other circumstances. But in this situation, I have to agree with the abbot and feel that this opportunity was granted us by God for no other reason but to do what we must."

"Yes Agobard. We have no other alternatives," Hincamar added.

Agobard looked deep into the abbot's eyes, searching for some sign, any appearance of a spark of humanity. There was none to be found. Hincamar's grey eyes were dead, dead of affection, dead without remorse. Something had happened to his paramour, but what? No words, no signs; absolutely nothing. Almost as if they had never been, never was, or never will be again.

"There are always alternatives," the bishop shook his head. "If we look long enough we can always find another means to an end. There are too many faults with your plan which must be corrected if it has any chance to succeed. You must know your adversary like I do if you want to avoid the glaring mistakes you have made."

The pope leaned forward in his chair, carefully examining the exchange between Bishop and abbot. There was an obvious tone of anger in their exchange which had not been there when he first arrived. He would have to delve into their relationship at a later date, he mentally made note, but at this time it would seriously hinder the total cooperation required to put Hincamar's plan into effect.

"So Bishop, enlighten us to the flaws which we have failed to detect. Consider this your opportunity to set right the wrongs we have made against you. Perhaps if you clarify the young abbot's mistakes it would serve to restore my faith in you. Redeem yourself Bishop."

Agobard did not know whether he should be pleased for the opportunity to salvage his career or angered by Leo's condemning tone. He decided it was best to hold his tongue and acquiesce to the Pope's privilege of omnipotence. He would play the game, if game this be and perhaps with a little luck he could turn the tables to his advantage. A wave of calm washed over him as he began to speak. "If you are to have any chance of success then I would suggest that you listen carefully to me. Only I possess enough knowledge regarding the family of the Almyeri and the logistical skill required to achieve your goals."

"My Lord," Leo exclaimed feigning shock, "this puppy has balls! Well, Bishop, for a man walking a very thin line, you have caught my attention. Let us hear what you have to say."

"Hincamar is mistaken if he thinks that a way can be found to persuade Guiberc to come to Bordeaux in order to give birth to her child. She is not some weak bladdered female who fears every shadow just because her husband is chasing enemy forces down in the Carcassonne's. His expeditions have taken him south since Emir Hisham crossed the border four years ago and burned the suburbs of Narbonne. He won't abandon his quest until he's avenged the death of his father and that will be a long, long time in coming.

Each setback that he is handed by Hisham's forces only makes him even more determined for revenge. Revenge is an often all-consuming emotion. How do you think he felt when Hisham suddenly died last year from an illness? Cheated? Betrayed? I know that's how I would feel. His heart's not in the battle anymore now that Alhaqam is leading the Saracens. If it were not for the fact that Alhaqam was Hisham's son, I think that William would have abandoned his personal vendetta a long time ago and returned to his city."

"What makes you so certain he won't do that now," Hincamar interrupted.

"A man in my position hears many things; knows many things that an abbot would not." Agobard slyly winked at his once close companion. "I have been informed that two of Alhaqam's uncles have joined ranks with William, Suleiman and Abdullah. It is also rumored that the Wali Zado of Barcelona is thinking of throwing in his lot with William. It won't be a personal affair for much longer. When the news reaches Charlemagne, he will turn this into another expedition of conquest."

"Can you be certain of this," Leo questioned. "If this is true then we will have an opportunity to assume total control of the country in the absence of its leaders. We must be certain of this information."

"It is true. General Worad came to me for confession not too long ago. Apparently he required forgiveness for several lapses into adultery which he felt were necessary if he was to return alive from the planned campaigns to reoccupy Ausona, Cardona, and Casseres. Charlemagne has already had his advisors prepare the strategies for the coming battles."

The chatter amongst the monks reached a feverish pitch. There surfaced a mixture of trepidation and anguish at the mention of another war. The hardships of battle were felt in the monasteries as well. Decreased food rations, pressures of providing sanctuary and hospitalization to the peasants and the soldiers. They would not derive the same benefits from warfare as they now entertained in peacetime. The bishop's revelation was not welcome by them at all.

"Silence!" the pope bellowed and almost immediately a deaf silence filled the antechamber. "Enough of these hysterics! You act like frightened little children. We are an army of the Lord and what we do, we do for all. Do not concern me with your petty little wants and cravings. You, of St. Jerome are our girded right arm. Fail us and you doom us all to purgatory. Succeed with us and all will find paradise in Frankia. Now, good Bishop, continue if you may. Yours is welcome news to my ears. You are more capable than I first gave credit."

"As you are most certainly aware, Excellency, Charlemagne is without the advice of his chief aide, Isaac Iskoi. He has recently been sent to Baghdad and to Jerusalem to reconfirm the Carolingian treaty with the Caliph, Harun al Raschid. This creates a predicament for our King as he cannot be certain how much support will be given by the Caliph for his campaigns. His hands will be somewhat tied, which translates into long delays and an extended war of attrition. Time will obviously be on our side."

Leo wrung his hands gleefully. "Good! Good! This is most certainly welcome news. But what of Hincamar's plan? We must know for certain if it is practical."

Raising the palm of his hand, Agobard signaled for a moment to explain before allowing

167

Hincamar to rejoin the conversation. The pope fell silent in anticipation, while Hincamar began to pace restlessly upon the spot he stood. "All in good time Excellency. I want you to be fully aware of the entire situation as it now exists. We must examine the total picture if we are going to make a move to change destiny." The Pope and Morenci nodded their heads in agreement.

"It must be known why it is unlikely to persuade Guiberc to come to Bordeaux. Several years ago, as you are well aware, Charlemagne granted a request by Theodoric that the Jewish princedom in Narbonne would be made a hereditary and permanent kingship. Two copies of the agreement were written. One is in possession of the family of the Almyeri, the other just happens to be in my vault in this cathedral. If the time should be right, how much value would a single copy in the possession of heretic Jews be if there existed no Church or State records to verify their claim?"

"Yes, I agree, but such a thing would not be possible as long as Charlemagne is alive," Hincamar argued.

"This is true, but not even Charlemagne will live forever and how many others will remember what documents he signed when it becomes well known that such knowledge would be detrimental to the mother Church? Gentlemen, I am not talking of a plan over a year or two. We have decades to put this into operation. We are the Church. We will be here long after our adversaries have returned to the earth as so much dust."

"Well put, Agobard," Leo waved for continuation which in turn silenced Hincamar who looked prepared to ask a further question.

"In this agreement between King and Jew, Charlemagne granted the Almyeri one half of the income from the salt flats, as well as the tolls and navigation rights to travel the Garonne. Over the years, this has translated into quite a sizable income of which you are also most certainly aware. William has used this income to his advantage. Our taxes have built his towering community of Gellone as well as purchased him the right of what we have come to refer to as the Judaeorum Colaphus."

"A most despicable evil," Leo spat, "of which I hold you still to be entirely responsible." Once again the Pope's anger was inflamed against the Bishop as he pointed his gnarled finger.

"If responsibility be earned because I could not bend the King's ear then so be it." Agobard had grown cocky, knowing that he now had the upper hand with the Pope and therefore refusing to cower from the insults any longer. "Charlemagne enjoyed the opportunity to put us in our place. After the controversy concerning Aribert, if he had not given the privilege to William, he probably would have taken it upon himself.

Who would refuse the opportunity of one day a year, of dragging a member of the clergy onto a podium before an assembly of the populace and administering a single blow in retribution for acts of sedition and hate mongering against any of the Frankish peoples. To be truthful, I do not think there is a man among you who would not accept such an opportunity to mete physical justice against an enemy, adversary or nuisance."

"Yes, yes, all very good but this William has either crippled or killed every priest, monk or archbishop that has come before him." Leo's eyes were glazed with hatred as he thought of all his chosen flock that had fallen to the Almyeri's justice.

"And precisely the reason you will never persuade Guiberc to come to Bordeaux. This mastery of the cupped fist in order to strike a killing blow to the ear or neck has earned her husband the hatred of all of us. She is no fool. She would never willingly place herself in danger by coming to us. And with the profit her family earns by the royal agreements, she will never need to look for aid from us either. If we are to carry out Hincamar's plan then it is imperative that we do it within their own palace in Narbonne."

"Absurd! Can't be done!" Monsignor Morenci bolted from his chair as he challenged Agobard's comment. The silver haired fox had remained quiet for the duration of the discussion but he felt he could no longer restrain his opinions. Leo motioned for him to remain calm but Morenci waved away the pope's cautionary hand. "We cannot walk into the lion's den in an attempt to steal the lion's food. That would be insanity. If the lion awakes, we will be its next meal. It cannot be carried out in Narbonne. The risks are too great. I must insist that we find a way to bring Guiberc to Bordeaux or else we abandon this fool's mission."

"You are wrong." Agobard rebutted the Monsignor's opinion without even a thought to Morenci's seniority. "It can be carried out in Narbonne, easier than you think. You all have in mind to force a situation and I suggest to take advantage of its natural course."

"Again, Excellency, I must insist that the Bishop's suggestions are absurd. Who but God knows the natural course of events? That is why it is imperative that we have Guiberc in our custody. With the use of shepen we can keep her oblivious to our intentions until the time is right."

"Now that is absurd," Agobard blasted his detractor. With a cavalier toss of his robes over his shoulders, the bishop strode defiantly to within a hair's breadth of the Monsignor. "As I see it, good sir, I have very little to lose but you have everything to lose. Take the bishopric from me and I shall be content with my lot in life. But if you commit this heinous crime of which your plotting and you fail in its execution then you will have lost everything; Papacy, Church, power, everything. Who will believe in you when the Church is shown to be under Lucifer's control?"

"Excellency, the Bishop intends to betray us!" Monsignor Morenci threw himself at Leo's feet, his forehead placed upon the instep of the pope's right foot.

"I think not," Leo tutted. "In fact I think the Bishop is handing us our reprieve if I am not mistaken?"

"That is so, Excellency," Agobard nodded.

"Please continue, I wish to hear more of your plan. You have intrigued me." Leo gave a little kick of his foot, knocking Morenci off balance so that he stumble backwards a step before catching himself from further mishap.

"Guiberc is a mistress of herbs and drugs. We are all aware of that. She possesses secrets from her homeland that we cannot even fathom. She would detect shepen in her drink before you could even place it down before her. And who is to say that she would not add a little something to all our drinks if given the opportunity. We have no love for her and she certainly has no love for us.

What you have been speaking of thus far is to in fact hold her hostage. If you attempted to do so, William would be on your doorstep by the morrow. It would not even surprise me if Charlemagne had his forces there to assist him. If we wish to succeed we must work from within the framework presented. The facts are simple. Guiberc is with child and the Duchess of Aquitaine is with child. So instead, we have Gisella sail from Bordeaux to Narbonne so that she can be with her close friend, the princess of Narbonne, while their husbands are both off on military excursions."

A broad smile returned to Leo's withered face. "Ah, I am beginning to see your intentions. But what of the timing? It has to be coordinated perfectly if both Guiberc and Gisella are not to know what occurs."

"That is what I have been trying to explain to you all along. Unlike Hincamar's plot, and the Monsignor's rejections, it can be done. I have seen it done and I know who can do it."

"Horse's ass," Morenci exclaimed from the withdrawn position he had taken in the corner of the antechamber.

169

"Shut up!", Leo exclaimed. "Please continue."

"Gisella will obviously take along her own midwives and doctor. Guiberc will be tended by her own assemblage of Jewish midwives but her doctor, fortunately for us is currently travelling with William. And it happens that Gisella's doctor is Rolard de Poitiers, the same doctor that was tending Theodoric's wounds when he died four years ago.

The same doctor who used to be Charlemagne's court physician until he failed to save the King's brother-in-law even though the wounds suffered were fatal and Rolard did all that he could. The good doctor has confessed to me many times that he would like the opportunity to redress that situation. He also wished to confess the sins of his taking life on countless occasions on behest of the court ladies. Apparently all these battles involving their husbands have made the ladies-in-waiting somewhat restless if you understand my meaning.

There would have been a lot of immaculate conceptions being explained to husbands upon their return. Rolard found a solution to that problem. He calls it astragalus and he makes it from the locoweed plant. Grind it up, boil it and then collect the fine paste left when the water has evaporated; tasteless, odorless, impossible to detect. Only a smidgen added to food or drink and the lady-in-waiting waits no longer. He has found that it will cause a miscarriage any time during the pregnancy. Even in the final stages. Better yet, it has a euphoric effect that seems to cause a temporary loss of memory at the time. No pain, no regrets, not even the slightest tingling of remorse."

The Pontiff clasped his hands wringing them repeatedly. "Surely this is the answer to all our concerns. We wait until one begins labor and then induce it in the other. The time interval of their natural pregnancies is so minor that it would not seem impossible that each enters labor the same day. But then, how do we switch the babies? And what if the children are of different sex?"

"Rolard will have to examine both children, especially the Jewish child because if it is a boy he has to be certified healthy if he is to be circumcised eight days later. As for the other matter, I suggest we keep several near term wet nurses available just in case we have to induce several more deliveries. No matter which child, Gisella will eventually return to Bordeaux with the Jew-child as her own."

"And thereby my initial plan reaps its results," Hincamar interjected. Bowing before Leo, the abbot attempted to accept the credit where he felt it was due. "As I have already stated, the child will be raised in the good Catholic home of the Aquitaines and then as he or she matures, the child will be married into the Carolingian household so that this so-called sacred blood of David will be an integral part of our monarchy and then we can dispense with these foreign interlopers once and for all."

Pope Leo tapped the knuckles of his closed fist to his tightly pursed lips as he carefully though of possible consequences. "And what of loose tongues?"

"Surely you cannot be suggesting that any of us would betray the Mother Church or yourself, Excellency!" Agobard tinged his voice with every drop of sincerity he could muster.

"Of course not," Hincamar responded.

The monks mumbled a communal consent that could only be interpreted as an affirmation of cooperation. "Good," Leo responded. "Now that that is all settled, you have my blessings to begin this plan of ours. Persuade Gisella to leave immediately. The sooner she is underway, the better. May God in his infinite mercy grant us success in the performance of his works. Amen."

"Amen," echoed the response.

"Now that things are settled, I wish to get back underway to Rome before my absence creates too great a stir. Morenci, help me out of this chair. I have sat here too long and my bones are paying the price." The Monsignor leaped forward to help the Pope on to his feet. With a wave of his hand, Leo dismissed the assemblage, urging them to leave the antechamber immediately. Only the abbot waited behind while the monks returned to their quarters and the bishop ascended the long, winding staircase that led back into the cathedral's main hall.

Stepping forward he kneeled politely and kissed Leo's ringed hand. "Have I done well Excellency?"

"Your performance was magnificent," Leo replied. "You have made your uncle and me very proud of you. At last we finally know whether the Bishop stands with us or against us. It also has given me an insight into Agobard that I never knew existed. He does not crumble easily. There is a quick and agile mind within that bloated head of his; a dangerous mind. Anyone who can think that quickly when reeling from a blow is a threat to my own throne. What we have seen him do this night, I am certain he could do just as easily in Rome. Let him have his moment of victory but we shall keep a close eye upon him. That I leave in your capable hands, Hincamar."

The abbot glowed in appreciation of the responsibility granted him. "I shall not fail you, Excellency."

"I don't think you will, my son. That is why I trust you to leave no witnesses to what we have agreed upon this night. See to it that all but the Bishop meet an untimely death. No one is to know! No monks, no midwives, no wet nurses. They are all to die. I don't want anyone left that can corroborate Agobard's confession in case he turns against us."

"What of the doctor, Excellency?"

"See to it that Rolard delivers his last set of children that night as well."

"It will be done."

"I expect no less of you, dear boy. You will be handsomely rewarded but I expect you to be patient. Everything will be yours in good time. Do you understand?"

The abbot nodded as he kissed the ringed finger once again.

"Now it is imperative that Morenci and my party which I have left standing at the mercy of the outdoors return to Rome. Careful with any documents but there must be a record to ensure that the legacy of the child in the House of Aquitaine not be lost or forgotten. One more thing, Hincamar, if the Jew-child born is a girl, see to it that Gisella names her Judith. If a boy, he is to be called Jacob. I want the child easily identified by any future popes in case I am not alive at the time of the child's marriage. I am certain that Gisella will be more than happy to cooperate, knowing that the child was born in the blessings of the Almyeri's palace."

Leo leaned forward and lightly kissed the abbot's head on its crown. "Be off with you before your absence leads to suspicion. And do not get to comfortable with Agobard just in case it's necessary to send him on his way to paradise. Come Morenci! We have a long journey ahead of us."

Into the shadows of the night, the Pope and his Monsignor disappeared down the cavernous mouth of the tunnel that led to the outside world that waited beyond the black stoned walls of the monastery. "That nephew of yours Morenci is a good lad. He'll rise rapidly in this Church."

"Thank you, Excellency," Morenci replied as he helped Leo into the waiting carriage. "And have no worries Excellency, he will carry out your orders exactly as you instructed."

"Very good, Morenci. I will personally reward him when he does so."

Chapter Seventeen

Toronto: 1999

"The good news is that there is some payback!" I respond to Pearce's fervent wish, that divine retribution should somehow befall all those in the story, that were nothing but evil incarnate.

"It's inconceivable," he rants, "that men of the cloth could be so heartless. It galls me. That this Pope would later acquire sainthood is outrageous!"

"Ah, I see you know your church history. Saint Leo is venerated for his beautifying of Rome. All the accusations of him being scum of the earth are recorded as being unfounded."

"But this situation they created is horrible. Indescribably horrible! How can everything get swept under the rug?"

Pearce appears obviously troubled. The fact that he knew some history of the papacy aided my suspicions of his strict religious upbringing. It would help explain some of his more emotional reactions.

"Not even they could have foreseen the relationship that would result. But when you start with a little lie, guaranteed that it will be monumental by the time it's finished."

"But what of this relationship! Even by the Church laws it's sinful. Blasphemous!"

"All the better to use to their own advantage, which by the way they did later on. But I'll get to that later. Right now, I'd like to tell you about them getting a little bit of their own brand of justice. Oddly enough, all those historical figures that bore the nom de plume of 'The Great' were better antagonists to the Church, than defenders of it. Constantine saw the Holy See as his personal plaything. He did what was necessary to unite and rule an empire. Whether he was a true follower of doctrine is highly debatable. Charlemagne wasn't any different. The Church, to him, sufficed as a means to an end. He did as he pleased. He did it with his marriages, his divorces, his polygamy, and his alliances with Islam and especially with his selection of Jews as both friends and advisors. I think the title really meant greater than the Church."

"Well, that worked fine for Charlemagne, but what about the rest of the people."

Pearce is still disgusted with the entire episode concerning Judith and Geberga. You can tell a lot about a man from the way he reacts to certain situations. I'll give Pearce some credit. He obviously has some moral standards. I like that.

"The rest received a share of retribution. It may not have been much, but at least it was something. William would get his once a year opportunity to take out a member of the clergy with a single blow. He had a good track record. Charlemagne had an even better record. Let me tell you a few more details about Charlemagne's coronation in 800 A.D., which you don't usually read about in the school texts. When you see the paintings, it would appear that he and Leo are the best of friends. In fact, Leo looks like quite a nice looking guy. Nothing could be further from the truth."

Rome: 800 A.D.

Seated within the conclave, the clergy huddled nervously, awaiting his arrival. They had been summoned under extreme urgency, compelled to attend by the knowledge that failure to do so, could result in excommunication. They had come to suspect, by the untimely passing of several colleagues over the last few months, that it could even result in their deaths.

These were troubled times, and once again the papacy was available to whomever could wrest the fisherman's throne through nefarious means . Thus far, Leo III had been in command of that exalted position for nearly five years, but having been found shamefully in the carnal embrace of a married woman, his grasp on the papacy had become tenuous at the most. He may have been old, but his proclivity for younger women still burned with youthful enthusiasm. What was more serious was this particular woman happened to be the wife of the Chief Magistrate of Rome.

Chief Magistrate Ruggilio marched with his cohort of pikers into the streets of Rome, where he forcibly removed Leo from his carriage while he paraded in the Procession of Litane. If Leo happened to be praying during the procession, his prayers had definitely gone unanswered. Dragged in front of a civilian tribunal, the pope was confronted with his numerous sins and found guilty. Sentencing was carried out swiftly by the civilians of Rome, who eagerly awaited their opportunity for retribution. After all, this was the same man who had taxed them excessively all the way into the grave and beyond. Though the money had been used to beautify the Vatican that meant little to those expecting that it would feed the hungry and provide shelter to the poor.

Carrying the writhing body of the Pope above their heads, the pikers flung the screaming vicar into the outstretched arms of the populace. For almost three hours he remained at the mercy of an unforgiving mob, who pelted him with stones, dragged him by his ropes through the streets, and when they finally exhausted themselves in front of the local smithy, they exacted their final punishment.

With iron tongs they clawed at Leo's eyes until blood streamed down the sides of his face. Between horrific screams he cursed and swore calling down heavenly retributions upon his tormentors. When the people could no longer tolerate his caterwauling, they took the blacksmith's pincers and while others forced his mouth open they cut his tongue in half so that they didn't have to listen to him any longer. Then they left him there, beaten and barely alive, stretched out on the smithy's cold stone floor.

Bruised and dazed, Leo dragged himself back towards the sanctuary of the Vatican Square. Every inch of ground he covered equaled a pound of flesh that he would exact in revenge. Feeding off his hatred, he found the strength to survive and plot his vengeance. Once safely within the Vatican enclave, he was bundled and whisked to the safety of Charlemagne's kingdom. His recovery took a full year, and during that time he became extremely obligated to the King of the Franks. Accompanied by a contingent of soldiers, Charlemagne sent the Pope back to Rome, to announce the Frankish king's own arrival, which would follow shortly.

To any that looked upon him now, all they saw was a creature of revulsion. Repulsively disfigured, his face a mass of scars, and barely able to speak, not even his own Holy See wanted him back. The council of cardinals sought to have him removed from the papacy, but they had failed to anticipate the degree of Leo's hatred for any that stood in his way. His soul had become black and foul. Satan's vicar would not allow anyone to defy him; he had sworn that they would all pay for what they had done to God's holy messenger. And if hundreds would have to die in order to achieve his goals, then so be it. It was God's will. He had become the spokesman of a dark god, passing judgment over life and death with impunity.

Though his mouth could not fully form the syllables of his edicts, his actions spoke in his stead. Red cardinal hats floated in a sea of crimson blood, until all that sought the downfall of Leo III, perished in a fiery storm of hatred and brimstone. Those voices promoting his abdication were stifled quickly. Those who objected to his papacy met with a bizarre series of fatal accidents.

None of those remaining would condone his excesses, but there were none fool-hearty enough to condemn him either. In a matter of weeks, Pope Leo III re-established himself as the Vicar of Christ without further objection, until just recently. Someone from amongst the papal enclave had sought the help of the Lombards after he had returned to the city, that same godless, unruly people which Pope Adrian with the aid of Charlemagne had finally brought under control. Chief Magistrate Ruggilio had also sought the sanctuary of this brazen race when he too learned of Leo's unexpected return to power.

The Papal insurgents requested that the Lombard king remove Pope Leo from Saint Peter's throne. In return the king would receive a healthy yearly tribute. If it had not been for the Pope's spies amongst his enemies, he may have never known about the lone rider heading south from Lombardy, carrying the anxiously awaited reply from the Lombard chief.

Now there would be a day of reckoning. The doors to the Great Assembly were pulled back by the Swiss Guard, as a deadly silence filled the hall. The angel of darkness was coming. Pope Leo had arrived. No sooner had the disfigured form wrapped in saintly robes entered he waved for the guards to seal the exits. None would be allowed leave without his permission.

His loyal adjutant, the Monsignor Morenci stood by his side. Morenci was more than just an aide; he had become the voice of the Pope. Whatever Leo wanted to say, it would be through Morenci's mouth that the words would be uttered. Into Morenci's ears the pontiff would mouth his message but the Monsignor would transfer the tortured whisper into a papal pronouncement. He had become a man to be feared as much as Leo himself.

The circus had started. Leo grunted and Morenci lectured. "Traitors! You have all become a nest of vipers. Like in olden days, you have made the Lord's house a den of thieves. If it was not for the Lord's mercy, he would have cast you all from the land of the living long ago. Do you think I do not know which of you have entertained these thoughts of my destruction? But you have failed. Last night my spies intercepted your reply from the Lombards.

Your kingly savior has decided to send a garrison to aid your uprising. Unfortunately for you it will not be allowed to happen. At this very moment I have sent my secretary to the camp of the Great Carolus Magnus, who is but a short distance from our city. What do you think his reaction will be when he hears of your perfidy with his most bitter enemy?

By the power invested in me I have offered him a marriage of Church and State. I shall appoint him as my right hand, my sword against infidelity, my scourge against treason by offering him the Imperatorship of the Holy Roman Empire."

A gasp went up from the hostage audience. "You cannot do this!" several of the cardinals protested. "The throne of God cannot be bartered with. There can be no mortal king to govern over the Church. This is sacrilege."

"Silence!" Morenci shouted. "I will brook no dissension in my house. You have behaved like foolish children and a stiff rod is necessary to return you to the path of righteousness. Charlemagne shall be a servant unto me and I shall be a servant unto him. The papal crown rests on my head and he shall be as a prince amongst the nations, as the Caliph of Baghdad is to the heretical world of the Mohammedans. The evil amongst you shall be uprooted and the Vatican will be purged of your blasphemy."

"A vote, a vote," the cry rose from the sea of scarlet caps. "We must have a vote!"

"There shall be no vote! Hear me! Hear me you harlots! "Wherefore art thou red in thine apparel, and thy garments are like those that tread in the wine vats? I have ridden the wine-press alone and from amongst all you people there is not one man with me."

"He quotes Isaiah, brothers," Cardinal Ricci shouted. "He is mad! He believes himself to be the prophet of old." The assembly began to scream their displeasure but the pope surrounded by the safety of his guard would not cease his preaching into Morenci's ear.

"I will tread them in my wrath and trample them in my fury. Their blood shall be sprinkled upon my garments and I will stain all my raiment. For the day of vengeance is in my heart, and the year of my redemption is come. And I looked and there was none to help. And I was amazed that there was none to uphold; therefore mine own arm shall save me, and my fury shall uphold me. I will tread down people in my wrath, and make them drunk in my fury. I will bring down their blood to the earth."

Now you all know that such matters are well within my authority, for did not Isaiah predict this day would come? I will tolerate no dissension from your ranks. Until you have repented and swear your undying loyalty to me you shall remain in this hall without food or water."

Turning on their heels, the Monsignor led the Pope by the arm, a clear sign that his vision had not fully returned, and they exited the stunned assembly, followed closely by the Swiss Guard. The massive iron doors were locked behind them.

Charlemagne commanded his four thousand Franks to establish camp on the Mars plain, across the Tiber and in full view of the city. Word of Leo's incarceration of the cardinals and priests made its circuit through informers and spies until it came to rest on the already overburdened shoulders of Einhard, Charlemagne's chief steward.

Einhard was alarmed by the news that Leo's intentions to make his master the new Emperor of the Church had already resulted in the deaths of several of the trapped bishops. Deprived of food and water, the most senior of the red-hats succumbed to their deprivation of basic essentials. True, it was only hearsay, but Einhard had learned to appreciate the accuracy of his intelligence gathering network.

The steward knew that his master would be seen as a lackey of the Pope by many. Having come to Rome with the understanding that he would be rescuing the papacy from the blood soaked hands of the Lombards, Einhard realized that his master would be viewed as the villain in this scenario. Most of the clergy were not in favor of Charlemagne taking the crown as Holy Roman Emperor despite what they had been led to believe in their earlier discussions with the Pontiff.

The Pope's secretary had duped them into joining the conspiracy under false pretenses. That was now patently obvious. An entire year of providing details from one perspective had tinged Charlemagne's view of the entire incident. Einhard was faced with the task of informing Charlemagne of what truly transpired over the last few days in the Vatican. The Frankish king would expect a wise solution to the predicament from his chief steward, but Einhard was at a loss for religious insights.

Charlemagne bid his steward to enter the large camel hide tent that had been a gift to him from the caliph, Harun al Raschid many years ago. Crawling upon his knees, Einhard approached his liege who was lounging comfortably upon a carved chaise of ebonwood.

"Whenever I have found you to be upon bent knee, Einhard, it has been my displeasure to have you present bad tidings. What is it you wish to tell me now?"

"It is true, my Lord," the steward agreed as he rose from his kneeling position. "I am afraid that we have come not as saviors of Rome but as its assailants. Pope Leo has misled us into believing that the city was being handed to the Lombards but instead he has used our presence here as a tool by which to assert his domination over the synod. I know that we agreed to this, but I am coming to suspect that we did not fully appreciate the situation that had transpired in Rome. Those that have resisted his tyranny have fallen to thirst and starvation but all that has come to naught as our deployment has caused the others to surrender fearing that we are vassals of Leo's madness."

"Madness!" Charlemagne spat the word at his steward while he sat himself upright, clutching the paw like arm of the chaise. "Do not think me to be the Pope's fool, Einhard! That would be an underestimation on your part. Do you think it is a madness that has brought me here, to this God-forsaken city? Leo was never an Adrian. His predecessor was a man of his word; Leo is a man of twisted truths. But whereas I would never try to supersede Adrian's authority or power, I have no qualms in doing it to Leo.

Once before I was pressured into accepting a crown when the Englishman, Alcuin, forced me into accepting the crown of the West and I have finally come to appreciate that decision. To bear that crown meant the beheading of over four and a half thousand Saxon prisoners. Do you remember that day Einhard? Their blood turned the River Aller red. It was over eighteen years ago, and I thought then to myself, what had I become? Is this what being a king was about? Did one have to be a butcher in order to rule; to become a monster whose blood lust knows no bounds?"

"I remember that you struggled with many a sleepless night after that happened, my Lord. How many times did the nights quake as you shrieked at the blackness that tried to take root in your soul?"

"Scared child that I was, I could not see the total picture. That crown and those deaths brought a peace upon the land. Together they gave me the power and the authority by which I could institute that peace. Ergo, we must look also at the total picture that exists here. I have come to claim yet another crown but this one is the most prestigious of diadems.

Leo has taken us to be fools but are we truly bereft of our senses? Did we not know all along of whom we were dealing with? We made a pact with a devil, a creature despised by his own people over which he claims to preside. We were aware of that the entire year that he was our guest. Were we also not aware that he had been mutilated by those same people that he has asked us to come and save? How is it that he would have any concern for their wellbeing? The answer is that he would not! You should have known weeks ago that I was not coming to Rome for Leo's sake but for my own. Usually you know my every whim, Einhard. I am surprised.

Leo has become a tool by which I am to be anointed as Holy Roman Emperor. If I have to offer him the gates of heaven in order to secure my crown, then I will do so. Then we shall see who will be the master and who the servant!"

Einhard poured a cup of water for his king. "I must admit that you have caught me unawares, my Liege. You have made me feel foolish for harboring these apprehensions. I should have seen the larger picture as you have so enlighteningly expressed. Once more I am the student learning from the master."

"Do not berate yourself so harshly, chief steward. I employ you as an advisor, not as a mind reader. And I know you to be far cleverer than you'd like me to believe. Listen to what I now wish for you to do prior to my coronation..."

The first of December arrived and in response to the public edict, the populace of Rome began to gather in St. Peter's square from the break of dawn. By the time the cock crowed, there were already several hundred, waiting excitedly as they shivered in the chill of the late autumn mist. Everyone in the city was electrified by news of the tribunal being conducted by the Franks. It had been clearly posted by Charlemagne's decree on every signpost, stretching well beyond the city limits.

His Eminence, Pope Leo was to be placed on trial before Charlemagne. In one quick gesture, the Frankish King had gone from being accused of licking the Pope's boots to being the savior of Christianity. Surely, Leo would be held accountable for his sins and this time no force of arms could save him. The people were elated that justice would finally be served.

By noon there was barely enough room in the square for anyone to move and still they waited. No one dared leave, afraid that they would lose their spot from where they could view the events. By now, the air had become warm and humid. With so many of the citizenry crammed into such a little space, it was becoming difficult for the people to even catch their breaths. A few with weaker constitutions had fainted, but the crowd was so tightly pressed upon itself that there was no place for them to even fall.

As soon as the sun had reached its apex, trumpets blared, heralding the start of the long awaited tribunal. On the concourse of the basilica's first floor, the lawyers and jurists, chief among them, Charlemagne, took their positions. Leo was brought out moments later, his arms and legs tethered in the manner of a runaway slave. The crowd jeered their approval of the Pontiff's humiliation. Justice was only a hair's breadth away from being administered. A hush settled upon the mob as soon as the bailiff rose from his seat to begin the proceedings.

The bailiff finally pronounced the formal charges that had been laid against Leo. Surprisingly, Charlemagne was not named as the prosecution, nor was the Holy Synod. Instead, the family and relations of the former Pope Adrian were cited as the plaintiffs. That it had been that particular family, exacting a blood feud, over a year ago, that tortured Leo as punishment for undetermined crimes. As such, if proven to be so, then there would be no need for further prosecution. Only an inquiry was deemed necessary into the cause of this supposed blood feud.

A cry of disbelief outpoured from the gathered crowd. Did the tribunal not realize that Ruggilio had sought the safety and security of his self-imposed exile with his Lombardian protectors and therefore it was the chief magistrate's fear for his own life that caused him to be absent to lay any formal charge against Leo? Soon they were hurling insults at the tribunal, accusing it of being nothing more than a sham.

Summoning forth the Vatican's elite guard, the bailiff called for silence from the spectators. The visual threat of the squadron with their raised pikes worked effectively. The guard had a reputation for brutality almost as infamous as that of Leo.

Once order had been restored, Monsignor Morenci rose and addressed the Frankish King. "To the great Carolus Magnus, King of the Franks and ruler of the Western Empire, I bid you peace. I who am so unworthy of thy charity request that I be permitted to speak in defense of my Pope, not only as his legal representative but as his voice in these matters as well."

Charlemagne nodded his regal consent, waving his scepter for Morenci to continue.

"If my master could speak clearly I know that he would say that he is grateful for this opportunity that you have provided for him to clear his name. This forum shall bear witness to truths which have failed to be made clear to the people of Rome due to a secret cabal amongst the cardinals which has worked endlessly to discredit my master through a series of perversions and distortions.

The Pope has worked tirelessly in his efforts to root out these villains which have made

God's house a den of thieves. It is praise for his actions which my master is deserving of, and not the ramifications of proceedings into certain alleged infidelities by which his enemies wish to deter him from his righteous mission."

Another series of catcalls and vile insults were hurled by some of the people in attendance. Within the blink of an eye, the Vatican guards were swathing through the crowd searching for the perpetrators. Along with their pikes they carried leather whips equipped with several iron tipped tails clenched in their hands, readied for the execution of punishment as soon as the culprits could be identified.

Charlemagne responded to the Monsignor's request as soon as the last guard had found one of the disrupters and delivered a series of near-crippling blows to an elderly man. "It would appear Monsignor that there are those amongst the people of Rome that doubt the sincerity of your righteous master. I will grant you permission to speak on his behalf but I must warn you to confine your arguments only to statements that can be demonstrated as being factual. I will not tolerate conjecture as a defense in a case involving monumental immorality. His Excellency, the Pope, as representative of our Lord Jesus must prove himself above such pettiness, such as pursuit of the flesh, of which we, the common man are constantly guilty. If he were not to demonstrate the heavenly forgiveness, which is the nature of God, as well as the Divine strength of restraint, then how are we to believe that such is the true essence and nature of the Lord? It could be easily assumed that a Bacchian orgy was more consistent with the Church's teachings."

Morenci nervously tapped his fingers against the table, while at the same time His Holiness, Leo shook his cane as a sign of his displeasure. Charlemagne's comments were clearly designed to limit Morenci's defense statements and the Pope was hardly amused. This had not been the agreed upon script that they had arranged in prior discussion.

"Excellency, may I ask permission to approach your chair to speak to you for a moment in private."

"Counsel for the defense has permission to approach." Charlemagne waved the Monsignor to come forward.

Morenci moved swiftly to the king's left ear and spoke softly so that he would not be overheard by the rest of the tribunal. "Your majesty, I am afraid that I do not fully comprehend the nature of your response. Are you implying that my master was mistaken in taking action as he deemed fit, or are you saying that he was justified by reason of his own guilt? It would appear that you are raising the issue of adultery, which we all acknowledged, never happened. Both His Excellency, and myself were led to believe that this entire matter of the tribunal would be superficial and would be dealt with as quickly as possible. Your opening comments are not at all what we had agreed on in our meetings concerning procedure."

Charlemagne cuffed his huge hand behind Morenci's neck and pulled the Monsignor's ear to within an inch of his lips. "I have changed my mind..."

Morenci pulled away with a startled gasp. "But...but," was all that he could say for the moment. "This is unacceptable!"

The king grabbed Morenci's ear this time so that he could not be so quick to pull away again. "I am certain that you and your master are frightfully aware of the position that you have willingly placed yourselves into. This tribunal can do exactly what it was established for, and thereby render a totally unbiased decision. I do not think that you, Monsignor, nor His Excellency, would appreciate such a decision. So play along nicely and perhaps you will get through the proceedings unscathed. Remember, by the powers invested in me, as rightful King of the Western Empire, I could possibly see to it that any charges against you were quickly dismissed upon your meeting certain conditions. Once exonerated, Leo will be free to pursue his other interests in the services of the Lord, of which I am told he has many. I will see to it that he has money a plenty to leaf the entire Vatican in gold, if he so desires."

"We will not tolerate this...this, blackmail! I must object to your perfidious intonations."

"I do not wish for you to think that this pontifically ordained tribunal is blackmailing anyone. Seen in the proper light, I am certain that you can understand how precariously you and the Pope are treading upon the deep and murky waters of iniquity. Your crimes against your fellow clergy are inexcusable. You have been responsible for the death of more souls than you have saved, and most of all, your master was found committing a carnal sin with another man's wife.

Murder and stealing are sins on their own but the act of coveting has always been the biblical doom of so many of the Lord's chosen. The question becomes not whether you and he can retain the Papacy, but whether you will somehow remain alive once the tribunal hands you master over to the people for sentencing."

Charlemagne grinned openly at the Monsignor and then turned to His Holiness to flash the same threatening smile.

"All this can be avoided if you join in the spirit of cooperation and heed my directions closely. Remember, whatever is finally decreed by this tribunal will be become law and the truth. I can make all of your crimes disappear, or I can use them to have His Excellency disappear and a new Pope appointed. Either way, history will see my participation as being righteous and my decision as being in the best interests of Rome, the citizenry, and the Church.

I have what you need and you in turn have what I require. Too long has your master, His Excellency Leo III, condemned my matrimonial status. I will settle for nothing less than a full pardon and a papal proclamation that my marriages are all sanctified before God and that no man can say nay.

Any past or future divorces shall be considered annulments and likewise sanctified. That all progeny of my loins shall be considered legitimate heirs to my empire and shall be duly recognized and respected as such by the Church. That all edicts passed in my name shall be honored and recognized by the Church. Thusly, the Gesta Caroli Magni ad Carcassonam et Narbonam will be honored and recognized by the Church.   The Carolingian-Abbasid treaty signed by my father and Al Mansur will be officially adopted by the Roman Catholic Church as limiting our sphere of influence in respect to the domains of Islam and the sovereignty of Baghdad. And, I insist that you cease your attempts to arrange a marriage between myself and the Empress Irene of Byzantium, because a unified Church is not in the best interests of my Abbasid allies.

I will be also expecting my due reward for saving your worthless hides when I come to Peter's tomb on Christmas day. Is that all understood before you relay my request to His Holiness?" The shock borne on Morenci's face ensured Charlemagne that his demands had been clearly understood. The moment he did so, Charlemagne released the painful grip upon his ear.

In defeat tinged with animosity, the monsignor rendered a partial bow and asked, "Is there anything more that his majesty requests of his lowly servants?"

"Now that you have asked, there is. Too long was my sister Alda burdened by your scar of excommunication because of her marriage to Theodoric. I want her, posthumously, and all her children granted a special dispensation by the Catholic Church which recognizes their dual heritage and thereby restores all privileges of the Equestrian order to them."

Morenci's anger was reaching the boiling point. He raised his voice so that everyone on the tribunal could overhear it.   "His Majesty has now gone too far! He must consider the possibility of his own excommunication as a result of his flagrant intimidation of God's holy ministry."

179

Leo began to tremble upon hearing the Monsignor's threat against Charlemagne. Morenci grew even more livid with anger. "This man who is the rock upon which Our Lord Jesus has placed his divine cloak of leadership shall not be held accountable by you and this farce of a tribunal."

Morenci stepped down from the raised dais and paced wildly about the courtyard screaming at the spectators as if he had gone mad. "There shall be no other judge but God! We will not allow any man to hold court over the Church! This cannot be tolerated nor permitted!"

Misinterpreting it as Morenci's own call for justice and a condemnation of the tribunal a droning chant of "death to the adulterer" surfaced from the mob, standing behind the guard's restraining line. Falling to his knees, Leo began to weep uncontrollably before Charlemagne, fearing that Morenci's outburst had now sealed his fate. As the mob began to surge forward, challenging the Swiss Guard to stop them, he knew instinctively that his survival now rested solely with the King of the Franks.

His words were barely discernable, formed as they were by his swollen misshapen stump of a severed tongue "Peaz, peaz! Oo as Charmay requez. Morezi, peaz. I mow him. He wihl kihl us if we om't."

Morenci ran back to the platform and wrapped his arms around Leo's sobbing frame. "Excellency, you don't understand. You do not know what he requested of us!"

Leo shook his head wildly back and forth. He did not want to hear any further refusal by his secretary. The chant of the agitated spectators grew steadily and was already looming over him like a dark and vengeful cloud. Leo feared an ignoble death at their hands above all else.

"Please, Excellency," Morenci begged, "Let me explain to you first what he said to me." Leo continued to shake his head in refusal. "Surely our lives our not worthwhile at any cost Excellency. If we agree we have merely taken the fetters from you and placed them upon the entire Church."

Shaking loose from Morenci's embrace, Leo crawled on his knees in the direction Charlemagne's chair. "We ahgrey, we ahgrey," he intoned. "Forgive uz, for I have simmed." His lifeless eyes stared pleadingly into Charlemagne's.

Rising from his seat, the king addressed the members of the tribunal and the assembled populace. Holding his scepter over Leo's bowed head he began to recite his proclamation. "This tribunal has come to a decision. In respect of His Excellency, Pope Leo's admission of guilt, we who sit in judgment and who are bound by the mercy and forgiveness of our Christian heritage, after receiving guarantees that certain demands that we have made shall be met hereby declare the following..."

Chapter Eighteen

Toronto: 1999

"This isn't the same Pope that was presented in my religious studies," Pearce objected. "In fact you've really done a number on the history books. Not even the pictures of the events show anything like this."

His objections do not bother me in the least. "Seriously, John, how much of that history, when you studied it, did you truly believe? If you had any intelligence you'd have to question what and why it was written. Let's take a look at those Vatican records. I just happen to know them off by heart. Leo is Pope for five years by the time he's attacked by the mob the first time. Adrian has been dead for five years. Adrian's memory is preserved and sacrosanct, due to various pronouncements by Charlemagne. So, why in the world, would anyone believe that a bunch of outraged relatives would storm a heavily guarded procession to inflict punishment on a Pope that had nothing to do with Adrian?

Can't you see? It's exactly the way Charlemagne said it would be. History is written by the victors. They provided you with a half-baked fairy tale that doesn't even make any sense. You don't get to see the true story!"

"Okay, Doc, I'll admit that I always had trouble with the story of his miraculous healing. They taught us that he was blinded and his tongue was torn out by the roots but as he lay hidden in an alley, God restored his eyes and his tongue."

"And you believed that?"

"I didn't know what to make of it."

"So you chose to believe it?"

"If you stop believing in the miracles then what's left?"

"How about the truth, Pearce? You know what that is, right? That thing you reporters are supposed to look for!"

"But you have shown that he could see and still talk," Pearce defends his misguided belief still.

"How much of his sight was restored will always be questionable. We can safely assume that his eyes were damaged by the mob but they weren't obliterated. And as for his tongue, you can still talk with half a tongue or what may have been a split tongue, just not well. But when you have a faithful secretary to do most of your talking, it doesn't really matter."

"But the pictures of the coronation!"

"What about them?"

"They portrayed him as completely healed. Why wouldn't' they portray the Pope as he really looked if he was really scarred like you say?"

"Who would want to believe in a Church with ugly old men? With blackened sockets for eyes and a serpent's tongue, he'd look more like a demon than a pope. Charlemagne certainly wouldn't want his coronation to be some grotesque mockery. So, you whitewash, you beautify, and you conceal! Those are the essential requirements for a religious movement. Any movement!

181

Let's get real John! You are well aware of the sins of your papacy but everyone just turns a blind eye to them. At least now you have some modern day Popes that are willing to apologize for all the sins committed in the Church's name."

"So you're saying everything a lie then?"

"It depends how you define lies. If we speak of half-truths, and alternate versions, then I would say yes. But if we consider that the essential truisms are contained within those alternate perceptions, then I would say no."

"You're just trying to confuse the issue and avoid the answer," Pearce accuses me.

"No, I'm being factual," I countered. "Let me tell you another battle story, since you like them so much. This particular siege is well recorded but there are elements in the story handed down to us that don't make a lot of sense. For example, it says that the siege army built themselves little wooden booths in which they resided for two weeks and wouldn't fight. It's written right there in their historical records, it doesn't make a lot of sense, and yet no one in twelve centuries has ever bothered to try and clear up this unusual anecdote. One of history's little mysteries most historians have commented. What historian worth his salt would make such a lame comment as that? But you'll be one of the first now to hear what it really was about. So, don't think of it as a lie on their part, it's just not the full truth if you understand my meaning."

Barcelona: 803 A.D.

The cool breeze off the Balearic Sea was a most welcome relief from the torrid and peeling rays of the Hispanic sun. Crossing the Pyrenees through ragged trails and along snow-drifting heights, had been almost euphoric in comparison to this constant withering dehydration suffered under the late-summer sun.

Count Bera had explored these parts exactly two years ago but made no mention of the intolerable, furnace-like midday temperatures that he may have been exposed to. It was an oversight which William would have to reprimand his son for, as soon as their forces reunited. The most serious consequence of the sweltering temperatures could easily result in the loss of ten percent of the fighting force, before they even exchanged the first blows. Without knowing the full strength of the enemy, the loss of that many men could be the difference between a victory and a rout.

Wearing their mail shirts and leather jerkins, his men suffered miserably as they crossed what they referred to as Hell's Infernal Gates. Fortunately, it was much too late for any of the soldiers to consider mutiny. The only thought they could afford at this juncture in time was one of simply staying alive and finding water. Once committed to the march in the dead of summer there was little else to do but to continue forward.

Wars were won in the mind long before they ended on a battlefield. The one hundred and twenty mile distance traversed from Narbonne had been fraught with dangers, ultimately transforming a campaign of what should have taken, perhaps a week, into a never-ending fortnight of physical torture.

Now they faced this maelstrom of Mephisto's twisted paradise. It was not that their prince was bereft of any compassion for them but he was far more aware of the awe in which they held him, willing to obey his every command even if such orders proved disastrous. Still they would obey him, even unto death. His men still found a bit of comfort when he reminded them that they did not have to take the highly regarded royal elephant with them. That honor had befallen Bigo, who had married Charlemagne's granddaughter. William held no great affection for the militarily inept Bigo, appointed co-general by his daughter-doting father-in-law. But not even an Almyeri could countermand an instruction from the Emperor.

Upon re-examination of his true feelings, William concluded that 'lack of affection' was probably an understatement. In fact he detested Bigo more than any other man. There were no redeeming qualities in Louis' son-in-law, which William could relate to. He was profoundly arrogant, constantly flaunting blood lines which meant very little in a land where every tribal chieftain had a score of illegitimate children. Stubborn to the point of excessiveness, there were several other words quickly came to mind; pompous, peacock and petulant.

The man behaved like a spoiled child. When confronted by the specter of war, after repeatedly voicing his less than negligible opinion against a military expedition, he insisted on taking Charlemagne's prize elephant along on the march. William promptly agreed to the absurd request as long as it wasn't his men that had to mind it. If that's what it would take to acquire approval to launch a twin armed campaign, then so be it.

At least the elephant, unlike Bigo, had a history of participating on the battle field, even if it was only to lend a physical presence. Perhaps the Franks with all their annoying superstitions had attributed it with some manifestation of good fortune. Elephants and luck in the same sentence he laughed, the mere thought to William was ludicrous.

It had been William's call for battle which won over the stalwarts at the Diet, held in the palace of Aix-la-Chapelle. It wasn't only Bigo that objected. Neither Louis nor Lupus Santio had the slightest motivation to fight. William on the other hand had every reason to attack the Spaniards. Not long before, the Saracens had slaughtered several hundred serfs under his protection, gutting them from crotch to sternum as was their sickening habit.

Perhaps Louis felt comfortable in claiming that they were only serfs, easily replaced and highly expendable, therefore war was not necessary. Serf or not it did little to erase the horrible memories of mutilated innocence that William had observed. Not to mention the loss of a sizable portion of his labor force, this was apparently only a concern of William's and not to any of the others.

There was no way any prince could turn his back on his own people who suffered on his behalf. In the worst case scenario he would have fought the forthcoming battle alone. This war was now a personal matter to be settled between the Nasi of Narbonne and the Emir Alhaqam of Spain. William had come to hate the son as much as he despised the dead father, Emir Hisham.

William knew, that somewhere, high in those mountains he and his men had just crossed, was Bigo and his prize elephant, wandering aimlessly. The mere thought made William mirthfully lightheaded. Combining that image with the fact that Bigo had placed his entire army in the hands of Count Rostagnus, a man who could get lost in his own house, and it was no surprise that the Bigo travelling circus was nowhere to be seen. It had not arrived and surrounded Barcelona as had been part of the prepared strategy. Fortunately it wasn't critical that the city be cordoned before William's arrival.

William started to roar hilariously at the wild imagery within his mind. It was even funnier than his first encounter with the beast. The elephant appeared with the Caliph's mission from Baghdad over a year and a half ago. Isaac Iskoi had returned from the East with wagon loads of gifts for the King of the Franks and Holy Roman Emperor. Gifts ranging from an amazing clock that ran on running water to the keys to Jerusalem's holiest sites. But in spite of all the marvels that the Caliph showered upon Charlemagne, no one could ever forget the elephant. Or to be more exact, no one could ever forget the quantity of excrement a single elephant could produce, while in audience before the throne of the Frankish King.

And there, assembled neatly in perfect stacks directly behind the elephant, had been all the gifts, those same gifts which confirmed Charlemagne's recognition as Holy Roman Emperor by Harun al-Rashid the Caliph and supreme Emperor of emperors. Officially, the world was now to honor the Carolingian dynasty as the second most important in the known world, even mightier than that of the Byzantine Emperor. The elephant had sealed the agreement!

Al-Rashid, by his gifts, had respected the gains that the Franks had made against the renegade Spaniards. Toledo, with its large Jewish population easily fell into the hands of William when an insurrection from within the walled city annihilated the Saracen guards. The rebel held city offered its allegiance to the Nasi of Narbonne but William had difficulty in accepting his prize. Toledo rested on the shores of the Tagus River, positioned in the center of the Spanish peninsula. To keep it within his domain would require a clear corridor between it and Narbonne; another reason for launching this most recent campaign against the Spaniards.

The Caliph had sent along a shipload of Moslem soldiers, as part of his gifts, to be garrisoned within that city and preserve it as part of William's own little empire. But there still remained the tactical problem of getting the Caliph's soldiers to their final destination. Perhaps that was what Al-Rashid had intended the elephant for? Whatever the reason for the gargantuan gift, it was Bigo's problem now.

As long as Bigo and his general remained lost in the mountains, it meant that William had one less problem to suffer, while he conducted his war against the Saracens. Heribert and Bera, his two eldest sons were dispatched with a force of three thousand men with instructions to set up a line along the Ebro River, eighty miles to the south. This would prevent any reinforcements or supplies moving north from the Saracen capitol of Cordova. Once word was conveyed to William that the line had been secured and was holding, then and only then would the siege begin.

The only other remaining problem, significant enough to scuttle the entire mission, had nothing to do with the enemy, the men, or even the war itself. It had everything to do with timing. The new moon would be appearing soon and when it did, the siege would have to be halted. Two holy men accompanied the force from Narbonne into the peninsula with the sole purpose of accurately determining the night of the full moon. They had already informed the Nasi that the most likely date would be the approaching Thursday, the twenty-first of September. That was less than a week away and Louis was expecting the siege to begin immediately.

Weighing out the odds of a successful conquest of Barcelona within a few days, William arrived at a fateful, strategic decision, with the aid of both his military and spiritual advisors. In any dispute between the ways of war and the requirements of God, it was reaffirmed there could only be one choice.

On the following day, William reached the outskirts of the city but instead of making siege towers and ladders, he set the Narbonnaise upon the task of building little wooden huts made from branches bundled and then tethered together. The men took lodging upon the large plain outside the city where they had assembled their crude domiciles. Palm fronds and ferns were used to make the sparsest of green roofs for these tiny cabins. The camp was set at a distance, far enough away from the city's walls that arrows would not reach the outer perimeter, but close enough that the inhabitants of Barcelona could watch the Narbonnaise eat and drink as they partook in their New Moon festivities. As for Bigo and his forces, he was still nowhere to be seen.

The supplies within the town dwindled once the siege was on. The Narbonnaise flaunted their food stores before the townspeople's eyes, as they sat eating within their wooden huts. Though, normally, the holy days were interspersed with weeks of normal days, William gave the order that they would continue to rest and enjoy the harvest festivities for the complete twenty day period.

When they were not celebrating the holy days in a festive manner, they prayed. Communing with God as their ancestors had done so often in the past; to pray, knowing that the outcome of the battle about to be fought hinged on an answer to their prayers.

On the evening of October fourteenth, William finally launched the attack. If God had seen their little huts, and found favor in their prayers, then Barcelona would soon be theirs.

Behind the massive protective of Barcelona's sandstone walls, the Moslem governor watched the movements of his adversaries as they set about the plain and forest belt, searching for tree limbs and branches. The behavior was most confusing to Zalmon ibn Hadiz, who tried to interpret their actions as having some military purpose but finally confessing openly to the Wali that he could not decipher their intent at all.

"There is nothing difficult to understand, my Lord," the Wali Zado responded, puffing his chest out confidently as he explained. "Once you realize that you are facing the men of Narbonne it is all perfectly understandable."

"Ah, yes, certainly, I almost forgot their little secret", the governor rubbed his pointed beard, drawing it tenderly through his fingertips. "You were a guest of this Jewish prince, were you not...?"

"I would hardly refer to myself as being a guest, my Lord. The madman sent me in chains to his king and lay charges against me that I conspired against the Caliph al-Raschid."

"And, wasn't it true?"

"Yes, I mean no. Perhaps! There's an explanation! Oh, by the prophet's beard, you understand!"

"Perhaps is such a confusing term, don't you think?" Governor Zalmon flashed a broken toothed smile in the Wali's direction. "I would not be here as overseer if everything was that simple." The Emir has difficulty in understanding the reasons for your release. In fact, Alhaqam can only surmise that they released you because they found that you were not guilty of conspiring against that bloated camel's ass, who dared to call himself caliph of Baghdad. What are we to think Zado? The answer should have been yes. You should have been dead. And all you can say to me is perhaps?"

The Wali began to twinge nervously, the highly perceptible tick in his right eye twitching uncontrollably. "How could the Emir even think such a thing?" The Wali cupped his hands and bowed respectfully. "I am his most trustworthy servant. I have served him faithfully." Zado placed his right hand over his chest in an expression of loyalty. "Have I not returned to Barcelona upon my release in order to lead the Emir's troops into glorious battle in Allah's name?"

The governor laughed in contempt. "Be serious, Zado! You came back in order to fill your pockets with whatever gold you could manage to stuff in them and then make good your escape before the Franks captured this town with the help of the maps you happily drew for them, stressing the weaknesses where the walls can be easily breached. We have spies in Aachen too. I bet you were surprised to see me here awaiting your return?"

"My Lord, how can you make such preposterous accusations? The reports from your agents in the Frank's palace are fabricated. I have always been our master's most trusted servant. As Allah is my witness I would not have been guilty of such terrible crimes. Surely you must know that? By the beard of the prophet, I swear my allegiance to Alhaqam, the benevolent and

185

merciful one."

"Do not grovel, Zado. It becomes you not. Although I have not mentioned any of this since you returned to us, it mattered little that you betrayed our faith in you. The truth is that we have need of you and for that reason we have let you remain as Wali. Had it been up to me, I would have sent you back in several little boxes to your Christian friends, but Alhaqam felt your military expertise was of vital importance to us."

"I am a faithful follower, Lord. I would not betray my faith in Allah. The prophet Mohammed said in the fifth Sura that we who are true believers should take neither Jew nor Christian as a friend as they are only friends to one another. If I had sought their friendship would I have not become one of their numbers as the Prophet said we would? You see, I am a believer!"

The governor spat contemptuously upon the ground before him. "You have already become one of them, Zado! Remember the second Sura. Jews love life more than any other people. Look at yourself on the ground! You whine like a Jewess whore, looking for her jewels in the dung heap. Where is your pride? Let Allah decide your guilt when you face him. Be a martyr for Allah as you lead his army into battle against these infidels from Narbonne and perhaps all will be forgiven. Now get up before you embarrass yourself any further."

"Yes, yes, Lord. Forgive me. I don't know what ever could have possessed me so. Perhaps an evil jinn has clouded my mind and caused me to behave so reprehensibly."

"Your chance to prove yourself will soon arrive, Zado. See to it that our faith in you is restored. At least let me eulogize over your pretended greatness. Perhaps if I tell enough lies I can convince even Allah to let you pass into heaven and lay by the seven sacred rivers."

"It would be most kind of you, Lord." Zado bowed repeatedly before the governor. "I will bring glory to our master in battle. We shall celebrate our great victory over the infidels who dare to invade our lands with such impudence and who have besmirched the name of Allah with their distortions of a God in their own image."

Zalmon ibn Hadiz sneered demeaningly at his bellicose associate. "Be serious, Zado. I suggested you go out from the city and fight a great battle. I said nothing of winning. I am pragmatic. The best you can do for yourself is to be carried off the battlefield in glorious martyrdom. We are out-manned, out-equipped, and it will not be long until our supplies are totally consumed.

From what I know of Jewish customs, this William is quite intelligent as far as Jew-dogs go. These New Year and Succoth festivals will consume the best part of three weeks before he'll launch an attack. Unless we can break through his lines and bring in supplies from Granada or Cordova, we don't even have three weeks' worth of minimal necessities. Whatever you do, you better do quickly, if there is any chance to save the city. Otherwise, prepare to die like the rest of us!"

"But my Lord, it would be suicide to go out from behind our defenses. William's archers would hew us down like so many trees as soon as we got one hundred yards from the gates. I think it best we wait for new troops from the southern provinces. I am certain that they will breech William's barrier at the river. It will be only a matter of time."

"Again, you bray like a jackass, Zado. Do you not understand? There will be no supplies, no reinforcements. None whatsoever. My informants have brought bad news over the last few days. Louis has engaged Alhaqam's main force near Burgos and General Sadiq has led our armies into the mountains blindly after some elephant. Allah preserve us! It is bad enough that for reasons I cannot even attempt to understand, this elephant is being followed by a legion of Frank soldiers. But now I must concern myself with the whereabouts of our own forces.

Even if they were to be ultimately victorious, there is not enough time for them to come to our rescue. But this is to be expected. I am a religious man and I know when the Koran speaks of events that we are now experiencing. The fortieth verse of the second Sura. If you are as devout as you claim then you will understand my trepidation.

Does it not clearly say that if the Children of Israel remember the favors that Allah has bestowed upon them and should they keep his covenant, then Allah will be true to His children? Well, look for yourself and see their field full of little booths. They have kept their covenant with Him and now He in turn will be faithful to them and grant them this victory. Their time has come again. As is written in the twenty-eighth Sura, twice shall He give the Jews their reward and that second time I believe is now. He will bestow that reward upon them.

Has he not carved a new kingdom from the barren rocks of this land for them? There is no way for us to fight against the word of Allah. Why even try? Whatever they do, let it be done quickly so that we can be rewarded in heaven. Let me lay by the rivers of wine, while the Hori caress my weary temples and pluck grapes from the vine to drop onto my hungry tongue.

So take whatever time is necessary Zado to prepare the men, but see to it that you engage our enemies before any of the citizens endure any horrific torment. Think not of yourself but of them. If I find even one child suffering because of an empty belly I will come to your house and cut yours out to feed it to them. Is that understood?"

"It is very clear, my Lord. I will prepare our defensive attack immediately."

"Defensive attack! You can still make me laugh, Zado. Do not let us down!" Turning upon his heels, the colorfully robed governor sped down the walled bridgework, followed closely by his two immense body guards.

Zado waited until the governor disappeared from view and then cursed repeatedly. "Bloated sac of camel dung," Zado fingered in the governor's general direction. If Allah wanted him dead, then let Allah tell him himself! Time was running short. He would have to plan his strategy with great haste if he was going to survive the fall of Barcelona. It would most definitely have to be planned very discretely if he was going to escape Zalmon's watchful eye. No telling who might be working for the governor. After all, he even had spies in Aachen of all places. Best to take as few people into his confidence as possible. Yusef! If anyone had a plan of escape it would be the captain of the guard. With that thought he scampered down the stairs to find his good friend. After all, the army of the Franks would be attacking the city at the weak points he had drawn for them. That should leave numerous other passages where there would be no fighting at all. Yusef would know where they were.

While William's men celebrated their festivities, the townspeople wet their swollen and cracked lips with envy, as they watched the burgeoning cart-loads of fresh fruit required for the harvest festival arrive at the enemy's camp. What little they could scrounge from bare shelves and the refuse piles located behind the garrison's mess provided their stomachs with their only sustenance. But to those old enough to remember, Barcelona had survived worse and the towns people were determined to survive once again.

Squalid conditions and constant harassment from street urchins and warring gangs, turned the once beautiful city with its stucco-walled structures and red terra cotta roofs into nothing more than a village plagued by fear and disease. The sickness spread even more quickly than the pangs of starvation throughout Barcelona. First evidence of the contagion was the vomiting, then came the spiking fever. That was swiftly followed by the debilitating diarrhea that the children and elders would succumb to first. It usually meant quarantining the affected home and sealing the inhabitants inside until death claimed them.

William knew that all he had to do was wait. Wait until those Spaniards trapped behind their three foot thick defensive walls fell victim to their own worst nightmares of which the cholera was probably the greatest threat.   No one would be spared.   Not the rich, not the powerful and most certainly not the innocent.

It mattered not that it would take weeks, perhaps even months before the spreading disease would claim everyone in Barcelona.   It didn't really matter that the stores of food contained in the city's warehouses, if they had been carefully rationed, could have tided the populace over for several more weeks.   Once the deaths started, the level of fear would rise to the point that instead of identifying the ailment properly, the fear of the plague word circulated within the city.   Once that unfathomable fear gripped the populace, they would literally destroy themselves from within only a matter of days.

The Wali was nowhere to be found. Those in the know had seen him go down into the caverns beneath the city along with Captain Yusef days ago and neither had been seen since then. Those of a quick mind that realized what the Wali had done, bribed the guards into allowing them access into the caverns from which they too would attempt to conquer the underground maze and find their freedom.

As soon as the governor heard of what had occurred, he immediately put an end to any further attempts to escape by sealing the entrances, and putting to death the guards that had profited handsomely from their little business.   Their public beheadings did not raise the city's morale, nor did it stem the flow of evacuees from the city.   It was only a matter of time before the populace found other ingenious means of escape; some of them proving successful, others not as ingenious as they first thought.   From catapulting oneself over the walls to stowing away in coffins so that they would be carried outside the city by the mortician's wagons, how many had died in their efforts would never be known.

As he watched the events from his little wooden booth, William of Narbonne made a simple assessment to his military staff, "Easier to take an empty city." The final days of Barcelona were numbered.

Chapter Nineteen

Toronto: 1999

"Now, you are one of the few men who even has an inkling of what the inclusion of the story about the huts in the taking of Barcelona was all about. The court historians certainly didn't have a clue or even if they did, they certainly wouldn't confess to knowing. And that was a plus because it seemed so innocuous that it escaped the later editors as well."

Pearce nodded his head in acknowledgement. "I guess there are a lot of historical records with unexplained incidents?

"We've lived through enough ourselves," I suggested. "Just take a look at the Kennedy assassination. We all know that there was a lot more going on than what the Warren Commission reported, and yet what we have from them is the official transcript. When our descendants read of the events in their history book, what are they to believe? Will they know about all the other documentation, the cover-ups, the theories, or will they just be presented with the one official version and that's it? What will they imagine when they read the reference to a commotion up on the grassy knoll?"

"I never thought of it."

"Precisely! We leave history to be written by those whose job it is to record it as they are instructed. We are indifferent and we allow it to happen!"

"But it can be corrected!" Pearce was emphatic that he was right.

"Sure," I responded. "Just as I'm correcting it now. You'll record everything for your readership, providing them with fact after fact, date after date, and when all is said and done, they'll accuse you and I of having wild imaginations. It won't matter that we will be providing answers to questions that have puzzled scholars for centuries."

"I think you underestimate the people, Doc."

"Do I? John, if there's one thing I've learned over the years, it's this; if you say the lie long enough, it becomes the truth!"

"Where's the truth concerning the baby being born to the Queen? You haven't gone back and explained to me how that was dealt with."

"History records that a fifty year old, and likely impotent king, fathered a second child through his second, and very young wife. This second child took four years to conceive after their first child, a girl. The delay is very significant. This second child grew up to look like none of the king's other offspring; so different in fact that at one point, the child was accused of being a bastard. And the mother was imprisoned in a nunnery by her husband, charged with adultery. What do you think about that, John?"

"But what about the brother and sister relationship?"

"What a perfect situation for the clergy. It provided the first real opportunity for the Church to gain total control of a descendant of Charlemagne."

"And how did they do that?"

"Strangely enough, the historians of the time did record that an accusation of patricide was leveled against Charles the Bald. Now, everyone agrees that Louis died from old age, so how could such a charge even exist by any stretch of the imagination? But because they don't know what you now know, modern historians fail to see that the accusation was very accurate and very true. They consider it just a bit of nonsense without substance that doesn't require investigation. I for one would think that a charge of patricide was very serious and would warrant investigation as to how it arose."

Pearce wiped the sweat from his brow and then knuckled his eyes in an effort to keep them open. "Patricide? Can this get any worse?"

"Again, it's a matter of perspective. To the Church, it provided a very effective means of controlling the King. Let's jump ahead in time and see what was happening with Judith Blanchfleur. After all, she's key to this entire episode!"

Paris: 844 A.D.

Judith sat alone in her chambers, having dismissed her servants with but a wave of her hand. Loneliness was a melancholy that she had grown all too familiar with. It was not the first time she had been confined through imprisonment within her own quarters. She remembered back almost fourteen years earlier when Louis, had decided in his divine and majestic wisdom that his queen was officially dead.

She had been a good wife, not entirely a faithful wife, but Louis for all his royal omnipotence could not give her the one thing her lover could, a royal heir. She never concealed her paramour and in some ways, Louis had given his tacit approval. It had now been twenty-three years since the birth of that heir, and Charles had now become her jailer, in place of his long dead, adoptive father.

Judith had devoted so much of her life to simply watching Charles grow and develop into the man he was now. She had been a doting mother, occupying every second of her being with her child's welfare. Only her desire for the lover she could never fully have, took precedent over her son. Charles matured to look so much like his true father that she knew it was only a matter of time before the resemblance between the young prince and his godfather, Bernard would be passed in comment upon the lips of the courtesans.

She always felt there would be time to reconcile the controversy if and when it should arise, never thinking that perhaps her son would not desire any form of reconciliation. She had misjudged her son severely. Where she thought he would be happy with the truth, she now found she was trapped, locked away in the hope that he could keep her from revealing the secret to the rest of the world.

There was only one recourse left for her. She began writing a continuous string of letters, in the hope that one day she could melt her son's ice-cold heart and make him realize that the truth was better than the lie he continued to live. With feathered squib in hand, she began:

> *"Charles, my son, please listen to your mother, this once. What matters the seed that plants the spark in the womb? You are King. You have achieved that which meant most to you and which other men can only dream about. Your true lineage will take nothing*

away from your right to rule. In actuality, the seed that gave you life is of an even more royal line than the myth you choose to preserve. Bernard of Septimania is your true father, of that there is no denial.

I should have told you long ago. No finer man could a child lay claim to paternal heritage. In deed and action he has been closer to you than Louis ever was. Who was it that taught you to ride, to bear arms, and to joust? It was none other than your natural father under the guise of being your godfather.

So where is the justice that he must now stand in your courtyard on the morrow and defend himself by means of arms? Your challenge has left him with no alternative but to be present. My God, Charles! He's your father! You have it within your power to withdraw the challenge. You have the authority to right this wrong. If it be known to all that Bernard be your sire, so what. He is of the nobility; he is a prince of his people. Better the lion cub than Louis's pup. Cast off those that have proclaimed differently to you, for they know not of what they speak.

I beg of you. Please do not do this! If you must punish someone, then punish me. Bernard has always wanted to tell you the truth. It was I who stopped him. No man loved a child more. He was there to guide you, teach you and protect you and I know that you loved him too. He was your mentor throughout your youth. Why is it that you cannot find it within your heart to love him now as you once did, back then? Whatever the fetid spawn of the Church have told you is a lie.

I gave myself willingly to Bernard. He did not force himself upon me. We were two souls in desperate need. Together we found that which we could not find apart. Was that so wrong? Was that a crime to be punishable by death? Do not think for the moment that Louis did not know. He knew from its very conception. The King knew he could not provide for me in all ways. He had become old and feeble shortly after he took me as his bride. The strain of planting the seed that became your sister was too much for him. He knew that he had become incapable of siring an heir.

Only through Bernard could you have been conceived and Louis was aware of this. Bernard his favorite godchild; Bernard his ward upon William's death. Do not think that Louis was such a fool that he did not know what would transpire when he sent me to stay in Bernard's home. He knew and it even had his blessing. And after your birth, did not the king name Bernard to the order of the garter and protector of the queen. Do not think that Louis was either blind or demented. For neither was the case. He had selected and appointed Bernard for this very task, for he loved Bernard as if he was his own.

None of his possessions would he deny him. Not even the queen, for I was not so much wife as I was queen. But as the Emperor grew older, his mind became poisoned and unclear. He lost all perspective and he could not separate truth from fiction; reality from the absurd. The talk within the court condemning Bernard and my illicit affair was suddenly like an apparition to him, a strange and foreign specter of which his weakened mind claimed no prior cognizance.

It was only a matter of time until the red hats were able to twist his altered senses and pervert them to their advantage. After all, it was against their wishes in the summer of 829 that Louis appointed Bernard to the position of Camerarius, second only in power to the Emperor. The positions of Chamberlain of the empire and treasurer were given to him as well. When Wala, Hilduin, Agobard, Bertmund, Hilisachar, and Hugh of Tours decided that Bernard was an obstacle of their own ambitions, they drafted the letter charging us with infidelity.

All were aware that Louis's stability had failed. Wala became bolder and had the church declare that Louis was under a spell cast by the heathen, Bernard. Agobard then delivered the writ declaring Bernard and myself to be adulterers, a crime worthy of execution. When Louis hesitated to take action, the conspirators under the guise of rescuing the Emperor and the empire, called for a rebellion promising your half-brothers Lothair, Pepin and Louis that once we were dead they would be given lands over which to be kings. They even promised to have you declared a bastard child so that you would not be entitled to any of these lands.

Although Louis realized your brothers were serious threats to his crown, he tried to appease them. By acting upon their demands he felt he could calm the uprising. Did he not attempt to imprison you? You were to be his sacrifice to them. Louis then stripped Bernard of all his earthly possessions and confined me to this very same convent of St. Marie de Leon.

And Heribert, poor Heribert; Bernard had made his brother an advisor to the court and all he received in payment was to be kidnapped without a trace. I, personally would have been content with my lot in life but it was Bernard that I grieved for. How do you separate the man from all that he is? Lands, given to his family by Charlemagne, but a people to rule over given to the Almyeri by God. By blood Bernard was born to be an everlasting king through a line of succession almost two thousand years old. How could that ever be stripped away? To be shed like a soiled garment. It cannot and could not be done! All knew that Bernard's exile to Barcelona would not be everlasting.

Did not Bernard still go to war against Pepin and Lothair on behalf of his Emperor? It was only when he had heard what Louis had done to me, did Bernard have a change of heart and joined forces with the squabbling brothers. They had forgotten that they had placed their allegiance with a clergy that began the entire affair, demanding the death of both Bernard and myself. But who was able to unite all of you? Who was able to take all four brothers and meld them into a cohesive armed force? Though you yourself did not fight, you still supported the rebellion led by Pepin.

And when all was over did you not all share in the spoils. Did not the Diet of Aix-la-Chapelle divide the empire amongst all of you? Did not Bernard ensure that you received your rightful share? Pepin became associate emperor while the rest of you were given kingdoms in which to reign. And what did Bernard take as his spoils of war. Only that which was rightfully his; Septimania and nothing more, except that for which he fought hardest for, my freedom.

Condemn him not for that which he did for love. Louis understood it well. Everyone knew that when I was given my freedom and Bernard was placed under my personal direction, that we were what we have been to this very day; lovers, in heart, in soul and in life. Is that a crime to be punished by death? Did Louis think so when he made Bernard Camerarius? And for all that he has done for both king and country, what does he get? Nothing more than your advisor, the bishop Radbert accusing him with his vile tongue of being the Antichrist!

The more I write this letter the more I feel it in my heart that you will slay your father. I can see how much your advisors have gained control of you. They must have some knowledge which they are wielding against you to have achieved their plans against Bernard and myself thus far. I know that you will let nothing stand in the way of you and the throne. That precious throne that you and your half-brothers have fought over incessantly since the day all of you were born. Could any crown tainted with this much blood be worth wearing?

Well, if I cannot stop you then at least let me tell you about the man that is and forever will be your father. No man in all the land had greater courage or passion. When Aizo the Goth attacked with his Saracen allies in the year of our Lord 827, it was Bernard that held off two attacks with his men, with absolutely no aid from the Commanders of Aquitaine.

And when you took his eldest son, William, as hostage, after Bernard sent him to you in the hope that you would recognize William's right to Burgundia, as promised by Louis, did Bernard retaliate in any manner? No, he did not lift a hand against you, swearing and pledging his fealty to you instead. And when you attacked his town of Toulouse recently, did he send his army out against you? No, he would not soil his pledge of fealty to you even though you were breaking your promises to him. Now, he is your prisoner and at your mercy. Will you not show him the kindness he deserves? Will you not tell your father that you love him and free him from this madness which the Church has created?

Take control of your life my son, take control of your kingdom. Seize your true heritage. Please, for the love of God, do not carry out this execution. It shall bring the wrath of heaven down upon your household. No man, in the eyes of God shall kill his father. Please, before it is too late, turn back your decree, and rejoice that you are Almyeri. You are the living spirit of the ancient kings of Israel. Yours is the kingdom to rule in heaven and on earth.

See the truth my son. Do so for yourself, and for me, your mother. I who have always been there for you from the day I first brought you into this world. Let your father live! I beg you. Should you not heed my plea, then know this, that I will join my love in the world beyond. You will mourn two parents in a single passing. Charles, walk not the path of patricide. To do so would damn you to everlasting hell. Not all the clergy's promises would free you of that sin."

Judith rolled the parchment and tied it with ribbon, her tears staining the outer covering of the scroll as she tipped the candle slightly, allowing the wax to drip onto the ribbon and edges of the letter. Removing the ring from her left index finger, she imprinted her insignia into the wax seal and rang for her assistant. Within seconds her servant had packed the letter into his pouch and was on his way to the king's palace.

Exhausted, afraid and defeated, Judith fell into her bed, her cries muffled by the pillow she held to her face. There would be no reprieve of slumber this night; only the emptiness of knowing what the morrow would bring.

Chapter Twenty

Toronto: 1999

"Being a grandchild of Natronai was an honor most could do without. Seems more of a curse than a blessing," the words are garbled as Pearce stifles his yawn.

"Are you going to make it through this?" He's tired and I know that I'm certainly feeling tired. My eyes are half shut and I felt myself drifting off several times during the telling of this story.

"What time is it?"

I look at my watch for the very first time tonight. It wasn't night any longer. "It's one thirty-four in the morning," I tell him.

"No problem," Pearce assures me. "This is still an early day for me. I've pulled all-nighters when I've had to. How about you?"

"Honestly, I'm tired. I could just as easily continue this tomorrow, but if you're game, I'll keep going as long as I can."

"We can't stop now, Doc! There's still so much I have to fill in. Like, what was this bit about the brother, Heribert? Judith mentioned in her letter something about his disappearance. Why not just kill him outright? What's the story there, Doc?"

"A simple one; his crime was that he loved life, women and a good pint of ale too much. And not necessarily in that order. So essentially, he's a lot like us." I hadn't any intention of discussing Heribert at this time. It wasn't as if he was a crucial player in my story, but Pearce is looking pretty insistent on getting the details.

"Sounds like he'd be a good contrast to all of the other characters in your story. Everyone you've discussed so far appears to have suffered undeserved punishments. They all come across as knights in shining armor, wearing haloes above their heads. At least this guy sounds a little more down to earth. So why not tell me about him?"

"And that warrants the punishment he received because he's different?" The pointedness of my questions set Pearce back a bit. He is still looking for some justification, for the atrocities delivered by the Church against the Almyeri. I can sense it. "Listen, John, I'll tell you about this particular son of William, but only because we have to come to an appreciation here, that this family was executed by the Catholic Church for no other reason than they all carried royal Jewish blood. That's all! That was their crime! Nothing else! They deceived, hunted and slaughtered members of my family without justification. End of story!"

"So, tell me about Heribert," he requests once more seemingly ignoring all that I had just said.

"He really doesn't have much to do with the rest of the story," I insisted.

"Doc, we have a saying; let the readers be the judge of that."

Anjou: 825 A.D.

Word ricocheted throughout the small hamlets along the south road. "Samson was coming. Samson was coming," the children would scream and the young maidens would swoon, hoping that this time he would stay a little longer in their village and perhaps they would attract his attention a little better than they fared upon his last visit. Hundreds of townspeople gathered along the roadside in anticipation of catching a glimpse of their favorite folk hero; the living legend in their midst.

As the subject of their adulation approached, sporting his trademark big grin, buried beneath a burly black beard, he waved to one and all. His enormous strides took him closer and closer to the town's limits. He basked in their admiration as they chanted over and over again, "Samson, Samson." Not his given name but he had certainly developed a strong affinity for it over the years. And he definitely preferred it to his real name. It wasn't that bad when pronounced in the Frankish tongue; it even had a melodious ring to it when pronounced correctly. But this Samson lived in Gaul and Pic country with its harsh guttural sounds and nasal twang. In both of those languages his given name sounded like bad indigestion.

Samson, they called out and Samson he preferred it to be. Heribert would always be his name of last resort; the one that close friends and family would address him by, as much as he disliked it. His Eastern title of Evarard sounded much better. If only he knew what had his father, William, been thinking at the time he was named? No way would he do anything similar to a child of his. Heribert! Who would call their child Heribert?

Heading directly towards the Tavern of the Two Moons, the crowd surged behind, forcing their way into the establishment as they trailed their hero. Samson had never proven to be a disappointment in the past, and there was no reason for the townsfolk to believe this night was going to be any different.

The last time he had come to the village, he lifted a solid oak table, with ten barmaids sitting upon its top, a full four feet above the ground. Balancing the table across his broad shoulders, he began to prance around the inn. Later that same evening, he had suggested that the weight be increased upwards to fifteen barmaids but he could find no one willing to accept the challenge on a wager.

As he strode through the entranceway, he was greeted by a hail of salvos and then shown to his favorite table, up against the wall, so that any who approached could only do so far from the front. Heribert still knew that as Almyeri you never let anyone approach your back. His father made certain he learned that lesson well.

The innkeeper leaned over the table. "I take it my Lord will have his usual brew? And could I make a small request that my Lord tries to leave my establishment in the same way he found it tonight." The balding man sheepishly awaited an answer.

"Tsk..tsk. What is this all about, Alfred?" Samson shook his massive mane of black curled locks. "Are you suggesting that I am no longer welcome in your good establishment?"

The innkeeper began to perspire profusely. Clearing his throat several times he responded timidly. "Of course not, Lord. You are always welcome here. But last time, after you could not find anyone to take your wager, you did put my table through the wall if you recall."

"To which I made compensation, Alfred. And you also know, that whenever I come to town your patronage triples."

"Granted, good sir, but it stresses me and my brothers tremendously when you tend to lose your temper. We are afraid that the consequences may bear directly upon us." In the distant corners of the inn's main hall, the two brothers nodded their heads in affirmation.

"Temper? I know not of what you speak, Alfred."

"Not that I had any affinity for the gentlemen, but after you damaged the wall, the Captain of the guard did try to place you under arrest, if you recall."

Heribert scratched his head trying to recollect the events of the evening. "He should have known better. I do not take kindly to being jailed. So, was I able to appease him?"

"You broke both of his legs, my Lord. The fines were levied against us, since you are not resident in our province. We cannot afford another such occurrence."

Heribert rose from the bench and stared sternly at the innkeeper. Alfred began to twitch nervously. Samson raised his right arm and the huge fist blocked out the light of the torch hanging on the wall behind him. Instinctively, Alfred raised up his arms to shield his face but instead, Heribert slapped him across the back and laughed. "Whatever the fine levied, I will have my estate pay double your loss. The son of Prince William will make good on all your losses. The scion of God will not let you suffer in his name. And while we're at it, drinks for everyone."

"Oh, thank you sir, thank you." Alfred bowed, especially grateful for not having suffered for his forwardness. His brothers also sighed with relief, having feared the worst, once they decided to approach young Samson about his indebtedness.

In the farthest corner from the prince, a hooded figure sat concealed in the shadows. Motioning to one of Alfred's brothers, he summoned him with a voice not unlike broken gravel. "Barkeep! Get over here!" No sooner had the tavern owner approached the stranger's table, he felt himself being pulled down by a hand firmly attached to his apron. "That man over there , the one who boasts of a divine essence. The insolent braggart," the stranger thought out loud. "Do you know who he is?"

Pulling away from the stranger, Alfred's brother collected his composure. "That good sir is Lord Heribert, the late Prince William of Narbonne's son. Everyone knows him."

"And does everyone believe his boasts?"

"Of course! We call him Samson. He has the strength of at least five men. I can attest to that myself. One day my good milk cow went down in the field. Young Heribert slung the beast over his shoulders and carried her all the way back to her stall. Last time he visited our establishment, he lifted that solid oak table over there," Alfred's brother pointed in the direction of the table, "and with a load of barmaids sitting upon it, he danced through the inn. I have never witnessed anything like it before and I doubt I'll ever see anything like it again."

"As far as I know these lands are not part of the Almyeri's holdings. What's the man doing so far astray?"

Straightening with pride, the barkeep looked around his inn. "Lord Heribert is a patron of our humble establishment. Although we have had our differences as you probably overheard, yet he'd be sorely missed if he returned to Septimania. There's many a young maiden's heart that would be broken if he were to disappear. Not to overlook the substantial loss to my business that would result. I can tell you; far more is spent here when Samson comes than any other time of year, even if we have suffered a few physical losses, as a result."

"And you think his absence would be a grave occurrence, do you? I have overheard that the man almost single handedly destroyed your tavern in the past. That sounds to me to be considerably more than the loss of a few physical assets. I would think that you would want him as far from your locale as possible."

"Lord Heribert has always compensated us well for whatever damage he causes. Men always come from the surrounding hills and villages to challenge him with feats of strength. Some come thinking that they can beat him, others come merely to lay claim to having fought

Samson and survived. Yes sir, Lord Heribert shall always be a welcome guest in our house."

"Then you are a fool," the stranger snarled. "These lands fall under the jurisdiction of the bishopric. Archbishop Agobard is the law here and he would not suffer such a disturbance within his holdings. It cannot be tolerated. It will certainly not be tolerated after he receives my report!"

"Then I would suggest sir that the archbishop comes to my establishment and tells Lord Heribert himself. Better yet, let Agobard challenge Samson to a fight. Loser leaves our districts, never to return. I can guarantee that there would be a lot more people backing Samson, than would ever miss the cleric." The inn keeper turned and left the customer to his thoughts, while he served the other patrons.

The stranger drummed his bony fingers against the top of the table, muttering inaudibly. "Oh, he'll be here soon enough you old fool. And when he comes he'll bring your downfall with him."

Agobard sat pensively in the carved chair while the magistrate from Avignon reported at length on the disturbance he had encountered in the town of Anjou. "And you say that this man is my old foe's son? Do you know that for certain?" The magistrate nodded his confirmation.

"You don't know how much that pleases me. William of Septimania has been the bane of my existence, even after he passed into the grave. His family's presence is an affront to the Lord, his son Jesus Christ, and his Holy Church. Now God has delivered his enemy's son into our hands and we shall deal with him accordingly. We are the flaming sword of the Almighty and we will do as we are commanded. In spite of the righteousness of our actions, we must make certain that the king knows of none of this. The Almyeri have been able to bewitch the Carolingian household and they cannot see the threat that this unholy family represents to the one, true faith."

"But my Lord, what of the differences of which I told you? This one, Heribert is gifted. He has the strength of ten men. He calls himself Samson, like the judge of the ancient Israelites. The people tell tales of how he slew a wild bull with his bare hands and then carried the carcass miles to the closest town. What if he is blessed?"

Agobard rose from the ornate chair and spread his withered hands heavenward. "Don't you see, it is a sign! Each time God has shown me the weaknesses of his enemies. One by one he shows me the means to eliminate them. He has set before us a means to destroy these false prophets. If Samson his calls himself, then Samson he is. The fruit of the vine and scented flesh shall be his downfall."

"You have a plan, father?"

"Of course I have a plan! Have you not been listening? I have just laid it out for you. From God's lips to your ears and you cannot comprehend!" The archbishop's voice rose an octave as he castigated his subordinate. "I presume you have learned your biblical passages of Judges, magistrate?"

"Most certainly, my lord," his lips pursed.

"Then we shall do until him what the Philistines did to the real Samson."

"We cut his hair ?"

"No, you imbecile!" Agobard swung his staff in the general direction of the magistrate, missing by several inches with his attempt. "No wonder the land suffers with the lack of stability when it suffers fools to govern its courts. Go and search the province for the most beautiful woman in all of Avignon.   One who is in the service of the Church preferably as she will not decline your offer.   Pay her in gold for her womanly wiles. We shall let Delilah slay our Samson."

"I will not disappoint you holy father."

"See to it that you have everything in place within the fortnight.   The bait must be ready if all else is to proceed.   This Samson from what you told me appears to be a wagering man.   We will attract him to the snare with a wager he cannot refuse.   Then the trap shall be sprung!"

"And once he has fallen into our trap?"

"What do I care?   Set him between two pillars if you want.   Just ensure me that he never sets foot in this land again.   I want him to suffer and in so doing, his father will suffer all the more in hell.   They are not to threaten the Church ever again.   Do we understand each other?"

"Perfectly, as you wish, Father.   Heribert of Narbonne shall no longer be a threat by the time of the new moon.   On that you have my word."

"See to it that I do, Magistrate.   I will provide you with all the support you need but do not disappoint me."   Agobard shook a gnarled finger as a final warning.   "You shall be provided with men and money to undertake this venture.   Now go!"

The patrons of the Tavern of the Two Moons were wild with anticipation.   Alfred and his brothers hastily prepared an arena in the courtyard.   They were almost certain that their establishment was about to be destroyed, but they weren't bothered.   From what they could see of the early betting crowd gathering, it would be well worth it.   This was going to be a promoter's dreams come true.

It was an event unparalleled in all of Frankia.   A battle of true titanic champions; godling against godling.   Where the initial money to arrange the event came from, no one could say.   But it was carefully managed and orchestrated, right down to the security that ringed the town.   Every available room in town was occupied, having been booked well in advance.   The late comers were seen spreading their belongings beneath tarps stretching across every inch of vacant land surrounding the tavern for which they were charged handsomely.

Eldritch the Burgundian had arrived earlier that afternoon with an entourage of a dozen followers.   It was a long tortuous journey, but Eldritch appeared to have done it in relative ease and comfort.   Anjou was a long way from the Burgundian border, located well to the north, in the lowlands of the Anglo Sea.   All along the course of his travels, the news spread quickly, that the giant barbarian of the forest was heading south to face an equally legendary opponent.

In all of the Northern provinces, there was no greater wrestler than Eldritch.   Many men had had their backbones cracked in two by his powerful grip.   Once caught between his barrel chest and trunk-like arms, there was no hope of escape.   In the presence of kings and emperors, time and time again he had demonstrated his feats of superhuman strength.   None had ever claimed to be his equal, until word came that Anjou's favorite son was prepared to challenge that claim.

Just who it was that presented the challenge was not clear.   This was still part of the aura of mystery that seemed to shroud the event.   How the challenge arrived simultaneously at both Eldritch's doorstep and Heribert's with neither having been the instigator only added to the suspense. Surely some undisclosed patron of the manly arts was sponsoring the event, perhaps the Emperor himself some guessed.   In spite of the controversy, both eagerly accepted, the promises of riches beyond measure thus sealing the contract.

It was early evening when Heribert arrived in Anjou, to the shouted praises from the townspeople. The chanting crescendoed as he approached the tavern. Like a deafening chorus, it shook the foundations of the stone buildings, and the hastily constructed visiting dignitary stands in the courtyard, now threatened to collapse.

The crowd grew giddy with excitement. Jugglers entertained the spectators, as did a variety of balladeers and magicians. The three brothers took the wagers on behalf of their patrons, carefully weighing the odds of the outcome in their favor. With enough, cross, counter and percentage bets they had ensured they'd make their fortune no matter who won. None could remember any event of such magnitude in their lifetimes. Travelling players and showman set up their small platform stages around the town, which had magically tripled its population over night.

As Heribert strode towards the courtyard, the crowd parted in a wave and then closed quickly in behind him like the crashing surf. The two opponents now stood at the center of the arena like twin giants surrounded by gnats.

Resembling all Burgundians, Eldritch sported his dirty blonde main tied into a long pony tail that extended to his waist. Several gold and silver clasps spanned the length of that tail. Stripped down to his loin cloth, his massive chest was shaved smooth and oiled, so that his finely honed muscles glistened in the flickering light of the surrounding lanterns. The two tree-like pinions, serving as legs, were wider in the thighs than most men's waists. While the bulging muscles of his arms appeared to be carved from solid granite blocks.

In every measure, Eldritch held the advantage over Heribert, though each combatant was a titan in comparison to any common man. Backs as broad as a bison's, every movement displayed a mass of muscle and sinew; all the right ingredients to thrill the crowd and send the women in attendance into frenzy.

Tavern maids flitted amongst the tables, serving food and drinks at a pace which made the three brothers ecstatic. This was truly going to be a night to remember.

The burgermeister of Anjou stepped into the center of the arena and called the two combatants to his side. He stood between them like a child gazing upwards into the faces of his parents, and the sight brought a spontaneous bout of laughter from the crowd.

"Gentlemen, may I have your attention," the burgermeister cried. "Tonight we will witness sporting history. Our town has been blessed with an event that has not even been seen in faraway Paris. The Emperor, himself, has sent word, wishing us a most fortuitous occasion and expressing his deepest regrets that he could not be here to witness this spectacle.

It is with great pleasure that I present our two worthy opponents, the one and only, Eldritch the Burgundian, Terror of the North " A round of applause sprinkled through the crowd but was quickly drowned by a chorus of boos. "And Anjou's favorite adopted son, the legendary strongman of Septimania, Prince of the Spanish March, and a man who needs no introduction, the one and only Samson!" The people exploded into a thunderous chorus of cheers and song. They screamed and shouted their devotion, chanting the name of their hero over and over again, as loud as they could.

Waiting for a momentary lapse of silence, the mayor broke in with his final comment then ran from the arena as quickly as he could. "Let the fight begin!"

Each wrestler circled the other in a carefully choreographed dance of elude and grab. Grasping for initial leverage, steel like talons searched for a stronghold, only to have their holds shaken off time and time again. Sparring with cat-like maneuvers, they would lunge for a leg or an arm, only to have their thrusts blocked or sidestepped.

Both men had been well trained in the art of hand to hand combat, neither willing to make the first mistake that would cost them the fall. At last fingers interlocked, hands spread above their heads, palm forced against palm with tremendous pressure, trying ultimately to bend their opponent's knees to the ground. The strain of their efforts ripped across their faces in horrible grimaces of mixed pain and pleasure, while the sweat sprayed from their bodies onto those that purchased the seats closest to the arena's edge.

The crowd continually worked itself into a feverish frenzy, anticipating that a fall was soon to happen. Feet scraped along the ground, searching for toeholds, seeking the leverage required to swing the battle. Each head fell across the other's shoulder, pushing, bulling, seeking to make the other give a step, but still no man gave an inch.

"They are too evenly matched," one spectator was overheard to say while trying to decide how to place his wager with one of the brothers.

"Nonsense," replied the innkeeper. "The odds are in favor of Lord Heribert. He has never been defeated. Bet on Eldritch."

"Well, Eldritch has never been defeated either," the man replied.

"A minor detail," the innkeeper snapped back. "Do you want to make some money or not?" The man placed his bet, chanting for the Burgundian, as soon as it was recorded.

Neither wrestler could gain the upper hand. They released their finger grips trying to latch on to each other's wrists but to no avail. Eldritch made a desperate clutch for Samson's waist, stumbling short by inches and almost going down before he quickly recovered his balance. Once again they began to circle the arena, bent forward at the waist, hands slapping against hands as they prepared to strike.

The Burgundian was once again first to make a move, springing forward with a speed that seemed impossible for a man his size. Initially, it appeared that he had missed his target, his head becoming lodged between Heribert's legs while his arms swiftly became locked behind his opponent's knees. And then to everyone's surprise he began to straighten his back, straining against Samson's weight, slowly lifting him from the ground.

Seemingly unperturbed by the event, Samson merely let himself go slack, falling across Eldritch's back until his arms were able to reach around the Burgundian's waist. Once Eldritch had raised himself erect, he found himself to be as much in a compromising position as his agile opponent. Neither could gain any leverage, nor could Heribert be shaken off. Eldritch had no choice but to release his arm lock on Heribert's legs, allowing Samson to flip himself harmlessly back on to his feet, three paces from his opponent..

Eldritch turned to face Heribert once again, settling back into his customary crouch. This time both men assumed the basic maneuver of the neck embrace. Both hands clasped behind the other's neck, with head nested alongside head. Such a move had often been the first lesson for any aspiring wrestler, creating a virtual deadlock, where neither party held advantage but in this case it was far more menacing. The strength being exerted by this evening's pair of wrestlers was beyond measure. A lesser man's spine would have shattered by now. Power enough to uproot trees was brought against the base of each skull, yet neither man would yield. Their faces contorted into distorted displays of agony. Neither man would release his grip, as they began to swing through a series of ellipses, taking them from side to side of the arena.

The crowd howled with delight, smelling the scent of blood, hanging auspiciously in the air. Whatever would happen would occur soon and all in attendance could sense the impending overture. Simultaneously, both man pivoted. Now they stood back to back, shoulder to shoulder, their hands still firmly locked about the other's neck but their fists balled below each other's chins. Each tugged forward, exerting maximum pressure on the attachment of skull to neck.

With the futile hope of flipping their opponent overhead now gone, both wrenched mightily on the other's jaw, but neither moved an inch in any direction. Still they refused to release their grips, straining with every ounce of strength they could muster. And then it happened. Some said it was like the sound of lightening striking a tree and shearing off a limb. Others could only describe it like the sound of an overripe melon dropping from a height onto a cobbled surface. But all knew that they had heard the horrifying sound of death.

Time stopped. The enormous crowd grew frighteningly silent. All eyes were transfixed on the wrestlers still standing, bent backwards, at the center of the ring. Slack jawed, their eyes opened wide with alarm, as they awaited an indication of the outcome. Some sign, any sign, that there was both victor and vanquished.

When the two giants collapsed to the ground, their arms falling slack by their sides, the shocked congregation broke into an audible moan. The lack of any movement by either wrestler continued for what seemed an eternity. Stunned into silence, the crowd collectively shook their heads in dismay.

The questions were fired from every direction. "What happened?" was met with the shrugging of shoulders. "Are they alive?" was answered with a shaking of heads. "Who won? Do we know who went down first?"

"Tie goes to the house," spouted one of the more callous brothers.

"Look!" someone shouted. "He's alive, he's alive." The crowd pressed forward to see who it was. Wild screams of jubilation rang in their ears. "Samson, Samson," was sung over and over again. His companions that had come with him swooped down and raised him up on their shoulders, carrying him aloft, above the outstretched arms of the masses. The three inn keeping brothers were ecstatic, having successfully convinced the majority of bets to back the Burgundian.

It was left to Eldritch's entourage, to drag the body of their benefactor from the center of the mob before it became mutilated beneath their stampeding feet. The glory days for the behemoth from the North Country were over; vanquished by the sport he loved most. He had all but been forgotten, except for his closest travelling companions, and those kicking dirt in his direction for losing all of their money. Such was the life of heroes, fleeting at the best of times, non-existent at the worst.

Ushering Heribert into the Tavern of the Two Moons, the throng of worshippers attempted to follow, only to have the three brothers bar their way. Only a select group was permitted to pass beneath their lintel. Once inside, Heribert was laid upon the large oak table. His body ached, especially his neck which was red and swollen, the arteries extend and pulsating just below his jaw line on either side. "Water," one of his attendants screamed to a tavern maid.

"Forget the water," Heribert barked in a voice that rasped and ached with each and every syllable. "Bring me some ale!"

"Bring him a keg," his friend shouted.

"Drinks for everyone in the house," Alfred shouted knowing that he and his brothers had already safely limited the number that had entered.

Standing over Samson's outstretched body, the burgermeister held a large brown sac. "To the winner go the spoils," he quipped. "It is my great pleasure and honor to present these one hundred gold bezants to you, Lord Heribert. The sponsors of the contest are grateful for your participation and extend to you a glorious opportunity to tour the continent with them as their main attraction."

Samson reached up and received the bag from the town mayor. With a voice still crackling due to the strain which had been placed on his larynx, he expressed his gratitude. "I appreciate the offer, but affairs of state would not let me tour about like a gadfly. I would thank them personally but I'm not certain who the sponsors even are. But I will definitely take their money."

"Actually," the burgermeister responded, "one of their representatives is right over there. May I introduce the provincial magistrate, his honor, Giscard d'Bois.

Tall and slender, the magistrate dressed in fur trimmed black robes and squared cap that covered his heavy lobed ears, stepped forward. Staring down at Heribert, he commented, "My associates and I are greatly pleased with your performance tonight. Although Eldritch had been under our management, such unfortunate accidents are to be expected from time to time. But it does leave us in search of another fighter.

Truly, yours was a contest that the balladeers will be singing of well into the next century. Never have I seen two more evenly matched contestants. We lesser men could only stare in awe at your Herculean feats. You have won your admirers this night and for me it has been a pleasure to meet the Prince of the Almyeri.

There is someone I would like you to meet. Allow me to introduce my daughter, Renate; she has spoken only of you since she laid eyes upon you. I think she has become one of your greatest admirers."

Waving his hand, the magistrate summoned the young lady from the shadows, extending his right hand as she approached. Taking his hand at its tip between her own thumb and fingers, she floated to the side of the table.

Heribert looked into the almond face of breathtaking beauty and suddenly forgot completely about his pain wracked body. Her raven hair fell across her shoulders in braids of scarlet silk while stark blue eyes gazed down invitingly at him. Her corseted dress accented the youthful body, curvaceous and firm. Heribert quickly propped himself into a sitting position, attempting to make himself appear more presentable. Before he could utter a word, the lilting melody of her voice filled his ears.

"My father has told me so much about you, my Lord." She flashed a smile of perfect white teeth that made his heart melt instantaneously.

"Well then, my gratitude to Magistrate D'Bois," Heribert replied. "I hope that I will have the opportunity to learn equally as much about you."

"All things are possible, my Lord," her eyes danced enticingly as she stroked his bulging arm in response. "Your arms are so powerful. They are like the branches of the willow; so strong and sheltering."

One of Heribert's friends frantically tugged at his tunic. "Sorry to interrupt, my Lord, but we did intend to head on to Aquitaine this evening. You do remember, don't you?"

"I think I've changed my mind, Remi. Go on without me and I'll join up with you tomorrow."

"Then you have also forgotten that as the prince, the Nasi must be present in Aquitaine to accept the properties being awarded to your family estate by the crown." The young advisor stood adamant with arms crossed, awaiting an answer. "It has taken this long for the Emperor to finally return the lands he held in trust for your father. It would not be advisable to be absent from the ceremony."

"Oh, Remi St. Jean, you worry too much. What if my fate had been that of poor Eldritch? Then I wouldn't have been in attendance at all. Gottshelm and Bernard will be there. Let my brothers preside over the ceremony." Samson clutched Renate's delicate white hand in his huge mitt with a tenderness that belied its great size. His gaze transfixed upon her soul searching eyes.

Remi shook his head in silent defeat, acknowledging a foe he could not compete against.

"I do not think this is wise, Heribert. My instincts say that this is wrong. Very wrong but I will try to delay the ceremony for a couple of days. If you fail to arrive, I will advise Gottshelm to stand in your stead."

"That will be fine, Remi." Samson dismissed his friend and advisor without even a backward glance as he departed. "I will join up with you in several days," he yelled to the exiting shadow by the door. "And now, my sweet one, where can a man who is feeling much better, dine in private with such a fragrant flower."

"Allow me to lead the way," the magistrate rushed forward forcing himself between Samson and Renate. "I have the perfect spot for you two to get acquainted, a small cottage outside of town belonging to my brother-in-law. It is vacant now and I know he would not mind if you used it. Quickly, go out the back where my carriage awaits. We shall see to it that your admirers do not follow. Quickly, quickly now!" The magistrate shooed them from the tavern, through the back door and into the black sedan.

While Heribert crouched low in the carriage, Giscard dictated the directions to the driver. The whip snapped and the carriage bolted down the dirt road towards the outskirts of town and into the shelter of the neighboring forest.

"Did anyone see us leave," Heribert questioned from his kneeling position beside Renate.

"No," she responded, "no one saw you leave. You are safe now."

"Good! Then I don't have to lie at your feet any longer." Heribert climbed into the sedan chair beside Renate. "Although, I would easily lie at your feet for an eternity if you so desired."

The woman's pale features blushed with embarrassment. "You are a flatterer, my Lord." Shyly, she turned her head from him to recover her calm.

Once again, Heribert rested his hand over hers. "My words cannot do your beauty justice. The moment I beheld you, it was as if I was in the presence of an angel. My heart cried out, 'this is the one!' It was as if I had been searching all my life to find a great treasure and now I have found it."

Renate held her hand up, pressing her fingers against his lips. "Please, you say too much. What the future bears, no man knows. My father asked that the cooks prepare a meal for this evening before we left for the contest. I know that it would be his intent that you eat his portion. After we dine, we will have our chance to talk about the future."

"Then you are admitting that there's a possibility that there may be future for the two of us."

"All I am saying is that after we eat, we will talk." Renate grew silent as the carriage approached the gates of the cottage.

"Good, we will eat and then we can discuss. I look forward to talking to your father."

Opening the carriage door, Heribert helped his companion down from the sedan. Together they entered the thatched cottage, where honeyed meadow wine and roasted quail adorned the petit-point clothed dining table. The aroma drifted about the cottage with its exotic blend of spices. Excited by the prospect of the evening, Heribert took great delight in the meal set before him, downing large quantities of the wine and several of the fowl. As he stared at Renate, he felt as if he had somehow walked in to a wonderful dream from which he hoped he would never be allowed to awaken from.

"Tell me everything that happened, magistrate. Don't leave out a single word." The archbishop wrung his hands eagerly together, the excitement dotting his forehead with beads of a cold sweat. "You do not know how happy you have made me. I have prayed for this for so long. One by one I will uproot the seeds of William until they will exist no longer"

"The plan went perfectly, father. It was as if we were guided by a divine presence. Everything went far better than could have been expected. The glutton drank so much wine and consumed so much quail that he was passed out within the half hour."

"But you did not slay him," Agobard chuckled. "You had a perfect opportunity and you did not take it."

"Why bring down the wrath of the Almyeri by slaughtering one of their princelings? You did say that his fate was in my hands to mete out his punishment." Giscard laughed only to be joined by Agobard with his mocking cackle of laughter.

"Yes, I did say that. I recall that well," the archbishop acknowledged.

"What better than fowl laced with the seeds of the thorn apple. The Devil's Trumpet has blown its bitter note. And meadow wine, fermented with wood shavings. The quail rendered him blind and the wine made it permanent. Knowing that his appetite would be excessive, I was not concerned with the effects ever wearing off. Just like the Samson of old, he filled his eyes with lust for a woman and as a result, he saw no more!"

"And the woman?"

"Let us say that she won't be a threat to expose our plot, father. Do you really need the details?"

"Of course not…and the ship?", Agobard exclaimed.

"I was in luck that there was a ship leaving port the next morning. Why not give the poor bastard a free voyage?"

"Splendid! Absolute genius! You have made me a very happy man! Where did you send him?"

"I believe their first port of call was somewhere in Italy."

"Oh, I wish I could be there when he wakes up!" Agobard clapped his hands together gleefully.

Chapter Twenty-one

Toronto: 1999

"Poor bastard is right," Pearce comments sympathetically. "I think I liked the guy. There was something about him that appealed to me."

I notice that Pearce appears to be getting his second wind which was a worry. He wasn't looking nearly as tire as he had, but I am beginning to feel more wasted than ever.

"Neither he, nor his brother Gottshelm are germane to the story. They both were dealt with cruelly but neither was really a threat to the Church or throne. With the passing of William, the kingdom was more nominal in nature than political. None of his children were as fervent in their religious beliefs or heritage as he was. Only Bernard ruled to a significant degree by the Davidic authority he inherited. He stayed in Narbonne until his exile I mentioned earlier. The others chose to go elsewhere and would have been eventually assimilated into mainstream society."

Pearce is shaking his head in disagreement. "But there was a threat! Bernard fathered a King of France. How can you say that the threat was only nominal?"

I can't believe it! Two fifteen in the morning and he wants to start a debate! All I want to do is sleep. I knew that I 'd better start tying everything together before we rambled well on into the second day.

"By this time the Church was more powerful than the Emperor. If they chose to eliminate the King, they could have done so. But it was in their best interests to keep a weakened monarchy because then they would remain as vassals of Rome. To reinstitute a new ruling family would have revived all the old issues that they had to resolve when they brought the Carolingians to power."

"So, Charles knows that Bernard was his father and that's perfectly acceptable to all concerned?"

"Absolutely not! Charles was devastated. For a long period he lost interest in ruling his country. The Church actually governed for good deal of the time using the threat of exposure to keep the King in his state of absentia. It was only when the country was being overrun by invaders that Charles snapped out of his melancholy and made a momentous decision."

"What kind of decision?"

"That's what I was going to tell you before you sent me off on a tangent and talking about Heribert."

"So tell me now."

Better make certain your tape is rolling and I'll give you the answer."

Aix-la-Chapelle: 845 A.D.

Concealed within the cavernous shadows of long forgotten rooms, burdened by the odors of mold-soiled tapestries and slate tiled floors, they met, exchanging adversarial glances, glossed over by the forced presence of sardonic smiles. Each man surrounded by his elite guards, warily eyeing the other's strengths and weaknesses, parrying each stare with icy belligerence. As allies, neither ever trusted the other; theirs had become an alliance of need, born from catastrophic events, and mutual fears, but little else. Measuring each other cautiously, they waited for a break in the deafening silence; circling, in ever smaller concentric rings until they had come within arm's reach of each other.

When the taller of the two, with balding pate and sunken eyes could tolerate the silence no longer, he spoke. "Damn you Gregory! This mess is your entire fault." The words were laden with harsh and bitter emotions. Charles waved a leathered fist in his adversary's face. "I never should have listened to you! Never! Now you and your damn fraternal order have cost me dearly." The King reared back, his clenched hands now bonded tightly to his waist, constrained only by the raging battle of conscience within his own mind. If not for the presence of Gregory's Lombardian guards and the uncertainty of who truly wielded the power in Europe, he may have abandoned caution and physically exhibited his true feelings.

Showing not even the slightest concern for the king's opening remarks, Gregory, moved slowly to the internal rhythm of his own desire, dabbing his linen handkerchief to his lips in preparation to speak. A carefully designed motion done not only to demonstrate how little he felt threatened but also to exhibit how little he considered the power and authority of the Frankish King to actually be.

"You know what your problem is Charles? You worry far too much. Here I am trying to help you with your problems and you do nothing but assail me with your accusations. Really now, aren't you ashamed of yourself? Don't I deserve better than this?"

Unable to hold his temper entirely in check, Charles rallied against his opponent. "The only shame I feel is that I ever listened to a swine like you," he swore. "What you really deserve I dare not say, lest I sacrifice my place in heaven. Ever since the day you entered my life, I have been cursed beyond the endurance of any mortal man! You have made my rule a mockery; my kingdom a shambles; my life a misery."

"Now, now, your majesty, let's not over state your situation." Gregory waved the linen cloth casually to and fro, mere inches from Charles's face, in a manner most annoying. "Is that anyway to speak to your Pontiff?" Gregory held out his right hand in supplication towards the king. "Would you rather have had me bury the facts of your conception, lie to you; conceal the sins from the Almighty? I didn't think so! Or would you rather just kiss my rings and know that all your secrets will remain with me." A sinister grin spread across Gregory's face as he stretched out his slender fingers. Each digit bedecked with a fabulous jewel encased in glittering gold.

The king ignored the mocking gesture. "You know what, Gregory, you can kiss my ass. I know now that it was not the facts concerning my birth that unsettled you most, Unholy Father. It was the knowledge, that your ability to rule the Papal See rests entirely with my being a good Catholic. All hell would break loose if your followers were to learn that the only military support you have been receiving came from a heathen bastard, as you have now threatened to expose me of being. You are as much a prisoner of my past as I am."

Charles watched for any signs of concern scrolling across the Pope's moon-shaped face but none was forthcoming. "My mother was right all along. You can't expose me. You would destroy yourself! You are powerless without me! She knew and I chose not to listen. I let my fears guide me, and even though she begged me to spare my father's life, the fears you instilled within me were far greater. I was a fool!

You must realize, that if I should throw my support to John, this Anti-pope, as you would like others to call him, he will then have the sanctioned right to call himself head of the Church. You must certainly be aware of that fact!"

Gregory tittered bemusedly, encouraging his entourage to join him in mirthful laughter. "I wouldn't be too certain of that your majesty. You wouldn't be here with me now if you thought supporting John would eliminate your problems. You are in far deeper than you're willing to admit. You see, I wasn't born to this position. I used my family's wealth to secure the papacy. Money has a way of excusing sin, hiding the past, even granting clemency. You on the other hand are only king because the people believe you to be the son of their former king. I would suggest you not take the gamble to see if either of us survives exposing the truth. I really don't believe it would be in your best interest."

"What would you know or care of my best interests," Charles retorted. "You've blackmailed me into placing your bishops in charge of all this country's domestic affairs. Even all the lands and rights of the Almyeri in Narbonne have been stripped and given to the bishop of that city. Your church has grown fat on land and taxes you have extorted from me. For that very reason the nobles have fostered this renegade pope and his following grows every day. And you talk of my interest. Surely you jest!"

"And what do you think of all this, Hincamar?" The elderly clergyman merely shook his head in disgust. "Did I ever mention how I came in possession of all this knowledge, regarding your conception? I owe it all to Hincamar, here. You see, the good Archbishop of Rheims was nothing more than an adolescent abbot when Charlemagne was still around. Got himself involved with some very interesting dealings between both Leo and Agobard, may God keep their souls." Gregory spat in disgust as he pronounced their names, belying his true feelings.

"It would appear that nothing was by accident as they played a little game of deception. They fooled you all. Nothing about you and you royal family is what it appears. You are all a creation, a fiction of the foulest kind. In fact, there's more about your birth and your mother that Hincamar has revealed that I haven't even bothered to expose to you. I'll save that information for when you behave naughtily. There's not any use to upsetting you prematurely when there's nothing to gain, at least not at this juncture in time."

Gregory's smugness was designed to infuriate. It was a game of cat and mouse that he was used to playing and winning. His ongoing battles with the King of the Franks, he wanted over once and for all.

Charles thought momentarily again about striking the Holy Father. And once again he just narrowly restrained himself, not wishing to challenge the authority of the See. Perhaps it did reign supreme, above all monarchies and earthly kingdoms, as it claimed, or perhaps it did not. But this was definitely not the time to find out. The king still required the recognition he received from Rome to rule the Franks.

"You truly are a despicable man," he commented. "Of all the vermin I have encountered in this empire, you are the lowest of them all!" As if in an attempt to emphasize the king's statement, the pontiff's shadow against the stone wall became grotesquely exaggerated in the flickering torch light.

"Yes, I am," Gregory responded coolly and collected. "And that's why I always have my way. But I am also a generous man and right now Charles, you need that generosity. After all you have Norsemen ransacking Paris? How could such a thing happen? A fleet of one hundred and twenty Viking ships sailing along the Seine. And to lose the city on of all days, Easter, my, my, Charles, what are the people going to say?"

Charles held up his hands, palms upwards towards heaven. "As I said to you once before, Gregory, it is divine punishment for the travesty you urged me to perform; the killing of my own father with these very hands. Why would God forgive me? Why should He forgive me? How could He forgive me? Perhaps our souls are meant to rot in hell and we're just prolonging the inevitable? But my knowing that you will be accompanying me into purgatory makes my fate bearable."

"Surely you're not saying that I forced you to slay your father. That I somehow guided that ghastly deed performed by your own hand? As I recall, you were so eager to prove to yourself that you were not his bastard pup, that you decided of your own free will to plunge the dagger into his blackened heart, all by yourself. And the man never even raised a hand to stop you. Truly shocking! You behaved like a wild animal, a rabid fox, striking at everything and everyone in your path.

Your attendants were aghast when they witnessed your murderous act of an innocent, unarmed man, standing before you as he made supplication to your benevolence. Embracing you as you brought down that craven blade and pierced the hollow of his chest. How can you say that I or the Church would condone such behavior? It was an appalling display that will condemn you to everlasting damnation unless the Church absolves you of the crime." Gregory was now waving the index finger of his left hand in admonishment, the long cuffs of his robes swinging freely as his arm moved up and down.

"All I am trying to tell you is that ever since the day Bernard died..."

"You mean killed," Gregory interrupted, clearing his throat as he did so.

"Ever since he died the world has been turned upside down; Vikings in Paris; the Britons seizing all of the Northern provinces; the Muslims raiding from the south. It is no secret that these attacks have not been random. Somehow, someone has coordinated the attacks." The king pounded his leathered right fist into the shielded palm of his other hand.

"And why look any further than the obvious. Your half-brother has openly sworn that he will bring you to justice, for the butchering of his father. William seeks revenge for Bernard. It is obvious that he must be behind it."

Charles carefully studied the Pope's expression as he spoke. Either Gregory was an excellent liar or there had been a ring of truth in his statement. It would not have been beyond William to mobilize a sizable force to attack the king but only if they were his own men. William still had the loyalty of his Narbonnaise subjects, even though he had been stripped of his family's holdings. The suspicion quickly departed. "I do not agree with you, Gregory. William is a fighting man but as a strategist at an international level, he would fail terribly. There is no way that he could have coordinated such an attack with both the Saracens and the barbarians."

"Are you so certain, Charles, to stake your life upon it? He's already attacked you once when he allied himself with your brother's son, Pepin. In case you have forgotten, they almost defeated you at Angoumois, last June. After they had completely annihilated your army, captured Toulouse, and expelled your governor, as I recall, you had to offer your nephew Aquitaine in order to appease his taste for conquest but you never bothered to offer William anything and that is an oversight that has come back to haunt you tenfold measure."

Gregory strode towards the king. "Have you forgotten that it was William whom allied himself with Abd ar-Rahman, the emir of Cordova and together they captured Barcelona and Appurias. I think that he is a far better strategist than you give him credit for. Whatever skills he may be lacking, his tutelage with the Saracens would have been more than enough to compensate for his deficiencies."

"William was never the one I assumed to be behind my demise. You still have not been able to convince me of his treachery. For you see, Gregory, I know for a fact that the revolt in Brittany was the result of the local priests putting wild ideas into Chief Nominae's head. I barely escaped with my life from that battle. I had to grant him and his people independence in order to secure his nominal recognition of my reign. Now suppose I had been killed in that battle, Gregory, what was your plan of action going to be?"

The tall, slender figure of the Pope circled gracefully around the much taller monarch. "Surely you jest Charles to suggest that the Church had anything to do with the revolt. Personally, I couldn't be bothered to waste my time with such a small fish in the pond. There would have been nothing for me to gain through any alliance with Nominae. And by now you should realize, I have much greater designs than some petty chieftain. Mark my words, Charles, William shall prove to be the bane of your existence. He may only be nineteen now, but he is driven by revenge and his mind is razor sharp. What he has achieved in his few years as a youth exceeds all the accomplishments of your generals in total."

Charles revolved on his heels, never taking his eyes off Gregory, as the Pope continued to circle around him. "Save your warnings and mongering for someone that wishes to hear your tales, Gregory. Next you will try to tell me that his younger brother, Bernard, is also a threat and he's only ten years old. I am tired of your lies. Whatever Jewish blood remains in my veins finds your vitriolic condemnation of these particular people tedious and boring.

Find some other excuse for extorting monies from the sheep, besides your impending threat of a Jewish seizure of the kingdom. Because in case you have forgotten, the very thing you have used to stir the populace is what you used to blackmail me into slaughtering my father and now you do have a part-Jew sitting on the throne of this Empire. The people have believed your lies, thus far, but do you think you can continue to use the Jews as the excuse for all the Church's inadequacies?"

"Dear boy, don't be so foolish. Firstly, we have looked at every contingency and we win in every situation. Do you think that I and my advisors have not evaluated this particular situation over and over again, weighing each facet in the balance?" The Pope held up two fingers before his face. "And have you ever thought that it may not be a part-Jew but a full blooded Jewess-begotten cub that sits on the throne." Gregory's second disclosure caused Charles to freeze in astonishment, his body stiffening as if hit by a lightning bolt.

"Yes, you heard me correctly," Gregory snickered. "As I tried not to say earlier, Charles, there are matters regarding your mother that you are not even aware of." A third finger was held up in front of his face. "And now do you see why you are going to be a good boy and listen to me and do what I say? If you wish to remain king then follow my instructions carefully. If you wish to be dead then continue with your fool heartiness."

Charles turned away, staring at the edge of the ceiling, into the nothingness that hung above the chamber like a heavy blanket. The King smiled and finally laughed, as he thought about this latest revelation.

Gregory looked on with concern. The King's reaction was not anticipated. "Perhaps you did not hear me correctly, your Highness. I suggest you take this seriously! You are in no position to laugh."

The King merely regarded the Pope's consternation with amusement, pointing at his face and laughing even harder. His belly ached with laughter. Finally catching his breath after several minutes, Charles approached Gregory. "You of all people should know what you have done, Your Holiness. After all, is not your favorite condemnation of the Jews that old adage that they are a stubborn stiff necked people? Now you will see just how stubborn I can be. Not without good cause, because if what you say is true, then I am all Jew. If I am to be my father's son then let's start as of now!"

The heavily leathered fist came seemingly from nowhere as it landed square on Gregory's left temple. Falling to his knees, the Pope momentarily lost consciousness from the sudden impact. His senses returned slowly and he shook his head in an attempt to clear the fog. Collecting themselves, the Lombardian guard began to surround the King, but Charles just as quickly signaled his guard to stem their approach.

"Unh-unh-ah," Charles waved a warning finger towards the Lombards. "Not a good idea. You don't want to lose your lives in this manner."

"Lower your weapons!" Gregory shouted to his men. "There will be no fighting today. Consider yourself unique in all of history, Charles," Gregory said as he struggled to his feet, helped by the aging Hincamar. You have struck a pontiff and you will live to talk about it. But I swear to you, it will be the last blow you will ever strike against me or my Church."

"You still don't understand, do you?" the King responded. "All my life I have felt torn between the Emperor, the Church, and my guardian. And of the three, Bernard meant the most to me and I never knew why until recently. He was not only my guardian, he was my godparent, my mentor, and just now I realize, my savior. You see, I thought I needed you and your church for forgiveness for the terrible act I performed. But you are nothing but lost souls, yourselves. You can't forgive me because there's no one that has forgiven you. You are hollow shells filled with the darkness.

I have already been forgiven. In my father's dying embrace, he held me until the ebb and torrent of his life's liquor finally ceased to flow. He knew this day would come and his spirit now courses through me. Prepare yourself, Gregory, because if I am what you say I am, then you're about to face the most powerful enemy you have ever met. I will battle you until the end of time. And now you have made it possible by freeing me of my adherence to the Church."

"Then you are as big a fool as your father was! You are nothing. You are the sand beneath my feet. We will sweep you away and you will be gone forever. That is the heritage you have inherited from your father. I will wipe you from the earth. History will have no trace of you. Do you truly think you are strong enough to fight my Church. No one is that strong! No one!"

"Then you have nothing to fear from me," Charles winked. "And if I start passing edicts that restores the rights and privileges of the Jews within my kingdom, then I'm sure you'll find some manner to convince the people that it is merely a transient re-establishment of the old ways. Isn't that correct, Gregory? It's all just transient. The same way that the Saracens have ransacked and burnt Rome, it's just a transient occurrence. I'm certain that you can recapture Rome without my assistance. After all, your Church is so very strong."

Gregory pointed a shaking finger at the king. "You made a promise before your nobles, Charles. You swore to send troops to liberate Rome. They will hold you to your word."

"My word? Since when has my word become the cement that binds the mortar of the Catholic foundation? You, yourself have implied the word of a half-breed is not accepted at full value. As a full-bred Jew, I have no fetters that force me to keep a promise to you and your church.

You and your kind are merely extortionists dressed in red. Call down your hail and brimstone upon me if you don't like the answer, but Frankia will not send a single soldier to your war unless you make certain concessions to me." Charles held out his left hand, the seal of his reign firmly attached to his middle finger. "Would you care to kiss my rings, Gregory?" He waved his hand to and fro as it hung limp at the wrist, his gesture mocking the Pope's previous action.

His face flushing bright red with anger, Gregory commanded his Lombardian guard to follow him from the chamber. "You have not heard the last of this, Charles," Gregory screamed as he hurried his men to pack their gear and return to the summer palace in which they were housed. "Mark my words, your Majesty, this is definitely not the last time!"

"First, last, it makes no difference," Charles responded. "All that matters is that I am the power in the land of the Franks. I rule here, and tonight I have made that point very clear. You and your cronies have seen me do the last of your dirty work. If Bernard's death has bought me any salvation, it is that I am my own man!"

Charles withdrew his sword from its scabbard and held it high above his head. "Tomorrow, Gregory you will see a new Frankia; a land where all men are treated equally. Christian, Jew, Muslim, it makes no difference. In honor of my father, I shall make his dream of Narbonne exist throughout all the land!"

"The only dream you shall nurture shall be a nightmare of my making," Gregory flailed a fisted threat. "You shall rue the day," the Pontiff cursed. "I shall see to it that your life is a living hell. I shall expunge the last trace of the Almyeri from this world!"

Charles merely laughed. "My life is a living hell, already. You have certainly seen to that! Do your damnedest, for there is nothing more that you could possibly do to me."

"To you, perhaps not, but upon your new found heritage I can bring down the wrath of the heavens. Every Jew shall tremble in fear upon hearing my name. The mention of Pope Gregory shall make them regret the days in which they were born. And it will all be because of you. And they will curse you themselves."

Shaking his head, the king dismissed the ranting of the Pope. "It shall not happen. You are powerless to do anything against them. There can be no new laws unless I approve of them. All that you are and all that you will be, will because I say so."

Gregory and his entourage began to shuffle through the archway into the corridor leading from the room. "And for how long do you believe you can exercise your control over the Lord's holy house? Do you plan to live forever? Who is to say which of us will live the longest? I will lay the ground work which shall spell the doom of your people. The laws that I will propose shall eventually come to pass. You cannot stop it from happening. It is the inevitable outcome. The time of the Jew has come and gone. This kingdom of theirs is an abomination. A farce! An event that should have never happened and now I will correct our error!"

"You are blind, Gregory, like all those that came before you and all that shall follow in your footsteps. Blind like I had been for so long. You made me feel ashamed of what I was, ashamed to be the bastard child of the only man I truly loved. And yet none were more proud of his heritage than Bernard. What did he know that I could not readily see? They are a people chosen by God, which is why you fear them. Because they have something you can never have; God's eternal blessing. That is what fuels your hatred. Is it not so, your Holiness? And let us just see who outlives the other."

Gregory turned back, taking a few steps towards the chamber and then dismissed the king's comments with a backwards wave of his arm. "Bah! I will show you what I think of their eternal blessing. Mark me well Charles, the day shall come when all that I have ordained shall come to pass! Throughout every church they will be read until even you would fear to withdraw a single one. My being alive will not determine their passing into doctrine. I shall see to that."

"State these ordinances you wish to pass, so that I can judge whether you are wasting my valuable time or not," the king challenged.

"I will do so gladly," Gregory exalted. "There will be no more owning of slaves by Jews.

And a Jew will no longer be able to serve as a soldier, lawyer, or hold public office. And a Jew found fornicating with a Christian shall be put to death. I will not allow them to show their faces during a Christian holiday. And when a Jewess has a child, that child will be seized from the arms of his hysterical mother and brought up in a monastery. This is what I shall do to them to so that they may pass into extinction. I will crush this vile race from the face of the earth. This shall be my legacy to them." Gregory's face distorted into a cruel mask of hatred.

"It will not come to pass," Charles casually dismissed the Pope's ravings. "I shall see to it, this morning! I will pass laws to protect all my subjects. Do not try to challenge me on this. I will prevail." The King signaled with an arrogant flip of his hand that Gregory was dismissed.

Almost out of sight, the last few words from the Pontiff drifted back into the chamber. "We shall see, we shall see. Patience is my virtue, your majesty. The Church is eternal, the Carolingians are not!" Gregory bowed in a mocking salute and disappeared into the shadows, the last word having been his.

Chapter Twenty-Two

Toronto: 1999

I have this intense desire to curl up in my chair and fall asleep. On the other hand, Pearce is busy pouring himself another cup of coffee. With the cup in one hand and his pencil in the other, beating against the air, he reviews what I had just told him in solemn silence, wandering about the room, searching for his next question. He spins on his heels to face me.

"Then it all worked out? Charles recognizes his birthright, he challenges the Church, and you have a descendant of David sitting on the throne. Correct?"

"You would like to think that's how it all ended," I advise him, "but sadly, it could not. I would like to have seen it end that way, because I'd be able to go to sleep now. Sleep is a good thing, John. But back to the story, you have to remember the people you're dealing with."

"How so Doc?"

"Charles was not a very strong individual. Oh, he had his moments, but that's all they were. He had enough difficulty dealing with the fact he killed his father. Likewise, he was finding it difficult to know that he was fully Jewish. Gregory was smart enough to keep the last detail in his back pocket of how that was possible. I don't know if Charles would have been stable enough to accept the knowledge of his mother and father being sister and brother. No, Pope Gregory held all the cards and most assuredly passed the deck on to his successor, Sergius.

Sure, history records Charles as going through a period of legislating anti-Jewish laws and confiscation of their properties, only to be followed by edicts to reinstate the Jewish land ownership and offer them court protection. But it doesn't explain why he had this sudden reversal. And yes, afterwards he did protect his Jewish citizenry until his death, just as he swore to Gregory he would do but it was all too late. He had broken the Almyeri power-hold in Narbonne. He had given the Church far more authority than they ever had prior and that sealed their doom.

So even when he tried to rescind many of his earlier decrees, it was too late. People that had lost their property were no longer found. Churches made half-hearted restitutions to rightful owners when they were actually located. But most of all, once you start a policy of anti-Semitism, nothing is going to reverse it. It just gains momentum until it steamrolls everything in front of it."

"So, it was over," Pearce acknowledged my sense of defeat.

"For all intents and purposes. Obviously, there were still a few loose ends. Gregory was extremely powerful and resourceful. He did have the last word. He was also determined to wipe out every last trace of the Almyeri. William, son of Bernard was still quite a visible threat and he was gaining momentum in his plans to lead a revolt."

"Gregory was right then," Pearce commented.

"If you make someone an outlaw, they become an outlaw. Charles didn't have much

213

choice in the matter either. William would always be at odds with the king."

"And that's where we began our story."

"I'll now bring it full circle and you'll see for yourself."

Paris: 850 A.D.

Completely encircled by the platoon of Goth soldiers, the pine framed wagon rolled clumsily over the rock strewn road. Dressed in their lamellar, handed down for almost a century, the patch-work contingent guarded their precious cargo religiously. Wearing discarded helmets, left behind from prior battles, which were considered too dented or damaged to be worth salvaging by the regulars. The Goths made a pitiful and scornful sight. Most of them were without swords, carrying instead an axe or pike, the trademark weapons of their infantry.

Two huge black shire horses drew the cart along at a monotonous pace while its human cargo tossed and rolled with every bump and turn in the road. With hands and legs tied, the prisoners were unable to steady themselves from crashing heavily into the sideboards time after time.

"This is my entire fault," William, Prince of Narbonne, apologized to his steadfast companion. The ropes burned into his flesh with each jostling of the wagon so that now a solid ring of welts cuffed each wrist.

"You're right," Charles grumbled. "It most certainly is your fault!" The next rock passing under the right front wheel sent the pair rolling the length of the wagon's rough boarded bed. Struggling back onto his side, Charles St. Jean barely recaptured his breath, having had one of the sideboard ribs strike him solidly in the abdomen. "If you had only listened to me, we would not be in this situation. I am supposed to be your advisor and you never listen to a word I say."

"You sound more like my wife than my advisor," William growled.

"You won't listen to her either, so what is the difference?" St. Jean struck back.

"Quiet down, you dogs," the driver grumbled in a heavy accented Frankish tongue, snapping his whip accurately against both their prone bodies further emphasizing his point.

"Well," William countered to his companion's first complaint, "it seemed like a good idea at the time."

"To whom?" Charles complained, "Certainly not to 'ar Rahman, when you mentioned it to him. And none of our other allies appeared too enthused either. They all stated the obvious. You can't trust the Goths! Do you remember them saying that William?"

William rocked back onto his side so that he was facing his friend. "I didn't recall hearing 'ar Rahman suggest that he was prepared to take back Aquitaine and Toulouse from the King's forces. Those cities belong to me! I am their lord and protector. Without enlisting the Goths, our forces were too small to mount an attack equal to the task! What choices did I have?"

"Perhaps the Caliph was being sensible, for your sake," Charles retorted as a possible alternative explanation. "Sometimes you just have to bide your time and wait for a better strategy. You weren't thinking clearly! Now don't get me wrong William. You know that I cared for your father deeply. That he and my father were as close as brothers. But tell me honestly, how much of this fight which we've carried on for the past five years has been for the sake of preserving your family's land holdings and how much has been purely for revenge?"

William stared coldly into his companion's eyes. "Are you suggesting that my motives have been purely self-indulgent? That all this could have been avoided?"

"In a simple word, my friend, yes."

The driver's whip snapped a glancing blow off William's cheek, as the Goth once again yelled for silence.

"Well I'll be damned," William cackled. "After all these years, you never said a word. You stood by my side through countless battles and never told me once that you doubted my motives."

Charles was surprised that his long time liege took criticism so well. It was a trait that he must have just recently acquired. "You know that I would march to hell and back with you. It is not for me to ask why, only to say that it may not be the best idea you ever had."

The expression on William's face grew grim as he focused his thoughts on the King of the Franks. "All that I know is that my father is dead because he thought he could reason with a madman. I know everyone is saying that the king has changed following that murder. If Charles the Bald has become a protector of my people, as a penance for his past deeds, then let it be said that I am not that easily fooled by neither his ploys nor his lies. He who was once my guardian, now and forever will be my enemy!"

"How can you be so certain that he hasn't changed? So much has happened lately. Remember, Pope Gregory died under mysterious circumstances. Why would you not think that the King had a hand in it? And what about his refusal to help Sergius when Rome was under attack?"

"Whether he was responsible for Gregory's death is not the issue. I don't believe it changes anything. Charles would not have killed Gregory in order to make our lives or the lives of my subjects any easier. All it served to do was remove one more threat to his retention of power. The same goes for his failure to aid Sergius. That is what this has all been about. Power! Who has it, who wields it, who keeps it!"

Charles edged closer to his master. "I do not understand how one pursues power by supporting another to the throne. That would appear to be no more than trading one evil for another. There is no logic in such an approach. Wouldn't you agree?"

"I supported Pepin on the advice of my father. He could see what fate had in store for us if Charles became king. Pepin was the most like his father, Louis. That meant he represented our best chance to retain our kingdom." William was able to dodge the whip which sailed once more in his direction, the driver laughing as he glanced back to gauge his accuracy and watch the prisoners struggle to roll out of the way.

"But your father abandoned Pepin. He wouldn't even take arms against Charles!"

William just shrugged his shoulders. "I don't know why he did what he did. All I know is that my father did everything with good reason."

"I wish we could say the same about ourselves!" St. Jean commented, his words tinged with self-ridicule. "Trying to ally ourselves with the Goths was totally insane. What were we even thinking?" Charles kicked himself into a sitting position, his back against the sideboard. "At least, now, we can see if King Charles has had a true change of heart when they hand us over to him." Charles scanned the view over the top of the wagon. "We are close. Look ahead, the gates of Paris."

William made an effort to right himself but lost his balance as the wagon passed over several large rocks huddled by the edge of the road. He sighed heavily, knowing that the road was soon coming to an end. Listening to the jeering in the distance from the top of the city walls, he knew was about to receive a warm welcoming. After years of warfare against the king, he was hardly the most popular man in the kingdom. And in spite of the King's rumored change of heart, he held no false hopes of redemption.

"I never thought the day would come when I could actually say that the battle is over for me. We gave them a good fight, Charles, didn't we?"

"That we did, my lord. We most certainly did!"

Chapter Twenty-Three

Toronto: 1999

"I guess that's it, then?" Pearce looked at me to see if there was anything further I wished to add.

"The rest is for you to search and verify," I comment. I stretch my legs and then planted myself upright. I was already moving towards the hall stand when it dawns on Pearce that I was ushering him from my study. I notice that he isn't too quick in rising from the couch. That could only mean one thing; he isn't ready to go yet.

"You know, Doc, I'm thinking. Here's this city occupied by a majority of Jews for over a thousand years and just like that, they're all gone. How's that even possible?"

"John, that's a question that every historian asks when an entire population of Jews seems to disappear. Three and half million Jews in Poland before World War II, and now there's only four thousand. How's that possible? The question grows tiresome after a couple of millennia. You and I know it happened, but given a century or so, there will be a lot more people saying it was impossible and before you know it history is rewritten to say that Jews never lived in Poland!"

"I wasn't trying to cast doubt on the claim, Doc. Believe me, I'm a reporter, I know that genocide is quite within the capabilities of the human race. All I want to know is how it happened. If King Charles was offering them protection, then what went wrong?"

"That's easy to answer. Like Natronai said to Charlemagne, good intentions last only as long as the person that made them remains alive. Charles the Bald wasn't going to live forever. Late in his reign, he started to make an appeasement with the Church, and the bad blood started to be swept under the carpet. His successors were even weaker than he was."

"So the Church regained control over all that they had lost?"

"John, as far as the Papacy was concerned, it was mere child's play!"

Paris: 899 A.D.

"Sign it!"

"But Guifred, I don't understand any of this."

Clenching his teeth in frustration and anger, Archbishop Guifred hammered his fist against the table. For an entire morning he had been fighting with the child in order to secure his signature. "Your Majesty, just sign the bloody edict already. Your father appointed me as your legal guardian before he died. Is that not so?" The fierce countenance relaxed into a patronizing smile.

"Yes, but I don't know if this is right," the youthful monarch questioned. The palace aristocrats had come to call him Charles the Simple, but the heir to the throne was proving that he was far more aware of events surrounding him than he had let on.

"You do not have the ability to judge what is right or wrong. Don't make feeble attempts to rule now. It will only give you a headache. It's not that difficult to understand," Guifred snarled.

"Your father had already confiscated the vineyards and salt works of the Narbonnaise Jews, before he died. He relied on my advice. You must do so as well." Spreading his long robes, Guifred cast an ominous shadow over the king.

"Now, sign the edict and we will finish off what your father started. All their houses and all their property shall be deeded to the Church of Narbonne. That was your father's dying wish. We shall rid the city of its Jewish vermin once and for all. It's what we all want."

Young Charles trembled beneath the Archbishop's grizzly shadow. "But they are my subjects too!" he rebutted, cowering slightly to avoid any blows that Guifred might shower upon him. Guifred had been a hard schoolmaster, teaching with an iron fist from the day he was first appointed as Charles's tutor.

Uncharacteristically, the Archbishop relaxed his posture and took a gentler position. "Yes, they are, your majesty. And that is why you must do what is in their best interests. They do not belong here, my king. They never did. They have never been accepted amongst us and because of that they have suffered terribly. Why let them suffer any more. As their king, you should help them find their way back home."

Charles scratched his head, a myriad of questions coming to mind. "But where is there home Guifred?"

"Who's to say, my liege. I don't even think that they know. But that is not for you to decide this day." Guifred's anger flushed his face. "Don't you think you've made enough decisions on your own today?"

"But Samuel of Avingnon says that they once had a kingdom, here in France. And that they even had their own king to rule over them."

"Mere fairy tales, your Majesty. You know how the Jews love to tell their tales of fancy and legend. They are famous for their art of telling fables. Just look at how they still claim to be God's chosen people. Would they be suffering if that was true? Would God let us hurt them over and over again if they were his chosen? We have to punish them just so that they can see how wrong they are and how ridiculous their stories are.

They're all just fairy tales. What their parents told them before they went to sleep as young children and now they have grown up to believe in them. If they had a kingdom, where is it now? Where are these Kings they speak of? Stories and nothing more!"

Once again, Guifred moved the candle closer to the document, illuminating his stern features in the dancing light as he did so. "You know that they were cursed by God to wander the four corners of the earth for an eternity. How could the homeless have ever had a kingdom? How could those who killed our Lord, Jesus Christ have been rewarded with anything more than scorn and hatred? You're a smart lad. You can see that none of it was ever the truth."

"I don't know," Charles replied his mind now befuddled and clouded, seen through characteristic behavior of flitting his eyes constantly about the room.

"They can't! You, yourself can see that there is no basis to their legends. And after you sign this, they cannot even own a grain of sand in all of France. Could this fate possibly befall a people that once had a kingdom? Surely, for the world to treat a people thusly, it would never have been possible if they had a kingdom. A monarch is a defender, an upholder of their liberties and rights. They have no such protector. It would be inconsiderate of them to place you in such a position."

Charles thought about it for a moment. "I guess not."

"Of course not! Do you think God would let you take away all their possessions if he was watching over them? He wouldn't let you. So if you sign this edict and it comes to pass that they lose everything and are forced from our lands, then you will know that you are enacting God's will because he did not stop you."

"God would stop me if it wasn't right."

"Exactly my liege. You are giving them exactly what they deserve. This will encourage them to go somewhere else and perhaps even start up a kingdom with a Prince or Duke to safeguard their privileges. But it's just not going to happen in a God fearing country like France." Guifred patted the young king on his shoulder.

Charles was about to put pen to paper then suddenly paused. "But it has been said that my grandfather was their protector. Perhaps that is an indication that it is my responsibility too."

Beneath the thin veneer of tolerance and patience growing ever more fragile, Guifred was seething with anger. "Many things have been said of Charles the Bald. Some are true, some aren't. But as you know, he became Holy Roman Emperor, twenty-four years ago when Pope John the VIII placed the crown upon his brow. You don't become the Emperor of the Church if you are following policies directly opposed to Church edicts. That is why I always tell you to listen with your ears but learn to discard half of everything you hear."

"If I do this, Guifred, will I become an Emperor as well?"

Guifred smiled and winked at the boy. "Let me put it this way, your highness. If you don't sign this paper, you will never become Emperor. Of that, I can assure you. But if you listen to me, perhaps the Emperor's crown will be yours in the future."

Charles took up the quill in his hand. "I would like to be Emperor."

"So would we all, your majesty, so would we all."

219

Chapter Twenty-Four

Toronto: 1999

"Don't look so glum!" Pearce was sitting on the couch looking totally dejected. Whether he admits to it or not, I knew the story had an effect on him. As gruff as his exterior was, he's got a heart.

"Ah..., I'm just sad to see it end like that. Like it never existed; all those lives, gone, disappeared forever!"

"Nothing is forever!" I comment with a glint in my eye, which Pearce must have perceived straight away.

"What do you mean?"

"Well, I'm telling you the story now. You're going to see that it gets published and the family of the Almyeri and the Kingdom of Narbonne will no longer be forgotten. So, nothing is forever."."

"No," Pearce says, looking introspectively at me, staring into my eyes. "That's not what you meant, Doc."

"How can you be so certain what I did or didn't mean?" He's definitely more perceptive than I give him credit for.

"I told you, Doc, at the beginning. I'm a good reporter. I know when there's a good story and I know when I'm not being told the full story."

I rub the point of my beard, giving the situation some very careful thought. How much do I trust this Pearce? I've revealed an awful lot already. Do I really want to tell him more? I began to weigh out all the possible permutations.

"I wasn't going to tell you this. But perhaps you should know. The Almyeri didn't completely disappear. It's been a very closely guarded secret for a millennium but the Church didn't win completely."

"What! All this time you have been telling me a story of the eradication of a family and it never really happened!"

"Of course it happened. Having a sole survivor doesn't mean that they weren't eradicated."

"You can't be eradicated if someone survives," Pearce corrects me.

"Don't sound so disappointed, Pearce! I only thought you would like to hear a somewhat happy ending? You can't tell me that you're not pleased that one survived."

"Yes. Sure. They missed one?"

"Fortunately, yes! They missed one; the last of his kind."

"Okay, tell me about it Doc. Who? Who was he?"

Narbonne: 877 A.D.

The mop-haired, bright-eyed boy sat nervously on his uncle's lap, fidgeting relentlessly under the scrutiny of the mysterious stranger, who had come telling stories of harrowing adventures in faraway lands. This time, it was not a joyous occasion which brought visitors to the house. It was quite the contrary. Events of the past week had been a traumatic experience for all, but for none more so, than the lad.

Exact details of what his uncle and the stranger were conversing about escaped him, but he knew instinctively that it would alter his life dramatically. The wails of the womenfolk in the manor could still be heard as they went about their duties as if in constant mourning. They were distraught, sullen and despairing, but for all their outward emotion, he knew only one fact, his father was never coming back. No miracle, no divine intervention, was going to alter that simple, undeniable fact.

The man, who had been like a beacon, guiding him through his infancy, following the death of his mother in labor, was never returning. As a young child, he did not fully appreciate just how special his relationship with his father had been; too young to comprehend the uniqueness of the bond they had shared. His father, Bernard, played both parental roles, excelling in each, with his outward displays of affection for his son. He had been a doting father, the younger Bernard his only child. To all, his father explained, his son was his raison d'être.

The child was the last vestige of the older Bernard's wife, the fair Blihilde, the most beautiful woman in all of Narbonne. When he looked into the young Bernard's face, he saw only the large doe eyes of his departed soul-mate, the same soft, delicate features that she possessed; the same warmth in their touch and tone of their laugh. A delicately turned smile that was infectious. He loved his son above all else.

To the child, life seemed to always be carefree, growing up in a home surrounded by relatives, servants and friends. But what had begun a week ago as a normal day, resulted in the shattering of a young boy's life. The reasons escaped him, but he knew from the conversations he overheard, that it was inextricably tied into the origins of his family. Although he had been nurtured on his family's unique history, the young Bernard only grasped the fundamentals. Most of the stories were handed down from his uncle, Solomon.

Legends claimed that his uncle was the horn blower of a great army. Solomon Bovo Cornebut he was called by those that served under him, the finest signal man in all of the Empire; a tactician of unparalleled abilities, even as a youth when he first joined the army.

Not just an uncle but a great-uncle, brother-in-law to his grandfather, William. To the sound of his trumpet, astounding victories were heralded, time and time again. As a young boy, his uncle had known the founding member of their clan. During his ninety odd years, Solomon experienced a world filled with such awe and splendor. His tales were so vivid, springing to life before the child's eyes. The son of the first Almyeri Natronai of Baghdad, of whom the epic songs heralded as William Nasi, was his military companion. Though William's conquests were of mythological proportions his uncle could confirm them all. He was there when the king turned to the east to find the one true love of his life after the death of his first wife. He returned with the beauteous Guiberc, daughter of a Yemenite potentate.

Alongside William, Solomon's trumpet sounded in the greatest of victories that wrestled the Spanish March from the hands of the evil Saracen Empire. That black robed, faceless horde, which attempted to steal away the civilized world and plunge it into a feudal chaos.

His uncle told him of how his great grandfather, William's son Bernard, was slain by the king of the Franks but in his dying breath he forgave Emperor Charles, whom he loved like a son of his own loins. In their naïveté the Almyeri had assumed that meant the royal family had also forgiven his family. Now, the error of that assumption was all too apparent. First it was his grandfather, William, to inherit the curse, perishing in a Paris prison just a day before his scheduled execution by the very same king that had murdered his great-grandfather. Though no one said so, he knew that the death of his own father was also related.

A diabolical plot shadowed his family and he knew that he too was under its spell. At his young age, the politics of man escaped him completely, his only comprehension of what was transpiring, as being the work of the devil. And this meeting of his ancient uncle and this aged stranger was mysteriously designed to protect him from that evil, which tormented his family. Now once could comprehend how uncle Solomon could live so long, having survived five generations of the Almyeri thus far. Most assumed it was God's will and only when his divine purpose had been met would God call him from this Earth.

The boy thought back to the last time he had seen his father. He had wanted so desperately to go hunting with his father that day. He begged and pleaded to go with, but once again his father refused, saying that he was still too young. Stag hunting was too dangerous he said; too many things that could go wrong if a bull stag was merely grazed or injured and not put down with the first arrow, his father warned. The elder Bernard joked that the best part of hunting venison was the eating anyway. The young Bernard relented to the obvious that he would not be going with no matter how much he begged his father.

Just as his father was about to mount his horse, the young Bernard rushed forward to embrace him. Holding on tightly, he wrapped his arms around his father's waist. "Don't go, please don't go," he said repeatedly, the tiniest of voices in his head, whispering over and over again that it was not safe for his father to hunt that day.

"Now, don't be foolish, little one," the elder Bernard cautioned as he removed the small arms that clung to him. "I know how much you want to go with me but you are too young. I promise, you and I will go hunting together when you're a little older."

"I'm scared," the boy whimpered.

"Scared of what? Nana will take care of you while I'm gone. And I'm certain that Uncle Solomon will have plenty of adventurous tales to tell you. I won't be gone long."

It was a lie. The younger Bernard knew it was a lie, but he was helpless to stop his father from encountering fate. The voices, he knew were real. And he knew his father was not coming back from the hunt.

He only heard the accident discussed once by his uncle. That was when the messenger first arrived that evening, at the manor. From the gesticulations made by Solomon, young Bernard knew it was a very serious matter. Solomon tore at his clothes and showered his head with a handful of ash. The messenger turned and began to walk away.

"Wait," Solomon yelled after him. "How did it happen?"

The messenger never sacrificed a single step, as he yelled back his answer. "An arrow shot by a yet unknown assassin. It planted itself square in Master Bernard's' back, tearing everything in its path. It was horrible, absolutely horrible; a most heinous murder, my lord. "

"What of the feathering," he recalls his uncle asking.

"There were no markings to be found on the arrow recovered from the body. I'm sorry. I cannot tell you anymore."

"No distinct feathering on the arrow? Bah! You have told me enough," Solomon sighed, "Too much for this old man to deal with." It was then that the shining light in his uncle's eyes dimmed, and even at his great age, Solomon appeared to grow even older.

Not long after, a courier was dispatched from the manor, but young Bernard never asked why or for whom. Then, after a few days, this stranger came to the house, partaking in the mourning for his father, as if they had known each other extremely well in the past. Like his uncle, the stranger's stories stretched back into the past, not as far as Solomon's, but well into the boyhood of his grandfather, William. And when the stranger spoke of William, it was as if he spoke of a brother, a loved one whom he missed terribly. Both of the men's attention turned and focused on the boy. The stranger held out his hand to Bernard, seeking to clasp the child's hand as a sign of affection.

"I am so pleased to meet you, young master Bernard. My name is Charles St. Jean. I have known your family for a very long time."

In a challenging tone, Bernard responded. "As long as my uncle? He's known everyone in my family."

St. Jean laughed, "No, not as long as your uncle. I don't think anyone could know all the people your uncle has known. He's been around longer than anyone that I know of. The Lord has definitely favored him with a long life."

"They say that my uncle Solomon will grow as old as Methuselah."

"Of that I have no doubt," St. Jean replied. Leaning in his chair towards Solomon, Charles St. Jean commented quietly, "he is a bright boy. He reminds me a lot of his grandfather. There is cleverness around the eyes."

"He is a quick learner," Solomon shot back immediately. "Like all of the Almyeri, his mind grasps concepts faster than most others. There is no doubt that he is his father's son. He's already displayed an aptitude for languages. But most of all he's a good lad; the best of them all." Solomon ruffled the boy's hair.

"Ah, uncle, don't do that. You know how much it embarrasses me." Bernard twinged under his uncle's sweet caress, screwing up his lips into a mew as he tried to hide his face in his shoulder.

"Would you deny an old man one of his greatest pleasures in life?" Solomon ruffled the boy's hair all the more. "It will break my heart to see him go, but I know that it is for the best. I can no longer protect him and the hand of his enemies has grown even closer. I knew this day would come."

"But why do I have enemies, uncle," the boy interjected. "I haven't hurt anybody. I don't want to leave here. Did the bad King's men hurt my father?"

"Do you know who I am boy?" St. Jean decided it was time to explain to young Bernard exactly what the situation was. The boy shook his head without uttering a word. "I am your guardian angel. What your uncle and I decide tonight is in your best interest. You must always believe that!

Along time ago, when your family first came to this part of the world, the Emperor Charlemagne put my family in service to yours. Where ever an Almyeri would go, a St. Jean would be there with him. Whatever battles you partook, my family's sword was there by your side. It has been that way for five generations. You are now the sixth. It is the way God willed it to be."

The boy's thin lips cracked into a comfortable smile. "Uncle Solomon has told me about your family. He said that one day one of the St. Jean's would come back to teach me the ways of knighthood. That the songs of the Almyeri say it is so."

"And he was right. I have come back. The last of the St. Jeans to serve the last of the Almyeri. I am your squire, your tutor, your mentor but most of all; I will be your friend. And together we will have adventures like the ones your uncle has told you all about. Would you like that?"

"But I am not the last of my family," Bernard insisted. "There are also my cousins William, and Samuel, and Adalinde as well. Tell him uncle, I am not the last. There are more like me." In the mind of the young boy, being the last of anything was very unsettling.

Solomon hugged his great nephew even closer. "Bernard, you are the last. My grandchildren are your cousins but they're not of the Almyeri. My wife Adalinde, whom your cousin is named after, was an Almyeri but I am not. Neither is my son Makhir Bernard nor his wife Ermengarde. The last of the Almyeri blood is yours. And Charles is here to help you fulfill your destiny. Only he can ensure that you survive to keep your grandfather's dream alive."

"I don't understand," Bernard began to cry. "I don't understand what destiny is. I don't want to leave here. I want my father!" The cries turned into a steady flow of tears as the boy clutched to his uncle's chest. "I don't want to hear any of this! Why are you sending me away? Why are you being so mean?"

"I don't understand it all, either," Solomon consoled, stroking the lad's long chestnut hair. "I don't think that I've ever truly understood this madness. But Charles understands. He can make sense out of it all. But to do that, you have to go with him and he will take you to where it's safe."

Charles St. Jean reached towards the boy and rested his hand upon Bernard's leg. "Your grandfather thought that he was the last. He could not believe that your father would become the man he had always hoped for. If William had one flaw it's that he failed to realize that who you are is not something you become but it is always inside of you, and exists from the time you are born. Mistakenly, he gave me this stone which I wear about my neck." St. Jean untied the cord and placed the stone into Bernard's hand. He then rolled Bernard's fingers until they enclosed the stone completely.

"It does not belong to me. It should be with you. I want you to go to bed now, but to sleep with this gift from your grandfather. This stone came from the original tablets that Moses brought down from Sinai. Your grandfather thought that the stone possessed great powers. Your grandfather dreamed of the twelve pieces reuniting one day, but he failed to understand the real magic. The true power he dreamt of would only exist when the twelve families possessing the stones came together. Not just the stones themselves. That is my quest and that is the adventure that you and I are about to set upon."

Bernard's finger traced the faint outline of the ancient characters etched into the stone. Worn almost smooth, there was nothing remarkable at all about the rock, but the boy could feel the warmth radiating the length of his arms as he held it. "I can feel the magic," he shouted, his sorrow lifting, the more he held the stone.

"Good!" St. Jean exclaimed. "The stone knows that it is home, that it is now with whom it belongs. Now run along and go to bed. We have a busy day tomorrow."

Bernard felt secure with the stone firmly in his hand. Puckering his lips he pecked his uncle's cheek. "Goodnight uncle, goodnight Master St. Jean." Receiving a pat on his behind from Solomon, the boy scampered off in the direction of his chambers.

Solomon waited until he could no longer hear his great-nephew's feet striking the stone floors. "So, Charles, now we talk of magic stones, do we?"

"The only magic is the magic within the Almyeri themselves. The stone merely unleashes their potential. The story of the stone I attest to you is true. I have wandered to too many distant lands, encountering the same legend over and over again to have any doubts. I only wish I knew back then, what I know now. The boy's father did not have the full benefit of my teaching. As much as I tried to tell him that he would never be safe, he could not believe the world could be so evil.

Perhaps, if he had stayed with me longer, seen as much as I came to see in the years following, he would have learned that he could never be accepted by the reigning powers in this land. He lulled himself into a false confidence and thereby fell into their trap. I know if I had only been here, he would still be alive and my taking the boy would not now be necessary. I let him leave me and I was absent when he needed me most."

"Nonsense," Solomon shouted. "No amount of teaching could have saved him. He thought he had all the answers. Whereas his great uncle, Bernard, died because he allied himself with the king's half-brother, this Bernard thought it best to support Charles. This was to be his sign that he did not hold the death of his father William against the King. Now it is merely his epitaph. The Almyeri chose to support both sides and all of them are still very dead. It made no difference. Death was the only reward they ever could expect."

"The elder Bernard, was very much like his brother William. He understood what being an Almyeri was all about," Charles St. Jean rebutted, "And because of his understanding, chose to make war against the crown. He knew there could never be an acceptance of what he was. Give him that much credit, Solomon. During my last days with William, I thought the King had changed his ways. William never agreed and his brother was proven right."

"And as right as he was, he is still dead," answered Solomon. "So what is your point, Charles?"

"Did you know how William's brother came about his ethnic name of Hayim Vitellus. The story was known only to a very few of us. As you know, it means the 'Living Life'. He came by it via a most interesting experience at the time of his birth. When he was born, his mother Dahouda stole off in the middle of the night to the abbey of Uzes. It was her intent to have the baby baptized into the church. It was as if she was saying, 'you have William, but I'm going to have this one for my own.'

But when Prince Bernard was informed of her scheme, he became enraged. Marshalling his forces, he sent his army to Uzes and threatened to burn the abbey to the ground unless the child was returned to him. The abbot had no choice but to comply. On the eight day after the birth, Bernard of Septimania had his son circumcised and the child was given the name Bernard Hayim Vitellus.

The child was to be the embodiment of the living spirit; a fighter against the evil in this land right from the first few days of his existence. And that is what he did! Your brother-in-law chose to fight every single day of his life. But when the King killed his father, and then his brother, he fought foolishly, thinking only of revenge. He forsook completely the concept of survival. It should have been his primary focus. Survival of the Almyeri! Survival of his people and their way of life! His passions consumed him and after so many battles, he lost his war.

I am determined not to choose the same path for this Bernard, his great-nephew. I will also call him Hayim Vitellus but he will live. His spirit will not be tainted with an all-consuming hatred. He will survive and as a result, your people will survive. This was the pledge I made to William, as he died by my hand, and I will keep that pledge until the day I too finally die."

"Then he will be like his father, who harbored no hatred for the king, and still he has fallen to an assassin's arrow. You cannot prevent the determined effort of the crown to eradicate their family." Solomon could find no comfort in St. Jean's story.

Urging his old friend to be patient, Charles motioned for calm to prevail. "There is so little that the Almyeri understood of their noble heritage. Just look at the stone which William passed into my care. He did not understand that it was not the stone that was blessed by God but the family that possessed it.

The Almyeri were a special blessing. God gave the Almyeri to the world and that is why it is important that I safeguard the boy. If the Almyeri and those other eleven families that possess the other pieces of the tablets were to all disappear, then darkness will fall over the world and evil will prevail."

"But if they do not fight, how will they continue to exist?" Solomon inquired.

Charles St. Jean rose from his chair. "It was never about fighting and winning," he advised. "None of the boy's ancestors understood that. It was a realization that only dawned on me after all my travels, encountering the remnants of a once great civilization. They still exist because they found a life beyond winning or losing. No other ancient civilization has ever made that same claim. The day when the Almyeri and the other Jewish princedoms cease to exist will mean the disappearance of your people. And yet you Jews cannot see the true necessity of those twelve families to ensure that you do not follow all those other civilizations into extinction."

"And if these families do not fight to win, then what?" Solomon asked.

"Survival, my friend, nothing more and nothing less. They must blend into the general populace for now, becoming imperceptible from all the other Jewish people. No one will know their secret. It will only pass from the lips of father to son until the time of revelation. That is why the boy must disappear with me, never to be seen in this land again."

"But for what end?" Solomon inquired, puzzled by the futile interpretation of his ninety odd years of existence being offered by St. Jean.

"I cannot tell you. Who am I to know the will of God? Who are any of us to do so? Whatever the Lord desires of this family must be of a colossal magnitude. The boy is undeniably God's anointed. Let him sleep well tonight, at sunrise we shall begin our adventure. I bid thee, a good night, good sir."

Apologia St. Jean

Long have been the years of my life and many have been my travels in search of that most holy of quests; true friendship.

These words I lay down so that once I have passed into the stillness that awaits me, others may come to learn of matters which I have always known but have recently been purposely forgotten by so many. I have seen much which has not been to my liking, much which has been condoned but which I knew in my heart of hearts was wrong. In all my years I have been devout in my faith only to learn that those who claim superiority over me in matters of religion have been less Christian than many I have known who were not Christian in faith at all.

I, Charles St. Jean, son of Remi, the son of Michael, the son of Pierre, who has dined with kings, befriended princes of Catholicism, Islam and Judaism have learned, although belatedly that the world is of two minds. Good and evil, and that no religion has a monopoly upon either. Long ago I should have spoken out regarding crimes perpetrated against those whom I loved but alas I remained mute against these transgressions.

Only now that I fear no man, because death so eagerly awaits me, do I find the courage to say that which should have been said long ago. What has been done in the name of my Lord, Jesus Christ, I disavow any part of, though my silence had made it possible. Forgive me William. If I have failed you, but it has taken a long time to understand that I learned more from you, a Jew, about being a good Christian than I ever was taught by the Church. I pray that in your death that you extended to me the mercy of forgiveness.

Since our parting, I have also learned more about myself than any man should ever know. And in so doing, I learned more about your family from its origins until its demise, as the lives of the St. Jeans and the Almyeri are inextricably intertwined. In your honor I have written down my findings for the sake of posterity but I jealously guard these pages from the prying eyes of the clergy who would not hesitate to destroy my efforts and thereby repress the message; a message of love, of freedom, and the rights of all men. This was the legacy of the Almyeri to me.

To those of my posterity who may read these notes long after I am gone, do not be confused. If the chronology appears disjointed then know full well that no man thinks sequentially. Too often we weave back and forth through memories within time that we end up often where we started. But my discoveries into the past were never so well organized that they were made in a consecutive order preserving time and dates. In fact, I found it more shocking to make a discovery long after I had assumed myself knowledgeable regarding a certain era. Suddenly a new light would be shone upon established fact casting it into an entirely different interpretation.

I have preserved my epistles much in the manner I discovered them, thusly preserving the impact of my initial discoveries. Feel the shock and the dismay which I suffered as each new discovery filled a gap until I realized that the family of my friend was doomed from its beginnings. That all along our lives were being manipulated by forces that I had been raised to assume were good and honorable. I had been deceived but I quickly realized that William of Septimania had left me a legacy which restored my faith and belief in the Almighty.

I am a Christian not by birth but by deed. I cannot say that you were without fault William, often you were driven to excess, but I know that your intent was always pure and even as you faced the end you did not falter in your beliefs.

Now I realize that you possessed what I have sought for so long. The undying love for God that bonds all men of all faiths. The Lord Jesus tried to show us this, but we who sermonize in his name have somehow forgotten it. Finally, it has returned to me and only because a Jew, whom I loved above all others, showed me the path to reach the Son of God. How ironic that I consider you of being more a Christian than those who have risen high in the Church.

I look forward to seeing you once again, upon my passing. There is so much to tell you old friend. They now sing about my adventures as I searched the four corners of the globe, in hope of finding more pieces of the stone puzzle you presented to me. I shall have to teach you the lyrics when we meet. I have followed the path of the Danites to the emerald isle of Eire, the Levites to the inland sea, and though I have no more of the puzzle in my possession, I have heard a myriad of stories and accounts of where I might find them. Some say that the Zebulunites crossed the great western sea and there I would find their section of holy relic. It may sound funny, but I believe them.

Since the interval of your death, I have seen and heard so much that it would astonish any other man, but I no longer doubt the veracity of these tales. Has not the Song of the Almyeri become a legend amongst our own people? The nature of the hero has been changed but the kernel of truth still underlies the verse. They sing of your family which they destroyed and they aren't even aware of it. If such a thing is possible then why should I doubt any of the legends of the twelve stones?

I will also tell you upon our meeting of events which have taken place amongst your descendants. Forgive me, but I did not honor your last request but instead chose to seek out him whom you cast off. Be not mad, but rejoice. He possessed a love for you that you had turned a blind eye to. Perhaps you are already aware of that if he should happen to be with you now. You would have been proud of him, old friend. I know that I was. He served you and your family with honor.

If my efforts have been successful then I will have foiled the intent of your enemies and saved a remnant of your family for perpetuity. It is your grandson that sits with me and records these words as I speak. He too would make you proud. You were wrong dear friend and I am glad. I pray that this shall be the legacy I leave behind. To those who mourn for me, I ask instead that you rejoice. I am going to see a long lost friend. Never have I been happier than when I was with him. Bid me success that we shall be together once I have crossed over to that other side. May the Lord be with you throughout all your days and may he teach you to see with your heart, as he did for me.

Epilogue

Pearce hands back the translation of Charles St. Jean's final letter. "And the original?" he asks, his eyes searching the shelf from where I had removed the translation.

"Lost. Only the copies exist but they are the reason I know that one child survived."

"I don't know what to say! It's been a remarkable story, Doc. Certainly made me rethink all that Jesus and Mary dynasty conspiracy mumbo-jumbo put out by books like the *Da Vinci Code*."

"Mumbo-jumbo that millions of people have bought into, don't forget," I remind him.

"Yeah, but this makes a lot more sense. There's history behind these guys."

"Well Mr. Pearce, how's that for you first installment? I hope you are satisfied that it's suitable for your readership." I am exhausted. My head hurts and my eyes can barely focus any longer.

Pearce rotates his shoulders and then twists his back, first right then left, trying to remove the cramp that had developed in his lower spine. "I was never one for history, but this saga of yours had me riveted." Pearce does a double take, craning his neck to stare out of the den window. "Is that the sunrise?" he inquires with alarmed surprise. "When did it get so late? I remember you saying a little past one, not so long ago."

I smile wryly. "It has been a long day and night's work. I hope that your wife will understand when you try to explain it to her."

"I can't believe it," Pearce mutters, "An entire day gone by. It seems like a few hours. Heck Doc! That was one hell of a story you told. The little woman's gonna have my hide but wait till she reads this exclusive."

"I'm certain that she will forgive you, John. After all, she now has the only audio tape of a book that hasn't even been written as yet. That should make her a big hit at her next tea party. You better hurry and push your publisher to sit down with mine so you can get this story into print.

Like you said, there is currently a lot of interest amongst the historical societies on what was transpiring at that particular time period in Southern France. They're all still caught up on Priors of Zion, Knights Templar and stuff like that but that's not to say that someone is not going to uncover the truth at some point. You'd hate to lose your exclusive."

"I don't think that's possible, Doc. Consider it as good as done," Pearce waves a perfunctory salute attesting that he will have everything in place for later that day. It was obvious that Pearce knows that he is on to the greatest story of his career. You can recognize his excitement. His hands just seem to go in every direction as he speaks, and you just know his heart is racing.

"So, Doc, what would you suggest for a title?"

"Whatever you would like John. Just so long that your readership knows that as far as the Kahana Chronicles are concerned, this will be your first book. If I'm going to do this then I'm going to do it right."

Pearce slaps the side of his head excitedly. "So when do I hear the others?"

"Another time, another place, perhaps even another life," I respond. "Right now, I'm tired and my head's pounding like there's a hammer thumping against my skull from the inside. I'm going to sleep and you're going to get out of my house."

I begin walking to the door for the second time that morning, so that Pearce will get the point. "Oh, and Pearce, a little advice for you if you don't mind...I know you said you would, but do go and check out the information I've given you. I want you to see for yourself that all these people I mentioned really existed, that the events are recorded but never the explanation of why some of the events did take place. Until now, that is. I want you to be a believer before you put a single word into print."

"Consider it done, Doc. I've got a lot of work to do." Pearce rises from the sofa and walks somewhat stilt legged to where I had hung his trench coat. Slinging it across his arm, he walks to the door, and rather unceremoniously I quickly usher him out onto the first step. Pearce begins a monotonous little whistle as he strolls down the pathway towards the street where his Chevette was parked. I knew it! I knew he would be driving a Chevette!

He opens the driver's side door and then shouts back in my direction. I have to lean out my door in order to catch his words. "There are two things you should know Doc. One is I'm already a believer and secondly, you know, I'm gonna be back for those other books."

"I know, John, I wouldn't expect any different from you," I yell back to him and then I slowly close the door as I watch his car take off down the road. Won't he be surprised to find out there's a lot more stories to tell than he could ever imagine. I guess I'll lay that on him at another time, perhaps even another life.

The End

www.ingramcontent.com/pod-product-compliance
Lightning Source LLC
Chambersburg PA
CBHW051954090426
42741CB00008B/1383